Grasping at Straws

First published by Sola Hill Press in 2021. For permission requests, additional information, or bulk sales, please visit LETTERSFROMTHEHOLOCAUST.COM.

Names: Wasserman, Steven, author.
Title: Grasping at straws : letters from the Holocaust / Steven Wasserman.
Description: Includes bibliographical references. | San Francisco, CA: Sola Hill Press, 2021.
Identifiers: LCCN: 2021920467 | ISBN: 979-8-9850308-1-5 (hardcover) | 979-8-9850308-0-8 (paperback) | 979-8-9850308-2-2 (ebook)
Subjects: LCSH Ichenhäuser family--Correspondence. | Holocaust, Jewish (1939-1945)--Germany. | Jews--Persecutions--Germany--Cologne. | Holocaust victims--Germany--Cologne--Biography. | Holocaust survivors--Germany--Cologne--Biography. | Jews, German--Biography. | Germany--History--20th century--Biography. | Germany--Social conditions--20th century. | BISAC HISTORY / Holocaust | HISTORY / Europe / Germany
Classification: LCC DS135.G33 W37 2021 | DDC 940.53/1809--dc23

This work depicts actual events as truthfully as can be verified by research and translation. All persons within are actual individuals; no names have been changed.

Cover photo, left to right: Sigmund Moses, Max Ichenhäuser (standing), Renate Ichenhäuser, Martha Moses, David Ichenhäuser, Trude Moses Ichenhäuser (standing), Erica Ichenhäuser, and Emma Ichenhäuser.

Book design and production assistance by Adam Robinson for GOODBOOKDEVELOPERS.COM

Grasping at Straws
Letters from the Holocaust

STEVEN WASSERMAN

SOLA HILL PRESS
San Francisco, CA

Contents

"We live as long as the memory of us is alive."

DEDICATION

To Renate, Erica, Trude, Max, Ernst, Heinrich, Martha, Sigmund, David, and Emma: Your memory is alive.

INTRODUCTION

I T WAS EARLY MORNING ON NOVEMBER 10, 1938, THE DAY after Kristallnacht. Streetcars moved slowly down Aachenerstrasse. They rolled past piles of shattered glass from storefront display windows and heaps of goods that mobs had looted from Jewish-owned stores and thrown into the street. Those passengers on the trolley who looked up from their newspapers saw—many with approval and some with horror and guilt—the word "Juden" scrawled on Jewish homes and commercial buildings. The air in Cologne was thick with smoke from the smoldering embers of Jewish homes and synagogues. The acrid plumes of smoke and bits of silvery ash curled slowly upward marking the spots where Nazi-inspired mobs had set match to fuel. The resulting fires had consumed livelihoods, homes, and any sense of belonging to which Germany's remaining Jews had been clinging. The city looked like a war zone, which in truth it was, a battlefield in the simmering war the Third Reich had launched against Germany's Jews that was now coming to full boil.

The SS pounded on the door of 412 Aachnerstrasse. Max, who had been shaving, wiped the soap from his face and opened the door. Without explanation, the officers arrested him. They said only: "Come with us." And suddenly Max and the grey-clad officers were gone. Max's daughters Renate and Erica had no idea what this meant; they were bewildered by their father's arrest.

Max's wife Trude, however, knew and she was filled with dread. She understood all too well what this might portend, not only for her husband Max and their family, but also for other Jews in Cologne. She immediately telephoned a colleague of Max's who had sons the same ages as Renate and Erica in order to warn him. Trude was too late; the SS had already arrested him.

Trude hastily packed two small bags for the girls. Although it was unusual for women to drive in Germany in 1938, Trude knew this was no time to adhere to custom. She had bucked convention by going to college, so she did not fear driving, nor was it something she was willing to forego in a crisis. She put the girls into the family's Opel sedan and drove through Cologne to pick up their friend's sons.

She drove the children out of the city and, she hoped, away from the Gestapo. What went through her mind as she drove? Perhaps she thought she should drive straight to Holland to get out of Germany. Maybe her best strategy was to try to save the children and herself and hope that somehow Max and his colleague would be released and could join them. But the border police would almost certainly detain her and the children since they did not have passports; the Nazis had seized their passports months earlier. Any effort to flee the country might result in all of them being arrested to await who knew what fate. Perhaps she should hide the children and return to Cologne to try to get Max released, but in doing so risk having all of them imprisoned. She drove onward with no good answer. Fear gripped her mind as tightly as her hands gripped the wheel; her lips were as white as her knuckles…

JEWS IN COLOGNE

T HE CITY OF COLOGNE WAS ESTABLISHED ALONG THE BANKS of the Rhine River, in what eventually became western Germany, during the first century A.D. The city began as a Roman outpost named Colonia Claudia Ara Agrippinensium. The city's name was derived from the first word of the Roman designation for the outpost—Colonia. "Cologne"—the French version of the name—eventually became standard usage for the city's name in English, as opposed to the German spelling of "Köln."

Researchers have found references to a Jewish population in Cologne as far back as 321 A.D. Jewish merchants frequently followed Roman legions as the legions moved northward through the Roman empire. The merchants often established small communities on the banks of the Rhine alongside Roman encampments and fortifications. Cologne, one of those Roman encampments, soon had a small Jewish community. The first Jews to arrive in Germany, "the country known as 'Ashkenaz'" in the Hebrew of the time, were merchants.[1] However, there are no further written references to a Jewish presence in Cologne until the Middle Ages, so it is not clear there was a continuous Jewish presence in Cologne from the 4th to the 11th century.

During the Middle Ages, Cologne was a major center of east-west trade in central Europe. Jews had a presence in Cologne during

---

1   *Pogrom Night 1938—A Memorial to the Destroyed Synagogues of Germany*, pub. Synagogue Memorial "Beit Ashkenaz," 2013, Vol. I, p. xiv.

this time. In fact, the Jewish community became large enough that it built a synagogue in approximately 1000 C.E. "By 1075, the town had a designated Jewish Quarter."[2] However, Cologne's Jews were subject to recurring periods of oppression, murder, and destruction of property. In 1096, during the First Crusade, several pogroms resulted in the murder of hundreds of Jews, while others were forcibly baptized.[3]

"[T]he Church enacted discriminatory measures against them in the early 13th century by ordering clergymen to restrict business transactions between Christians and Jews. Jews were also forced to wear a distinctive yellow badge…to pay heavy taxes and were forbidden to hold public office."[4] The local populace attacked and murdered Jews during the Black Plague in the 14th century, accusing them of bringing the plague and poisoning local wells in order to sicken the area's inhabitants.[5]

In 1424, Cologne's city council barred Jews "for all eternity;" the council justified its action by claiming the city's Jews were responsible for crime and poverty.[6] The council confiscated Jewish properties, including the Jewish community's lone synagogue, which the city converted into a church.[7] No longer able to reside in the city, Cologne's Jews settled in neighboring villages. The largest such community was in the town of Deutz, which was immediately east of Cologne on the far bank of the Rhine River. The Jewish community of Deutz was comprised mainly of people with limited means. Jews were not restricted to a ghetto in Deutz, but rather were allowed to live among the community at large. Cologne, however, restricted Jewish access to the city. Cologne allowed Jews to cross the Rhine during daylight hours, but only to do business; the city required that Jews return to their homes in Deutz in the evening. In light of

---

2   *Id.*

3   *Pogrom Night* at xv.

4   *Pogrom Night* at xvi.

5   *Pogrom Night* at xvi.

6   *Pogrom Night* at xvi.

7   *Pogrom Night* at xvi.

the ongoing hostility to their community, many Jews left the area entirely and resettled to the east in Poland and Lithuania.

Germany was the home of Martin Luther, born in 1483 in the central German town of Eisleben. Luther became a professor of theology, a priest, an Augustinian monk, and, eventually, a leader of the Protestant Reformation. He challenged the authority of the Pope to speak the word of God. Luther translated the Bible into German, an event that helped spread the word of the church and standardize the German language. Luther was also a vicious anti-Semite. He wrote venomous texts blaming Jews for the death of Christ, deemed them blasphemers for not accepting Jesus, and advocated burning synagogues, destroying Jewish prayer books, seizing Jewish property, and killing Jews. Since his religious texts were widely read, Luther played a major role in spreading anti-Semitism throughout Germany. Centuries later, the Nazis used his writings to justify their murderous agenda against the Jews of Europe.

In 1799, the first Jew since the 1424 expulsion requested and was granted permission to settle in Cologne.[8] Within a few years, enough Jews lived there to establish a small congregation. They did so notwithstanding the fact that Jews in central Europe during the Middle Ages did not have civil or property rights. For example, Prussia, in what was later eastern Germany, did not permit Jews to become full citizens with equal rights until the late 1860's.[9] While Jews were allowed to settle in Cologne at the end of the 18th century, this was not due to a German epiphany about tolerance and equality. Rather, Jews were allowed to return to Cologne because the Rhineland, where Cologne was located, had come under French rule by virtue of Napoleon's conquests.[10] Napoleon had given French Jews full citizenship a few years earlier; he directed the authorities in the Rhineland to comply with French law and abolish many of their discriminatory laws that restricted Jewish life.[11]

---

8   *Genealogy of the Family Dülken*, Ernst Dülken, (circa 1974) p. 2.

9   *Dülken Genealogy* p. 2.

10   *Pogrom Night* at xv.

11   *Pogrom Night* at xv.

As part of the French Revolution, the 1789 Declaration of the Rights of Man and of the Citizen guaranteed freedom of religion and free exercise of worship provided those freedoms did not contradict public order. Napoleon came to power in 1799 and crowned himself emperor of France in 1804. He extended the Declaration's dictates and overrode laws requiring that Jews reside in ghettos, removed limitations on Jews' rights to own property and worship, and removed strictures barring Jews from practicing certain occupations. When Napoleon annexed German territory west of the Rhine, where Cologne was located, Cologne's Jews became equal citizens in that part of Germany for the first time.[12] Unfortunately, after Napoleon's defeat at Waterloo in June 1815, Germany reverted to its discriminatory treatment of Jews.[13]

Thirty-three years later, the German revolution of 1848-49, in which many Jews participated, led to the Frankfurt Parliament issuing the "Basic Laws of the German People."[14] These laws stated that religious affiliation should not affect the civil and political rights of individuals; this allowed Jews to participate fully in German life for the first time.[15] While Germany was still suffused with anti-Semitism, Jews, at least in purely legal terms by the end of the 19th century, had come much closer to being full German citizens.

In 1815, the Congress of Vienna established the German Confederation, an association of thirty-nine German-speaking states, to coordinate the economies of German-speaking countries. The Confederation replaced the Holy Roman Empire which had been dissolved in 1806. The Confederation designated Cologne as a defensive "fortress city," which led to the construction of two "ring belts" of fortresses around it. Cologne and the Rhineland were predominantly Catholic, as opposed to the German state of Prussia to the east which was overwhelmingly Protestant. The city grew rapidly

---

12 *Pogrom Night* at xvii.

13 *Pogrom Night* at xvii.

14 *Pogrom Night* at xviii.

15 *Pogrom Night* at xviii.

in the 19th and 20th centuries; by the time of the first World War, it had some 700,000 inhabitants.

Being a Jew in Europe entailed living with risk as a constant companion. Nevertheless, by the time World War I began, German Jews were, by most standards, largely assimilated into German society. Germany's Jews did not consider themselves to be distinct from other Germans; they certainly did not think that within a generation their non-Jewish countrymen would seek to annihilate them. Most German Jews thought of themselves as Germans at least as much as they thought of themselves as Jews. They were active in many professions and enjoyed Germany's rich cultural life. "By the middle of the 19th century, Cologne developed into a scientific, economic, and cultural center, and the Jewish population had a strong part in this development."[16] "In Cologne, the late 1800's marked the beginning of the vibrant Jewish community life that flourished from the 1920s to the early 1930s."[17]

The Jewish Reform movement had begun in Germany in the 19th century. Reform rabbis wore vestments similar to those worn by Protestant ministers. Instrumental accompaniment became part of the services at Reform congregations; the Hebrew prayer book was replaced by one written in German.[18] The Reform movement did not consider observance of Kashrut to be important. Reform Jews became more and more "German" and less and less "Jewish" in many aspects of their religious observances and daily lives. Germany's Jews by and large believed themselves to be assimilated into and a part of the German population. The family of David and Emma Ichenhäuser in Cologne was just such a German-Jewish family.

---

16   *History of the Jews in Cologne*, Jesse Russell, Ronald Cohn, Pub. Lennex Corp., (2012), p. 15.

17   *Pogrom Night* at xxi.

18   *History of the Jews in Cologne* at 33.

THE ICHENHÄUSERS

T HE HISTORY OF THE ICHENHÄUSER FAMILY BEGINS IN THE mid-18th century in the small town of Ichenhausen. The town, situated in the heavily forested Bavarian district of Günzburg, is near Germany's southwestern border with France. Ichenhausen, filled with the timber and stucco buildings common in Germany, straddled the River Günz, which flowed north through Bavaria before becoming a tributary of the Danube.

Jews had lived in Ichenhausen since the mid 1500's. By 1687, there were enough Jewish families to support construction of a synagogue and establishment of a Jewish cemetery. By the mid-19th century, Ichenhausen's Jewish community was the second largest in Bavaria, with some 900 Jews living there. Ichenhäuser family records begin with Isachar Bar aus Ichenhausen ("Isachar Bar from Ichenhausen") who lived in Ichenhausen in the early 18th century. Jews in Germany were not allowed to take last names until after the Napoleanic Wars. When the prohibition ended, many Jews took the name of the town in which they lived as their last name. Isachar followed suit and took his surname from his hometown of Ichenhausen.[19]

---

19   By 1933, thirteen percent of Ichenhausen's population was Jewish. During Kristallnacht in November 1938, Nazi mobs destroyed the town's synagogue and Jewish cemetery. Many Jews left Ichenhausen for large cities in Germany or fled the country altogether. The Nazis deported or killed on site those who stayed in Ichenhausen. In 1942, the Nazis deported eighty-two Jews from Ichenhausen to Lublin and sent another twenty-eight Jews to Theresienstadt. In 1943, the Nazis

In the early 18th century, Isachar left Ichenhausen and settled in the town of Fürth, where he died in 1790. Fürth was wedged between the Pegnitz and Rednitz rivers in northern Bavaria's administrative division of Middle Franconia, a few miles northwest of Nuremberg.[20] Fürth was established near a river ford; the town's name was derived from the German word for "ford." One of Fürth's most imposing sights was St. Michael's church, which the faithful constructed in the 11th century. St. Michael's black stone spire and red-tiled roof could be seen from all points in the town and the surrounding area.

The first mention of Jews in Fürth was in 1440, when the town allowed two Jews to settle there, albeit while subjecting them to higher taxes than other residents of the town. Notwithstanding this disparate treatment, by the 17th century Fürth's Jewish population had grown and prospered to such an extent that the community had a well-known Yeshiva (an Orthodox Jewish college or seminary). The Jewish community also established a Jewish cemetery on Weiherstrasse in 1607; it was one of the oldest Jewish cemeteries in Germany.[21]

Fürth's Jewish community erected a synagogue in 1617. In 1653, the community built the first Jewish hospital in Germany, which also happened to be the first hospital of any kind in Fürth. By the early 1800s, Jews made up nearly twenty percent of Fürth's population. After periods of restrictions on Jewish life and Jewish immigration to the town, Fürth rescinded its anti-Jewish laws. By the mid-19th century, more than 2500 Jews lived in Fürth, making the community large enough that it could build and support Jewish

---

deported ten Jews from Ichenhausen to Auschwitz. Only one Jew from Ichenhausen survived the war. (Wikipedia—Ichenhausen, Germany.) Yad Vashem has a memorial named "The Valley of the Communities" listing the Jewish communities the Nazis largely or completely destroyed. Ichenhausen is identified as such a community on one of the steles comprising the memorial.

20   Nuremburg would later become one of the areas in Germany with the most ardent Nazi sympathizers. It was the city for which the virulently anti-Semitic "Nuremberg Laws" were named and was the location for the war crimes trials of Nazi leaders in 1945-46.

21   The Nazis almost completely destroyed the cemetery; it was restored in 1949.

primary and high schools. In short, by the mid to late 19th century, Fürth had a thriving Jewish community.[22]

Isachar Ichenhäuser's son Simon married Gitel Schlenker. Gitel's father, Isak, was born in 1697, demonstrating how far back a Jewish presence existed in Fürth. Simon and Gitel's son, Joel, was born on October 19, 1768. Gitel died in 1775, when Joel was only seven years old. Simon lived another fifteen years before he passed away in 1790. No records have been found showing what trade Simon plied to support himself, Gitel, and Joel.

Joel Ichenhäuser married Bella Schwelheimer; Bella gave birth to a son, Elias, in 1794. Bella passed away in 1836; Joel died fifteen years later in 1851. Elias married a woman by the last name of Hechinger; family records do not disclose her birthdate, first name, or town of origin. Elias' son Jacob was born in Fürth on December 20, 1824. As a young man, Jacob parted his long, dark hair on the left, with a ring of curls circling the back of his neck. He wore a beard that wrapped around his chin. His dark suits were sometimes set off with a floral vest and cravat. Jacob later grew a full beard and moustache, which made him look quite distinguished when his hair and beard turned grey.

Jacob Ichenhäuser's wife Babette Ollesheimer was a strikingly beautiful woman with blond hair and blue eyes. They were married on August 31, 1853, when Jacob was twenty-nine and Babette was twenty-one. Babette's parents, David Ollesheimer and Sofie Rindskopf, like many Jews at the time, maintained a strictly Orthodox home.

The Orthodox Jews of Fürth lived in their own world largely cut off from the community around them. Jacob went to daven (pray) every morning, as was customary for Orthodox men. When the minyan (Jewish law required ten men in order to hold a Jewish prayer service) completed Schachrit (the morning prayer service)

---

22   On November 9, 1938, roving Kristallnacht mobs destroyed Fürth's synagogue. The SS arrested and sent 132 Jews from Fürth to the Dachau concentration camp in the immediate aftermath of Kristallnacht. Those Jews still in Fürth after Kristallnacht either fled or, if they stayed in Fürth, ultimately died in the death camps. By 1944, fewer than twenty-five Jews remained in Fürth out of a population of some 1200 Jews prior to Kristallnacht. (Wikipedia, Fürth, Germany.)

the men schmoozed for a few minutes before sitting down to study Torah. On brisk winter mornings, the members of the minyan might throw back a shot of schnapps to fortify themselves against the cold before they left. Whether drinking schnapps was primarily social or was intended to serve as anti-freeze, or both, the fiery shots were as much a part of the men's winter morning ritual as the prayers.

Jacob operated a business, Elias Schwelheimer & Company, that the family had established in 1788. The family named the company after Jacob's father Elias and Jacob's paternal grandmother's surname Schwelheimer. Jacob sold Nuremberg and Taudwaren toys. His wares included Nuremberg's famous "Tand" toys such as furnished dollhouses, wooden soldiers, toy horses, drums, and small brass cannons. "Tand" means a toy or trinket made by hand, as opposed to the toys manufactured by machines once Germany's toy industry became mechanized. Tand is an old-fashioned word that was originally applied to tin toys. In the 18th and 19th centuries, Nuremberg was world-famous for high-quality mechanical toys made of sheet metal.[23]

Jacob and Babette's first child, David, was born in Fürth on September 24, 1854. David had six brothers and five sisters: Siegmund, Jeanette, Klara, Julius, Cilly, Simon, Maurice [Moritz], Raphael, Louise, Hermann, and Sofie. Jacob and his seven sons were almost their own minyan. Jacob and Babette maintained a strictly Orthodox home just as their parents had. This meant attending services, observing Jewish holidays, and keeping a kosher home. Cooking in most kosher homes involved using a lot of chicken schmaltz (fat). Brisket, chicken, onions, potatoes, and potato or noodle kugels would have been mainstays on the family dinner table. Babette likely diced chicken skin and fried it in schmaltz to create the crisp, delicious, but artery-threatening treat known as gribenes, a Jewish version of chicharrons. Babette died on December 7, 1877, at age forty-four, barely one year after the birth of her twelfth child. Jacob lived another twenty-one years before passing away on October 6, 1898, at age sixty-four.

---

23   The tin toys are still made today in Germany by Schuco Toys and Arnold Toys.

David attended the Jewish parochial school in Fürth. "Jewish schools and Jewish education for children and young people were of paramount importance in Jewish communities in Germany. Many synagogues started out as schools and became synagogues only later on. This is where the Yiddish word for synagogue, 'Schul', meaning 'school,' comes from."[24]

Upon completing his schooling, David went to work at Jacob's toy store. David wore a full, but well-trimmed, beard and moustache. He parted his dark hair in the center and applied a dash of pomade that made it glisten. His appearance was one of dignity, gentility, and composure.

In November 1881, at age twenty-seven, David became engaged to Emma Dülken of Cologne-Deutz. They were married in Cologne on May 22, 1882, when Emma was twenty-two. Emma, the youngest of five siblings (Lina, Joseph, Julia, Isidor, and Emma), was born in Deutz on December 19, 1860. Emma was trained as a pianist and singer. It is unclear how she and David came to know one another, since Fürth was some 250 miles southeast of Cologne-Deutz.

Emma parted her dark hair in the middle and pulled it back, while a few curls in front broke free and spilled over her forehead. Her dresses had brocade on the front, while the collars were made of lace. She pinned a cascade of lace to the front of her dress, while a pendant dangled from her necklace. Emma had a calm, steady gaze and appeared to be deep in thought in family photographs. In November 1882, six months after David and Emma were married, David became a partner in Elias Schwelheimer.

---

24 *Pogrom Night* at xx.

THE DÜLKENS

E MMA DÜLKEN'S ANCESTORS HAD LIVED IN COLOGNE-Deutz for generations. The first Dülken to reside in Deutz and the namesake of the family, Joseph Dülken, moved to Deutz around 1700. Joseph's wife Feigel Rachel was a native of Deutz. Joseph was a well-respected member of Deutz's Jewish congregation and served as a representative of the Jewish community in dealing with local authorities. Joseph's son Abraham also served as the head of the Jewish community for a short period. The men of the many generations of Dülkens in Deutz worked as teachers, butchers, barbers, musicians, bakers, merchants, shoemakers, and manufacturers.[25]

In 1712, "The books of the City Hall of the City of Deutz state that the Jew Salomon Rindskopf asked permission of the Mayor of Deutz to settle the widow of Joseph Dülken and her two children in Deutz."[26] Joseph's widow had previously lived in Moers, a small town near the German border with Holland.

Another Joseph Dülken (a descendant of the family namesake who had moved to Deutz around 1700) and his wife Jeckeibel Wallach had a son, Moses, in 1807. Joseph died on May 19, 1812, when Moses was only five; Jeckeibel died on February 2, 1819, when Moses was twelve. Young Moses Dülken became a baker. Perhaps

---

25   *Rundgang Durch Deutz* ("Tour of Deutz"), Das Jüdische Köln—Geschichte und Gegenwart ("Jewish Cologne: Past and Present"), Author Barbara Becker-Jákli, 2012.

26   *Dülken Family Genealogy* at 1.

he baked the heavy loaves of rye and pumpernickel bread that were common to Jewish communities in Germany and eastern Europe. Moses and his customers may have eaten the dark bread with pickled herring from Germany's North Sea coast or with fresh herring imported from Denmark and Holland. Perhaps Moses' customers spread chicken schmaltz on his breads and topped the schmaltz with thinly sliced onions, or perhaps they ate thick slices of his dark bread with "schmeers" of cream cheese. Records do not disclose whether Moses sold his goods in a shop in Deutz or peddled them from a pushcart. Perhaps he took his baked goods across the wide, fast-flowing Rhine to sell them in Cologne during the day before returning to Deutz at dusk.

Moses Dülken and his wife Liselle Wallerstein had two sons: Anselm Heinrich Dülken, born in 1808, and Joseph Moises born on September 15, 1813.[27] Anselm and Joseph were the fifth generation of Dülkens in Deutz. Anselm became a schoolteacher, but he also founded a small trading business in 1837. Anselm initially sold goods as varied as bone meal and millstones. He purchased guano from Chile for use as a soil conditioner and fertilizer. He also sold cotton and woolen goods to local farmers.[28] Anselm later branched out into selling wood and scraps of building material. He was so successful selling lumber that he eventually founded A.H. (Anselm Heinrich) Dülken & Cie "Wood and board dealers, bones and artificial fertilizers." A.H. Dülken & Cie expanded over time; the lumber trade eventually became the most important part of the business.[29]

Anselm Dülken was a clean-shaven man with a strong chin. He had a wave in his hair which he brushed back from his high forehead. He wore wire-rimmed glasses and displayed a stern visage. Anselm dressed in black, three-piece suits featuring wide lapels, along with a vest, upturned shirt collar, and black cravat. At times, Anselm served as a Deutz city councilor. For many years, he was chairman of the

---

27 Moses Dülken died on May 8, 1839; Liselle passed away twenty years later on September 22, 1859.

28 *Rundgang Durch Deutz.*

29 *Rundgang Durch Deutz.*

Deutz Jewish community, which he led with an iron fist.[30] Given his reputation as a resolute leader, it is easy to envision him as a stern school master who always had a wooden ruler ready to rap the knuckles of recalcitrant or ill-behaved students.

Anselm Dülken married Jeannette ("Netta") Baum on November 2, 1842, when Anselm was thirty-five and Jeannette was twenty-one. Netta's father Isaac Baum was a butcher; her mother Caroline Salm tended the home. Netta, born in 1819, had dark hair that she parted in the middle and pulled back, with long curls cascading down to her shoulders. She pinned a hair covering on the back of her head. She wore dark, floor length dresses, with a small white bow tied tightly at her neck. Anselm and Netta lived at 65 Freiheitstrasse ("Freedom Street") in Deutz with their five children: Joseph, Isidor, Lina, Julia, and Emma.

Isidor and Joseph joined their father working at A.H. Dülken & Cie. Joseph, the oldest brother, was a tall man with a moustache and mutton-chop sideburns. Isidor, clean-shaven, was several inches shorter than Joseph; he attired himself stylishly in three-piece suits and crisp bow ties. Emma's older sister Julia wore full skirts with a jacket cinched tightly at her waist. She had long dark curls that fell over her shoulders.

Anselm's brother Joseph Moises Dülken became a master butcher. Moises likely dealt mainly in chicken, along with lamb, goat, ox tails, and perhaps some fish. Beef was expensive and, accordingly, rare. Of course, customers would never find pork in the shop of an Orthodox Jewish butcher. The carcasses hung from large hooks in the shop; Moises butchered the various cuts as his customers desired. Joseph Moises made his home and maintained his butcher shop at 73 Siegburgerstrasse in Deutz. With his wife Jennifer Baum, they had eight children: Elisabeth, Helena, Julianna, Herrman, Eva, Marianne, Rosa, and Sibilla. Eva, born in 1856, married Hermann Capell, a shoemaker; they settled in Cologne. Eva's daughter Else Capell married and lived in Cologne with her daughter Lore, who was born in 1917.[31]

---

30   *Rundgang Durch Deutz.*

31   Eva, Else, and Lore did not leave Germany before the onset of WWII. The

After Anselm Dülken passed away in 1887, Joseph and Isidor ran A.H. Dülken & Cie, eventually moving the business from Deutz to Cologne. In 1897, after Joseph passed away, Isidor ran the company and purchased a lot in Porz on the east bank of the Rhine where he built a modern sawmill at which the company could cut and plane lumber. The business thrived and steadily expanded the markets it served. The Dülkens and their families were well-established and financially successful. Their futures seemed to be secure.[32]

Nazis deported Eva to Theresienstadt; she was reported missing after the war. The Nazis deported Else and Lore to the Jewish ghetto in Riga, the capital of Latvia. Elsa and Lore survived concentration camps and forced labor. After being liberated, they spent a short period in Cologne in 1947 before emigrating to Palestine. Lore moved back to Cologne in 1957 and opened a butcher shop with her husband. Lore died in Cologne in 1998 and was buried in the Cologne- Bocklemund Jewish cemetery.

32 When Isidor Dülken died in 1932, his two sons took over management of the by-then international lumber company. The Nazis forced the sons to sell the business pursuant to the Nazi Aryanization program; the Nazis confiscated the entire sale price. (Rundgang Durch Deutz.)

THE ICHENHÄUSERS IN COLOGNE

ALTHOUGH DAVID AND EMMA ICHENHÄUSER WERE MAR-
ried in Cologne, they established their household in Fürth,
where David had his business. Life in Fürth proved to be difficult for
Emma. She was used to the freedom of life she had enjoyed in the
Rhineland. Deutz was just across the river from Cologne, the latter
being a bustling, cosmopolitan area replete with shops, museums,
and cultural events. Emma had trouble adjusting to the small-town
life of Fürth, which offered little by way of such amenities, let alone
an active social life such as that to which Emma was accustomed.

After several years in Fürth and likely at Emma's urging, David
and Emma moved to Berlin where they opened a branch of Elias
Schwelheimer at 70 Ritterstrasse. On October 2, 1887, David
and Emma had their first child, a son, whom they named Anselm
Heinrich.

David and Emma soon left Berlin and moved to Cologne,
where their second son, Ernst, was born on October 19, 1889. Their
third son, Max, was born in Cologne on December 4, 1892. David,
a quiet man, was known as a skilled mechanic who often fixed
mechanical problems at the homes of friends and neighbors. With
three young sons and David's business up and running, David and
Emma were well settled in Cologne.

In 1897, David, with the assistance of Emma's brother Isidore,
started a lumber and wood products business ("Holzhandlung"—
timber trade) under the name Lentzen, Meyer & Cie. His lumber

yard was located at 409 Aachnerstrasse in the village of Braunsfeld, roughly two and a half miles west of Cologne's imposing Gothic cathedral (the "Kölner Dom"). The Gothic structure, with a height of 515 feet, was the tallest twin-spired church in the world and the second tallest church in Europe. Begun in 1248, it was not completed until 1880. To get to Lentzen, Meyer & Cie from the Deutzer Brücke (Deutz bridge) that spanned the Rhine from Deutz to Cologne's downtown, customers headed west along Augustinerstrasse, which became Cäcilienstrasse, which then became Hahnenstrasse, and the thoroughfare was ultimately dubbed Aachenerstrasse just past Cologne's West Habsburger Ring Road (the "Habsburgerring"). It was there, in the village of Braunsfeld, that David operated his lumber company.

In 1906, David and Emma's eldest son Anselm Heinrich (who went by Heinrich but whom friends and family referred to as "Heini") passed the high school "leaving exam" that students took upon completing high school as a prerequisite to attending university. Heinrich then studied law at the University of Freiburg. In 1914, at age 27, Heini passed the assessor's examination to become a "Rechtsassessor," a title held by law graduates who had passed the first and second state examinations (finishing law school and a two-year legal clerkship) to qualify for a career as a judge, prosecutor, attorney, or civil law notary.

Heinrich was a handsome young man with a straightforward gaze. Unlike his father, who had a neatly trimmed goatee and a moustache that almost qualified as a handlebar, Heini's thin moustache was short and neatly trimmed. His dark three-piece suits featured small lapels. Heini topped off his outfit with a black bowler on his wavy hair; he also carried a walking stick. David's and Emma's second son, Ernst, became a merchant in 1905 after serving one year as an apprentice. Ernst kept his hair cropped short, had his moustache neatly trimmed, and wore a high collar shirt and cravat with his dark suits. Heinrich and Ernst seemed well positioned to pursue their chosen careers in law and business.

MAX ICHENHÄUSER

DAVID AND EMMA'S YOUNGEST SON, MAX, SPENT HIS EARLY summers with his mother visiting the village of Ilsenberg at the foot of the Harz Mountains in central Germany. Ilsenberg was nestled in a valley surrounded by mountains to climb and forests to explore. Max often played with his cousin Sophie Cohn from Berlin; she was two years older than he. They were thick as thieves and could often be seen walking arm-in-arm through the town. Max wrote to his mother Emma to tell her how he was faring while away from home:

> Dear Mom!
>
> I drank up everything in my cup—also ate an egg and bread roll. Later, I ate a lot too. I've already gotten a little fatter. By the time you come back, I will have gotten so fat you won't recognize me. So far, I'm behaving myself really well. I wrote this myself. If Dad is still with you, then please give him my greetings—sending you warm greetings and kisses too,
>
> Your Mäxchen [diminutive for Max]

In 1898, when Max was six, David and Emma enrolled him at the pre-school of the Oberrealschule in Cologne. The Oberrealschule was a secondary school that emphasized mathematics, natural sciences, and modern languages to prepare students for university, as opposed to other schools' emphasis on the classic languages of Latin and Greek.

In 1901, when Max was nine and Ernst was twelve, the two of them spent the summer in the village of Oberdorf, near Bopfingen in Bavaria, where their uncle Hermann Kroner had a farm. They stayed at a boarding house owned by the Lehmann family, where Therese Lehmann looked after them. Max and Ernst were avid stamp collectors; they competed with one another rooting through paper waste at Uncle Hermann's home looking for postage stamps. Max and Ernst also loved to play with Mingo, Uncle Hermann's black and white-spotted dog.

Max and Ernst frequently got into trouble, such as one day when Ernst returned from a walk in the forest brandishing a snake he had found, much to the consternation of the family and neighbors. When Ernst approached, horrified townspeople scattered as if he had a huge serpent in tow. Uncle Hermann, not a lover of snakes, quickly inflicted a premature death upon the poor creature, causing it to give up, in Max's words, "its black soul."

On another occasion, Uncle Hermann was hosting an important meeting at his house. To eliminate distractions, Uncle Hermann banished Max and Ernst from the home. Thoroughly peeved at being exiled, they sought retribution by slamming shut the wooden window shutters on the outside of the house leaving Uncle Hermann and his guest in the dark. Their prank did not earn Max and Ernst much in the way of good will, although Uncle Hermann eventually came to see the humor in it.

Ernst wrote to Martha, David, and Heinrich to fill them in on his and Max's adventures. "We are doing well and hope that you are too. Max just dances around and is in such high spirits that he doesn't know what to do with himself. Have a good Shabbat. With warm greetings and a kiss from your son Ernst who loves you." Max added a few lines: "I also send you many greetings and kisses. We like it a lot here. We are very happy and are having lots of fun. And yesterday we went swimming. Greetings again, Max."

Ernst wrote again a few days later: "Monday we sent you a postcard with a picture of Baldern (castle) on it and yesterday another letter. So, dear parents, there's no need to worry about us and be warmly greeted by your cheery son Ernst." Max was also quite pleased with their visit: "We are very healthy and well and doing great. Everyone says we look better since arriving here. We haven't been out and about with Uncle Hermann yet. Today, we are going to the forest with Hortensia (Lehmann) and many others. An always cheerful Max sends you warm greetings and kisses." Hortensia, or Therese to those who knew her well, added a postscript to let Max and Martha know the boys were well; apparently Max and Ernst had failed to write to their parents for several days, sparking some alarm in the Ichenhäuser home. When Ernst wrote a few days later, he again wished his parents a good Shabbat. Ernst's regular references to Shabbat suggest that David and Martha were sufficiently attentive to Jewish tradition that observing Shabbat was part of their lives.

During the summer of 1902, by which time Max had reached the sixth grade, he and Ernst were together again in Euskirchen, southwest of Cologne in North Rhine-Westphalia. They built dams of twigs and mud and hand-dredged canals along the banks of the Erft River. They played in nearby ponds where they caught frogs, lizards, and fish. In 1903 and 1904, the family spent their summer holiday in Bad Brückenau, a spa town on the Rion River in the Rhon Mountains of northern Bavaria. Max and Ernst loved clambering around the rock falls and catching salamanders in the icy mountain streams. Max was interested in all things in nature. He collected any fossils and crystals he came across during his exploration of the forests and mountains the family visited.

In 1905, Max began attending the Oberealschule associated with the Reform Real Gymnasium on Humboldtstrasse in Cologne. Max and his schoolmates Fritz Kauffmann, Otto May, and Karl Hirsch stuck together "like glue." Years later, they became fraternity brothers. Max eventually attended the Reform "Gymnasium," the German version of a college preparatory high school. Max's favorite subjects were math, natural sciences, and astronomy. These interests led Max to join the school's literary science club.

The Ichenhäusers played tennis, or at least so it seemed based on an undated photograph taken at Bad Brückenau showing them with tennis rackets and wearing what presumably were their tennis clothes. David, with his carefully groomed goatee and upturned handle-bar moustache, wore a three-piece suit, white shirt, tie, and a watch chain dangling from his vest. Emma sat holding an umbrella while wearing a long-sleeved silk blouse and full-length skirt. Heinrich and Ernst wore suit jackets, vests, and ties. Max, in addition to sporting the only smile of the group (perhaps the others took their tennis more seriously), wore a sailor outfit with what were either knickerbockers or trousers hiked up to his knees, and high-top leather shoes.

During the summer of 1905, by which time Max was twelve, Emma, Max, and Heinrich vacationed together on Norderney, one of the seven populated East Frisian Islands along Germany's North Sea coast near the Dutch border. The boys played on the beach and splashed in the waves notwithstanding the chilly North Sea water. Max spent his days building huge sandcastles and collecting starfish and shells. By the time the family returned to Cologne, Max was tanned to a dark brown. David and Ernst had opted not to go to Norderney, instead returning to Bad Brückenau for their vacation.

Back in Cologne, Max and his friends Fritz, Otto, and Karl founded the Nature Study Club. They called the Club's initial meeting to order with great ceremony. Max gave the first lecture; he selected radium as his topic. The boys invited the Erica Club—a girls' club whose members were Resi Lobbenberg, Grete Silberbach, Liesel Marx, and Billa Lyon—to attend. Despite giving his best effort, Max was convinced the girls were eminently bored by his lecture. (Max's Green Diary.)

The first family home Max could remember was a second-floor apartment at 46 Roonstrasse in Cologne's Latin Quarter. The apartment, located at the corner of Roonstrasse and Beethovenstrasse, was southwest of central Cologne just outside the Ring Road. The Ichenhäusers eventually moved a few blocks up the street to an apartment on the first floor of a building at 17 Beethovenstrasse. The building had a garden featuring a sandbox in which the boys enjoyed playing. The building manager allowed the boys to keep kittens as pets, which they were very happy about. The family later moved again, but this time only across the street to an apartment at 8 Beethovenstrasse.

Max had his bar mitzvah in December 1905 at the new Reform synagogue at 50 Roonstrasse. The synagogue, constructed in 1899, featured a substantial central tower flanked by two, smaller, peaked towers separated by a rose window. The shul was southwest of central Cologne near Ehrenfeld. The Ichenhäusers could reach the shul in ten minutes by walking southwest from their home on Beethovenstrasse and then turning north onto Roonstrasse. The Roonstrasse synagogue was the largest in Cologne and soon became the center of Cologne's mainstream, liberal Jewish community.[33]

The winter of 1905 saw Max learn how to dance. It is not known whether this was to allow him to dance at bar mitzvah parties (if such even occurred then) or was simply training for adult social life. However, during the winter of 1906, Max broke one of his shinbones on the playground at school and spent several months recuperating at home, putting his nascent dancing career on hiatus. Max did not seem at a loss from his injury; he enjoyed the long break from school.

As a teenager, Max's interests began to change:

> The following year, 1907, my parents and I again spent the autumn holidays in Brückenau. I was by then a young man [age fifteen], wore long pants, and played the role of young cavalier. I romanced two young ladies, Nelly Walter, age 16, from Bamberg, and Ida Haas, 19 years old from Frankfurt. A few months earlier, in May, my parents celebrated their silver wedding anniversary. In order to avoid any festivities, they took a trip with Heini and Ernst to the Berner Oberland [the higher elevations in the Swiss canton of Bern]. I stayed in Cologne and was a guest at Aunt Clara's while they were gone. (Max's Green Diary.)

Max clearly felt he was coming into his own as a young man about town with real pants to wear and romantic endeavors to

---

33 *Pogrom Night* at xix.

pursue. He joined the Kölner Gymverein, an athletic club, where he maintained a membership until he went to college.

By the time Max was fifteen, his artistic talent was evident. In art class, he sketched a beautifully detailed image of a grey heron. The drawing shows the feathers on the heron's head and wings, its rust-colored neck, white belly, and black, webbed feet. The level of detail was so fine that it included a white dot on the cornea of the heron's eye to show the reflection of light. Max also produced a skillful sketch of his father with fine pencil strokes detailing David's moustache and beard.

In 1908, at age sixteen, Max passed the so-called "one-year exam" and received an exemption from having to take the otherwise required oral examination.

> The following winter, as *obersekunder* (second year student in the Gymnasium), I took dancing classes in the Kromerschen Wednesday Club…There was a new year's party and three balls that took place; at the first, Luise Lowenberg was my partner, (at) the last one Greta Bieler was my dinner partner. At one of the balls, I performed for the first time with my minimal talent; I sang a song for the concert. In addition, there were a number of private parties at the Feilchenfelds, Lowenbergs, Gottschalks, Biebers, Silberbachs, and at Carnival at the Levys. A number of the members organized a tennis club in the spring, in which I participated. (Max's Green Diary.)

Max was keeping more than busy with his interest in science, astronomy, singing, tennis, dancing, art, and a calendar full of parties.

Max was also an inveterate diarist, and he was quite thorough in his entries. As an example, his notes included lists of the young men and women who participated in his dance classes, fraternities, and other activities. He displayed this attention to detail in the diaries he kept throughout his life. Max continued to sketch and write doggerel poetry. His busy social life included a New Year's party and three balls in 1909.

Max was becoming quite a young Renaissance man given his many interests and activities. As evidenced by the Nature Study Club, dance classes, tennis club, parties, and balls, Max's segment of Cologne's Jewish community had an active and varied social life. Although the Ichenhäusers' lives were largely conducted within the Jewish community, the family felt they were very much a part of Cologne and Germany.

In 1909, at age seventeen, Max decided to forego further education in order to become a merchant:

> During this year, I made the decision to leave school and to become a merchant. Two teachers [had] made my life miserable. Since my father wanted an apprenticeship for me which would leave my Saturdays free, I didn't have much choice. At Easter 1909, I apprenticed to the wholesale hat shop David and Geldern. The son of the owner, Alfred David, was a good friend of my brother Heini's. The business required three years of apprenticeship, paid 15, 20 and 25 marks. In August I got a week vacation. Parents, Heini and I went to Harzburg [a spa town in the Radau Valley in Lower Saxony] for summer break. Here we ran into Leonard Cohen from Berlin, and his wife-to-be, Miss Elsbeth Glaser. We took many lovely excursions, to the Radau and Ockertal, Steinerneu Renne, to Goslar (Schloss), to the top of the Brocken, and into the Hermannus cave. I worked in the shop for a year, but finally this occupation became so unpleasant for me that I decided to make a change. I vacillated for some time as to which profession I should engage in. I always had a great interest in science, engineering and architecture, but since there didn't seem to be many opportunities in these fields, I decided to go into medicine. (Max's Green Diary.)

And so, as the result of an unhappy apprenticeship at a hat shop and process of elimination more than anything else, Max decided to embark on a career in medicine.

UNIVERSITY BECKONS

TO STUDY MEDICINE, MAX HAD TO PASS THE REIFEPRÜFUNG
"leaving-school" exam. The examination Max had taken
upon completing the Unterprima (the second to last year of the
Gymnasium) was not sufficient. Max did not want to return to
school to study for the examination, so he decided to prepare under
the guidance of a tutor. When Easter arrived in 1911, he applied to
take the Reifeprüfung examination as an "external student." Through
a Provincialschule colleague, he was sent to the Realgymnasium in
Krefeld, near Düsseldorf, to take the test. He passed the required
examinations in German, Latin, French, English, history, geography,
mathematics, physics, and chemistry and obtained the qualification
necessary to begin studying medicine at the universities in Bonn and
Freiburg.

Max wrote in his diary about his many fraternity brothers and
friends in medical school. Some of his fondest memories were of
trips he and his friends took to Bonn that included enjoying the
wonderful "Bowlen" he and his friends drank at Bellinghausen in
Königswinter and at Annchen's in Goesberg. Bowlen calls for mixing a bottle of Rhine wine with a bottle of Moselle wine in a punch
bowl, then adding fresh strawberries and letting the wine and berries chill and steep for several hours. When guests arrive, a bottle of
champagne or sparkling wine is added to create the bubbly beverage.
The resulting punch is sweet and goes down easily, for some a bit too
easily. Most of all, Max loved his fraternity's "Founding Banquet"

that took place in August in Mehlem, just south of Bonn, along the banks of the Rhine.

Toward the end of the academic year in 1912, Max wrote a scholarly paper entitled "The Concepts of Race, People, Nations and Special Aspects of Judaism." The notion of Jews being a race distinct from Germans was already in vogue in Germany, which led Max to explore the concept in his paper. Unfortunately, no copies of his paper have been found.

In the summer of 1912, Max, now twenty, went to the University of Freiburg to study. The city made a good impression on him due to its lovely location at the foot of the Schwarzwald (the Black Forest), its many buildings constructed during the Middle Ages, and its magnificent Münster (cathedral). Max wrote that "this city with its romantic magic is the proper environment for young students." However, he felt the university buildings and theaters, while wonderful examples of modern architecture, did not fit with the rest of the town.

On weekends, Max occasionally drove to Strasbourg. He took excursions to the Black Forest, the Feldberg (a peak in the Black Forest that was the highest mountain in Germany outside of the Alps), the Belchen (another peak in the Black Forest), and the Höllental (a deep valley in the Black Forest). He finished the summer with a week of strenuous hiking in Switzerland. Max was overwhelmed by the beauty of the Lauterbrunnental's (the Lauterbrunnen Valley) feathery waterfalls cascading down the mountainsides, the steep valley walls draped with green foliage, and the snow-capped peaks all around.

For the winter semester, Max stayed in Freiburg. This was a wonderful time for him, in no small part because of his busy social life. A Jewish women's boarding house was situated near the university. That was where Max and his fraternity brothers sought companions for the many parties they attended. They belonged to a dance club which they frequented with their lady friends. They went to a Karnival ball, as was traditional in much of Germany. Their fraternity hosted a ball "which everyone agreed was wonderful." (Max's

Green Diary.) On Sundays, he usually went to the mountains to ice skate, sled, or ski.

Over the holiday break from school in December 1912, the Kartelltag took place in Bonn. The Kartell Juedischer Verbindungen (KJV) was an umbrella organization of Jewish university fraternities in Germany.[34] The KJV was composed of two groups. One group, the Bund Juedischer Corporation, had been formed in 1901. Its purpose was "to function as the meeting center of all Jewish students who consciously feel themselves Jews and are willing to collaborate in the development of living Judaism."[35]

The second group, the Kartell Zionistischer Verbindungen (KZV), had been formed in 1906. The KZV was the first explicitly Zionist student group in Germany.[36] In 1914, the two groups merged into the KJV "which was dedicated to educate its members to strive for 'national unity of the Jewish community' and for 'a renewal in Eretz-Israel'."[37] Max and one of his friends were delegates to the Kartelltag from the university in Freiburg. "This Kartelltag had a special feeling due to the boycott and press of the Kölner liberals and assimilationists. The big assembly took place in Cologne in the (Rhineland) Lodge, which was completely sold out. Particularly the Orthodox would not be denied the opportunity to protest the leadership of the liberals. With the flags of the various groups and the thirty leaders in [undecipherable word], the ballroom was a colorful and exhilarating scene." (Max's Green Diary.)

The Kartelltag sought to meet the need many German Jews felt to band together to protect themselves from anti-Semitism, as well as to pursue Zionism as a solution to the unsettling times in which German Jews found themselves. The Kartelltag also reflected a deep split in the Jewish community. On one side were those Jews who felt deeply German and who believed that, despite increasingly anti-Semitic rhetoric and threatening behavior towards Jews, they

---

34 Encyclopedia.com, Kartell Juedischer Verbindungen.

35 *Id.*

36 *Id.*

37 *Id.*

would be able to continue their lives in Germany. That group was opposed by a faction who increasingly felt that Jews had no future in Germany. This faction believed that German Jews needed to find a new home, which Zionists argued should be in Eretz Yisrael—the land that would ultimately become the State of Israel.

In the summer of 1913, Max registered with Infantry Regiment 113 in Freiburg. He expected to be turned down for military service because of the leg fracture he had sustained, but, to his surprise, the army accepted him. (It is unclear whether Max registered due to a general requirement to register for military service or whether increasing tensions in Europe led to the requirement that he register.) He then buckled down to study for his exams. Max passed the preliminary examination in medicine in Freiburg with a grade of "sehr gut" in all subjects. In Germany, to this day, schools do not award letter grades. Germans use a point system. "Sehr gut," which means very good, is often translated as excellent and was the highest grade that German schools awarded. At the end of the semester, David and Emma picked up Max at school and the three of them spent a week hiking in Switzerland.

Upon returning to Cologne, Max applied for a transfer from Regiment 113 in Freiburg to Infantry Regiment 160 in Bonn. This required another medical examination. In October 1913, the transfer came through and Max joined Bonn Infantry Regiment 160 for a one-year tour of duty. However, because of his leg fracture he was dismissed on October 13 and left for Berlin to continue his studies.

Max spent one semester in Berlin:

> The semester in Berlin I did not enjoy. The big city life and the rushing around all the time were not to my taste. Berlin is not the place for a pleasant student life, in particular since a student simply disappears in the big city…I was often invited by the numerous relatives, at Cohn's routinely Saturday noon, so that I was able to save on many dinner and supper costs…From old habits and customs, Uncle Hermann preserved many Jewish traditions. Therefore, the doggies (his King Charles Spaniels) had to sit very quietly at the table for the Kiddush and to eat their matzo… (Max's Green Diary.)

Max was not impressed by the architecture in Berlin. "The Museums and the Royal Theater made externally a very Prussian-sober impression on me. The Dom (cathedral) is a tasteless unharmonious mishmash." However, Max enjoyed Berlin's art museums and theaters, including productions of "The Merchant of Venice" and "King Lear." He also saw "Der Rosenkavelier" and "Aida" at the Royal Opera House. He went to the movies almost every Friday evening, but still sometimes felt lonely. He did not find a way to become comfortable with Berlin's active Jewish social life, even though he attended many balls and activities. "I have really learned to cherish and appreciate Cologne's lovely lifestyle."

A SMALL ADVENTURE

MAX TRAVELED OFTEN THROUGHOUT 1912 AND 1913. HIS hiking excursions frequently took him to Switzerland, where he visited Lucerne and marveled at its stunning wooden bridges bearing dozens of frescos painted on overhead wooden panels. He enjoyed the highly ornamented Baroque, Jesuit cathedral alongside the Reuss River. He watched the elegant swans paddle along the riverbanks waiting for passersby to toss bread to them. He visited the Aare Gorge in the nearby Hasli Valley. He went to Mt. Rigi outside of Lucerne, which offered expansive views of the Swiss Mitteland, Interlaken, as well as further into Germany and France. Other days he visited Switzerland's stunning Lauterbrunnen Valley, fashionable Zurich, the Tamina Gorge in eastern Switzerland, Lake Walensee, Klosters, and Davos. Max also traveled to the Strela Pass and the 2970 meters high Mt. Schilthorn, which offered views of the Eiger, Mönch, and Jungfrau peaks. His wanderlust and passion for hiking took him to St. Moritz, Alp Giop, Pontresina, Morteratsch, and the Brenner Pass on the Italian-Austrian border. He also traveled to the Bavarian Tyrol in southern Germany to climb the 2962 meters-high Zugspitze, Germany's highest mountain, which afforded views of four hundred Alpine peaks in four countries.

Max spent the next semester studying in Munich. "No other city pleased me as much." He loved the city's rich culture of museums, theaters, and its many sights, in particular its beautiful fountains. He also enjoyed Munich's relaxed, gemütlich (cozy) lifestyle, and the nearby Alps. Max and several fraternity brothers took advantage of the mountains for frequent hikes. On one outing, they stayed overnight in a tiny alpine hut. "When we awoke the next morning, the weather was wonderfully clear—above us a deep blue cloudless sky, all around us, covered with blindingly white new snow, the high mountain world." (Max's Green Diary.) Although the temperature hovered around zero, "the sun was so strong that we were able to sunbathe with only a pair of pants on." They sat outside the hut and watched avalanches crash down the mountainsides around them.

Max had a close call on one of their hikes:

> There was deep snow on the path and so the crossing was rather exhausting. On the descent to St. Jakob, I had a small adventure. We wanted to walk away from a rather steep snow mass; I, in order to show off bravely forged ahead. When the snow field ended and I hit the brakes, I couldn't stop. With great force, I skidded and slid across the adjoining, diagonally dropping rocks. A scary situation. I didn't know if ahead of me there was a vertical drop-off. With all my strength I braked on the rock face. I must have skidded twenty meters across the rocks, then reached another diagonal snowfield. I steered towards the middle where the snow had melted, and the dark earth was exposed. I finally, with further ahead braking, was able to bring myself to a stop. Further on, where the snow stopped, it was joined by green meadows where cattle grazed peacefully. So, I sat on the ground to assess the damage—the bones were all in one piece, pants and socks were threadbare, hands and knees scraped, but I got away fairly well. However, my backpack was gone, hat was gone, (walking) stick was gone. (Max's Green Diary.)

Small adventure indeed. Fortunately, Max's friends, who had taken a more careful path down the mountain expecting to have to collect his bones for burial, found his hat, pack, and walking stick. Only later did Max realize that the gold watch he wore on a vest watch-chain had been torn off during his slide and been lost. And yet, in a minor miracle, after Max left word with the parish priest about his watch (there was no police force in the Alps to whom he might report his loss), someone found it after the snow melted in the spring and mailed it to him, undamaged and running perfectly.

On another occasion, Max was hiking in the Alps when a storm blew in:

> A little way past the Höllentalhütte a thunderstorm broke loose; in the narrow wild valley it was quite a scary experience. Right next to me ran the steel cable of the Zugspitzhütte, which until now I had used as an anchor rope on the steep narrow path; not a particularly comforting feeling to have the lightening rod (steel cable) directly beside me. I speedily turned around and fled into the Höllentalhütte. (Max's Diary.)

The Höllental ("Hell's Valley") was a deep valley in Germany's Black Forest region of Baden-Wurttemberg which narrowed to a gorge in places. The "hütte" was a mountainside cabin owned by a German Alpine Club in the district of Garmisch-Partenkirchen. Max certainly selected challenging hikes. His aggressive decisions along with the vagaries of nature and weather added more than a little drama to some of his outings.

THE POLITICAL CLIMATE GOT
DARKER AND DARKER

DURING SPRING 1914, MAX PASSED THE OBERSARTZ senior medical commission examination. He then registered for the doctors' military draft. Max had been planning a trip with Ernst to visit the Dolomites in the fall, but such was not to be:

> When Austria gave its ultimatum to Serbia, I was in Munich. I'd had the intention of hiking through the Dolomites with Ernst at the end of the semester, but things were to turn out differently. The political climate got darker and darker. Since prospects of resolving the conflict were quickly non-existent, I decided with a heavy heart to return to Cologne on August 1, 1914. On that same day, we were informed that the outbreak of war was imminent. Railroads, bridges, etc., were already under watch by armed guards. When I arrived in Deutz, the Hohenzollern Bridge [which crossed the Rhine and connected Cologne on the Rhine's west bank with Cologne-Deutz on the east bank] was already closed to passengers; only the tram was still allowed to take passengers across the river with its doors locked. I immediately reported to the district command, where an immense crowd of people was waiting, and I received my induction orders for the second day of mobilization. (Max's Green Diary.)

The spark that gave rise to World War I was struck on July 28, 1914, when a Serbian nationalist assassinated Archduke Ferdinand of Austria. Heinrich, age twenty-seven, promptly enlisted in the army. Ernst, age twenty-five, followed Heinrich's lead and enlisted. Germany declared war on Austria on August 1. Ernst was quickly ordered into the field and Heinrich followed soon after. On August 3, 1914, less than a week after the war broke out, the army ordered Max, age twenty-two, to report for service as an Unterarzt ("Assistant Doctor"):

> I immediately reported to the district command, where an immense crowd of people was waiting, and I received my induction orders for the second day of mobilization. I was to report to the garrison hospital. Even Heini and Ernst had to report for duty in those days, though Heini was allowed a brief leave to go to Berlin to take his civil servant exams. Ernst marched off into the field after a few days, Heini soon followed.

> When I reported to the garrison hospital on August 3, eight medical graduates as well as a large number of stretcher bearers had assembled there. We marched immediately as a unit to the barracks in Riehl [a district of Cologne], where we were outfitted with old, white cuirassier uniforms.[38]

> Then, cheered on by the crowd, we returned to the military hospital. Once there, we let the garrison doctor know that we were medical graduates. So, he separated us from the others and divided us into two groups to serve as assistant physicians [doctors in training] at the two garrison hospitals. I and a corps brother, Katznellenbogen, who'd previously worked at the asylum, were sent to the military hospital in Deutz. The next day we took up our duties. Because we did not yet have a military rank, we started out as civilians. I was assigned to the surgical ward. (Max's WWI Diary pp. 1-2.)

On August 4, Germany invaded Belgium and initiated combat that quickly spread across much of Europe.

The German army required that each soldier maintain a Soldbuch, which started out as a pay record and evolved into a

---

38 Cuirassiers, derived from the French cuirassier, were cavalry that first appeared in the 15th century. They last took the field of battle in the early stages of WWI. The cuirassiers had a storied history of mass cavalry charges but were no longer viable in the face of artillery and machine gun fire.

booklet containing basic information about the solder as well as listing the soldier's deployments. The army categorized Max's religion
in his Soldbuch as "Israelite." This categorization, more racial than
religious, would resurface in Germany a few decades later with disastrous consequences for the "Israelites."

The army decreed that in order for medical graduates to be promoted to field physicians they had to take a six-week training course.
Accordingly, from early September to mid-October, Max and his fellow graduates took two hours of training each day. When they completed their training, they put in for promotion to become "acting
medical officers," who were also known as assistant field physicians.
On December 4, 1914, Max's twenty-second birthday, the promo-
tions were posted allowing Max and his fellow graduates to wear
army doctors' uniforms. (Max's WWI Diary pp. 2-3.) On January 7,
1915, the army assigned Max to Fortress Hospital No. XIII which
had been set up in an elementary school. As an attending physician,
Max lived in the hospital, but he was allowed to go home for meals.
(Max's WWI Diary p. 3.) However, the army soon sent Max into
the field.

In May, Max wrote to David and Emma while he was stationed behind the front for a few days of rest in a small village in
the Ardennes near the Belgian border. "When we were replaced [on
the front], we, of course, didn't look like human beings anymore,
but like pigs; on top of it, we were de-loused with every imaginable
de-lousing agent. It was a blessing to be able to wash oneself from
head to foot...The first 11 days in the trenches we had good weather,
but then a second rainfall brought an indescribable muck with it and
people had to stand more than knee deep in mud in some places."
(Max letter to David and Emma, May 20, 1915.) David and Emma
sent several packages to Max filled with potatoes, punch, and a can
of salami. However, the package containing cherry cake had, unfortunately, gone missing.

On September 17, 1915, the army summoned Max by telegram to deploy and assist the doctor for the Army of the Bug, named
after the Bug River in eastern Poland. Two days after receiving his
orders, Max and two colleagues left Cologne to traveled eastward

by train towards Warsaw. They eventually began to see evidence of the war: "houses [were] riddled with bullet holes, trenches, barbed wire barriers, etc." Warsaw did not show damage other than that the bridges over the Vistula River had been blown up, presumably by Polish soldiers or perhaps Russian defenders trying to delay the German army's advance. However, the Germans quickly replaced the destroyed bridges with two solid bridges and one pontoon bridge, while also repairing the bridges that had been blown up.

As far as Max could tell, life in Warsaw seemed to be normal, with elegantly dressed women strolling the streets, including chic women in beautiful furs, and the elite seeming to carry on an active social life without any cares. However, Max also saw "pictures of poverty and misery the likes of which are unknown at home." Warsaw "is teeming with beggars, some in fact only wearing tattered rags that just hang from their bodies, and with door-to-door salesmen, peddlers who hawk everything on the streets from postcards and matches to rubber coats and gold watchchains." (Max letter to David and Emma, Sept. 25, 1915.) He also took note of Warsaw's large Jewish population; the Jewish men were easily recognizable in their "black caps, long coats and high boots." (Max's WWI Diary at 5.)

Max continued traveling eastward towards Brest-Litovsk in what is now Belarus, but which at the time was just within Russia's western border. On this leg of the trip, he saw substantial evidence of the war; most of the towns had been burned down, including the train stations. (Max letter, to David and Emma, Sept 25, 1915.) However, he also saw farmers still trying to till their fields. Max arrived in Brest on September 23, 1915, after six days of travel, to find a city that had been burned almost to the ground. (Max's WWI Diary at 4-5.) His journey continued to the city of Kobryn. Along the way, he observed that "dead horses and other animals are lying around on the road, polluting the area. We passed some swamps and saw the legs of horses sticking out from below the surface. We were also struck by the many civilian graves by the roadside; it looks like people died like flies on the way. Jews are almost the only people to remain behind." (Max letter to David and Emma, Oct. 2, 1915.)

Because the poor water quality in Russia posed a threat of

cholera, Max and his colleagues drank coffee and wine to slake their thirst. They also drank a good deal of schnapps, while provisions were comprised of canned meat, bread, zwieback, and cocoa. "You quickly get used to little things like sleeping fully dressed without a bed, not bathing for four days, and not eating a proper meal for one day." (Max letter Sept. 25, 1915.)

The group next joined a food supply column made up of "small, abominable vehicles with no suspension" such that Max and his colleagues were thoroughly tossed about as they rode across Russia's rough roadways. They spent many nights sleeping on piles of straw or straw mattresses in barns and homes, with the unfortunate result that they frequently were plagued by fleas. (Max letter to David and Emma, Sept. 25, 1915, p. 5.) Max continued traveling towards the eastern front to join his regiment. After two and one-half weeks of travel, he located the regiment in Linewo, just in time for the army to order the regiment to board trains to return to Germany. The troops headed west, visited a delousing station along the way, and continued towards the Western Front. (*Id.* at 7.)

On October 9, 1915, Max and his regiment crossed the Belgian border into France. They disembarked at Poix-Terron, south of Charleville, and marched west to Villers-sur-le-Mont where they rested for several days. They continued by foot and train until they reached Manre in France's Ardennes region. They soon dropped into trenches through which they continued marching westward. At night, they slept in the trenches by finding spots to curl up in dugout shelters which soldiers had scraped into the sides of the trenches. The stench from so many unwashed men crowded together, sleeping in the dirt, was overwhelming.

By this point, the regiment was close enough to the front that it was exposed to French gunfire and artillery barrages. They began to incur casualties from a French attack that came to be known as the Champagne fall offensive. The offensive eventually stalled, which allowed Max and his regiment to advance. However, the chalky ground was soon wet with autumn rain that made the soil slippery and difficult to traverse. The German troops taking part in the advance were subject to intense French gunfire and, when traveling under cover of darkness, frequently lost their bearings and had to wait for daylight before they could move forward. (Max WWI Diary at 9-10.)

By late October 1915, Max's regiment was exhausted from artillery barrages, rifle fire, trench digging, and frequent marches. The intense artillery barrages, referred to as "drumfire" because they sounded like the beating of heavy drums, made it difficult to sleep. (Max WWI Diary at 12.) The regiment eventually made its way to the village of Pomacle seven miles northwest of Reims. Max and two colleagues were able to avoid sleeping in trenches by locating a comfortable room in a house. The room even had a wood-burning stove to provide heat. The army's "kantine" (the enlisted men's mess) in Pomacle was incredibly well-stocked. Max and his colleagues were able to choose from champagne, wine, liqueurs, canned fruits, cookies, and, when not attacking the French, enjoying the classic French treat of macarons.

After a few days, Max's regiment relocated to Witry-les-Reims, six miles northeast of Reims. The battalion headquarters were situated in the village of Cernay in France's Alsace region. Cernay had been heavily damaged by artillery fire. However, much of the housing stock had survived and provided quarters in which the German soldiers could billet, even though, as Max observed, the town was "crawling with rats." Max noted in a letter to his parents that he had not yet heard from the "mishpocha." (Max letter to David and Emma, Nov. 3, 1915.) Mishpocha is a Yiddish term meaning extended family. "In Russia, it was only fleas (that we had to deal with), but here in the Champagne I have to deal with lice in a big way—and powders and sprays don't help. You have to search for every single one and pull them out individually—and on the next day there are new ones to catch. Therefore, I will temporarily refrain from sending you laundry. Please send me water-resistant gaiters at the earliest opportunity—you get wet feet on every march, since it rains almost every night.—Also send condensed milk and wool to darn socks." (Max letter to David and Emma, Nov. 14, 1915.)

In late November, the regiment dispatched Max to inspect frontline positions where he observed trenches that had been dug for communications and to shelter reserve troops. When the weather cleared, he could see Reims' High Gothic cathedral, the traditional site for the coronation of French kings, although fire had destroyed its beautiful gabled roof. Max's regiment typically spent several days at a time in front-line trenches, followed by a rotation of several days of relief away from the worst of the shooting. On some days, the French unleashed artillery salvos. On other days, the Germans initiated barrages which, without fail, prompted a devastating French response in kind. (Max letter to David and Emma, Nov. 14, 1915.)

Max updated his diary as 1915 drew to a close:

> Christmas Eve [1915] went by without incident. I visited the casino [the officers' dining area which was more akin to a restaurant than a mess hall], but nothing much was going on there. At midnight, the French all of a sudden delighted us with an idiotic attack of shellfire directed at our trenches. In fact, the artillery on both sides had recently begun to engage in more activity. But it's our side without a doubt that started this; for one thing, our artillery wanted to practice shooting, for another, the gentlemen of the 4th Infantry D[ivision] wanted to act like 'the dashing August.'[39] Due to mutual tacit agreement, however, our [two] towns were spared this exercise.—On New Year's Day [1916], we were back in Witry, where we put on a nice little party at the casino. (Max's WWI Diary at 17.)

In January, the French, foregoing artillery barrages, subjected the German troops where Max was stationed to a surprise attack of small arms fire. A few weeks later, Max wrote: "Since we were stationed at the front on the emperor's birthday, we made up for it on February 5th with a celebration in Witry. Every officer received a bottle of champagne, all of which we drank in the evening in the casino. At the end, everyone was massively drunk; convenient, that it was a Saturday night. (Max's WWI Diary at 19.)

In late February 1916, the Germans initiated the battle for Verdun. For weeks, months, and then years, the war had become predictable. One side or the other launched artillery barrages. A response in kind from the other side soon followed. "As long as we

---

39   The reference to "dashing August" was an idiom connoting a "tough guy."

remained in Witry, the French fired grenades [artillery shells] at us every morning around 6 a.m. and every evening starting around 8 p.m. with about a 15-minute interval between them." (Max's WWI Diary at 20.) Occasionally, one side or the other launched gas grenades. The Germans shelled Reims and the French retaliated with barrages at the German positions. This state of affairs continued well into 1916. Heinrich, like Max, wrote to David and Emma, but he was under strict orders not to disclose where he was stationed. Ernst was on leave due to an injury; according to David he was limping badly. His limp may have been due to exposure as the result of Ernst having to sleep outside without shelter for seventeen months.

In April, the army ordered Max to go to Bergnicourt in northern France southwest of the town of Sedan. While there, Max and several colleagues had a day of respite, which they used to visit Rethel, a small town on the Aisne River northeast of Reims and southwest of the Ardennes. The area around the town's cathedral had been destroyed, but other parts of the town had survived. Since this area was further back from the front, the living conditions were in some respects much better. One of Max's colleagues invited him to have lunch at the officers' casino in Rethel:

> It was a veritable feast, and the food was delicious. After first drinking a glass of beer to quench our thirst, we ordered a glass of liqueur as an aperitif; then we had soup, salmon from the river Rhine smothered in mayonnaise, roast beef with potatoes and vegetables, all of this accompanied by a bottle of white wine; followed by omelets with jam, some dark beer, and to top it all off a cigar for 50 (francs) and a cup of coffee. Our excuse? That it was Sunday. (Max's WWI Diary at 24.)

In late April 1916, the army ordered Max's regiment to take up positions in front of Hill 304 near the city of Verdun in the Meuse district of France not far from the French border with Belgium and Luxembourg. The French made the defense of Verdun a major component of their defense strategy and to that end had constructed a series of forts to defend the city. As a result, the German military believed that taking Verdun would deal a mortal blow to both the

French defense and the French army's morale. The Germans hoped to make their attacks on Verdun so bloody and costly that the French would have no choice but to surrender.

Two other nearby rises, Hills 265 and 295, dominated the area and provided extensive fields of vision over the surrounding hills and fields. The Germans took up positions near Hill 304 beginning in late February 1916 and began to attack Verdun. The French responded with massive artillery barrages that caused extensive German casualties. The Germans continued to attack notwithstanding the enormous cost. They repeatedly rushed and occupied French trenches, only to be driven back and forced to yield the trenches to counterattacking French troops. The Germans eventually elected to attack Hill 304 directly in order to gain an advantage and be better situated to launch attacks on other nearby hills.

Max and his regiment marched to their designated positions in front of Hill 304. They could hear the rumble of cannon and see flashes of gunfire. They reached the forwardmost trenches and searched for carve-out shelters in which to sleep. On April 29, 1916, Max went to an artillery lookout post to survey the area. What he saw was frightening:

> The downhill grade was mild, walking downhill, you got to Forges Creek; on the other side of the creek there was another small hill called Bear's Paw. A little bit further south, there rose the infamous Hill 304, which has an elongated shape; to the east of it you can see the Dead Man.[40] East of the Bear's Paw lie the sad ruins of Bethincourt; halfway to the west of 304, those [the sad ruins] of Malancourt. Bear's Paw and 304 were a terrible sight; both of them had been raked by grenades [artillery] to the point of looking like a lunar landscape with a thousand craters. There was no trace of the green grass that once grew there. The woods to the east of 304 looked strange; the crowns and branches had been completely ripped off so that only the naked tree trunks still stood. Hill 304 and our positions that

---

40   Dead Man's Hill had been named after a traveler who got lost there and died during a storm.

were located in front of it were exposed to constant artillery fire, so that the smoke sometimes rose like a fog to cover the entire hillside. (Max's WWI Diary at 28-29.)

On May 2, the French attacked:

[f]iring heavy artillery at our trenches again, at times using large caliber weaponry. Our own trench got its share of hits as well. Some of the ordnance struck really close by so that the dugout shook hard, and rocks fell down from the wall and ceiling. All of a sudden there was an especially loud bang and the entrance suddenly went dark. At first, we thought it had completely caved in and started reaching for our shovels and picks. But we had been relatively lucky. The grenade had struck the front lip of the trench; it had been totally torn into; the trench was completely leveled so that we couldn't use it any more in the daytime because whenever the French saw something move in our trenches, they immediately shot at us with heavy artillery fire. (Max's WWI Diary at 31.)

Since the entrance to the dugout had only caved in "to a small degree," Max and his regiment were able to crawl out. However, they became more and more concerned by the condition of the trench and their exposure to French gunfire. Suddenly, another shell struck. Rocks rained down from the ceiling of the dugout, but the ceiling held. Although the men recovered from this terror, they were agitated by their close call, a concern that lingered. (Max's WWI Diary at 31-32.)

On another day, Max had to move through a communications trench that French artillery barrages had caused to collapse in numerous areas. In many spots the trench was only knee deep because of the dirt and debris that had fallen into it. As Max moved along, he had to make his way past corpses lying throughout the trench. (Max's WWI Diary at 34.)

The Germans attacked French positions day and night during early May 1916, with the assaults resulting in many casualties whom Max and his colleagues treated in field stations. The number of wounded grew tremendously. In mid-May, it began to rain heavily;

the trenches turned into marshes in which the troops stood in mud up to their knees. Troops returning from the front were covered with dirt from head to toe. (Max's WWI Diary at 35.)

> The fact is that the battles at Verdun have so far been the most dreadful battles fought. If you yourself haven't experienced it, you cannot imagine what it was like…The terrain on both sides is literally spiked with ordnance from artillery shells to large caliber weapons, and the artillery fire continues uninterrupted, day and night, for weeks, making it impossible to estimate how many rounds of ammunition were fired. We took up positions here on the 27th [of April]. We were finally replaced yesterday [May 8]. It is impossible to describe what our soldiers had to endure in their time spent on the front. In badly developed positions, largely without shelters, constantly lying in the heaviest artillery fire without being able to think of sleeping, without hot food, that is something the strongest nerves can't endure for more than a few days. If we aren't dead, injured, or sick, we are physically and mentally so down, so exhausted and nervous, that we have more than earned a period of rest…We had to care for the wounded all night long, because you can only collect and bring back the wounded at night; a few hours rest in the morning; then it's time to examine the very many sick and the ones who want to be sick. (Max letter to David and Emma, May 9, 1916.)

Finally, on May 18, fresh troops arrived to relieve Max's regiment. After the "hell in Verdun," they moved to the rear towards the tiny village of Euilly, southwest of Sedan near the French-Belgian border, to rest in what felt like a paradise. The countryside was gently rolling grassland not yet devastated by artillery barrages. The weather was glorious. Food was readily available, including such rarities as milk, butter, and eggs. (Max's WWI Diary at 37.)

In July, Max's regiment took up positions at Fosses Ravine. The French battered their encampment with almost daily artillery barrages. A daily stream of dead and wounded troops passed through the camp. (Max's WWI Diary at 38-39.) Stationed in the Chauffour Woods near Verdun, Max hunkered down in the trenches. The stench from the rotting bodies of dead horses wafted over the battlefield and settled into the trenches, creating a nauseous miasma that made it difficult for the soldiers to breathe.

> The Chauffour Woods look as though the trees had all been chopped down; there's nothing left but some very short tree stumps…The medical station is likewise an open hole in the ground with a tarp on top, which means not even shrapnel proof; a small tunnel links up to it, just big enough to let us two doctors sleep in it…Every day, the Ravine of the Dead is the target of heavy caliber weapons; there are frequent sudden artillery assaults; every day there are new dead and wounded troops. Because we don't have enough space, we have to keep our injured troops outside in front of the medical dugout…It must be terrifying up there. There are no trenches; the men are taking cover in grenade craters. The various blocks are under heavy enemy fire, especially the infantry block. The entrance and back wall made of bricks face the enemy; there are constant barrages of artillery fire around the infantry block and machine guns fire at the entrance. The French shot a hole in the wall and they managed two bull's-eye hits that landed right inside the infantry block; the building has to be evacuated but is still full of injured soldiers who cannot be recovered…On the 23rd [of July], the aid station almost got hit; I could see the glow of the fire through the tarp and was splashed with mud all over; but I got away with just a bruised eardrum. Some shrapnel went right through the tarp. I was in the middle of bandaging a wounded soldier; the medical sergeant next to me had his left hand punctured by a piece of shrapnel; my wounded soldier was hit again, this time in the leg. (Max's WWI Diary at 40-42.)

The opposing armies waged the Battle of Verdun from February 21, 1916, until December 1916. It was the longest battle of the war and one of the longest in history. The stupendous artillery barrages from huge guns, along with enormous infantry attacks, murderous machine gun fire, and bombardments with gas shells, resulted in some 377,000 French casualties and 337,000 German casualties.

On August 4, 1916, the German army awarded the Iron Cross, Second Class, to Field Doctor Max Ichenhäuser of the III Battalion, Regiment No 149. Max's regiment granted leave for him to go home for a few days. Ernst had developed a case of rheumatism from the cold and damp he endured while fighting on the eastern front in Russia. As a result, Ernst had spent a good stretch of time in a field hospital, but was now serving close to home in a reserve battalion. Heinrich, who had been wounded at Verdun, was also serving in a reserve battalion nearby. Both Heinrich and Ernst were able to join Max while he was home with David and Emma. (Max's WWI Diary at 44.) They were thrilled to have a few days together as a family, as there was no way to know when, or whether, they would be together again.

In late August, Max returned to action. The army dispatched him to the battle of the Somme. (Max's WWI Diary at 45.) The Battle of the Somme raged from July 1 to November 1, 1916, and resulted in more than one million casualties, including 300,000 deaths. British troops suffered nearly 60,000 casualties during just the first day. The battle began as a joint Franco-British offensive to relieve the pressure German troops were applying on Verdun further south. The French and British, like the German strategy at Verdun, hoped to inflict enough casualties on the Germans to force them to capitulate. In the end, while the battle cost Germany 550,000 casualties, the combined French and British attack gained only seven miles of territory and did not bring an end to the war.

In late September, Max wrote "there is heavy gunfire with barrages of gas grenades; the entire terrain is covered with a large cloud of gas. We have to put on gas masks. On the 25th in the morning, drumfire. No doubt, the French want to attack. Suddenly, there's news that the French broke through and are already behind us. We are cut off and locked in." (Max's WWI Diary at 50-51.) Max could hear heavy machine gun fire behind his position. The battalion staff made a last-ditch effort to escape the French encirclement, but they were thwarted by French and British artillery barrages:

> French fire by now has come really close; it was just behind our dugout...After about ½ an hour we got the order: Get ready, leave your gear behind, patrols will be right back. Then we moved out, very quietly, but very quickly, to head back [retreat]. It was pitch-dark and we couldn't see a thing. I stumble and fall twice into deep grenade craters and lose contact with my

battalion. So here I am all alone between both frontlines. Thank God that the artillery fire has died down quite a bit. I throw away my coat and backpack so I can walk faster; I wander about heading right and now completely lose my sense of direction. I lie down in a crater for a while to try and get my bearings or maybe someone will come by. Grenades are hitting the ground not too far from me. That's when I think I can see the tall trees lining the Rancourt-Sailly country highway by the glow of the star shells. [Star shells explode high in the air to illuminate a battlefield.] So, I had made a wrong turn and gone in the exact opposite direction. I walk towards the highway and hope that I won't run into any Frenchman or, in case I stumble upon the German trenches, that nobody shoots me… Now it is essential to identify oneself loudly and to do so in a timely fashion. After a little while, I hear a noise ahead of me; I don't see anybody, there's just shrubs in front of me; I prefer to detour to the left to get around the spot. Then suddenly I hear German words said behind me. I run towards them as fast as I can before I lose track of where they were coming from; because it is pitch-dark, and I call out to the [speakers] so they don't mistake me for a Frenchman. I catch up with them in no time flat. They are snipers from another regiment; they were on their way back and know the way; thank heaven, so I was safe! (Max's WWI Diary at 51-53.)

Max stayed close to the snipers as they snaked through the trenches. Along the way they pick up wounded soldiers. They came across one soldier who had been "torn apart in an explosion." They eventually took shelter for the night in a trench near Manoncourt, just a few miles northeast of the town of Nancy and southwest of Metz.

When September 27 arrived, Max and his unit headed to their next deployment. The men were by then drained of every last ounce of strength, but they had no respite from battle. The French attacked again and again; the Germans responded with drumfire salvos. The noise from the exploding shells was so loud it almost drove the men crazy. (Max's WWI Diary at 54.) By early October, the regiment reached a position close to Soissons, seventy miles northeast of Paris and due east of Compiegne, mercifully away from combat. The troops were finally able to rest and recuperate. Like at Verdun, the terrain at the Somme had been utterly destroyed by shelling. The French were on the offensive; the German troops in the most forward positions "end up dying or being taken prisoner." (Max letter to David and Emma, Oct. 6, 1916.) Max nevertheless was able to collect his thoughts, despite the horrific battle, to ask whether his parents had received the one hundred Marks he had sent to them and to wish them well for Yom Kippur.

Max reported further the next week regarding the battles at the Somme, including his regiment's timely decision to move their position further to the rear:

> It turned out that we had good reason to do this, because the following night the French advanced several hundred meters forward, passing right through our former shelters. Time really hardens you. When we moved into position, we were fully aware that if attacked, we would have to prepare to be taken prisoner. So, we weren't surprised when it [the attack] happened; at most we were surprised by how sudden it was. (Max letter to David and Emma, October 12, 1916.)

Max asked David and Emma to send him some books, as "good reading material is as hard to come by as butter is for you at home." He asked for his copy of "The Vicar of Wakefield," or Mark Aurel's "Meditations," or even his copy of a commentary on Goethe's "Faust." Max had taken advantage of a lull in the action to write to the entire mishpocha and wish them a belated happy Rosh Hashanah. He sent his best wishes for David and Emma to enjoy a lovely Sukkot, which he assumed they would be celebrating at home.

In late November, after the British and French had halted their disastrous Somme offensive, Max and a colleague drove to a synagogue service in Blerancourt, fifteen miles northeast of Compiegne, but they arrived too late to participate. On December 21, Max decided to try again and requested leave to go to Laon, thirty-six miles northwest of Reims, to attend a Hanukah service. Two hundred people participated. The fact that these services occurred and were well-attended demonstrated the significant participation of

Jewish men in the German army during WWI, a fact to which the German nation would soon enough give short shrift. On Christmas eve, Max and his colleagues were able to briefly escape the war by somehow securing an opulent dinner of oxtail soup, roasted rabbit, and chocolate pudding with whipped cream. (Max's WWI Diary at 58.) To enjoy a meal like this was to enter a parallel universe, light-years away from life in the trenches.

Word soon arrived that the regiment was to be relieved from the front lines during the first week of January. Max also learned by the end of 1916 that he had been promoted from Assistant Field Doctor to the rank of Field Medical Officer. As a medical officer and pursuant to Article 20 of the Geneva Convention, Max was authorized to wear the sign of neutrality, that is, a white armband with a red cross identifying him as medical personnel.

In late January 1917, Max and his regiment marched to Clermont to board a train for Chauny, roughly thirty miles northeast of Compiegne. Their work in the hospital there was mentally and physically draining due to the huge number of casualties they were treating. With the war's massive battles and trench warfare causing hundreds of thousands of casualties, scores of dead and wounded soldiers passed through Max's deployments whenever he was stationed near the front. Allied planes regularly bombed the German positions. The impact was so devastating the Germans eventually had no choice but to retreat eastward to set up defensive positions. As they retreated, they planted mines and bombed everything they left behind, leaving nothing but destruction in their wake. They reduced to rubble the villa where the German officers had stayed in Chauny. It did not matter what was there. They destroyed houses, streets, railroads, and canals. (Max's WWI Diary at 60-61.)

In April 1917, Max was assigned to Reserve Pioneer Company 18, which was stationed at a camp in the woods near Fleuricourt-Ferme. One of the soldiers had obtained a gramophone; the sound of music went a long way towards lifting the soldiers' spirits. The troops self-medicated whenever they could: "Alcohol in whatever form is consumed frequently and in large quantities." Nevertheless, despite the copious, liquid self-medication, the camp was in perfect order and the troops were well-disciplined.

However, in April 1917, the United States declared war on Germany, presaging a change in the balance of combatants that would lead to the end of the war. By late June, American troops began landing in France and deploying towards the front.

In late May, the army relieved Max's division from combat after its frontline troops returned in a state of exhaustion from battles on the River Aisne. However, after allowing the troops to spend time in the rear to recuperate, the army ordered them to move forward again. In mid-July, Max found himself stationed once again near Hill 304, where he had been stationed in devastating battles two years earlier. As before, the armies ruthlessly bombarded one another with artillery. In August, the French attacked across a broad front and were able to advance up both sides of the hill. While the Germans were able to fend off the attack, they eventually vacated the hill, rendering the casualties they had suffered in repulsing the French offensive all for naught.

In September, Max was able to obtain leave to attend Rosh Hashanah services in Charleville, the capital of France's Ardennes province, situated on the banks of the Meuse River. The service took place in a theater which was much too small for the 1500 Jewish soldiers who attended. The familiar tunes and prayers took the soldiers, however briefly, away from the war and transported them to their homes and families as they davened (prayed) and remembered peaceful holidays from the past.

After a brief stint in Berlin during which Max was trained regarding gas warfare, of which Max had already seen a great deal, he returned to the front. The army then transferred Max from the Infantry to an Artillery division. He continued to write frequently to his parents, telling them about the situation at the front to the extent the army's need for secrecy allowed him to share information. He sent two packets of butter to Emma for her birthday, a gift which he no doubt chose due to severe food shortages at home. Max also continued to send money to his parents from his army pay. He asked Emma and David to send him more Reclam books to read in his spare time. Reclam was a publisher specializing in small, paperback literary classics.

By January 1918, Max was stationed, for the third time, in the same area near Reims where he had been two years before. March 1918 saw Russia withdraw from the war. Russia's new Bolshevik government and the Central Powers comprised of the German Empire, Austria-Hungary, Bulgaria, and the Ottoman Empire, signed the Treaty of Brest-Litovsk on March 3, 1917. The Treaty's terms were extremely harsh to Russia as they called for a substantial loss of Russian territory and for Russia to pay huge reparations to the Central Powers. It also meant German troops fighting in the East could be redeployed to the Western Front.

The Allied forces and Germans continued to exchange artillery barrages, gas attacks, incendiary raids, and gunfire throughout March and April 1918. The troops were now fighting mobile warfare after three years of static, trench warfare. In late May, Max's regiment once again moved towards the Western front near Reims. The Germans were taking heavy casualties. The situation was so dire and the need for reinforcements and medical care were so great that Max had to set up an aid station in a trench dugout. The Germans managed to advance to a point close to the Marne River. However, they were again unable to take Reims because their troops were simply too weak and exhausted to press forward.

In early September, the army transferred Max to an infantry division that was to be stationed in Auberchicourt, well to the northeast of his previous deployments and only ten miles west of the French border with Belgium. On September 7, he reached Lille in northern France near the Belgian border.

> In the afternoon at 3 p.m. I attended the gathering of the National-Jewish Students hosted by the army rabbi. Special meals were served for the Jewish soldiers which were utterly excellent and very plentiful and that I'd no intention to miss out on. Lille is a real big city; you can get everything you want there, and the prices are just incredible. By chance I ran into Leo Teitz [a cousin], who went on vacation right after Yom Tov. The army rabbi organized everything beautifully. Our meals were served

in a large hall; among other things, there was apple wine, as much as one wanted to drink!—Grape compote, schnapps; supposedly these were all gifts sent from Frankfurt. Quite a large number of prisoners also attended: Russians, Englishmen, etc., who probably thought the food was very unusual. All in all, about 1,000-1,500 were in attendance. (Max's WWI Diary at 88; Max letter to David and Emma, Sept. 11, 1918.)

Lille was a welcome respite for the German troops because food was plentiful and available at rock-bottom prices. Max was able to find raspberry and vanilla ice cream for three francs and pastries for one franc. Boots were also available, although some appeared to have been worn. Max wrote that he hoped to able to attend services for Yom Kippur and Sukkot and that Heinrich might be able to join him.

On September 12, the Allies launched what was to be their final offensive of the war. Only three weeks later, on October 6, 1917, the German troops were surprised to learn of a peace proposal: "We hadn't had any clue that things had become so disastrous." (Max's WWI Diary at 90.) But things soon became much worse for Max. "On October 13, I received the shattering news that my brother Heinrich had died in direct hits to the battery where he served near Valenciennes. The next day, I went to the division's physician to ask him for a brief leave. However, this overstuffed lard-ass who surely didn't get a red nose from drinking water denied me my request with absolutely no scruples; he didn't have anyone to replace me since there were only three of us [medical officers] in the Regiment." (Id at 91.)

Max's regiment continued to retreat towards Germany, first to Tournai in western Belgium and then further east to Leerbecke. On November 11, 1918, the German troops received news that the warring nations had signed an armistice that day ending hostilities. The combatants' representatives signed the armistice in the forest in Compiegne in the train car used by Allied Supreme Commander Marshal Ferdinand Foch. The armistice called for, among other things, the cessation of hostilities, the withdrawal of German forces eastward to behind the natural barrier provided by the Rhine River,

Allied occupation of both the German Rhineland and bridgeheads further east, the surrender of German war materials and weapons, and for Germany to pay reparations.

On November 28, 1918, four years after the Kaiser's army had called Max to active duty, the army discharged him. He boarded a train to Cologne and arrived home that night. Over the course of four years, Max had seen extensive battlefield service. On the western front, he had tended wounded soldiers in combat zones with artillery shells crashing all around. He had been stationed along the front in France and Belgium, sheltered in trenches and bomb craters from deafening drum salvo barrages, and marched through the French countryside dodging sprays from French small arms and machine guns.

Max's service records show that in 1915 he was involved in numerous battles in Champagne. In 1916, he was at the battle of Verdun, the battles at Hill 304, Zwischenwerk Thiaumont, and at the Maas River.[41] Max had been stationed at the battle of the Somme in 1917. His service included stationary battles (static, trench warfare) at Aisne, Reims, Soissons, and between the Marne and Vesle rivers. He had been in assault battles (forward attacks) on the Marne and in Champagne. In 1918, his deployments included battles on the front lines at Armentieres-Lens, battles between the Deule Canal and the Scheldt river in northeastern France, and retreat battles in front of the German Antwerp-Maas position from May to November 11, 1918.

Max wrote in his diary:

> At the end of October 1918, I was discharged from the army in Gross Königsdorf. My brother Ernst had returned home earlier. The joy of reunification was dimmed by a giant shadow—my brother Heinrich had not returned home. In loyal fulfilment of his duty, without befitting thanks, he was killed on October 5, 1918. Neither his promotion to officer, nor the transfer to

41   The Maas [the Meuse in French] was a major river that originated in France and flowed through Belgium and the Netherlands before emptying into the North Sea. The Meuse and its crossings would be a major objective of the German army during the Battle of the Bulge in 1944-45.

> E.K.I., which he had applied for some time earlier, was he fated to live to see. He is buried at Auberchicourt. His memory will be unforgettable for us. (Max's Green Diary.)

Auberchicourt is in northeastern France, south of Lille, not far from the Belgian border.

Heinrich had been wounded by shrapnel only a few months after he had enlisted and been sent to active duty. The army awarded him the Iron Cross, second class, in recognition of his service and wound. He returned to active duty after recuperating. After nearly four years of service, the Army nominated Heinrich again, this time to receive the Iron Cross first class; he was also to be elevated to the rank of officer. However, before the army acted upon Heinrich's nominations, he was killed in action on October 5, 1918, five weeks before the war ended by virtue of the armistice on November 11. Heinrich was thirty-one years old when he died.

David and Emma Ichenhäuser's sons were testaments to the fact that in the early twentieth century Jews could prosper in Germany. Heinrich had passed the bar examination and was ready to begin a career as an attorney, prosecutor, or judge. Max was a physician. Ernst was a successful businessman. They were able to travel throughout Germany and enjoy the spas and mountains of central Europe. They had busy social lives, albeit primarily through Jewish organizations.

While they were not fully welcome into German society due to its centuries-long, always smoldering anti-Semitism, Max, Heinrich, and Ernst nevertheless served with distinction in the Kaiser's army. More than 100,000 Jewish men served in the Germany army in WWI; 12,000 of them were killed. During the "Great War," the German people had few qualms about allowing Heinrich, Ernst, and Max to bear arms on behalf of Germany, with each of them receiving an Iron Cross in recognition of their service; Heinrich received two such awards. Heini had been nominated to become an officer. Yet he died for a country that barely a generation later would betray his memory, dishonor his sacrifice, and try to murder his family.

RETURNING TO CIVILIAN LIFE

ERNST RETURNED TO COLOGNE AND JOINED HIS FATHER David's lumber business. By then, David Ichenhäuser was a partner in two companies in Cologne specializing in lumber and wood products: Lentzen & Cie in Cologne-Ehrenfeld and Lentzen, Meyer & Cie in Cologne-Braunsfeld. Since the Ehrenfeld district adjoined Braunsfeld, it was easy for David and Ernst to tend to both locations.

Max returned to Bonn to resume his studies. "After Mr. Max Ichenhäuser from Cologne has solemnly pledged himself with a handshake oath to observe faithfully and conscientiously the laws and regulations for students, he is accepted as a Student of the Medical Faculty and is included among the academic citizens of the university." (Medical School Certificate of Admission, signed in Bonn on December 20, 1918 by the Dean of the Faculty). In August 1919, Max passed the medical board examinations. He took an internship in the Frauenklinik (women's hospital) for two months while he worked on his dissertation: "The Spontaneous Rupture of the Caesarean-section-cicatrice after fundal cross-section and the Secondary Belly Cavity Pregnancy occurring as a Result." The medical faculty bestowed the title of Doctor of Medicine, Surgery, and Obstetrics on Max on December 5, 1919.

Having obtained his medical license, Max went to work as an assistant doctor from January 1920 to January 1921 in the surgical department of the Israelitische Asylum (the Jewish hospital was frequently referred to as the "Asyl") in Cologne-Ehrenfield, a sub-urb northwest of Cologne. The Chief Physician in the Department of Surgery noted that Max conducted himself with diligence and prudence, was able to obtain the confidence of his patients, had mastered the surgical treatment of wounds, and independently conducted minor surgeries.

In the summer of 1920, Max and Ernst returned to vacation at Norderney. Many German Jews went there to enjoy the sea and sun. Max and Ernst swam daily, working up a healthy appetite for the tasty and ample food at their hotel, the Rheinsichen Hof. They enjoyed bowls of whipped cream in the Konditorei ("cake shop") for dessert. Visitors rented beach cabanas in which they changed clothes and where they could shelter from the wind if the breeze off the North Sea picked up too much for comfort. The visitors that summer let themselves go in uninhibited joy, perhaps still enjoying a manic release from the destruction and death of the War.

Back at the Asyl, Max indulged in his penchant for writing doggerel poetry. He wrote a humorous poem for the hospital's Hanukah party which he performed with two nurses. The three of them dressed as elderly street singers. Their performance was met with peals of laughter from the hospital staff. Max loved to write and enjoyed performing for friends and family.

In 1921, Max took a position at the University Women's Clinic in Bonn, whose director noted that "he has done his service to the greatest satisfaction." Another director commented that Max had "improved himself very well in the physical and chemical research-ing methods and has acquired good knowledge of the Diagnostics and the Therapy of Internal Diseases. He showed great skill at the treatment of patients and was liked very much by them." (Certified Copy of Translation of Max's university degrees and certificates by Johann Kempf, 9 Adolf Hitler Plaza, Sept. 9, 1938.) Max returned to Cologne on weekends, where "I gave myself to the sport of kaya-king." He wrote several articles that were published in medical journals, including articles in "Obstetrics and Gynecology Monthly," "German Medical Weekly," and the "German Magazine for Surgery."

Max worked at the Women's Clinic until July 1921 when he

decided to specialize in obstetrics and gynecology. He searched for an internship in those specialties. However, there were very few opportunities due to the devaluation of the Mark. This was the period of Germany's Great Inflation: "The value of money plummeted incredibly; the non-government-related professions were as good as ruined; all savings were worthless." (Max's Green Diary.) The ensuing financial disaster crippled the German Republic and set the stage for a racist, authoritarian leader who believed, in fact proclaimed, that "only he could fix it."

A Toxic Brew

THE COMBATANTS IN WWI SIGNED THE TREATY OF Versailles on June 28, 1919, in the Hall of Mirrors at the Palace of Versailles. Thousands of Germans participated in demonstrations urging the German government not to sign. The protesters were furious over the onerous financial terms and disarmament the treaty imposed on Germany. However, the enormous casualties and economic devastation Germany had suffered meant Germany did not have the military strength to resist the Allies if Germany refused to sign and the Allies initiated further military action. At the urging of the nation's military leaders, the government of the Weimar Republic signed the treaty.

Germany's post-war hyperinflation stemmed from several causes. Germany had expected to win WWI. It had planned to pay the cost of the conflict from the spoils of war it expected to extract from its defeated enemies. Therefore, instead of raising taxes to pay for the war, Germany borrowed. It also abandoned gold backing for the Reichsmark.[42] When Germany lost the war, it had to pay reparations in gold or foreign currency. The government decided to run its printing presses to generate Reichsmarks it could use to buy the gold and foreign currency it needed. However, the more Reichsmarks that were in circulation, the less value they had, meaning it took more and more Reichsmarks to purchase everything. Germans began to

---

42   *Paper Money*, by Adam Smith, Summit Books, (1981) at p. 56.

buy things, anything, in order to get something for their money, since the value of their Reichsmarks declined monthly, weekly, daily, and, eventually, hourly.

The assassination of Walter Rathenau, Germany's moderate foreign minister, on June 24, 1922, shattered the public's faith in both the Weimar government and the stability of German society.[43] In January 1923, when Germany defaulted on deliveries of timber to France that were called for by the Treaty of Versailles, the French responded by occupying the Ruhr Valley, Germany's industrial heartland, dealing a tremendous blow to the German economy.[44] Germany's inflation became so catastrophic that the government eventually issued a 1,000 billion Mark note. By November 1923, one dollar was equal to one trillion Marks. A wheelbarrow full of money would not suffice to purchase a newspaper.[45] By 1923, a loaf of bread cost two hundred billion Marks. Savings were worthless. Germans were chasing goods in the face of hourly price increases. According to one account, a waiter at a café told a customer that if he thought he would want two cups of coffee he should buy them both right away before the price went up for the second cup.[46] Never was the phrase "time is money" more apt.

German anger and resentment regarding the situation in which they found themselves during the Great Inflation were also fueled by the Allies' occupation of the Rhineland, which included the British occupation of Cologne pursuant to the Treaty of Versailles. The Rhineland encompassed the German territory west of the Rhine River up to the German border with France and Belgium. The Allied occupation served as a daily reminder of Germany's defeat and contributed greatly to the bitterness of the German populace.

Max had no luck finding an internship because the impact of the hyperinflation was particularly hard on physicians and academicians. Since tradespeople were faring at least somewhat better than

---

43   *Paper Money* at 58.

44   *The Rise and Fall of the Third Reich—A History of Nazi Germany*, William L. Shirer, Simon & Schuster, (1959) at 61.

45   *Paper Money* at 57.

46   *Paper Money* at 59.

professionals, Max briefly returned to the family lumber business. However, after a month and a half, he realized it simply was not for him. Instead, he left Cologne and went to the Medical Clinic in Bonn to study internal diseases. He attended daily rounds regarding every patient the physicians were treating in order to learn as much as possible.

Max eventually decided it was time to get on with opening his own practice. He took up residence at his parents' home and opened his practice on July 1, 1922 at 8 Beethovenstrasse in Cologne. He had been purchasing medical equipment for some time to avoid the ever-increasing prices caused by the ruinous inflation. On October 1, 1922, the pertinent authorities issued a license to Max allowing him to operate a practice that accepted state-funded health insurance. Being able to treat insured patients was crucial to developing a viable practice. While Max was busy trying to establish his practice during the week, he enjoyed rowing on Sundays since he was still an avid kayaker. He also frequently spent weekends hiking in the hills near Cologne.

While Max was not a regular at synagogue, he nevertheless had an active Jewish social life. In December 1922, he attended a Chanukah party hosted by friends from Bonn. He also joined the Rhineland Lodge, which was a Jewish fraternal organization:

> In Cologne, the later 1800s marked the beginning of the vibrant Jewish community life that flourished from the 1920's to the early 1930's. In 1888, the Rhineland Lodge, which financed and managed numerous charitable and cultural organizations (including a mobile library), was founded; its purpose was to fight anti-Semitism, to strengthen Jewish identity and spiritual awareness, and to encourage good deeds and charity. The Lodge established Cologne's first Jewish youth organization in 1903.[47]

Max attended the spring Purim Ball sponsored by the Jewish Gym Association. The Ball was held at Cologne's zoo, which offered plenty of room for dancing. Apparently, Max's childhood shin

---

47   See www.germansynagogues.com. and Pogrom Night at xxi.

fracture was no longer an impediment to him taking a spot on the dance floor.

By 1924, the German Mark had stabilized, and a semblance of financial normalcy returned to Germany. The government had introduced a new currency, denominated the Rentenmark, in November 1923.[48] Issuance of the new currency caused inflation to stabilize as Germans simply decided to believe in the value of the new currency and stop increasing prices for goods and services. One Rentenmark replaced an old one-billion-Mark note, alleviating the need for residents to carry literally bushels of money to make even the most meager purchases.[49] Since money once again had value, goods and services could be paid for with valid currency. However, the enormous financial harm the Great Inflation had wrought and the attendant destruction of savings it had caused created deep resentment throughout the country.

On March 26, 1924, Max, by then thirty-two years old, moved his practice to 30 Raschdorffstrasse in Cologne-Braunsfeld near the busy intersection of Raschdorffstrasse and Aachenerstrasse. Max publicized his new location by placing notices in local newspapers; he made sure to include the crucial information that all state insurance funds had approved him to provide care. Having practiced for several years at the Medical and Gynecological Clinic of the University of Bonn, as well as at the Israeli (Jewish) Asylum in Cologne, Max decided to focus a portion of his practice on obstetrics. He took a furnished room in a home at 567 Aachenerstrasse and moved his office and practice there. By October 1924, his practice was thriving.

In October 1924, Max attended a party sponsored by the "Himmel und Erde Society." Himmel und Erde ("Sky and Earth") was a traditional Rhineland dish consisting of black pudding (blood sausage), fried onions, mashed potatoes, and applesauce. Its name came from the combination of apples—the sky—and potatoes—the earth. Max attended the Karneval parties Himmel und Erde hosted in the spring as well as a "H&E" masked ball held at Cologne's Ring

---

48   *Paper Money* at 61.

49   *Paper Money* at 61.

Café. Karneval in Germany was a pre-Lent celebration of excess. Karneval was the name given the holiday in northern Germany, while Fasching was the name used in the southern part of the country. Karneval celebrations typically involved parades, costumes, and balls. Satiric plays and writing were popular, especially those mocking political figures. While Karneval was not a national holiday, it was a huge event in primarily Catholic cities such as Cologne, where many shops, schools, and businesses closed for the festivities.

Max continued to row and hike in his spare time. He took excursions with Ernst to Merano (a spa town in the Tyrol region of northern Italy), the Mendel and Penegal mountains, and the Karer Pass in the South Tyrol. Max and Ernst also visited the Vigiljoch and Haflingerjoch passes in the South Tyrol which they reached by means of an aerial tramway. Max's medical practice was growing. He had a busy social life. He was able to take vacations throughout central Europe, as well as hike and kayak. Life was good.

However, all was not well. Germany had a centuries-long history of anti-Semitism that was always simmering and sometimes violent. The Great Inflation had inflicted enormous financial harm on the nation and destroyed the value of savings, causing deep resentment that percolated throughout the country. Many Germans harbored a visceral need to blame someone for the catastrophic financial losses they had suffered.

Adolf Hitler would soon exploit this resentment. He paired German resentment over the post-war financial disaster with the "stab in the back" conspiracy theory many reactionary Germans had spun to explain Germany's defeat in WWI. The combination created a toxic brew. Hitler railed that Germany's small Jewish community was to blame for the nation's military defeat. Anti-Semitism, which in the best of times was never far below the surface in Germany, surged.[50]

---

50 *The War Against the Jews 1933-1945*, by Lucy S. Dawidowicz, Bantam Books, 1975, p. xxi, 45, 47; *Pogrom Night 1938*, Vol. I, p. xxii.

In the years right after the First World War, many Germans could not reconcile themselves to their country's defeat. Blinded by nationalist arrogance, they could not concede even the possibility, let alone the grim reality, that Germany's resources had, in the end, been exhausted. These Germans had, in fact, become so deluded as to believe that their nation had been defeated only because of a "stab in the back," a conspiratorial betrayal by Jews, in their eyes, the arch conspirators of history.[51]

Many Germans, fueled by anti-Semitic harangues, believed "the Jews" were responsible for the Bolshevik Revolution in Russia and that "the Jews" wanted to achieve the same outcome in Germany. These harangues created a dangerous environment for Germany's Jews. They also fueled the Jewish community's interest in Zionism, as many German Jews began to suspect they might someday, and perhaps soon, need to find another country in which to live.

Hitler, despite being Austrian, served in the German army during WWI. He, like many Germans, could not bear the thought that his beloved, adopted "Fatherland" had been defeated. After the war, he returned to Munich where the German army assigned him to investigate political parties. The army, which was aligned with deeply reactionary forces in Germany, was deeply worried that Socialist and Communist influences might seek to inspire a Soviet-style revolution in Germany.

One of the parties the army assigned Hitler to investigate was a small political party named the Deutsche Arbeiterpartei (the "DAP" or "German Workers' Party"). Hitler first observed the party and then joined it in 1919. By 1920, the party had changed its name to the Nationalsozialistische Deutsche Arbeiterpartei (National Socialist German Workers' Party or "NSDAP"). Hitler, by the sheer force of will that he later wielded with such disastrous effect upon Germany and all of Europe, forced himself upon the small group as its leader. It was from this minuscule political party that the Nazi movement would arise.

On November 13, 1919, Hitler made his first public speech

---

51   *War Against the Jews* at xx-xxi.

in the dubious setting of the cellar in a Munich beer hall.[52] In what was more a feverish diatribe than a speech, he blamed Germany's wartime defeat on Jewish "treachery." Presaging the Final Solution, he exhorted the small crowd by raging that "We will carry on the struggle until the last Jew is removed from the German Reich."[53] He fulminated against the "November criminals" who "stabbed the nation in the back" and caused it to surrender and end WWI. He blamed Germany's Jews, who made up barely one percent of the country's population, for Germany's problems. He also argued for a "greater Germany" to be achieved by incorporating all Germans living in Europe within the German nation, regardless of where those Germans lived.

While the beer hall crowd was small and Hitler was a political non-entity, his paranoid rants were representative of the ravings of Germany's political far right. German anti-Semitism, which went as far back as Martin Luther and beyond, became mixed with German nationalism in the 1920s and 1930s to produce an even more virulent and dangerous form of anti-Semitism.[54]

> The Weimar Republic, which emerged from Germany's defeat, was based on a new constitution which gave Germany's Jews full equality. However, the rabid anti-Semitism that emerged during and after the war and the defeat which nationalists tried to pin on the Jews, substantially undercut this victory. On February 24, 1920, just six months after the Weimar Constitution was enacted, the NSDAP issued its twenty-five-point program, which asserted that no Jew could ever be a member of the German Volk, that only persons of German blood could be regarded as members of the Volk and citizens of the German state." [55]

"Deutschland erwache, Juda verrecke" ["Awake Germany, Jews

---

52 *War Against the Jews* at 17.

53 *War Against the Jews* at 17.

54 *War Against the Jews* at 23.

55 *War Against the Jews* at 46. Volk translates to "people," but as used by Hitler it connoted Germans as a people to the exclusion of others.

leave"] became a commonplace slogan.[56] Anti-Semitism moved further into the open. It rapidly became part of the national discourse; it was becoming mainstream. Unapologetic, virulent hate, far from being shameful or whispered about in dark places, came out of the shadows and became part of Germany's daily political discourse.

Hitler had dreams of leading Germany to a future free of Jews. However, he was not willing to wait for elections to bring him to power. He held a rally at a Munich beer hall on November 8, 1923, at which he urged the attendees to revolt against the Weimar Republic.[57] The next day, he led 2,000 NSDAP thugs to try to take over Bavaria's state government. Many of the thugs were members of the Sturmabteilung ("Storm Division"), commonly known as the "S.A." or "brown shirts" due to the brown uniforms they wore. The S.A. began as a band of NSDAP ruffians who were always spoiling for a fight. It evolved into a paramilitary force the NSDAP used to intimidate political parties and individuals who opposed the Nazis. Local police quickly put down the attempted rebellion after a confrontation in the streets that resulted in the death of sixteen Nazis and three policemen. The authorities arrested Hitler, who had fled the scene, along with the other leaders of the NSDAP.

A panel of three judges tried Hitler for treason for his leading role in what became known as the "Beer Hall Putsch." The right-wing court allowed Hitler to mount a defense in which he railed hysterically, often and at length, against "the Jews" and other perceived enemies of the German state. Notwithstanding Hitler's ravings and purported nationalist justifications for his actions, the court convicted him of high treason and sentenced him to five years in prison. Hitler was incarcerated in Landsberg prison, forty miles southwest of Munich in Bavaria.[58]

Hitler served only eight months of his five-year term. However, during his time in prison, as he stewed in a mental cauldron of fury

---

56   *War Against the Jews* at 47.

57   www.HolocaustResearchProject.org., Munich: The City at the Heart of Nazism; Rise and Fall at 68.

58   After WWII, the Allies used Landsberg prison to hold Nazi war criminals awaiting trial.

and hate, he composed much of "Mein Kampf" ("My Struggle"). In Mein Kampf, Hitler crystalized his hatred of Jews as the source of Germany's troubles. He wrote that Jews were responsible for Germany's defeat in WWI and were leaders of a Bolshevik conspiracy planning to take over Germany and, ultimately, the entire world. However, since the Nazi party had been banned by the time Hitler was released from prison in 1924 and the economy was starting to recover from the Great Inflation, there was, for the time being, limited public appetite for Hitler and his ravings.[59]

---

59 *Rise and Fall* at 111-112.

Appear in Mass; Stop the Indifference

For many years, Germany's Jewish community had looked for ways to address the nation's deep-seated anti-Semitism. The longstanding prejudice was becoming a rapidly increasing threat to the Jewish community. The German people's shame over the outcome of the war, their resentment over the punitive sanctions which the Treaty of Versailles imposed on them, and the world-wide Depression in the 1920s would soon make many Germans receptive to someone who claimed he could identify the causes of their misery and offer solutions. While Max's life was rich and much of Germany's Jewish community was thriving, danger lurked.

The Rhineland Lodge was the largest Jewish fraternal organization in Cologne. In January 1922, members of the Lodge invited Max to join. His induction took place on February 12, 1922, in the Lodge's reading room at 18/22 Cäcilienstrasse. The invitation for the Lodge's January 9, 1924, meeting included an agenda announcing that Max would give a presentation regarding Hans Friedrich Gunther's book "Racial Science of the German People." Gunther was a German author, professor, and eugenicist who was sometimes known as "the Race Pope." He specialized in Rassenkunde—"racial science." Rassenkunde was a pseudo-science popular in the context of the nineteenth century European interest in physical anthropology, which purported to study the racial-physical characteristics of humans, primarily in terms of a "civilizational hierarchy." The Nazis used Rassenkunde to justify their racist and anti-Semitic policies. Gunther's "Short Ethnology of the German People," which he wrote in 1929, advocated a theory of racial history based upon purported Nordic/Aryan superiority. Max used his lecture to address Gunther's writings and what they meant for Germany's Jews.[60]

In addition to joining the Lodge, Max was a member of the Reichsbund of Jewish Front Soldiers ("Imperial Society of Jewish Front Soldiers") composed of Jewish WWI combat veterans. The Reichsbund distributed a notice regarding a Rheinland Lodge meeting set for April 7, 1924, at which Max would reprise his talk about Gunther: "Comrade Max Ichenhäuser gives a talk on the academic, anti-Semitic book by Hans Gunther: 'Racial Science of the German and Jewish People.'"

By 1924, German anti-Semitism had become sufficiently alarming that the Reichsbund sent an urgent appeal to its members:

> We have deliberately spared our members and friends in the recent past urgent invitations in order to address to you all the appeal today:
>
> **Appear in mass! No one should miss it!**
>
> It applies to you, as well as to all of us, to hold together in order to face the Jew-baiting with united forces. Immeasurable money and resources are available to our German opponents, while we only have the weapon of spiritual defense. A victory of the reaction [reactionary forces claiming Germany had been "stabbed in the back" and betrayed by the Jews] would at once destroy our painstaking work and cause the worst harm to our German fatherland, for which you also fought and bled.

---

60   Gunther joined the Nazi party in 1932 and became a leader of its racial thought. In 1935, he joined the University of Berlin as a professor where he taught racial science, human biology, and rural ethnography. In March 1941, Gunther was an honored guest at Alfred Rosenberg's "Institute for the Study of the Jewish Question." Rosenberg was a leading Nazi anti-Semite and propagandist. In his book "Racial Science of the German People," Gunther categorized Germans as belonging to the Nordic races, while Jews were "other" and "a thing of ferment and disturbance." He advocated against "racial mixing" and urged the "Nordic races" to unite to secure their dominance over lesser races and peoples.

Help us with advice and action and prove yourself worthy of your name as a front-line soldier and support our efforts for the common good!

Stop the indifference!

Into our meeting!

Let's go to work!

We need you! (Reichsbund of Jewish Front Soldiers' flyer, March 30, 1924.)

The flyer listed agenda items regarding "the opposition's activities in Köln" along with guidelines for electoral work. The Jewish community, aware of the growing danger, was mobilizing to defeat the NSDAP and other reactionary forces at the polls.

TRUDE MOSES

A T ONE OF THE GATHERINGS OF THE HIMMEL UND ERDE social club, Max met Trude Moses. They soon became an item. Born on July 3, 1901, Trude was attending the Rheinische Friedrich-Wilhelms University in Bonn in 1924 where she was majoring in art history. It was unusual at that time for women to attend university. However, Trude was a strong and independent young woman who refused to let convention stand in the way of her desire to study. Trude was conducting research for an art history paper which required that she travel throughout central Germany. The Director of the Art History Institute at the University in Bonn wrote a letter of introduction for her:

> Bonn, March 31, 1924
>
> Miss Trude Moses, a full member of the Art History Institute of Bonn University, is planning a study trip through Central Germany and Berlin for the Easter holidays.
>
> We are taking the liberty of recommending Miss Moses, who on this trip intends to view several monuments relevant to her work, to the appropriate Directors of the Museum and administrative authorities. At the same time, we respectfully ask you to also allow her free access to the monuments and collections that are important for her to see.
>
> The Director of the Institute
>
> P. Clemen

Trude's family can be traced to Wolfgang Phillip Moses (1827-1876) and his wife Amalie Hoffman (1828-1912). Wolfgang and Amalie lived in Stommeln, a village fourteen miles northwest of Cologne in North-Rhine Westphalia. Stommeln was best known for a large windmill on a hill outside the village. Wolfgang and Amalie Moses raised five children: Karl, Sigmund, Johanna ("Hannchen"), Antoinette ("Nettchen"), and Moritz. The Moses family was large, with the offspring of Wolfgang and Amalie's five children resulting in an extensive network of cousins throughout Germany.[61]

Trude's father Sigmund Moses was born in Stommeln on September 25, 1859. Trude's mother Martha Oberlander was born to Joseph and Fanny Oberlander (maiden name Aberle) on November 14, 1880, in the town of Mannheim, 154 miles southeast of Cologne. Mannheim, situated at the confluence of the Rhine and Neckar rivers, was unusual in that its streets were laid out on a grid, which led to the town being referred to as "The City of Squares." Mannheim's Jewish community consecrated the town's main synagogue in 1855. Mannheim's Jews achieved full civil rights in 1862. By the 1920's, Jews were active in Mannheim's social, cultural, and political life.[62]

For many years, Sigmund operated an importing business, E. Oberlander & Cie, at 20 Glockengasse in Cologne. Sigmund specialized in fabric for menswear. In addition to importing fabric, Sigmund made custom clothing. The Oberlanders owned a nearby

---

61   The descendants of Sigmund's siblings—Karl, Johanna/Hannchen, Antoinette/Nettchen, and Moritz—were Trude's cousins. Several of these cousins were to figure prominently for the Ichenhäusers during subsequent events.
Antoinette/Nettchen Moses married Hermann Roesberg from the small town of Rommerskirchen, seventeen miles northwest of Cologne. Nettchen and Hermann had five children: Helene, Anna ("Aanchen" or "little Anna"); Otto; Wilhelmina ("Mitze"); and Paul. Helene Roesberg, known as Lene, married Max Berlin. Wilhelmina/Mitze Roesberg married Hans David Rothschild, who was from Bonn. Although it was not common, it was also not unheard of, for cousins to marry during that time, and so it was with Mitze. Her father's sister, aunt Johannah Roesberg, married Emil Rothschild. Their son, Hans David Rothschild, became Mitze's husband. Thus, Hans and Mitze were first cousins. Mitze and Hans had a daughter—Hannah. Tragically, Mitze died, along with what would have been her and Hans' second child, during childbirth. Hans later married Helen ("Leni") Strauss, with whom he had two children—Annelise and Peter.

62   The Jewish Community of Mannheim, dbs.bh.org.il/place/Mannheim.

restaurant where many businessmen went for lunch and dinner. Martha Oberlander worked at the restaurant and that is where she met Sigmund Moses.

Sigmund and Martha married and had one child, Gertrude, who was known by the nickname "Trude." The three of them lived in Cologne at 16 Kamekestrasse, a few blocks from the intersection of Bismarckstrasse and Venloerstrasse, just outside the inner Ring Road, in the city's Belgian Quarter. Given the nature of her father's business, Trude learned her way around a needle and thread early on and was able to operate a sewing machine skillfully.

Sigmund's store was in an elegant structure downtown near Cologne's enormous, riverside cathedral. The building where Sigmund had his business came to be known as the 4711 building because it was where the famed 4711 perfume manufacturer first operated. The namesake "4711" cologne was Trude's favorite fragrance. As a purveyor of fabric and bespoke menswear, Sigmund always wore well-tailored suits with a watch chain on his vest and a pocket square in his suit jacket. He rarely smiled in family photographs. However, despite his dour appearance, he was much beloved by family members.

Max and Trude enjoyed Cologne's rich cultural life. Max loved the performing arts, while Trude was a fan of painting and sculpture. On September 9, 1925, Trude's parents Sigmund and Martha Moses celebrated their silver wedding anniversary. Two weeks later, Trude and Max announced their engagement in the Cologne newspaper; Max was thirty-three and Trude was twenty-five. They were the proverbial odd couple in terms of physical stature; Trude was barely five feet one inches tall, while Max was an imposing and athletic six feet.

Max loved writing funny poems, parodies, and songs. He frequently illustrated them with sketches and cartoons. Max enjoyed playing to crowds by reciting poetry and participating in skits in college, medical school, and social groups. Trude had a more serious nature,[63] but she loved music and art. She was not opposed to dressing up in costume for Karnival or performing modern dance. Max

---

63   Certainly, Trude was very serious later in life, but that may have been due to subsequent events more than a product of her initial nature.

was quite the outdoorsman, always ready to go hiking or kayaking. There is nothing to suggest that Trude and her parents were great fans of the outdoors beyond strolling through Cologne's parks prior to Trude meeting Max. However, Trude happily joined Max on hikes throughout central Europe's mountains all year round. Max was still interested in collecting fossils and minerals; he and Trude carried a hammer and chisel on many of their walks in case they found a specimen Max wanted to dislodge and take home. Despite what seemed to be differences in temperament and interests, they became a close couple.

On October 25, 1925, Trude and Max held a party and festive dinner to celebrate their engagement. Max's parents David and Emma Ichenhäuser, Max's brother Ernst, Trude's parents Martha and Sigmund Moses, Karl and Irma Oberlander, and Max and Trude's friends Heinz and Margot Abraham, Hilde Wolff, and Edith Hahn joined them. Trude wore a white sweater and knee-length white silk skirt with a cutout overlay. Max was sharply dressed in a three-piece suit, silk tie, and white pocket-square in his jacket. Both fathers wore impeccably tailored suits. David Ichenhäuser could have passed as Sigmund Freud's brother with his neatly trimmed, but substantial, moustache and goatee. He carried his trademark cigar in his right hand. Sigmund Moses kept his small moustache neatly trimmed. He looked dapper in his suit, no surprise given his career as a haberdasher.

The reception room for the engagement party featured two long tables covered with bouquets and wedding gifts. The gifts included crystal, serving plates and bowls, decanters, sherbet bowls, and wine goblets. Max and Trude received gifts from the Oberlander side of the family, including Uncle Karl from Bonn, Eduard, Leopold, Fritz, Erma, Helen and Otto, and Frau Sigmund Oberlander. The Lissauers, Ashkenazys, David Teitz, Lene and Max Berlin, and Carl and Hilde Spier also attended.[64] Of course, Dülken and Ichenhäuser family members were part of the celebration, including Sigmund and Ernst Ichenhäuser along with Karl and Ernst Dülken.

Max and Trude were married six weeks later in a civil ceremony

---

64   The Lissauer, Berlin, and Ashkenazy families were cousins on Trude's side of the family.

on December 10, 1925, only two months after they had announced their engagement. However, the religious ceremony had to be postponed because Max became ill. Their Jewish wedding was conducted in a small ceremony six weeks later on January 26, 1926. Trude's parents, Max's parents, and Max's brother Ernst attended. Additional relatives and friends joined them, including Karl and Irma Oberlander from Bonn, Heinz and Margot Abraham, Hilde Wolff, and Edith Hahn. Trude wore a knee-length white dress. Her hat featured a ribbon of flowers above the brim and a white gossamer train that trailed on the floor behind her. Max wore an evening coat with white tie and vest, while a watch chain dangled from his left vest pocket.

The newlyweds honeymooned for three days in Wiesbaden, the capital of the state of Hesse in west central Germany. Wiesbaden, literally "meadow baths," was one of the oldest spa towns in Europe. It was famous for its hot springs; at one time it boasted more than forty-six active springs. A few days in the spa town allowed Trude and Max to relax, enjoy one another's company, and plan their lives together.

When they returned to Cologne, Max and Trude set up housekeeping in a furnished apartment at 31 Raschdorferrstrasse. Their home was west of central Cologne, just north of the Braunsfeld district, and southwest of Ehrenfeld. Max continued his medical practice in the rooms he rented from the Weiss family at 567 Aachnerstrasse. Trude maintained the books for his practice. Trude elected not to return to the university in Bonn to finish her studies, although one of her professors was anxious to have her continue. He wrote to her and asked that she please consider returning to finish her research on 13th century Gothic art along the Rhine River. He even sent roses to induce her to return, but Trude's focus remained on her new life with Max.

Max and Trude soon moved to 346 Aachenerstrasse in Cologne-Braunsfeld, a few blocks from their first apartment. Max moved his practice to their new home. His card read: "Dr. Med. Max Ichenhäuser, UV Light Therapy and Diathermy."[65]

---

65   Diathermy involved the use of electrically induced heat or high-frequency electromagnetic currents during physical therapy and surgery. It was commonly

Max and Trude's first year of marriage included a trip in June 1926 to Montreux, Switzerland, to stay at the Hotel Continental. They continued to the Hotel Schweizerhof in Kanderstag, a town situated in central Switzerland's Bernese Oberland. At 1200 meters altitude, Kanderstag, a small village comprised primarily of wooden chalets, was renowned for summer hiking. The chalets in the village sported flower boxes bursting with bright red geraniums at every window. The highlight of the trip was a visit to the village of Les Avants with its stunning fields of daffodils showing off their butter-yellow trumpets, while narcissi blossoms formed blankets of white in the mountain meadows. Les Avants, just west of Montreux in the Swiss canton of Vaud, boasted stunning views of Lake Geneva from the peaks above the town. The summits could be reached via a funicular built in 1910. Ernest Hemingway visited Les Avants in 1925 and reportedly was enthralled by the bobsledding, which visitors started from a point 2100 meters above the village, from which they sped down the mountain right into the center of the town.

The following spring, in May 1927, Max and Trude traveled to Lake Lugano in northern Italy. From there, they went to Milan, Lake Como, and Engelberg—an alpine town in central Switzerland, where they stayed at the Hotel Titlis. The Italian lakes' cerulean waters were surrounded by mountainsides dotted with stunning villas. Max and Trude took advantage of the spring weather to enjoy the lakes before traveling to bustling Milan.

In December 1927, Trude and Max left Cologne for a winter break. They visited Gstaad, where they spent the winter holiday at the Bernerhof Hotel. Bundled in heavy coats and wool caps, they pulled on hiking boots insulated with thick woolen socks. They walked the roads and paths around Gstaad using their alpenstocks (alpine walking sticks) for balance on the frosty trails. Max wore a thick, woolen scarf for additional warmth. He hitched his pants legs

---

used for muscle relaxation and to induce deep heating in tissue for therapeutic purposes. The procedure originated from research by Nikola Tesla, who noted in 1891 that high-frequency currents produced heat in the body. Tesla suggested this phenomenon might have medical applications. Diathermy was ultimately developed into three forms of treatment—ultrasound, short wave, and microwave therapy.

just over his knees to the top of his heavy socks. A crisp blanket of fresh snow made the fields around Gstaad glisten; the bright winter sun made the hills sparkle. Their lives and futures seemed to be as bright as the ice-encrusted fields.

Jakob Ichenhäuser (1824 - 1895)

Babette Ichenhäuser nee Ollesheimer

Jakob Ichenhäuser 1895

Dülken Family– Standing, Joseph, Isidor, Julie;
Seated– Jeanette, Emma, Anselm Heinrich Dülken

David Ichenhäuser

Emma Ichenhäuser nee Dülken, 1881

Standing– David and Emma Ichenhäuser;
Seated– Isidor Dülken and wife; children– Netta, Ernst, and Carl Dülken

Anselm Heinrich Dülken

Jeanette Dülken nee Baum

Emma Ichenhäuser with toddler Max, 1893

Max Ichenhäuser, 1893

Heinrich, Max, and Ernst Ichenhäuser, circa 1897

Gertrude "Trude" Moses, circa 1907 - 08

Ichenhäuser family at Bad Brückenau
L-R Ernst, David, Emma, Heinrich, and Max

83

Heinrich Ichenhäuser

Ernst Ichenhäuser

Max Ichenhäuser (L) and fraternity brothers

Max Ichenhäuser in Cuirassier Uniform WWI

Heinrich Ichenhäuser in uniform WWI

Ernst Ichenhäuser in uniform WWI

(L-R) Ernst, Max, and Heinrich in
uniform circa 1914 – 1917

Max (far left) in camp near Fleuricourt, 1917

Max (L) and army colleagues by
ruins of building during WWI

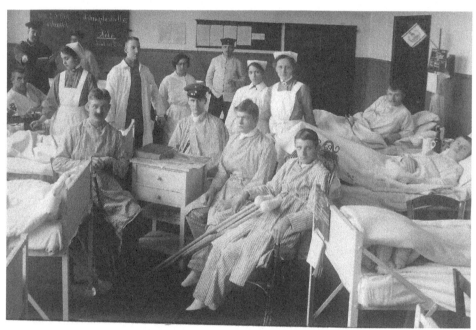

Max (standing left-center) in recovery ward WWI

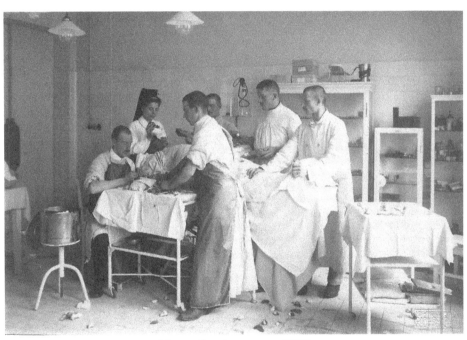

Max performing surgery WWI

A page from Max's WWI diary showing
Reims and nearby towns and battle lines

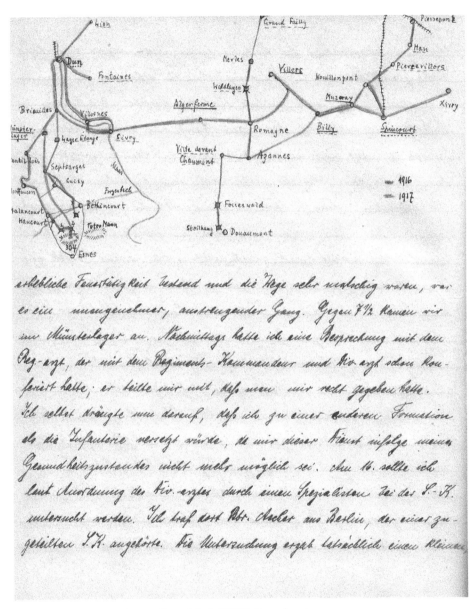

A page from Max's WWI diary showing map,
towns, and battle lines in 1916 and 1917

German newspaper article about the battle for Hill 304

Max's painting of a young woman with a feathered hat

Max's sketch of a woman
wearing a hat and veil

Max's sketch of a girl with roses

93

Max's sketch of a heron, done in 1907 at age 15

Max's sketch of a still life

Max (seated on floor lower right) with medical school classmates

Trude seated second from left; setting and context of photo not known

Trude Moses circa 1923

Max and Trude's engagement party, October 25, 1925. Seated L-R David and
Emma Ichenhäuser and Martha and Sigmund Moses, Ernst (with moustache)
standing in rear center-left, and Trude and Max seated on the floor

Announcement that Max's practice qualified to participate
in German medical insurance programs

Max and Trude in Gstaad, December 1927

Max hiking in Gstaad, December 1927

RENATE

T HE FOLLOWING YEAR SAW THE ICHENHÄUSER FAMILY expand by one. Max and Trude's daughter, Helga Renate,[66] was born at 2:20 a.m. on March 7, 1928, at their home in Cologne-Braunsfeld. Notwithstanding Max's specialty as an obstetrician, Dr. Max Samuel attended the delivery; he was assisted by midwife Helen Novak-Lange and maternity nurse Miss Emma Paul. Renate was a butterball with a shock of black hair that stood on end as if she had seen a ghost or stuck a tiny finger into an electrical socket. Trude and Max had planned to call their daughter Helga if she had blonde hair and Renate if she had dark hair. Given their baby's raven-colored locks, she was known as Renate.

Friends and family deluged them with good wishes. Carl and Hilde Spier, Lene and Max Berlin, Hans and Leni Rothschild, Emil and Luise Teitz and Dr. David Teitz from Fürth, the Roesberg family from Rommerskirchen, Tante (Aunt) Clara Cohen in Amsterdam, Dr. Max Samuel, and Meno Lissauer and Meta Lissauer sent congratulations and flowers. Renate received gifts from, among others, Edith and Clotilde Hahn, Lilly and Netta Dülken, Onkel (Uncle) Isidor Dülken, Tante Hermione Oberlander, Onkel Eduard Oberlander, Tante Nettchen Roesberg, and Hans and Leni Rothschild.

Renate soon had her first outing in a stroller. The pram appeared large enough, with its spacious interior and huge wheels, to hold a

---

66   Renate is pronounced "Re-*nah*-ta."

good portion of a nursery school enrollment if need be. Renate's shock of dark hair continued to grow, making for quite a sight as Max and Trude took their plump baby for outings in the neighborhood. By the time she was four months old, Renate's hair finally began to settle down, which made her look far less alarmed as she sat in her pram with her favorite toy, a painted, wooden duck.

In August 1928, when Renate was six months old, Max and Trude took her with them to Zermatt, high in the Swiss Alps, where they stayed at the Zermatterhof Hotel. Max and Trude seemed intent on introducing Renate at an early age to their love of the outdoors and hiking. They spent a few nights at the Hotel Vermala in the Swiss village of Adelboden in the Bernese Oberland. For Max, the highlight of the trip was taking the train to the Gornergrat summit to enjoy the spectacular views it afforded of the Swiss Alps. The summit, at 3089 meters, had developed into a top tourist destination starting in 1898 when tourists became able to reach the peak by means of the Gornergrat Bahn, the world's first fully electrified cog railway. The railway took visitors from the center of Zermatt to the summit while passing through tunnels, over vertigo-inducing bridges, across mountain meadows, and through forests of stone pine and larch.

At the summit, Trude and Max took photographs of Zermatt nestled in the valley below with the glaciers surrounding the village grinding down the mountainsides. Even for summer hiking, Max and Trude always carried their alpenstocks. Trude wore a floral print dress, while Max wore a wool suit and bow tie, with his trousers hitched up to his knees. As they walked down the mountainsides towards the valley, the bright sunshine led Max to shed his suit coat and drape it over his shoulder. They occasionally stopped to take advantage of the alpine streams cascading alongside the footpaths, where they took a few moments to drink the icy water from cupped hands and splash their faces to refresh themselves for the remainder of their hike. When they reached the village, they rewarded themselves with substantial lunches of rosti (shredded potatoes fried in a round pan with bacon, ham, onion, cheese, and sometimes apples) and dinners of raclette or cheese and meat fondue.

Max and Trude took side trips to Edelweisskopf for a nature

hike, to the Schwarzsee—Switzerland's Black Lake so named because, legend has it, a giant washed his apparently very dirty feet in the lake, as well as to the Schonbulhütte, Zmattgletscher (Zermatt glacier), and Riffelalp—a hamlet halfway between Zermatt and the Gornergrat situated at 7,290 feet. They clambered along the trails with their Alpenstocks, enjoying the brilliant sunshine and cloudless days. The trails took them through flower-filled pastures. The hillsides and meadows were populated by brown and white cattle wearing large brass bells that hung from colorfully embroidered leather collars. The cows seemed content to chew their cuds and lazily eye the hikers who had invaded their mountain pastures. Trude and Max strolled past herds of bleating goats and continued across footbridges that traversed rushing mountain streams.

By October 1928, Renate had grown into a happy toddler with a big smile. Her hair, cut in a page-boy style with bangs straight across her forehead, now rested flat against her head. Her nurse (in effect, a nanny) took her on daily outings to Cologne's Stadtwald park with a white Steiff bear as Renate's companion. Her crib included a wooden parrot that hung from a ring. A small wooden dog with a white muzzle rounded out her companions. Renate's plump cheeks were the result of a diet of rich milk, butterfat included. No skim milk for this child, who was sufficiently plump at eleven months that her snow suit practically burst at the seams when the family went sledding in Cologne's parks.

By May 1929, Renate had begun walking. She was no longer content to be pushed in her pram; walks with her nurse often resulted in Renate pushing the pram by herself, grinning all the while. Some days, Trude's parents Sigmund and Martha took Renate on outings. Renate wore short dresses while her grandparents were dapper in their suits and hats; Grandpa Moses strolled with his walking cane. The family often spent warm spring days at Cologne's municipal swimming pool or visiting friends. Trude occasionally weaved a small wreath of daisies for Renate to wear like a floral crown.

In the spring of 1929, Max and Trude took a brief break from their parenting duties to travel to Merano, in Italy's South Tyrol region, where they stayed at the Hotel Emma. Peaks of up to 3,335 meters (10,942 feet) surrounded Merano, best known for its spas, which had seen visitors as diverse as Franz Kafka and Ezra Pound. (Max's Green Diary.) Max and Trude took side trips to Karersee (a lake in Italy) and Trafoi (a tiny village in the Italian Tyrol).

Max and Trude purchased their first car—a Ford Model A sedan—that summer. The Model A was Ford's second huge success, coming after its initial success with the Model T. The Model A featured a four-cylinder engine that generated forty horsepower and had a top speed of sixty-five miles per hour. The Model A had a manual transmission and running boards, along with a rear-mounted spare tire. In September, Max, Trude, and Renate took the car for its first long outing by driving to Zons, a small, ancient German town on the lower Rhine between Cologne and Düsseldorf. Max did not like to drive, so Trude did most of the driving. When Max made house calls, Trude drove and waited in the car while he tended to his patients.

On November 25, 1929, a year and a half after Renate was born, Trude gave birth to a second daughter, Margot Erika Ichenhäuser, at 2:00 a.m. in the Ichenhäuser apartment at 346 Aachenerstrasse. Dr. Samuel and Nurse Emma Paul attended the birth, just as they had for Renate. Erica weighed in at 3730 grams (an impressive 8.2 pounds) with a length of 50 centimeters. Erica's hair was much lighter than Renate's. Its more relaxed posture suggested less alarm at being born than had Renate's bolt-upright shock of black hair. The family-sized pram was now put to good use as it was large enough to hold both Renate and Erica during their daily outings.

The Ichenhäusers' apartment building featured a sandbox in the rear garden where Renate and neighboring girls played. Trude kept an eye on the girls while she tended to Erica, whose strawberry-blond hair was a striking contrast to Renate's dark locks.

By the summer of 1930, when Erica's first teeth started to come in, Renate and Erica were old enough to stay with Trude's parents Sigmund and Martha while Max and Trude went on vacation. They headed off to the Hotel Giardino Riviera in Meroi in Italy's northeastern Friuli-Venezia Giulia region, with excursions to Rapallo, St. Margherita, Portofino, and Genoa. Though on holiday, Max toured in a wool suit, tie, and wool cap, while Trude wore patterned cotton dresses. They took every opportunity to swim given Italy's warm summer weather. Max wore black trunks and a black shirt, while Trude sported a cream-colored swimsuit and bathing cap as they swam from the rocky shores of the Italian lakes.

Max and Trude then enjoyed a Mediterranean cruise on the MS Monte Olivia, a two-funnel steam ship. They passed their days reading in deck chairs with striped canvas backing. Max occasionally donned white shirts and trousers instead of the dark suits he typically wore. Trude wore comfortable outfits comprised of a white vest and skirt. On days when the sea air was chilly, they reverted to suits and overcoats.

Max's medical practice flourished. While he drew patients from the community at large, he also came to be the "house doctor" for the American and British consulates in Cologne. The U.S. Consul General, Alfred W. Klieforth, had a son, Les, who was one year older than Renate. The British consul also had children the same age as the girls. The children sometimes played at one another's homes. Renate and Erica eventually spoke English fluently, which allowed the consuls' children to play with them, as the British and American children's mastery of German was a work in progress.

Max's practice was doing well enough in 1931 that he and Trude were able to purchase a new Ford. However, for their summer travel they took the train to Switzerland. They first stopped at the Hotel Vereina in Klosters near the Swiss border with Liechtenstein. They continued to the Hotel Steffani in St. Moritz and the Hotel Engadinerhof in Pontresina just north of the Swiss-Italian border. Their excursions included visits to Alp Giop, Lake Hahnensee, the Maloja district in Switzerland, the Morteratsch Glacier, the Bovalhusse in the Bernina Range above the Morteratsch Glacier, and the Roseg Valley in the Swiss Alps. While they enjoyed the rich cultural life in Cologne, they loved the fact that in a few hours they could leave the city and be in the spectacular alpine scenery of Switzerland or the Italian Tyrol.

Trude and Max soaked in the view of the Morteratsch Glacier from across the valley while sitting on wooden benches outside the Bovalhüsse, an alpine hiking hut at an altitude of 2459 meters.

Notwithstanding the huge river of ice close by, the air was warm enough for Trude to enjoy the day in a short-sleeved dress, while Max relaxed enough to loosen his tie. The view was enhanced by trays of cheese and sausage which Trude and Max washed down with mugs of hot coffee from the Bovalhüsse. They ambled through the high meadows and picked bouquets of Alpen Rosen (alpine roses similar to oleander blossoms) in the Rosegtal. The trip included frequent swims in the frigid glacial waters of Lake Stazersee in Switzerland's Engadin Valley. Lake Stazersee, also known as Lej de Staz, was beautiful in its own right, but was made even more so by the Stazerwald Forest and mountains that surrounded it, which combined to make Lake Stazersee a spectacular destination.

Trude and Max wrote to the girls frequently:

June 19, 1931

Dear Good Renate:

We are sitting across from these glaciers (Moreteratsch Glacier at Piz Bernina) and we just went through an ice cave carved in the glacier. We look forward to being able to take you and Erika along. You and Erika and your grandparents get a big kiss from your mum and a big hug and kiss from your dad.

Your Mutti (mother)

June 24, 1931

My dear, dear children!

Look at the hut (Tschierva hut, an alpine climbing hut at 2472 meters in the Rosegtal near Pontresina). On the bench to the right, we are sitting and enjoying the magnificent view of the Bernina and the craggy glacier. In four days, I will be with you again. Be good until then. Say hello to grandpa, grandma and Tetta. Sending love and a thousand big kisses from your mother.

Dear children, hugs and kisses from father.

While they enjoyed their children and their travels, life for Trude and Max was not without its challenges. In September 1931, Erica contracted scarlet fever. The following year she swallowed a hairpin that had to be surgically removed. Nevertheless, their lives were full and happy.

By 1932, Max's practice was doing so well that he and Trude could afford to build a house. On April 1, they broke ground at 412 Aachenerstrasse to build the first home they would own. The contractor completed the four-story house, situated on a corner lot, in just over four months. Max, Trude, and the girls moved in on September 1, leaving their cramped apartment behind.

The house, which architect Franz Seuffert designed, was quite modern given its Bauhaus style. It had a flat, white exterior. The stark design did not lead to universal acclaim from local critics. Nevertheless, the home's fourteen rooms, along with a basement which held the furnace and space for a garage, served many purposes for the family. The coal-fired furnace provided heat throughout the house via steam radiators. The house faced onto Aachenerstrasse, which was important since Aachenerstrasse had a streetcar line that allowed patients to take public transit to Max's office on the ground floor.

The second floor contained the living room, dining room, kitchen, and a small pantry. It also contained rooms where Trude's parents, Sigmund and Martha, lived. Sigmund had retired and sold his fabric-importing business, so he and Martha joined Max, Trude, and the girls in their new home.

Martha supervised the house cleaning. She was also in charge of the kitchen, where she helped the live-in maid prepare meals. Since Martha supervised the cooking, she also did the grocery shopping. Her usual purchases included beans, cabbage, fish, veal chops, and hamburger. Breakfast was typically a simple meal of puffed rice cereal. The main meal of the day, dinner, was at one o'clock. It featured meat or fish, a vegetable, and potatoes—boiled, mashed, or fried. Baked or fried kugel (noodle, potato, or bread pudding) was also a common dish among German Jews.[67] Four o'clock was teatime, which always included some sort of pastry with the tea or coffee. Dessert kugel, once a staple at tea, had been replaced by cake.[68]

---

67   *Jewish Daily Life in Germany, 1618-1945,* edited by Marion A. Kaplan, Oxford University Press, (2005) at 278.

68   *Jewish Daily Life* at 278.

Seven o'clock in the evening was time for supper. This was typically a light meal of open-faced sandwiches on thin slices of heavy rye or pumpernickel bread topped with cheese, sardines, liverwurst, or bologna. Treats might involve a bit of rich chocolate or some of Germany's marvelous marzipan candies made from a gooey almond paste. The marzipan confectioners frequently shaped the candies to look like various foods. The confectioners painted each piece of faux meat, fruit, or vegetable with food coloring to give the candies a colorful, lifelike appearance. Lébkuchen, German cookies made with ground nuts, chopped dried fruit, cloves, nutmeg, sugar, and cocoa, were available for dessert or a daytime treat.

Erica was particularly fond of Martha's lentil soup, made with lentils, onions, and large chunks of mild sausage. Erica had another reason for being pleased that Martha and Sigmund lived with them. Trude and Max did not allow the girls to leave any food on their plates. Whenever Erica had trouble finishing one of the dishes, Martha kept her company until Erica was able to finish her portion, making Martha a special grandmother indeed. Renate had a similar issue whenever her culinary nemesis, pea soup, was on the menu. If she did not finish it at dinner, the green soup distressingly reappeared for Renate's breakfast the next day.

The home's third floor contained the master bedroom, children's bedroom, nursery, playroom, and a bedroom for a nanny. The fourth floor held the maid's quarters, laundry area, guest bedroom, and a bathroom. The fourth floor also had a small, open-air sun deck and garden where Renate and Erica could play. Renate pedaled around the deck as fast as she could in a red, three-wheeled "racer" while Erica tried to keep pace on a two-wheeled scooter. While playing on the roof, the girls could see the Kölner Dom's massive, black spires looming in the city's center to the east.

Trude cut Renate's dark hair in a pageboy style. Erica's blond, almost tow-headed hair, gave the girls the appearance of a matched pair, like pepper and salt. They wore white, lace-up, over-ankle shoes with stockings that reached to mid-calf, along with white, long-sleeved shirts, and play dresses that featured embroidered patterns on the hems and pockets. The play area contained planter boxes with trellises on which vines grew, possibly including the clematis vines which Renate came to love. The girls played on the rooftop if going to the park or roller skating on the sidewalk in front of the house were not options. On cool days, Renate wore a white coat with a capelet, while Erica wore a white coat with standard lapels.

The girls dressed up for Karnival each year. Their satin costumes featured bright fabric panels with circles of color sprinkled across them. The girls topped their outfits with peaked caps like Merlin the magician might have worn. When it came time for the girls to exercise, they donned athletic gear. Renate's jersey had a lightning bolt and Erica's tunic had a stripe down the side. The girls smiled readily and enjoyed one another's company, holding hands for photographs and playing together nonstop.

The family home was only a few blocks from the Stadtwald Forest. The Stadtwald was a municipal park in the Cologne borough of Lindenthal. It was part of the "Aubree Grüngürtel," which was Cologne's outer "green belt." The city established the Stadtwald Forest in 1895 on the grounds of a former manor house and later enlarged it by adding several other parks. The forest, which included several ponds, was extremely popular with Cologne's residents. The Stadtwald was populated with stately beech and oak trees, along with ash, lindens, and maples. The trees provided cool shade during the summer and brilliant red, yellow, and orange foliage when autumn arrived.

The Stadtwald offered a variety of activities, including walking paths, pony rides, a petting zoo, and an animal park. The forest was well-known for its almost fully domesticated, white-spotted, fallow deer, which visitors could feed and pet. The park also had a population of roe deer, which were a bit smaller than the fallow deer and lacked the fallow deer's palmate antlers and white spots. The park had a lake where visitors could rent rowboats and watch swans gracefully float by. Since Trude worked in Max's office, the girls had a nurse from an early age who took them for daily walks in the park. By the time Renate was five and Erica was four, they rode matching scooters to the Stadtwald and wheeled along the paths that traced the riverside. They rushed ahead of their nurse, who huffed along trying to keep up with the excited and energetic girls.

On weekends, Max, Trude, Renate, and Erica clambered into the family car and headed to the parks, lakes, and hills outside of Cologne. Sometimes they found a grassy glen and spread out a blanket to enjoy lunch and play. Other times they used portable picnic furniture Max put together by screwing the removable legs into the tabletop and chair seats. Their picnic basket, which Martha filled with roasted or fried chicken, sausage, cheese, and fruit, kept them well fed. The girls washed down lunch with water while Trude and Max enjoyed a bottle of crisp Rhine or Moselle wine. The girls frequently brought a ball to toss with Max. When they tired of that, the girls scrambled through the forest and played in the grass until it was time to return home. Occasionally, Max's parents David and Emma joined them. Trude frequently brought a camera to record the day's events and later put the photographs into albums for the family to enjoy.

Later that spring, David and Emma Ichenhäuser, who were married on May 26, 1882, celebrated their golden wedding anniversary. The three generations of Ichenhäusers gathered to commemorate this milestone that few couples are fortunate to achieve.

In September, Max and Trude drove for a short visit to Schlangenbad, a spa town nestled in a small, wooded valley in Hessen province, near Wiesbaden. Schlangenbad was known for its thermal springs and moderate climate. Trude and Max penned a short note to the girls:

> My dear Renate:
>
> We are sitting in the rain in Schlangenbad and thinking of our little girls at home and wondering if both are being kind and obedient and making grandma and grandpa happy. Give all in the house our greetings, for you and Erika many big kisses from your mom.
>
> Hugs and kisses from Daddy. (Max and Trude letter to Renate and Erica, September 27, 1932.)

Within the parameters of their homes, their family, and Max's medical practice, life was good for the Ichenhäuser and Moses families.

However, all was not well in Germany. Hitler's anti-Semitic attacks and conspiracy mongering had begun to draw large crowds. His diatribes focused on the "Volk" as the essence of the nation. In Hitler's worldview, Jews were not members of the Volk, nor could they be. Hitler's Volk was composed of people with Aryan blood, as opposed to the Volk being German citizens whatever their religious or racial heritage might be. Hitler believed Jews were an inferior, alien race who, he claimed, sought to undermine and exploit the Volk and, therefore, should not be accepted as part of the German state. It was difficult to square Hitler's fear that those with weaker bloodlines would control the destiny of Germany with his belief that the Volk was the superior "race." How a small, inferior group (Jews made up less than one percent of the German population) could control and subjugate the "superior" ninety-nine percent of Germany's population was a mystery.

Nevertheless, the NSDAP grew in popularity while Germans suffered through the hardships of the post-WWI years and the Depression. From 1929 to 1932, German industrial production dropped by one-half; in July 1931 one of Germany's banks failed, causing the government to close all banks temporarily.[69] The German people looked for someone to blame for their unhappy situation. The NSDAP was more than ready to assign responsibility. It offered up Germany's Jews as scapegoats, the hatred of whom would quickly flourish in the already fertile ground of long-standing German anti-Semitism. The Nazi party sponsored electoral slates throughout Germany. It steadily increased its share of the vote from a tiny fringe party in 1923 to being one of the country's major political parties in March 1932 when it received thirty percent of the vote.[70]

On July 19, 1932, Germany's Minister of Defense, Lieutenant General Kurt von Schleicher, gave a speech in which he declared that Germany would, "if necessary," rearm in violation of the Treaty of

---

69 *Rise and Fall* at 136.

70 *Rise and Fall* at 158.

Versailles. German politicians used the crippling economic sanctions the Treaty of Versailles imposed, along with the attendant humbling of German pride, as justifications to breach the Treaty, including, most importantly, the provisions limiting the size and nature of Germany's military forces. A common refrain among German nationalists was that Germany should resume its "rightful place among the nations of the world." To the German nationalists, this meant, among other things, rearming to place German military forces on a par with those of England and France. Lieutenant General von Schleicher was not an advocate of democracy, nor was he a supporter of the Weimar Republic established after WWI. He believed that only a militaristic, authoritarian state would allow Germany to rise to glory again.

Von Schleicher's July speech was spectacularly ill-timed and very poorly received outside of Germany since he gave it only weeks after France waived its claims to further German reparations payments. France, having acceded to German demands for a reduction and then elimination of the financial burdens the Treaty of Versailles placed on Germany, was furious when Germany responded to those concessions by declaring it next wished to breach the arms limitations of the Treaty.

In the Reichstag election of July 1932, the NSDAP received the largest number of votes and became Germany's largest political party, putting Hitler and the Nazis close to taking power. In elections held in November 1932, the NSDAP garnered one-third of the vote, again better than any other party. The upward arc of German nationalism, threats, and rearming continued. Von Schleicher plotted against then Chancellor Franz von Papen and succeeded him as Chancellor on December 3, 1932. The Weimar Republic was tottering and close to collapse.

On the other side of the world, in the United States, Franklin Roosevelt won the 1932 presidential election in a landslide. However, the United States was still in the depths of the Great Depression. Following WWI, the United States' national sentiment was severely isolationist. While some U.S. politicians viewed developments in Germany with alarm, few had the stomach to address the issue and, even less so, urge U.S. action. In light of public sentiment against another "European adventure," which is how many Americans regarded WWI, and the pressing need to get the United States back on its economic feet, there was little appetite to get involved in a fight over what many regarded as "internal" German political issues.

THE JEWS ARE OUR MISFORTUNE

THE YEAR 1933 MARKED GERMANY'S FULL-THROATED descent into National Socialism. Germany had roughly 500,000 Jewish residents, most of whom were citizens.[71] Some 15,000 Jews lived in Cologne.[72] Jews constituted less than one percent of Germany's population. More than 100,000 Jewish men served in the German army in WWI; eleven thousand were killed. The army recognized many Jewish servicemen, like Heinrich, Ernst, and Max, for their service. Many Jews held positions in government and taught at leading German universities. "Of the thirty-eight Nobel prizes won by German writers and scientists between 1905 and 1936, fourteen went to Jews."[73] That is to say that while Jews made up barely one percent of Germany's population, they received more than one-third of the Nobel prizes awarded to Germans. These Jews who lived and worked in Germany, including many who had died fighting for the nation, considered Germany to be their home.

At the start of 1933, Chancellor General Kurt Von Schleicher was ill; he was unable to cobble together a ruling coalition. He resigned and recommended to German President Paul von Hindenburg that Hindenburg appoint Hitler to take Schleicher's place. After several inconclusive elections in 1932 had failed to result in any party

---

71   *The Holocaust Encyclopedia*, Jews In Prewar Germany.

72   *The Holocaust Encyclopedia,* Jews In Prewar Germany.

73   *The Holocaust Encyclopedia*, Jews In Prewar Germany.

obtaining a majority in the Reichstag, the NSDAP agreed to enter a coalition government with the Conservative party, which gave the alliance a majority in the Reichstag. And so, the disaster of Nazi rule began. At noon on January 30, 1933, when Renate was five and Erica was four, Adolf Hitler drove to the Chancellery Building on Berlin's Wilhelmstrasse to meet with Hindenburg, the ailing President of the ailing Weimar Republic. Against all odds, Hitler had risen to a point at which Hindenburg at last decided to administer the oath of office to him and make Hitler the Reich Chancellor of Germany.

> That evening from dusk until far past midnight the delirious Nazi storm troopers marched in a massive torchlight parade to celebrate the victory. By the tens of thousands, they emerged in disciplined columns from the depths of the Tiergarten, passed under the triumphal arch of the Brandenburg Gate and down the Wilhelmstrasse, their bands blaring the old martial airs to the thunderous beating of the drums, their voices bawling the new Horst Wessel song and other tunes that were as old as Germany, their jackboots beating a mighty rhythm on the pavement, their torches held high and forming a ribbon of flame that illuminated the night and kindled the hurrahs of onlookers massed on the sidewalks.[74]

"Hitler had been appointed Chancellor under Article 48 of the Weimar Constitution, which granted the President the authority to invoke dictatorial power to protect the democratic order from overthrow, a clause originally inserted to ensure against a feared Communist revolution."[75] This was the power Hitler would soon use not to defend Germany's democratic institutions from a Soviet-style revolution, but rather to destroy those institutions and make himself

---

74   *Rise and Fall* at p. 4-5. The Tiergarten is a district in central Berlin featuring a huge park. Horst Wessel was a violent young Nazi who joined the Party in 1926. He eventually came to the attention of Joseph Goebbels. Wessel was killed in a brawl in 1930. Goebbels and Nazi propagandists elevated the low life S.A. thug to martyr status. At his funeral, a choir sang lyrics Wessel had composed which the choir named "Horst Wessel Lied," meaning "Horst Wessel Song." The Nazis adopted the song, also known as "Raise the Flag," as their official anthem; they played it at all official occasions.

75   *War Against the Jews* at 49.

a supreme dictator with no political opposition. Hitler and the Nazi party would waste no time implementing their policy of excluding Germany's Jewish population from the nation's economic, social, and political lives.[76]

On February 27, 1933, less than one month after Hitler was named Chancellor, the Reichstag (capital building) in Berlin burned down in a suspicious fire. The origin of the fire was unclear, but suspicion was rife that the Nazis were responsible. Hitler took advantage of the fire to exercise the powers Article 48 granted to the Chancellor. Claiming that Communists intent on carrying out a Bolshevik revolution had set the blaze and arguing that the inferno demonstrated the fate of the nation was at risk, Hitler issued a decree the day after the fire suspending "all fundamental freedoms of speech, press, assembly, freedom from invasion of privacy (mail, telephone, telegram) and from house search without warrant."[77]

Six days later, on March 5, 1933, the NSDAP garnered forty-four percent of the vote in a national election in which roughly ninety percent of the eligible population voted. The NSDAP formed a coalition with a nationalist party that had secured eight percent of the vote, giving the Nazis control of the government.[78] Hitler's bloc won the largest proportion of the vote in the Reichstag and won an outright majority in the Prussian Diet (Germany's largest state legislature): "[s]uppression and intimidation have produced a Nazi-Nationalist triumph. The rest of the world may now accept the fact of the ultra-nationalist domination of the Reich and Prussia for a prolonged period with whatever results that may entail."[79]

"In the city of Cologne, the Catholic capital of Germany, under the influence of an unexpected 25% increase in the total vote—three fourths of which has gone into the Nazi column—Herr Hitler's party has come within an ace of seizing control there."[80] The Ichenhäusers'

---

76   *Pogrom Night* at xxii.

77   *War Against the Jews* at 50.

78   *Rise and Fall* at 196.

79   *The New York Times*, March 6, 1933, p. 1.

80   *The New York Times*, March 6, 1933, p. 1.

home city teetered on the verge of a Nazi takeover of the municipal government. What had seemed impossible was now coalescing into the actual.

By 1929, the S.A. had grown into a force of several hundred thousand men. It served the party by attacking the Nazis' political opponents through beatings, disruption of rallies, and destruction of opposition offices and publications. However, the S.A.'s members were unruly, and its leaders were of questionable background, loyalty, and ability.

Hitler decided to remedy this by creating a quasi-military force in 1925 named the Schutzstaffel ("Defense Corps"). This force came to be known as the "SS."[81] The mission of the SS was to be an elite, ruthless, and wholly dependable bodyguard for Nazi leadership. It also served as a spy force to detect anyone who opposed the regime, be it by word or deed. In order to distinguish the SS from the S.A., the SS adopted black uniforms, which served to make it even more intimidating than the S.A.'s brown-shirted thugs. In 1929, Hitler appointed Heinrich Himmler, a chicken farmer from a small village near Munich, to lead the SS. Under Himmler's direction, the SS became a tightly organized counterweight to the S.A. The SS would eventually come to terrorize all of Europe.

By the time Hitler came to power in 1933, the SS had thirty thousand members; by 1939, it boasted 250,000 members. The SS eventually gave rise to an even more frightening force, the Totenkopfverbände ("Death's Head Units"), who were responsible for administering the concentration camps. The Death's Head Units adopted the skull and crossbones as their insignia.

Hitler demanded unwavering allegiance from SS storm troopers: "I demand of a Storm Troop Leader, just as from a Storm Trooper, blind obedience and unquestioning discipline." SS troops, upon being inducted, took the following oath: "I swear to you, Adolf Hitler, as Führer and Chancellor of the German Reich, loyalty and valor. I pledge to you and to the superiors whom you will

---

81   *Rise and Fall* at 120.

appoint obedience unto death, so help me God."[82] Hitler required that all armed forces take an oath of loyalty to him: "I swear by God this sacred oath, that I will render unconditional obedience to Adolf Hitler, the Führer of the German Reich and people, Supreme Commander of the Armed Forces, and will be ready as a brave soldier to risk my life at any time for this oath."[83] The armed forces were now sworn to be loyal not to the nation, but to Hitler. This pledge of blind obedience to Hitler—not to the German nation or German Constitution—became emblematic of the German people's response to and acquiescence in Hitler's murderous policies: obedience to Hitler personally, untethered by conscience or moral grounding.

On March 20, 1933, Himmler announced that plans had been completed to construct the regime's first concentration camp. It was to be constructed in a former gunpowder factory near the town of Dachau, not far from Munich.[84]

Himmler soon took control of all police functions in Germany. This included the Gestapo ("Geheimes Staatspolizeiamt"—"Secret State Police"). The Gestapo, initially under the direction of Hermann Goering, was used to intimidate and eliminate political opponents. But when Goering appointed Himmler to head the Gestapo, it became a vastly larger and more deadly domestic terror organization wielding the power of life and death over every German. The Gestapo was now within the purview of the SS, which meant the Nazis controlled virtually all state security functions.

After the fire destroyed the Reichstag building, the Reichstag convened in alternative quarters on March 20, 1933. On March 23, the Reichstag passed an Enabling Act entitled "The Law for Removing the Distress of People and Reich" which gave Hitler's government the authority to promulgate legislation *even if it was contrary to the Constitution*.[85] The disturbing, in fact astonishing, reality was that the Reichstag had voluntarily abandoned its constitutional

---

82   *War Against the Jews* at 74; *Rise and Fall* at 120-121.

83   *Rise and Fall* at 226-227.

84   *War Against the Jews* at 51.

85   *War Against the Jews* at 51.

role and ceded all legislative and executive powers to the Chancellor. While Germany still had a democratic Constitution, it was now meaningless since it could be contravened by Hitler and the NSDAP at will. One week later, Hitler used the Enabling Act to dissolve all German state governments and appoint Nazis as governors in each state. Germany was no longer a democracy. It had, in practically the blink of an eye, become a dictatorship.

By this time, the S.A. had grown to 400,000 members, four times larger than what the Treaty of Versailles allowed for the German army. The S.A. had been pursuing a campaign of terror for nearly a decade aimed at intimidating Communists, Socialists, members of trade unions, and Jews. It was becoming more and more unrestrained in using violence. Hitler ramped up his campaign of anti-Semitic incitement and defamation by branding Jews as traitors, as leaders of attempts to carry out a Bolshevik revolution in Germany, and as responsible for the nation's defeat in WWI.

In March, "The Bund Nationalsozialistischer Juristen [League of National Socialist Lawyers] demanded that legal firms become 'Jew-free.' Jewish lawyers and public prosecutors were strongly urged to take leaves of absence."[86] "Nazi squads occupied court buildings, hunting down and beating up Jewish lawyers."[87]

On March 28, the NSDAP called for a boycott of Jewish businesses to take place on April 1. The NSDAP organized a "Central Committee for Defense against Jewish Atrocity and Boycott Propaganda."[88] The party placed guards outside Jewish stores and businesses to "advise" prospective customers that the enterprises were owned by Jews.[89] Some S.A. thugs wielded cameras to photograph and thereby intimidate and shame anyone who dared to patronize Jewish businesses. The S.A. brown shirts painted anti-Semitic graffiti across the windows and doors of Jewish establishments. "On the day of the boycott, Storm Troopers stood menacingly in front of Jewish-

---

86   *Germans No More, Accounts of Everyday Life 1933-1938*, Edited by Margrete Limberg and Hubert Rubsaat, Berghahn Books, (2006) at 17.

87   *Germans No More* at 17.

88   *War Against the Jews* at 54.

89   *War Against the Jews* at 54.

owned shops. The six-pointed "Star of David" was painted in yellow and black across thousands of doors and windows. Signs were posted saying 'Don't Buy from Jews' and 'The Jews are Our Misfortune'."[90]

While some non-Jews continued to patronize Jewish enterprises, most adhered to the S.A. troopers' "recommendations" and stopped doing business with long-time Jewish friends, neighbors, and colleagues. Barely three months after Hitler became Chancellor, the first Nazi-instigated, nationwide attack on Jewish commercial life had taken place. While the boycott lasted only one day, it marked the beginning of a national effort to disenfranchise Jews from the German economy.

The boycott had a tremendous impact on how German Jews regarded themselves. Their reactions "ranged from shame for having considered themselves German and having misinterpreted the Germans, to doubts about their Germanness and turning against those Jews who some considered to blame for anti-Semitism, to sudden feelings of hatred toward non-Jewish Germans."[91]

On April 7, 1933, the Reichstag passed the first anti-Jewish laws of the Nazi regime. The first such legislation was the "Law for the Restoration of the Professional Civil Service." Paragraph 3 of the law, which came to be known as the "Aryan paragraph," provided that: "Civil servants of non-Aryan origin are to retire..."[92] This was followed shortly by an edict which supplemented the original decree and provided that a non-Aryan was "anyone descended from non-Aryan parents or grandparents." Jewish civil servants, as "non-Aryans," were dismissed from their jobs, except for those who had held their positions since August 1, 1914, who had fought at the front in WWI, or whose father or son had been killed in action during the Great War.[93] Civil servants who belonged to one of the exempt groups were required to show proof of eligibility to retain their jobs. The fired Jewish civil servants included government workers as well

---

90   *The Holocaust Encyclopedia*, The Boycott of Jewish Businesses.

91   *Jewish Daily Life* at 314.

92   *Nazi Germany and the Jews, 1933-1945*, Saul Friedländer, abridged by Orna Kenan, Harper Perennial (2009) at 11.

93   Nazi *Germany and the Jews* at 11-12.

as teachers in public schools and universities. The Reichstag amended the decree in May to extend the term "civil service" to include the postal service, railroads, communal health insurance systems, professional associations, unemployment and salaried employees' insurance, miners' guilds, trade guilds, and chambers of commerce.[94]

The regime adopted another decree that day, which it published on April 11, prohibiting Jews from being admitted to the bar.[95] Those Jews who had already been admitted were barred from practicing law.[96] The decree had the same exemptions as the civil service law—combat veterans and attorneys whose fathers or sons had been killed in action in WWI or who had become attorneys by August 1, 1914 were exempt.[97] Due to the exemptions, "the initial application of the law was relatively mild." Roughly three-quarters of Jewish attorneys were able to continue to practice. However, "Jewish lawyers were excluded from the national association of lawyers and listed not in its annual directory but in a separate guide; all in all, notwithstanding the support of some Aryan institutions and individuals, they worked under a 'boycott by fear'."[98]

The regime also barred Jews from being lay assessors, jurors, and commercial judges.[99] Litigants could refuse to have Jewish judges preside over their cases on grounds of purported bias. As a practical matter, this disenfranchised all Jewish judges, regardless of how long and honorably they had served on the bench, because litigants were loath to be seen "consorting" with Jewish judges, just as shoppers feared being seen doing business with Jewish merchants.

On April 21, the Reichstag passed legislation banning the kosher butchering of livestock, which made it nearly impossible for most Jews to observe kashrut.[100] Although families of means could

---

94 *Jewish Daily Life* at 309-10.

95 *War Against the Jews* at 58.

96 *Nazi Germany and the Jews* at 13.

97 *Nazi Germany and the Jews* at 12.

98 *Nazi Germany and the Jews* at 13.

99 *War Against the Jews* at 58.

100 *War Against the Jews* at 60.

import kosher meat from abroad, the increasing impoverishment of the Jewish community due to Jews having been excluded from much of the German economy made this impossible for most people.

The Nazis' desire to purge the German economy of Jewish participation did not spare the medical profession. Jewish physicians were suddenly, by unspoken practice, barred from clinics and hospitals run by the national health insurance program. "On April 24, 1933, Jewish doctors were dropped from the public insurance system, ruining countless careers. The large private insurance companies soon followed suit, and the exclusive companies paid only for non-Jewish patients."[101] Non-Jewish patients stopped seeing their Jewish physicians, fearing retribution from the SS. In early June, Jews were barred from being dentists and dental technicians associated with health insurance.[102] "By the middle of 1933 nearly half of all Jewish doctors had abandoned their profession."[103]

The Reichstag added to these prohibitions on April 25, 1933, by enacting the "Law Against the Overcrowding of German Schools."[104] This Orwellian turn of phrase masked the true intent of the law, which was to limit Jewish enrollment at all German schools and universities to 1.5% of new applicants.[105] Children of Jewish World War I veterans and of Jewish-Aryan couples were, for the time being, exempt. The law meant that thousands of Jewish children had to withdraw from the schools they had been attending and enroll in Jewish-only schools. Many Jewish children were subject to terror on the streets as they made their way to and from school each day, and were subject to abuse in school as well, such that, regardless of the legislation, their continued attendance at public schools was no longer feasible.[106]

---

101 *Germans No More* at 18.

102 *War Against the Jews* at 59.

103 *Germans No More* at 18.

104 *War Against the Jews* at 186.

105 *War Against the Jews* at 59.

106 *War Against the Jews* at 186.

Young Hilma Geffen-Ludomer, the only Jewish child in the Berlin suburb of Rangsdorf, recalled the sudden change: The "nice, neighborly atmosphere ended abruptly...Suddenly, I didn't have any friends. I had no more girlfriends, and many neighbors were afraid to talk to us. Some of the neighbors that we visited told me: 'Don't come anymore because I'm scared. We should not have any contact with Jews.'" Lore Gang-Salheimer, eleven in 1933 and living in Nuremberg, could remain in her school as her father had fought at Verdun. Nonetheless, "it began to happen that non-Jewish children would say, 'No, I can't walk home from school with you anymore. I can't be seen with you anymore.'"[107]

New regulations provided that, to the extent any Jewish children remained in public schools, they were to be penalized if they missed classes on Saturday, which meant that if they were observant, they had to violate Shabbat to avoid the penalty.

"[F]or Jewish children it was almost impossible to understand why their playmates were no longer allowed to play with them, why they were excluded from swimming lessons and from field trips, why people shouted insults at them or even beat them up for being Jews."[108] "My homeroom teacher, Herr Walter, had recently begun noticing that my classmates were shunning me; no one wanted to sit next to me, no one wanted to play with me during recess. We always had to leave the classroom in pairs to get to the courtyard. To go from the courtyard to the classrooms the pupils also had to walk in class formation and in pairs. I always went alone, and I was always last."[109]

As recounted by a student at a Jewish school: "The school administration always warned us to behave inconspicuously on the street and never to appear as a group but only in pairs. We should never stand in front of the school. A teacher always stood at the entrance before the first bell and after the last bell to make sure we never formed groups in front of the school."[110]

---

107 *Nazi Germany and the Jews* at 14.

108 *Germans No More* at 95.

109 *Germans No More* at 100.

110 *Germans No More* at 102.

Most Germans soon stopped having any interactions with Jewish friends, colleagues, or businessmen due to fear of both personal and professional reprisals.[111] "This was particularly hard for older people who had long lived in familiar surroundings and now felt rejected, and for Jews for whom involvement in clubs or organizations had been a central component of their lives...The social climate was poisoned. Jews, when they were identified as such, were increasingly insulted and even abused in public."[112]

The Nazis pursued a relentless policy of excluding Jews from Germany's commercial, social, and political lives. On May 6, the regime extended the Civil Service law to apply to honorary professors, university lecturers, and notaries.[113] "The Cologne city council broke off all its contracts with Jewish suppliers and businessmen; Jewish sports clubs and athletes were banned from sports fields and facilities."[114] The point of these laws and regulations was to make life for Jews so horrible that they would voluntarily leave the country, sparing the Nazis from having to devise further efforts to remove Jews from German life. The regime's strategy was that by increasing the impoverishment of the Jewish community, its members would have no choice but to emigrate to wherever they might find a new home. That outcome assumed, of course, that Germany's Jews could find another country to admit them, which turned out to be an invalid assumption with fatal consequences.

In May, the regime abolished trade unions, eliminating another potential counterweight to Nazi policies. In July, the regime banned all political parties except the NSDAP; attempts to maintain or start other parties were punishable by imprisonment.

On September 29, 1933, the regime established the "Reich Chamber of Culture" which promptly barred Jews from cultural and entertainment enterprises such as art, literature, theater, and motion

---

111 *Germans No More* at 55.

112 *Germans No More* at 55.

113 *War Against the Jews* at 59.

114 *Pogrom Night* at xxii.

pictures.[115] On the same day, the Reichstag enacted the National Hereditary Farm Law, which barred Jews from owning farms or engaging in agriculture.[116] "[O]nly those farmers could inherit farm property who could prove that their ancestors had no Jewish blood as far back as 1800."[117] The Nazis also barred Jews from membership in the Journalists Association and from being newspaper editors. On October 4, the National Press Law placed political newspapers under state supervision and applied the prohibitions of the "Aryan paragraph" to bar non-Aryans from being members of the press.[118]

The effects of these laws were twofold. First, they excluded Jews from the German economy at large. That, in turn, caused Germany's Jews to create an entirely separate and self-reliant economy in which Jews could patronize only other Jews. To fill the void the exclusionary laws created for artists, the Jewish community established the "Kulturbund" in 1933 to act as a Jewish cultural organization. Its goal was to provide jobs for Jewish artists, musicians, writers, and performers who were barred from their previous employment. The Kulturbund, by organizing and sponsoring performances and galleries, also created employment for those whose jobs provided technical support to the artists, such as those involved in stagecraft.

The Jewish community also established the Federal Representation of Jews in Germany, known as the Reichsvertretung der Juden in Deutschland, to serve as an umbrella organization for local and national Jewish associations.[119] Rabbi Leo Baeck of Berlin served as its head. Since Jews were no longer allowed to work in virtually all trades, professions, and businesses, and Jewish children could no longer attend German schools, Germany's Jews decided to form an organization to coordinate their efforts to address the welfare and education of the Jewish community.[120]

---

115 *War Against the Jews* at 59.

116 *Nazi Germany and the Jews* at 14.

117 *War Against the Jews* at 61.

118 *War Against the Jews* at 59.

119 *War Against the Jews* at 105.

120 *War Against the Jews* at 105.

Max kept a wary eye on these developments. He noted in his diary that "Spring 1933 brought decisive political changes with it." (Max's Green Diary.) Max wrote that, "as a soldier who fought on the front, I was, however, licensed to run a medical practice for people covered by state health insurance." However, he knew many colleagues whose medical practices had been shut down and whose livelihoods had been destroyed because of the new laws. "By the middle of 1933 nearly half of all Jewish doctors had abandoned their profession. Many emigrated, while others attempted to survive as masseurs, nurses, and midwives."[121] At least for the time being, Max could continue practicing medicine.

Given the uncertainties the new regime had created, the Ichenhäusers did not go on vacation in 1933. Going out was becoming too uncomfortable in light of the worsening hostility towards Jews, not to mention the uncertainty regarding where the family might be able to stay or eat given the widespread refusal of Germans to have any kind of dealings with Jews. "In many a town the Jew found it difficult if not impossible to purchase food. Over the doors of the grocery and butcher shops, the bakeries and the dairies, were signs, 'Jews Not Admitted.'…Pharmacies would not sell them drugs or medicine. Hotels would not give them a night's lodging. And always, wherever they went, were the taunting signs 'Jews Strictly Forbidden in This Town' or 'Jews Enter This Place at Their Own Risk.'"[122]

Instead, the Ichenhäusers limited themselves to day trips by car. They drove to Attendorn (to see the Limestone Cave), Altenahr (a resort in the Rhineland north of Cologne), Kirchen on the River Sieg (Kirchen was a spa town in Germany's northern Rhineland-Palatinate region), Hohe Acht (the highest peak in Germany's Eifel Mountains), and the Eifelhohenweg (a beautiful forest along the Belgian border). Despite the intense political ferment and economic turmoil, they tried to enjoy the summer and continue their activities within the restricted living space the new laws afforded to them.

---

121 *Germans No More* at 18.

122 *Rise and Fall* at 233.

Max and Trude tried to give the girls a normal life at home as well. Renate and Erica had a "Braunsfeld Costume Party" on February 18, for which they sent "entry tickets" to their friends. The invitation promised "big surprises," with the doors opening at 3:30 and prize giving starting at 4:00, including a prize for the most beautiful costume. For the girls' birthdays, Trude purchased cakes from Café Eigel on Brückenstrasse in downtown Cologne; the Café offered a dizzying array of rich cakes and pastries from which Trude would make her selection.

On May 10, the extent of the increasing Nazi hold on the German psyche became evident in a frightening scene—the book burnings began. At the University of Berlin, a torchlight parade ended with students throwing thousands of books onto a huge bonfire. The authors whom the regime determined were no longer acceptable included German authors such as Thomas Mann, Erich Maria Remarque, Walter Rathenau, and Albert Einstein. Foreign authors whose works the mob destroyed included Jack London, Upton Sinclair, Helen Keller, H.G. Wells, Sigmund Freud, Andre Gide, Émile Zola, and Marcel Proust.[123]

The disastrous impact of the Nazi decrees caused widespread despair in the Jewish community. Many Jews, having lost their jobs and businesses, were left with no means to support themselves. Venturing into the streets put them at risk of beatings and verbal harassment. The Jewish community saw a sharp increase in suicides. The increase was sufficiently dramatic that community leaders issued a call for Jews not to give up hope, but rather to persevere.[124]

The Nazi-induced political ferment continued without respite. New turmoil erupted a few months later when, on October 15, 1933, Hitler declared that Germany was withdrawing from the Disarmament Conference and League of Nations. President Hindenburg dissolved the Reichstag by proclamation and ordered new elections. "These, however, will not be elections in the normal sense because there exists no organized opposition to the present

---

123 *Rise and Fall* at 241.

124 *Pogrom Night*, Vol. I at xxiii.

government. All parties other than the National Socialist have vanished—they have been either self-dissolved or forcibly suppressed."[125]

Hitler declared he would refuse to adhere to any conditions in the Versailles Treaty. "Repeated and studied refusals to accord Germany moral and material equality, he (Hitler) says, have deeply humiliated the German people and their government."[126] After replacing all state governments with Nazi party members, Hitler ordered the dissolution of all German state governments and declared they would not be replaced. As a result, Germany's only government would be the national government with Hitler as its head. There would be no state governments to fight a rearguard action against the Nazis, had any been so inclined, or to provide forums in which viewpoints other than those of the National Socialists might be heard. Over the course of seven months, the German nation had devolved into an autocracy. There were no unions, no political parties (but for the NSDAP), and no state governments. There was no Germany; there was only Hitler.

Even more troubling was the fact that, by the end of 1933, the Nazis had established fifty concentration camps (proto-KZ or Konzentrationslager) in which the regime was holding tens of thousands of inmates in "protective custody" for political offenses. The camps were Hitler's solution to what to do about political dissenters. The Nazis would later use the camps to solve another "problem."

---

125 *The New York Times*, October 15, 1933, p. 1.

126 *The New York Times*, Oct. 15, 1933, p. 1.

1934 — GERMANY TRANSFORMED

A S 1934 BEGAN, GERMANY WAS A NATION TRANSFORMED:

When Hitler addressed the Reichstag on January 30, 1934, he could look back on a year of achievement without parallel in German history. Within twelve months he had overthrown the Weimar Republic, substituted his personal dictatorship for its democracy, destroyed all the political parties but his own, smashed the state governments and their parliaments and unified and defederalized the Reich, wiped out the labor unions, stamped out democratic associations of any kind, driven the Jews out of public and professional life, abolished freedom of speech and of the press, stifled the independence of the courts and "coordinated" under Nazi rule the political, economic, cultural and social life of an ancient and cultivated people. For all these accomplishments and for his resolute action in foreign affairs, which took Germany out of the concert of nations at Geneva and proclaimed German insistence on being treated as an equal among the great powers, he was backed, as the autumn plebiscite and election had shown, by the overwhelming majority of the German people.[127]

Despite the political turmoil, Trude and Max tried to maintain a normal life. In June of 1934, after some of the shock from the initial anti-Jewish legislation had worn off, they took a road trip to Switzerland. Max had a sore hand, so Trude drove, even though

---

127   *Rise and Fall* at 213.

women drivers were few and far between at the time. They stopped in Heidelberg, on the Neckar River in southwestern Germany, and continued to Zurich, Lake Walensee, and the Hotel Engadinerhof in the Swiss canton of Graubünden.

They spent part of their vacation with their close friends the Hartmann-Schmidts, a couple from Cologne-Braunsfeld, whose friendship they would one day call upon in an hour of need. They continued south to Lake Como before circling north through Strasbourg, where they visited Edith Wachs, a cousin of Trude's, and Edith's husband Siegfried. They visited Speyer, one of Germany's oldest cities, which had been founded by the Romans. Located on the west bank of the Rhine in the Rhineland-Palatinate district, Speyer was dominated by its cathedral in which eight Holy Roman emperors and German kings were buried. Their last stop was at Worms to see the extraordinary Romanesque cathedral there.

Notwithstanding the fact that Max could, at least for the moment, maintain a semblance of his medical practice, Trude and Max realized they needed to consider what type of future, if any, Germany held for them. In light of the accession of the National Socialists to power and the wide-ranging anti-Semitic legislation Hitler and the NSDAP had forced through the Reichstag, the lives Trude, Max, and the Jewish community at large had enjoyed were gone. While the Nazis had only recently come to power, there was no ignoring their brutal, often violent tactics, nor was there any avoiding their threatening rhetoric and vindictive legislation targeting Jews. Max and Trude spent many nights contemplating what these developments might portend for their family.

Many Jews took a "wait and see" approach. They wanted to hold on and wait out the new regime, believing it could not remain in power for long. German Jewry was, by and large, native to Germany with Jews having lived there for centuries. Many of Germany's Jews were urban and most had a profession or worked in a business. Many Jews identified very strongly as Germans, sometimes even more than they identified as Jews.[128] However, the advent of the National Socialist regime "sent tremors throughout this Jewish

---

128 *War Against the Jews* at 170-171.

population from right to left. On the one hand, panic and flight, despair and suicide. On the other, steadfastness and solidarity, courage and a stubborn will to resist."[129]

After Renate and Erica went to sleep at night, Max and Trude sat at the kitchen table, sometimes with Trude's parents, assessing their future and trying to divine what the Nazi regime meant for their family. The thought of leaving Cologne, and worse yet Germany, was frightening. The Ichenhäusers had lived in Cologne for generations and in Germany for centuries. David Ichenhäuser owned two flourishing lumberyards in Cologne. Sigmund had operated a successful business in the city for decades, while Max had a thriving medical practice there. Trude and Max had lived their entire lives in Cologne. Their roots in Germany ran deep. It would not be easy to give up all of that for an unfamiliar life in a new country.

"Jewishness" manifested itself in the Ichenhäuser family in various ways. David Ichenhäuser came from an Orthodox background. His family was somewhat observant, going to synagogue at least occasionally. They observed the High Holy Days and Passover, but they did not keep a kosher home. David and Emma gave their sons a Jewish education, although the extent of their adherence to Jewish law such as Kashrut is not known. However, they ensured that Max was bar mitzvah. Max's correspondence to his parents as a child and even more so during WWI is full of references to Jewish holidays, including wishing his parents a good Sabbath, describing his efforts to attend services for Rosh Hashanah, Yom Kippur, Sukkot, and Pesach, and his comments about the "mishpocha." These references display a familiarity with the Jewish calendar, Jewish and Yiddish terminology, and observance of Jewish holidays. Max had become a Zionist, no doubt spurred by what he saw happening in Germany and the resultant need for Jews to have a safe harbor somewhere in the world if life for them in Germany continued to deteriorate.

The Moses family was far less observant, although Trude's paternal grandparents observed the High Holy days at synagogue and celebrated the Passover Seder. However, they, too, did not keep a kosher home. Trude's maternal grandparents, the Oberlanders, were

---

129 *War Against the Jews* at 172.

fully assimilated and agnostic in their attitudes. Trude was not observant in the least.

Reform Judaism originated in Germany early in the 19th century. The movement sought, in part, to create a Judaism that was more in line with the manner in which German Jews' non-Jewish neighbors worshipped. This included adding choirs and music to the synagogue services, performing much of the prayer service in German, and dispensing with the observance of Kashrut. This led Reform Jews to feel even more "German" and less "overtly Jewish." However, the intensity of one's Judaism and the extent, if any, to which one observed Judaism's rites and practices failed to insulate Jews from the harshness of Nazi rhetoric or the physical and economic threats emanating from the National Socialist regime.

Prior to the rise of the National Socialists, Max and Trude had Jewish and non-Jewish friends, although their closest friends were Jewish. Max belonged to a Jewish fraternal organization and both he and Trude were members of Jewish social and civic organizations. However, they were not affiliated with a synagogue and the synagogue was not the cultural or religious center of their lives. Synagogues operated differently in Germany than in the United States. They did not operate on a dues system; instead, all religious organizations were subsidized by the state. Attendance was not dictated by a financial commitment to a synagogue. As a result, some Jews felt less connected to houses of worship. Even so, Cologne had five synagogues. Several of them were beautiful, architecturally significant buildings, such as the Roonstrasse shul where Max had his bar mitzvah.

Max and Trude had always taken advantage of much of what "non-Jewish"' Cologne had to offer. In addition to socializing with friends at restaurants and cafes, they attended many cultural events. They frequently went to the theater, opera, and concerts. Trude, who had majored in art history, loved visiting Cologne's museums. They enjoyed a rich life in Cologne. However, there was no ignoring the sense of foreboding that permeated their thoughts as the crisis enveloping Germany's Jews continued without respite.

In 1934, Max and Trude had not yet decided to emigrate, even though tens of thousands of Jews had left the country in the first year after Hitler rose to power. Max believed the storm would pass. He was not yet prepared to leave the country where his family had lived for generations. He was a decorated officer in the German army and a veteran of WWI. Max had difficulty believing the Reich would turn on its Jewish citizens, including so many who had served the country in wartime. He thought the National Socialist "troubles" were a phase Germany was passing through and that, eventually, the Nazi regime would fall.

Trude, however, saw the handwriting on the wall. "It was usually women who pushed for emigration, due to the burden on their children, whereas men could often not imagine how they could possibly 'really leave all this behind to enter nothingness.'...Women generally assessed the situation far more critically than did men, who refused to emigrate as long as they still had ways to earn an income or made themselves believe they did. In addition, women were prepared to accept a lower standard of living for the sake of safety.[130]

Even though they were as yet undecided about whether to leave Germany, Trude and Max began to prepare for life in another country should it come to that. Trude threw herself into her daughters' education, striving to give them the broadest education she could. Having been an art history major, Trude took the girls to many art museums, so many that it is a wonder they did not swear off art for the rest of their lives. Afternoons spent looking at medieval and renaissance art somehow did not capture the young girls' imaginations.

Trude maintained a strict schedule of activities for Renate and Erica. The girls took a gymnastics class every week. They had music, art, and dance lessons. The dance lessons were, in a sense, courtesy of Shirley Temple. The first movie Erica saw was a Shirley Temple film. When she got home from the theater, she demonstrated to the family, as best she could, the dance moves Shirley had performed. Erica's enthusiasm for young Shirley Temple's dancing was the impetus for Trude to enroll the girls in tap dance classes.

By the time Renate and Erica started school, the Reichstag had enacted legislation requiring Jewish children to attend Jewish-only

---

130 *Jewish Daily Life* at 357.

schools. At age six, Renate began attending school in the spring of 1934 at the Städtische Israelitische Volksschule on Lützowstrasse. Class ran from nine in the morning to one in the afternoon, when the girls went home for dinner and then did their homework. The Cologne Städtische was the largest public, Jewish Volksschule in Germany. A Volksschule ("people's school") was an elementary school. The Volksschule was not far from the Ichenhäusers' home, as it was situated a few blocks west on Aachenerstrasse and south several blocks on Lützowstrasse, between Cologne's Latin and Belgian Quarters. Renate trundled off to school each morning wearing a skirt and sweater while shouldering a leather backpack to carry her books and school supplies. Renate typically took the streetcar to school.

Mr. Hirschfeld taught Renate's class. He was a severe-looking man who wore a suit and tie, a brown fedora with a ribbon around the brim, and a pocket square. Judging from the expression on his face in one of Renate's class photographs, he appeared to brook no foolishness. Given that his class had almost forty students, most of them displaying facial expressions in their class picture running a spectrum from glum to grim, it appeared that discipline may have been the subject Mr. Hirschfeld taught most frequently. Renate was, by her own admission, a "talker," so she spent a good bit of time standing in a corner of the classroom as punishment for her chatty transgressions. Of course, all of the Volksschule's teachers were Jewish.

Renate studied Hebrew and Latin as part of the curriculum. The students also learned about Kashrut and the Jewish holidays. Renate, an eager student, did very well in "order," cleanliness, attention, and diligence. She also did well in Biblical history, reading, and arithmetic. As to spelling, she oscillated between satisfactory and good.

Erica, a year younger than Renate, attended a different school where her class was taught by a Mrs. Schloss. One of Erica's subjects was bible study, in which the students took turns telling Bible stories to the class in their own words. This was, to put it mildly, not Erica's favorite subject. Although the Ichenhäusers were not religious, Trude had the girls read portions of the Old Testament at home. As a result, Renate and Erica became at least somewhat familiar with the books of Genesis and Exodus, in addition to whatever Bible lessons they had at school.

Despite the increasingly grim situation in Germany, in August 1934, Trude, Max, and the girls spent three weeks in Manderscheid, fifty miles south of Cologne. The girls hiked with their parents every day; one of them carried a canteen, while the other shouldered a small backpack. Each girl used a walking stick, although Erica and Renate did not yet have the formal, carved alpenstocks that Max and Trude carried. Manderscheid offered opportunities for the family to swim in ponds and lakes and for the girls to play with other children whose parents had taken them to the mountains for summer vacation. Their trip included a visit to Himmerod Abbey, a Cistercian monastery founded in 1134. The Abbey was located in the Salm Valley in the Eifel, a low mountain range that ran from western Germany into eastern Belgium.

German political life was becoming more fraught and violent. On July 1, 1934, Hitler crushed a suspected revolt by Nazi radicals during a purge that came to be known as the "Night of the Long Knives." He ordered the SS to murder General von Schleicher, one of the purported ringleaders, whom Hitler denounced as having plotted to overthrow the government. The SS murdered former members of the government, while some committed suicide after learning Hitler claimed they were part of a cabal to overthrow the NSDAP. Hitler ordered the murder of virtually the entire leadership of the S.A., of which Ernst Röhm had been the leader. Röhm had been both an early ally and friend of Hitler's and was a co-founder of the S.A. Nevertheless, as the S.A. swelled in size to over three million men, Hitler came to see Röhm as a potential rival and, therefore, ordered the SS to murder him during the purge. The regime placed machine gun nests on the streets of Berlin and ordered armed soldiers to take up positions around public buildings. Police with machine gun attachments stationed themselves in Berlin's historic Potzdammer Platz near the Reichstag.

Nazi violence soon spilled over into neighboring Austria. On July 26, 1934, one hundred and forty-seven Nazis attacked the Austrian Chancellery and killed Austrian Chancellor Dollfuss.

They seized numerous Cabinet members as hostages. The official, but utterly transparent, German position was that this was entirely an internal Austrian affair. In truth, Hitler simply wanted to avoid blame for the assassination, even though the Austrian Nazi party was little more than an arm of Hitler's National Socialist party.

The other shoe soon dropped in Germany. On August 2, 1934, President Paul von Hindenburg died. Reich Chancellor Hitler assumed the Presidency. "No new president was appointed; instead, the powers of the chancellor and president were combined into the office of the Führer…The army also swore an oath of loyalty personally to Hitler, giving him power over the military…"[131] This meant that Hitler would be, in effect, an absolute dictator since he would be in charge of the nation's political and military arms. With Hindenburg gone, there were no politicians of sufficient stature to push back against the Nazi political onslaught and street violence.

Max and Trude still tried to get away from Cologne for an occasional respite from the crushing tension permeating the city. The girls, ages five and six, were old enough to write to them:

> Dear Mummy and Daddy: I am going for a walk this morning. Hugs and kisses. Erika.

> Dear Mummy and Daddy: How are you? Here it is raining. We cannot go for a walk. Love and kisses. From Erika.

> Dear Mum,

> For your birthday I send you many kisses. I'm fine in school. When you are back here we want to cheerfully celebrate your birthday. Kiss. Renate

> I was in the fairground. Kisses. Renate

In September 1934, the family set aside their worries long enough for Trude and Max to host a birthday party for their fathers. Sigmund Moses had turned seventy-five and David Ichenhäuser had turned eighty. Sigmund, with his trademark dour face, was

---

131 *History of the Jews in Germany,* Jesse Russell, Ronald Cohn, Pub. Lennex Corp. (2012) at 35.

dapper in a dark, three-piece suit. David matched him in a black, double-breasted suit. Crisply starched collars and silk ties completed their outfits, with Sigmund adding a pocket watch and chain to his vest. Emma Ichenhäuser wore a floor-length patterned skirt, white blouse, and sweater. Martha Moses dressed for the occasion in a black dress that reached to mid-calf; she paired her dress with a white blouse featuring a scalloped collar and a bow that draped down the front. Emma and Martha wore simple necklaces to complete their outfits. Notwithstanding the Nazi attacks on Germany's Jews, the family was happy, as they were together in their home to share the joy of the occasion and honor the two patriarchs. The three generations of Ichenhäusers luxuriated in the day.

This celebration would be one of the last joyful family events. With Hindenburg gone and the Nazi regime firmly in place, the Ichenhäusers' Germany of mountain vacations, cultural events, and walks in Cologne's leafy parks, was disappearing. Max's prosperous medical practice, David's lumber businesses, and family gatherings with few cares would soon be distant memories.

Oddly, in light of the Nazis' anti-Semitic legislation and propaganda, in February 1935 the regime announced a further honor to Max for his service during WWI:

> In the Name of the Führer and Chancellor, Doctor Max Ichenhäuser of Köln-Braunsfeld has been awarded the Cross of Honor for Front Line Fighters on the basis of the decree of July 13, 1934, in commemoration of the World War 1914/1918, established by the Reich President General Field-Marshal von Hindenburg. (Certificate awarding Cross of Honor, Feb. 1, 1935.)

A further notice provided that:

> On behalf of the Führer, you have been awarded the Cross of Honor by the Chief of Police. You are cordially asked to meet at the 11th Precinct on the 9th of February 1935 at 4:00 to receive the Cross of Honor.
>
> Heil Hitler!

The regime that was characterizing Jews as the root of the German nation's troubles and the cause of its defeat in the Great War, was, at the same time, commending Jews for their military service to the Fatherland. In light of the daily, overt hostility to Jews on the street, one could hardly fault Max if he thought long and hard about the advisability of accepting even a "cordial" invitation to visit the local police.

On March 16, 1935, as Hitler was repudiating the provisions of the Treaty of Versailles that had disarmed Germany, he also announced compulsory, universal military service.[132] In late March, the regime renewed terror attacks and boycotts against Jewish businesses. As the summer of 1935 approached, "Jews were prevented from going into cinemas, theaters, swimming pools and resorts."[133] In October, the regime banned the public sale of Jewish newspapers.

The Nazis took further steps to eliminate any Jewish presence in the country's music. "Jewish performers such as Artur Schnabel, Jascha Heifetz, and Yehudi Menuhin were no longer heard either in concert or on the radio. Jewish conductors had fled, as had the composers Arnold Schoenberg, Kurt Weill, and Franz Schreker. After some early hesitations, Mendelssohn, Meyerbeer, Offenbach, and Mahler were no longer performed."[134] The systematic exclusion of Jews from the country's economic, social, and cultural lives continued apace.

---

132 *War Against the Jews* at 62.

133 *War Against the Jews* at 62.

134 *Nazi Germany and the Jews* at 42.

KATHLEEN

G IVEN THE INCREASING EVIDENCE THAT JEWS DID NOT
have a future in Germany, Max and Trude continued to prepare for a future somewhere else. It was customary for Germans to
have French-speaking nannies since Cologne was close to France and
French-speaking Belgium. However, Trude did not believe there was
a future in speaking French. She did not see France and Belgium as
safe havens to which the family might flee if life in Germany deteriorated further. If they could not stay in Germany, Trude believed that
only an English-speaking country would be safe for Jews; therefore,
she decided the girls should learn English.

As part of Max and Trude's efforts to prepare for life in another
country should it become necessary, in March 1935, they hired
Kathleen Goff, a lively twenty-three-year-old Englishwoman, to live
with them as the girls' nanny and English teacher. Kathleen was from
Harrow Weald, a village northwest of London. Kathleen was a bright
young woman who had been a good student growing up in Harrow
Weald. Unfortunately, her parents could not afford for her to continue her education. In those days, educating boys was seen as the
priority, so whatever money her parents had for school was directed
towards her brother Bernard's education. Therefore, even though she
was at the top of her class, Kathleen left school at age fourteen to go
to work. While Kathleen felt she had learned all her school had to
offer, she nevertheless regretted that her parents lacked the financial
means to continue her education.

Kathleen's first job was in a milk churn factory working as the office "junior," which essentially meant she was an errand girl. Unfortunately, she developed pneumonia from spending a good bit of time outside the factory office shuttling messages from one building to another, often in miserable weather. To ensure she did not succumb to another bout of pneumonia, her father secured a job for Kathleen in a drawing office where draftsmen drew scale plans for engineers and architects. She must have hated the job since she harbored a desire to be an explorer and travel the world.

At age twenty, Kathleen left England for France to study French and work for a French family as a nanny. Unfortunately, she became so ill with jaundice that she had to be hospitalized. By the time she recovered, her French family decided it no longer wanted her services and so, after four years in France, she had to develop a new plan to secure work.

After some deliberation, Kathleen decided to study German, which eventually led her to take a job in 1935 with the Ichenhäuser family in Cologne. While it is not clear, she may have obtained this position through German priests who lived in Harrow Weald. Kathleen entered the Ichenhäusers' lives in a marriage of necessity—she needed a job and the Ichenhäusers needed to learn English.

Trude believed the only effective way to learn a language was to speak it on a daily basis. Hiring Kathleen to live with the family was Trude's solution to finding an immersive learning experience. Kathleen joined the family on March 23, 1935. From then on, the family spoke only English at home, except when they addressed Trude's parents—Sigmund and Martha. The local police required that Kathleen fill out a Registration Form which called for, among other things, her family name, marital status, occupation, birthplace and date of birth, citizenship, religion, and the purpose and planned duration of her stay in Germany.

Kathleen, with her unruly, auburn hair and infectious laugh, soon won the girls' hearts. They played on the rooftop play area at home blowing bubbles, roller skating, riding scooters, and occasionally having lunch al fresco. They played in the rooftop sandbox and poked at the vines curling their way up trellises from the planter boxes. Kathleen taught Renate and Erica to sing in English, including one of Kathleen's favorite songs—"The Bonnie Banks o' Loch Lomond." Kathleen read to them in English, including one of her favorite books, "The Adventures of Winnie-the-Pooh." Perhaps they laughed at Pooh's adventures, bounced around the play area like Tigger, or thought of ways to cheer up gloomy Eeyore. Hopefully, no one got a hand or head stuck in a honey pot. Eventually, the girls took to calling Trude "mummy" as English children did with their mothers, courtesy of Kathleen's lessons.

Kathleen took Renate and Erica to the Stadtwald for walks and, occasionally, rides in row boats on the lake. The rowboats were challenging as the girls struggled to pull the oars while Kathleen sat wedged between them. Sometimes they took their scooters or roller skates to the park. On other occasions, they played Whip Stop (a game similar to Snap-the-Whip) with other children in the Stadtwald meadows.

Some days the three of them went to the Cologne zoo. Prior to one visit, they gathered chestnuts to feed the animals. In the spring, they donned costumes for Karnival. Kathleen joined the fun by wearing an outfit reminiscent of Salome in the Arabian Nights. Kathleen taught the girls how to play Bezique, a 19th century, French "trick-taking" card game played with a double pack of sixty-four cards from seven through ace.[135]

Most evenings after the girls had gone to bed, Kathleen studied with Trude and Max. She taught them to read and write English and they helped her improve her German. Some evenings Kathleen and Trude knitted. Occasionally, they played "66," a card game, while they practiced English and German. Kathleen studied Spanish when she finished working with Trude and Max. Trude was also taking Hebrew lessons, perhaps as a linguistic backstop in the event that emigrating to Palestine was their only option if and when they decided to leave Germany.

---

135 Bezique was one of Winston Churchill's favorite card games; he played it during WWII as a way to relax.

Kathleen occasionally ventured into Martha's kitchen to make marmalade or mince pies. Some evenings Ernst visited. He taught Kathleen to play Skat, a three-player, trick-taking card game that had been developed in Germany and quickly became the nation's most popular card game. Other times, Ernst and Kathleen played rummy. Kathleen quickly became a de facto member of the close-knit Ichenhäuser family.

In June of 1935, the family tried to escape the troubles at home by going to Switzerland. Renate had recently recovered from the measles. Trude and Max hoped the mountain air would help her regain her strength. Erica, who contracted the measles after, and likely from, Renate, stayed home with Sigmund and Martha to recuperate. Trude, Max, and Renate went to Pontresina, Worms, Bad Herrenalb (a spa town), Freudenstadt (a health resort in southern Germany), Villingen, and Donaueschingen. They went to Schaffhausen in northern Switzerland to see the Rhine Falls, which was the largest waterfall in Europe. Schaffhausen had lovely Renaissance buildings decorated with frescos on their outer walls. Trude, Max, and Renate also visited the Julier Pass which separated the Rhine and Danube drainage basins. The Pass was still covered with deep snow, which excited Renate immensely, notwithstanding that she was still a bit weak from the measles.

Kathleen, who stayed home to help care for Erica, wrote to Trude:

> Dear Mrs. Doctor (in German, this was the polite way to address a doctor's wife):
>
> Erika is quite happy and plays very nicely with us. She seems to be doing really well and is already starting to speak more English. The letter she wrote is very good, isn't it? The X's are kisses. I will write you a letter. Please say hello from me to Renate and the Doctor.
>
> Kathleen

Trude, in turn, wrote to her parents from the Hotel Engadinerhof in Pontresina:

My dear, good parents!

Today we received your long, detailed letter with all of the enclosures…Kathleen writes error-free German; I wish we knew that much English…Today we went for a long walk and took our lunch along…Renate goes along with everything playfully. She hikes through the snow drifts much more confidently than we do, but despite that I still hang on to the back of her skirt so that I always have a hold of her…Today she got quite a tan from the sun reflecting off the snow…You, dear mother, should see how much Renate eats, especially at night. She lies down and is fast asleep in five minutes, it's just wonderful. I wish I could give her half a year like this to recover.

Unfortunately, today is the start of our last week here. I am frightened of the environment at home…

Trude was right to be frightened. She was a strong woman with an iron will, which meant conditions in Cologne had to be terrible to have such an effect on her. Indeed, the environment at home was frightening. Life was changing in ways large and small as the regime enacted more and more anti-Semitic legislation. In the summer of 1935, Jews were forbidden to use swimming pools and other bathing facilities.[136] Daily life became more and more of a struggle. What had been normal was being relentlessly chipped away. Germany's Jews were like pebbles in front of a glacier. The Nazi program of terror and disenfranchisement of Germany's Jews moved forward inexorably, with unstoppable force, crushing everything in its path. So far, the Ichenhäusers had managed to stay ahead of the crush, but time was not on their side.

Being seen with a Jew was now toxic, an association to be avoided at all costs. Trude had been close friends with a schoolteacher named Olly whom Trude had known throughout her adult life. They were sufficiently close that they had traveled together. Olly married a pastor, Carl Kohler, whom Trude came to know well through her friendship with Olly. The time soon came when, if Trudy ran into Pastor Kohler on the street, he refused to acknowledge her. It was too dangerous to be seen in conversation with a Jew. If Jews and

---

136 *Nazi Germany and the Jews* at 38.

non-Jews were still friends in theory, in practice non-Jews were no longer willing to be seen with Jews. Just saying hello was more than many Germans were willing to risk. This was how long-time friendships died in Nazi Germany.

Even for children, Nazi Germany was dangerous. Weekday mornings, Renate walked several blocks to the streetcar to take the train to school. One morning while on her way down the street, a group of children started yelling anti-Semitic insults and throwing stones at her. At age seven, this dark haired, dark-eyed, gentle child faced a new reality in which being hated and fearing for her safety were part of her life. From that day on, she and the other Jewish children in the neighborhood took a taxi to school; the streets were no longer safe for them. The rooftop play area at their home, which had been designed as an amenity, was now a refuge. It became a place where Renate and Erica could play in safety, without having stones thrown at them or being chased down the street by non-Jewish children whose faces were twisted by hatred.

THE NUREMBERG LAWS

ON MARCH 16, 1935, HITLER ISSUED A DECREE CALLING for universal military service. He also called for a standing army of five hundred thousand men. Germany was rearming in defiance of the constraints placed on it by the Treaty of Versailles. While France, England, and Italy protested, they did nothing further to test Hitler's resolve or try to reverse his decree.

The Reichstag continued its disenfranchisement of Germany's Jews. Beginning on September 15, 1935, and continuing through December 1935, the Reichstag, while in session in Nuremberg, passed the invidious anti-Semitic legislation that came to be known as the "Nuremberg Laws."[137] The Bavarian city of Nuremberg became infamous for the massive Nazi rallies Hitler held in the city from 1927 to 1938 as well as for the racial laws the Reichstag promulgated there. Pursuant to the 1935 legislation, all remaining Jewish civil servants were dismissed from their positions, including those previously exempt because of military service during WWI. Many businesses dismissed their Jewish employees, even though the legislation did not call for it. The proprietors concluded it was simply too dangerous to employ Jews. Aryan business owners were unwilling to risk a visit from the SS or the Gestapo, and they certainly were not willing to face a boycott because they elected to employ Jews.

The Nuremberg legislation known as the "Law for the Protection

---

137 *War Against the Jews* at 63.

of German Blood and Honor," enacted on September 15, 1935, prohibited marriage between Jews and non-Jewish Germans.[138] All such
marriages already in existence were annulled. The decree banned
extramarital relations between Jews and non-Jews. The law stated:

> Moved by the understanding that purity of the German Blood
> is the essential condition for the continued existence of the
> German people, and inspired by the inflexible determination
> to ensure the existence of the German Nation for all time, the
> Reichstag has unanimously adopted the following Law, which
> is promulgated herewith:
>
> 1) Marriage is prohibited between Jews and citizens
>   of German or racially-related blood. Marriages
>   contracted in spite of this are null and void even if
>   they have been contracted abroad in order to avoid
>   this law....
>
> 2) Extra-marital relations between Jews and citizens of
>   the German or racially-related blood are prohibited.
>
> 3) Female citizens of German or racially-related blood
>   under the age of 45 may not be employed in Jewish
>   households.
>
> 4) Jews are prohibited from hoisting the Reich's or
>   national flags and from displaying the Reich's
>   colors. They are, on the other hand, permitted to
>   display the Jewish colors. The exercise of this right
>   is protected by the State.

The decree further provided that any person who violated the
prohibition under Sec. 1 would be punished by a prison sentence
at hard labor, any male who violated the prohibition under Sec. 2
would be punished by a prison sentence with or without hard labor,
and any person who violated the provisions under Sec. 3 or Sec. 4
would be punished by a prison sentence of up to one year and a fine,
or with one or the other of those penalties.

The legislation also prohibited Jewish families from employing
women under thirty-five years old as domestic help if any men lived

---

138 *War Against the Jews* at 67.

in the household.[139] The regime was "concerned" that Jewish men would take advantage of Aryan or "like-blooded" female employees and taint the "purity" of their German blood. The legislation was to take effect immediately, with the exception of the ban on employing non-Aryan women which was to go into effect on January 1, 1936.

The Reichstag also enacted the Reich Citizenship law stating that German citizens were those having "German blood." This meant Jews, whom the Nazis deemed not be part of the German "Volk" or "blood," were no longer German citizens. Instead, they became, as a legal matter, aliens. Jews who had been born in Germany and who had lived their entire lives there suddenly were no longer citizens:

> THE REICHSTAG HAS ADOPTED by unanimous vote the following law which is herewith promulgated.
>
> ARTICLE 1.
>
> 1) A subject of the state is one who belongs to the protective union of the German Reich, and who, therefore, has specific obligations to the Reich.
>
> 2) The status of the subject is to be acquired in accordance with provisions of the Reich and the State Citizenship Law.
>
> ARTICLE 2.
>
> 1) A citizen of the Reich may be only one who is of German or kindred blood, and who, through his behavior, shows that he is both desirous and personally fit to serve loyally the German people and the Reich.
>
> 2) The right to citizenship is obtained by the grant of Reich citizenship papers.
>
> 3) Only the citizen of the Reich may enjoy full political rights in consonance with the provisions of the laws.

The law went into effect on September 30, 1935. The law required that citizens be willing to serve and be loyal to the Reich,

---

139 *Jewish Daily Life* at 280.

whatever a Gestapo or SS officer might deem service and loyalty to mean at any given moment. It is worth noting that the first paragraph refers to obligations the "subject of the state" owes to the Reich. The concept of the German populace as not really citizens, but rather as subjects who live to serve the state and who must show they are fit to serve the state—which was now embodied in Hitler—could not have been more explicit or frightening.

On November 14, 1935, the Reichstag amended the Citizenship Law to provide that subjects of German or kindred blood who had the right to vote in Reichstag elections when the Citizenship law went into effect would, for the time being, have the rights of Reich citizens. The amendment provided that the law would apply to subjects who were of mixed Jewish blood, which was anyone descended from one or two grandparents "who, racially, were full Jews."

The legislation removed any doubt about whether Jews were part of Germany: "A Jew cannot be a citizen of the Reich. He cannot exercise the right to vote; he cannot hold public office." The law provided that "Jewish officials will be retired as of December 31, 1935." The supplemental legislation defined "Mischling" or "hybrid" as a person with two Jewish grandparents, a member of a Jewish religious community, a person who was married to a Jew, or someone born from a marriage with one Jewish parent. Such individuals were deemed to be Jewish and subject to the restrictions and prohibitions applicable to Jews.

Jews—regardless of whether they had been born in Germany and lived their entire lives there, and ignoring whether their families had lived in Germany for generations, and tossing aside whether they had previously been enfranchised and voted in German elections for years—now, by legislative fiat, were no longer citizens of the Reich. Even worse, they could never be citizens because of their "race and blood." So, what were Germany's Jews? They were, at best, German subjects. They were now, by definition, aliens—foreign, dangerous, and something to be feared.

"On December 21 a second supplementary decree ordered the dismissal of Jewish professors, teachers, physicians, lawyers, and notaries who were state employees and had been granted exemptions."[140] Any debt the nation owed to Jews who had served during WWI was now cancelled. The statute of limitations on gratitude had expired. "The Nuremberg Laws completed the disenfranchisement of the Jews of Germany."[141] The Nazis had removed Germany's Jews from the nation's economic, cultural, and political lives. Jews were, in a sense, gone, but they had certainly not been forgotten. Hitler soon would have more to say about them.

---

140   *Nazi Germany and the Jews* at 50.

141   *War Against the Jews* at 69.

1936 — THE SHACKLES REMOVED

RENATE FIRST BECAME OF AWARE OF HITLER AND THE changing political situation in Europe while watching her father shave one morning. Max had the radio on and was listening to the news. The Rhineland, the area on the west side of the Rhine that extended from the river west to the German border with France, had been part of Germany prior to WWI. After the war, although still technically part of Germany, it was occupied by French, British, and Belgian troops under the Treaty of Versailles, which called for the Rhineland to be demilitarized of all German forces in order to provide a buffer between France and the German military. The demilitarized zone was made up of all German territory west of the Rhine as well as a fifty kilometer (thirty-one mile) wide zone east of the river. The German military was required to stay well east of the Rhine and far from the Franco-German border. Germany, France, Italy, and Britain reconfirmed the demilitarized status of the Rhineland in the Treaty of Locarno the four nations had signed in 1925. The treaty reconfirmed Germany's boundaries following WWI and included a provision that Germany would never go to war with the signatory nations.

The Rhineland was Germany's major industrial area; the region contained coal deposits, steel mills, and other heavy industry. The Allies' occupation of the Rhineland was intended not only to provide a military buffer zone, but also to prevent Germany from using the Rhineland's industrial base to rearm. Cologne, situated on the west bank of the Rhine, was within the Rhineland, some eighty-six kilometers (fifty-three miles) east of the German border with France.

In 1929, after Germany threatened to stop paying WWI reparations if Allied troops remained in the Rhineland, the Allies reached an agreement with Germany for the Allies to leave the Rhineland, which they did by June 1930. On March 7, 1936, on Renate's eighth birthday, in his first major military-political gamble, Hitler ordered German troops to reoccupy the Rhineland in violation of the Treaty of Versailles. Nineteen German infantry battalions with air support occupied the region by marching west towards the Rhine. Several battalions continued across the Rhine and marched to within a few kilometers of the French border. "When German troops marched into Cologne, a vast cheering crowd formed spontaneously to greet the soldiers, throwing flowers onto the Wehrmacht while Catholic priests offered to bless the soldiers.[142] Cardinal Karl Joseph Schulte of Cologne held a mass at Cologne Cathedral to celebrate and thank Hitler for 'sending back our army.' In Germany, the news that the Rhineland had been remilitarized was greeted with wild celebrations all over the country…"[143]

Britain did virtually nothing in response. The French threatened to act but did not. Hitler seized the Rhineland without firing a shot and demonstrated to the German nation how he could bloodlessly restore German territory and glory. Hitler then offered France a 25-year non-aggression pact, a fig leaf he used to conceal his further territorial ambitions in Europe. France and Britain, desperate to avoid military conflict, ignored Hitler's brazen breach of the Versailles treaty. "Germany today cast off the last shackles fastened upon her by the Treaty of Versailles when Adolf Hitler, as commander-in-chief of the Reich defense forces, sent his new battalions into the Rhineland demilitarized zone."[144]

Hitler claimed he ordered German forces to occupy the Rhineland in response to France and Russia having signed a mutual

---

142 The Wehrmacht were the German armed forces, made up of the army (Heer), navy (Kriegsmarine), and air force (Luftwaffe).

143 *Hitler Hubris*, Ian Kershaw, Norton Press 1998, pp. 587-590.

144 *The New York Times*, March 8, 1936, p. 1.

assistance treaty. He characterized the pact as an effort to "encircle" Germany. He told the Reichstag that, since the Reich had restored German sovereignty over all German territory by occupying the Rhineland, Germany was ready to rejoin the League of Nations.

The New York Times reported on Hitler's speech and military gambit: "A few minutes before Hitler began to announce this move [the occupation of the Rhineland] to the world in his speech before the Reichstag, the first military flying squadrons already were circling Cologne's cathedral spires. As he began to talk, infantry, artillery, motorized cavalry, tanks, machine gun units, anti-aircraft artillery and all other paraphernalia of modern warfare were already crossing the Rhine bridges, and two hours after he had finished, his advance guards already had reached Saarbrücken, their westernmost point, only three kilometers from the French frontier."[145] The Times mused that this westward march could well be seen as a dress rehearsal "for more serious business." The Times foresaw the threat to which Britain and France were turning blind eyes.

While Renate, at age eight, certainly did not understand the implications of Hitler's threats or the significance of Germany's re-occupation of the Rhineland, she realized that important things were happening. The family lived only a few miles west of the Rhine. Their home faced onto Aachenerstrasse, one of Cologne's main east-west boulevards. Aachenerstrasse stretched due west from the Hohenzollern Bridge, one of the major bridges that crossed the Rhine from Germany's eastern territory to the Rhineland in the west. Given where the Ichenhäusers lived, Renate likely saw and heard the German tanks, armored vehicles, and troop transports rumbling past their house towards the French border to carry out the occupation. She likewise would have heard German aircraft flying west from Cologne to provide cover to the advancing troops, and she may well have seen them while she and Erica played in the rooftop garden.

Soon there was less and less conversation at the Ichenhäuser dinner table. The political situation was so fraught that neither Max and Trude, nor the Moses grandparents, were inclined to discuss current events at the table. A quiet tension settled over their meals. The

---

145 *The New York Times*, March 8, 1936, p. 1.

family had been disenfranchised, the streets were no longer safe for Jews, and German troops were on the move.

How to Cope

T HE REGIME CONTINUED TO TIGHTEN THE VISE SQUEEZING
the life out of the Jewish community. In January 1936, the
Reich's "Executive Order on the Reich Tax Law" forbade Jews from
serving as tax consultants.[146] In April, the Reich "Veterinarians Law"
expelled Jews from the veterinary profession.[147] Nazi functionaries
labored to identify aspects of the economy in which, if Jews had not
already been precluded from participating, the functionaries could
step in to rectify the situation by issuing further bans.

In March 1936, Max and Trude went to Holland for a few days.
Shortly after Max and Trude returned, Erica came down with chicken
pox with Renate following suit two weeks later. The girls recovered
after each suffered through several miserable days. Kathleen continued to take them for daily walks in the Stadtwald. Grandpa Sigmund
occasionally joined them on their outings wearing his well-tailored
suits and carrying his walking cane. They stayed close together and
tried to avoid drawing attention. Their goal was to remain "unseen"
while in plain sight.

The increasing restrictions on Jewish life were taking a tremendous toll on Jewish communal activities. The Rheinland Lodge wrote
to its members in mid-July 1936 that "As a result of government regulations, we are forced to restrict our events to a minimum for the

---

146 *The Holocaust Encyclopedia*, Anti-Semitic Legislation 1933-1939.

147 *The Holocaust Encyclopedia*, Anti-Semitic Legislation 1933-1939.

time being." (Rheinland Lodge Memo, July 15, 1936.) The Jewish community was under extraordinary financial stress due to the regulations barring Jews from most professions and trades along with the informal boycotting of Jewish businesses. Therefore, the Lodge was under severe financial pressure: "Brothers are urgently asked, both themselves and friends and acquaintances, to consider the possibility of using our outside facility. It is to be expected that the brothers will support the budget at every opportunity and in particular will hold festivities of all kinds in the facility."

The notice from the Lodge continued: "The vacation break of the Kölner Jewish school youth is particularly urgent this year due to growing economic hardship and is much more difficult due to the elimination of some public funds." The notice stated the Lodge had "a list of the Jewish restaurants and dining houses in Rhineland and Westfalen" available to lodge members. It is not known whether the purpose of the list was to identify kosher restaurants for members or provide a list of establishments whose owners were willing to serve Jews and at which it was safe for Jews to dine. Jews needed to find establishments where they could not only get in the door, but where they could also get out the door in one piece.

In July 1936, Kathleen took the girls to England to visit Kathleen's family. The trip was a welcome respite from the tension that was palpable throughout Germany and a constant in the Ichenhäusers' daily lives. The trio traveled by train through Belgium and boarded a ship at Ostend to take them across the English Channel. The ferry was two hours late. When they reached England, the train from the coast to London was running three hours late, which delayed them to the point that they did not arrive at Victoria Station until 12:35 in the morning. Given the late hour, they took a cab to the Goffs' home northwest of London at the then significant cost of fourteen shillings and six pence.

Spending time with the Goffs was a welcome tonic for Renate and Erica. The girls enjoyed inspecting the Goffs' vegetable garden, which included rows of parsnips and brussels sprouts, as well as pear and plum trees. They had never seen a garden like that and really had no understanding of how the food they ate was grown. The patch of neatly kept lawn behind the house provided a safe place to play in lieu of the rooftop play area at home and the Stadtwald park, the latter of which had become less welcoming as overt hostility became more evident on the angry faces and in the harsh words of other visitors to the park.

Kathleen took the girls and Kathleen's younger sisters Josephine and Dorothy on numerous outings. They rode the train to London to see Tower Bridge and the changing of the guard at Buckingham Palace. From there, they visited Selfridges, an enormous department store on Bond Street in the heart of London, only a few blocks from Speaker's Corner in Hyde Park. The roof at Selfridges featured terraced gardens, cafes, and a mini-golf course. The roof also offered views across much of the city, making it a favorite place to relax after shopping and/or touring central London.[148] One day, the group went to the London Zoo, where Josephine and Erica took a ride on a camel. The change of scene and the warm embrace of the Goff family made for a wonderful respite from the tension at home.

Kathleen and the girls returned to Cologne on July 27. Dorothy and Josephine went with them for a two-week visit. The trip to Cologne was a bit of an adventure. As Kathleen later wrote to her parents, the 10:30 a.m. train from Victoria Station to Dover on the English coast was crowded, but they managed to find enough seats so they could sit together. However, Renate and Erica decided to stand in the corridor and look out the windows for most of the ride.

The Channel crossing from Dover to Ostend in Belgium was smooth, with little wind and the surface of the North Sea like glass. They took sandwiches and other provisions with them for the journey, but they had the misfortune to break the thermos of milk on the ferry. Kathleen purchased bottled water for the girls, but they refused to drink it because it was carbonated. The trip soon got to be too long for Renate and Erica. They could not stay in their seats and before long were filthy from clambering around the train. Erica got so fidgety that Kathleen was soon at her wits' end. Several passengers thought the four girls (Renate, Erica, Dorothy, and Josephine) were Kathleen's children. They were amused at how Kathleen switched

---

148 During WWII the store's basement served as a bomb shelter.

from English to German to French depending on with whom she was speaking (she used French with the Belgian conductor.)

By the time they got to the platform in Cologne, Renate was so anxious to get off the train that she crawled out the window of their compartment straight into her parents' arms. The rest of them gathered their bags and joined Trude and Max for the ride to the house. Trude wrote a thank you note to the Goffs in perfect English (Kathleen was apparently quite a good teacher):

Dear Mrs. And Mr. Goff!

We met Kathleen with her four children safely at the station yesterday evening and even the train was on time. I was very sorry for you, that you both had to wait for such a long time, when they came to England. The reason why I am writing to you is to thank you heartily for everything you did for the children. They have already told me such a lot about you, they seem to have been quite happy in your house. They have seen so many things, they have not yet stopped telling us about London and the River Thames and the Tower Bridge and so on. I am sure they won't forget the weeks they spent with you.

I thank you very much for the lemon cheese (lemon curd) and the marmalade. I like them both very much. And our Grandpa was ever so pleased with the beet roots. Even the flowers arrived very well and are still alive. Kathleen thinks it's very funny to walk around Köln with her two sisters. For us it's alright, we only hope the weather will get better, so that your children will come home with red cheeks and brown arms and legs, especially Josephine looks a bit pale. When the sun is shining, we will put her in a deck chair on the roof garden.

We are very pleased to have our children back home again. We will try to show Dorothy and Josephine as much of our town and country as we can during the short time they are going to stay with us. But in any case, we must have better weather. Today we had a thunderstorm after dinner and now it's raining too. It's late now, I must finish. My husband and I thank you once more very much.

With kindest regards,

Yours sincerely,

Trude Ichenhäuser

(Trude July 28, 1936 letter to the Goffs.)
Renate also corresponded with Mrs. Goff:

Dear Mrs. Goff:

Thank you very much for the letter you sent me. D.&J. (Dorothy and Josephine) have gone for a daytrip up the Rhein with K. (Kathleen). We had a marvelous day last Sunday and we enjoyed it very much. D.& J. are having a nice time.

Love,

Renate XXXX

Like most younger siblings, Erica was not going to let Renate do anything without Erica trying to keep up with her. Thus, Erica wrote to Mrs. Goff:

Dear Mrs. Goff:

Thank you for your letter. We went to the photo shop, but the pictures were not ready yet. We went out on Sunday and it was very nice. Today we expect an American boyfriend for tea.

Erica

In August, the family and Kathleen took a road trip, this time to Egmond in northwestern Holland. They took excursions to Amsterdam, Alkmaar, Volendam (a Dutch town on the Markermeer Lake northwest of Amsterdam, famous for its colorful wooden houses and the old fishing boats in its harbor), Marken (formerly an island in the Zuiderzee), Katwijk (on Holland's central coast) and Nordwijk (also on Holland's central coast). In Alkmaar, they visited the cheese market. They watched workers load cheeses the size and shape of cannon balls onto sledges. Two men carried each sledge, one man in front and one in back, with the sledge supported by harnesses tied to yokes draped over the men's shoulders. The girls, wearing matching black sweaters, lifted several of the cheeses and rolled them down wooden chutes onto barges for transport along Alkmaar's canals.

They also visited the beach on the North Sea where they rented small cabanas to use as changing rooms. Renate and Erica, usually pale, were deeply tanned after only a few days playing on the beach. Erica enjoyed wading in tide pools to watch shrimp and other sea creatures. Many families piled walls of sand around the areas they occupied on the beach in order to have some privacy. The family was on the beach one day when a German woman walked up to them. Seeing blond-haired Erica, the woman pointed to her and said that Erica was the only Hitler Jugend on the beach, that is, with her blond hair she looked to the woman as if Erica could be one of the blond Hitler youth.

While in Amsterdam, the family visited Walter and Chelly Emanuel. Chelly was a cousin of Trude's; Walter was originally from South Africa. Max's concern about the family's safety in Germany had increased dramatically. His belief that the Nazi regime would never harm those who had served in the Kaiser's army had been severely eroded by the Reichstag's anti-Jewish laws, in particular the Nuremberg laws. Max began to smuggle currency into Holland whenever he visited in order to build a nest egg in the event the family eventually had to flee. This was extremely dangerous since it was illegal to take currency out of Germany. Attempting to export money was a criminal offense that, if discovered, resulted in immediate and lengthy prison sentences. The Nazis frequently conducted body searches and disassembled cars at the border to seize currency and other items of value. The Nazis bribed Germans to spy on friends, acquaintances, and neighbors and report them if they suspected someone was hiding anything of value. Each trip to Holland placed Max at risk of arrest and the family at risk of disaster.

In July 1936, war broke out in one corner of Europe. After the election of a left-wing government in Spain, General Francisco Franco led units of the Spanish army stationed in North Africa into Spain. He attacked government forces in a reactionary coup, initiating the Spanish civil war.

Germany hosted the Summer Olympics in August 1936. Hitler

and his propaganda minister Joseph Goebbels saw the Olympics as an opportunity to show the world a false face and counter negative news reports regarding Germany's anti-Semitic and anti-democratic regime. They hoped to present Germany as a modern, well-run country that was fair to all. They temporarily mitigated anti-Semitic attacks in the press, took down anti-Semitic signs and postings in German cities, and stopped the beatings and arrests of Jews. They instructed the German press to spin what soon turned out to be fantasies regarding Germany's peaceful intentions in Europe. Of course, it was quite a challenge to square the Olympic ideals of international goodwill and fair competition with the Nazi ideal of Aryan superiority. This was certainly the case during the prelude to the Games when the NSDAP newspaper was vigorously arguing that Jews should not be allowed to participate. German propaganda may not have been awarded any medals, but it was superlative in convincing many visitors that Germany was a modern, civilized nation.

And yet, in October 1936, the Ministry of Education in this purportedly modern and civilized nation banned Jewish teachers from public schools.[149] With the Olympics having concluded, the Nazi regime, pleased with how it was able to bamboozle the international community, quickly got back to the business of further implementing the regime's racist and anti-Semitic ideology.

---

149 *The Holocaust Encyclopedia*, Anti-Semitic Legislation 1933-1939.

I Must Go

THE NUREMBERG LAW THAT FORBADE JEWS FROM EMPLOY-
ing Aryan women under age thirty-five in their households
brought about the end of Kathleen's employment in 1936. The legislation, along with the willingness of many Germans to report those
whom they suspected were not complying, made it impossible for
Kathleen to stay with the Ichenhäusers. The police came to the family's home on September 14, 1936 and ordered Kathleen to leave.
She wrote in her diary: "I must go." Kathleen left that afternoon and
spent the night at a friend's home.

Kathleen visited intermittently over the next few months. Some
days she took walks with Trude and the girls. She joined the family
when they visited David and Emma Ichenhäuser to celebrate David's
birthday. On other days she stopped by the house for tea or to make
plum jam or cheesecake. Some evenings she came by to see the girls
and chat with Max and Trude. One day, they went on an outing to
gather hazelnuts.

Although she had been forced to leave the Ichenhäusers' home,
Kathleen was not ready to return to England. Instead, she purchased
a bicycle and began taking cycling trips through Germany. Since
she was fluent in German, Kathleen was able to pass herself off as
German. This was crucial because the Reich had issued travel restrictions; Kathleen could have been arrested if the authorities discovered
she was British. Her German must have been superb because she was
never, as the British would say, "rumbled" by the police for being a

Brit cycling around the countryside. Kathleen was tough as nails, so much so that even though she had to spend the occasional night sleeping in a field, she was not deterred from continuing her trip.

In mid-October, Cologne held air raid drills. While war did not seem imminent, the drills suggested to those willing to face reality that preparations for war were proceeding apace—at least in Germany.

On December 18, 1936, Kathleen visited the Ichenhäusers to say her farewells. Kathleen had obtained a position working at a German school in Italy. On December 27, 1936, Kathleen left for Florence. Kathleen had been a tremendous addition to the Ichenhäuser family. Trude wrote in a letter of recommendation:

> Miss Kathleen Goff lived in our house on March 23, 1935—September 15, 1936. She came to us to learn the German language in our family and it was a pleasure for me to help her. She now masters the language perfectly.
>
> Conversely, my then 5 and 6 years-old children, like me, learned English from Miss Goff. Thanks to her great pedagogical skills, she managed that our children could express themselves well in the English language after only 2 months and now speak fluent English after 1½ years.
>
> Miss Goff has been exemplary in caring for my children in both healthy and sick days, so that both of them are attached to her with devoted love. I personally have the utmost confidence in Miss Goff. I would like to mention that Miss Mademoiselle is excellent at sewing and knits especially well. She takes care of all her responsibilities. Her happy sunny nature made her a dear friend whom I will miss very much.
>
> Our very best wishes for her happiness in life accompany her on her further journey.
>
> Mrs. Trude Ichenhäuser

Kathleen's departure was tearful for all concerned. The Ichenhäusers felt more alone than ever. With Kathleen gone, the family had to find another way to maintain their proficiency in English. Trude hired a Mr. Franklin to come to the house once a week to speak English with them. He also had the girls write short essays in English. While he was helpful in the narrow task of teaching English, Mr. Franklin could not fill the emotional void left by Kathleen's departure.

THE ROTHSCHILDS LEAVE

HANS DAVID ROTHSCHILD AND HIS WIFE LENI WERE COUS-
ins on Trude's side of the family. They were very close to Max
and Trude, having attended their engagement party and wedding
and sent gifts when Renate and Erica were born. Hans was a successful businessman; he owned two metal fabricating plants, one in
Germany and one in Belgium. Hans' first wife, Mitze Roesberg, gave
birth to Hannah Rothschild on September 2, 1922. Mitze tragically
died, along with her baby, giving birth to what would have been her
and Hans' second child a few years later. Several years later, Hans
married Helene ("Leni") Strauss. They had two children: Annelise,
who went by Anne, was born in Bonn on July 5, 1927, making her
one year older than Renate; and Peter Emil Leopold, who was born
in Cologne's Braunsfeld suburb on March 7, 1931.

As matters became worse and worse for Germany's Jews in 1936,
Hans and Leni, fearing for their family's future, decided it was time
to leave. By January 1937, they had made sufficient arrangements
and prepared to leave their home at 14 Corneliusstrasse. Hannah
was fifteen, Anne was ten, and Peter was six. Hannah was the first to
depart. She fled to Holland with members of a Quaker organization.
The rest of the family followed soon after, packing a few bags and
driving to Holland via Aachen on the Dutch-German border. They
told the border guards they were only going on vacation, so as not to
raise any suspicions. They left everything else in their home, telling

162

their neighbors they planned to return. Despite this, the Nazis confiscated everything they had left behind.

The Rothschilds became more and more concerned as Hitler enlarged the Wehrmacht. Leni, in particular, wanted to put more distance between the family and Germany. Therefore, they made the decision to go to London, where they were safely ensconced by September 1938. They set up housekeeping at 58 Armitage Road in Golders Green, an area roughly eight miles northwest of central London that had a substantial Jewish population. Their two-story house, clad in brown brick and with bay windows facing the street, had several bedrooms, so the family had enough room to be comfortably situated. Golders Green was close to Hampstead Heath, a huge park where the children could play and Hans and Leni could take walks free of the fear associated with being a Jew on the streets of Cologne. There were enough Jews living in Golders Green, including German-Jewish refugees, that shops and bakeries sold goods and foods familiar to the Rothschilds, easing the adjustment to their new home.

Hans and Leni eventually were able to purchase, that is, ransom their household belongings and furnishings from the Nazis and have the items shipped to England. While Nazi law forbade Jews from taking assets out of Germany other than a pittance in Reichsmarks, Hans was able to use his Belgian factory as an asset from which he could generate funds to support the family as it began its life in exile. They breathed deeply of the fresh, free air in Golders Green, stopped looking over their shoulders, and settled into a new life.

1937 — Time to Prepare

On November 8, 1937, an exhibition opened in Nuremberg entitled "The Eternal Jew." It portrayed Jews as taskmasters for international Bolshevism with the goal of enslaving Germany in a Soviet-style system.[150] According to this insidious exhibition, Jews were not only responsible for Germany's defeat in WWI, but they now were trying to subjugate Germany to Russia.

Tens of thousands of Jews had fled Germany by this time. Some Jews committed suicide rather than emigrate or continue facing the hate and violence permeating Germany. The Nazis had curtailed their freedoms, slashed their incomes, and taken away the right to practice their professions and trades, leaving many Jews destitute. The world that Germany's Jews inhabited grew smaller, harsher, and more worrisome day by day.

The Ichenhäusers tried to maintain a routine. Renate and Erica continued to take their toys to the rooftop where they played with Steiff bears, a stuffed dog, a plush squirrel, and dolls of various sizes and attire. They added a tricycle to the scooters and the three-wheel "roadster" that they rode around the play area squealing with delight. On days when the girls did not go to the Stadtwald, but instead dared to roller skate on the sidewalk in front of their home, they took the chance of having to endure verbal abuse from passersby since

---

150 Holocaust Education & Archive Research Team, "Nuremberg."

Jewish children were as likely to be victims of hateful comments as were Jewish adults.

Trude added accordion lessons to the girls' schedule. Their teacher, Miss Conrad, came to the house. Erica enjoyed the lessons, Renate not at all. They started learning with a small accordion; Trude and Max eventually purchased two larger ones. They practiced on the rooftop so as not to disturb Max and his few remaining patients. The girls eventually performed in a recital at the Cologne Jewish Community Center, with Erica featured as a soloist.

The girls also played board games. A favorite game involved a turntable with a small opening in it and a stack of 25-30 cards, each card having a question or category written on it. One player would read a question or category from a card while another player spun the turntable and announced the letter of the alphabet that was revealed when the turntable stopped spinning. The players tried to be the first to answer the question beginning with that letter of the alphabet.

"Halma" was another board game they enjoyed. Similar to "Chinese checkers," Halma involved a playing board divided into six or eight triangular sections that surrounded a divided area roughly sixteen inches across. Each triangular section had holes for ten small, wooden playing pieces. Each set of pieces was a different color. A player rolled a die and moved his or her playing piece a correspond-ing number of marked areas to get the piece to the opposite side of the board, the object being to be the first player to get all one's pieces to the opposite side of the board.

One of the family's favorite card games was Bezique, a two-player melding and trick-taking game that had been invented in Sweden in the early 1800s. Bezique was played across Europe and was very popular in Britain. The object was to score points by meld-ing and taking tricks containing aces and tens. Another card game they played was "Quartet." The deck included four cards each nam-ing a work by various composers. If a player had a card for a given composer, the player asked another player for a card of that com-poser. If the player had the requested card, she had to give it to the person who requested it, who could then request another card. The object of the game was to obtain as many sets of four cards as possible. It was a sort of music-based gin rummy or "Go Fish."

Another game the girls played required a pencil and paper for each participant. The players took turns announcing a subject, which could be the name of a country, fruit, flower, or type of bird. Within a time-limit, the players wrote something for each category, the aim being to think of something unusual that no one else would think of. If two players wrote the same thing, they did not get any points.

In spring of 1937, the family took a brief road trip starting in Trier, a small city on the banks of the Moselle River. Trier, close to the German border with Luxembourg, was nestled in a valley with vineyards cascading down the surrounding hillsides. From Trier, the family drove to Luxembourg. With the weather still chilly, the girls wore matching double-breasted coats and wool caps as they walked through the tiny country's forests and visited the Roman Catholic cathedral in Luxembourg City.

Renate and Erica stayed in touch with Dorothy and Josephine Goff by way of postcards:

> Dear D. and J.:
>
> We send you love and kisses from our Easter trip.
>
> Yours, Erika
>
> We are just leaving Trier for Luxembourg. We had snow in the Eifel and it is still mighty cold over here.
>
> Love and kisses from,
>
> Renate xx (Renate and Erica postcard to Dorothy and Josephine Goff, March 28, 1937.)

Renate and Erica wrote to Kathleen as well, who responded via a postcard from Siena: "Dear Renate and Erica! Thank you very much for the nice letters—the pictures are very sweet. I hung them up straightaway in my room…Hope you enjoy Luxembourg. Love to Mummy and all."

Renate and Erica wrote to Dorothy and Josephine again a few months later:

Dear Friends,

We are very sorry indeed that you can't come to see us. Joan called on us the other day. Love and kisses to all of you from Erika

Love and kisses from Renate. xxxx (Renate and Erica postcard to Dorothy and Josephine Goff, July 22, 1937.)

The summer of 1937 offered the last days of normalcy for the Ichenhäusers, or at least what passed for normal given the state of affairs by then for Jews in Germany. The family visited Kanderstag in the Swiss canton of Bern. Located in a valley alongside the Kander River just west of the Jungfrau massif, Kanderstag was idyllic. The town was populated by plaster and timber houses. Stone-roofed chalets dotted the hillsides outside of the town. Small stone bridges spanned the burbling Kander River. The brown-shingled roofs and wooden beams of the hotels and chalets were set off by window boxes bursting with red geraniums. Horse-drawn carriages transported visitors through the town, clip-clopping past bakeries whose windows enticed passersby with strudels and tortes while candy store windows beckoned with chocolates and colorful marzipan treats.

The alpine lake nestled among the spectacular peaks above Kander was an iridescent turquoise; the electric hue of the water was due to glacial silt that rain had washed down the granite mountainsides. Hiking paths provided access to the surrounding hills and mountains, calling out to Max who had never met a mountain he did not want to climb. As the family hiked alongside mountain streams, herds of white-coated, black-faced goats jostled them as the goats sought handouts from the family's well-stocked picnic basket.

Renate, now nine years old, wrote to her grandparents Sigmund and Martha:

Dear Grandma and Grandpa,

It was wonderful on our trip. We drove through Siegburg, Limburg, Frankfurt, Darmstadt, and Heidelberg. When we were on the Frankfurt motorway, we had a good view of Frankfurt. But we couldn't make out Darmstadt at all because everything was overgrown with trees…When we arrived in Heidelberg, we met Aunt Clotilde. We weren't at all tired and even visited the castle…In Bern, we happened to pass right by the Bern bears.[151] They danced and caught the bread we threw to them. After Bern, we drove through Thun, Spiez, Frutigan, Kanderstag… We did go on some really beautiful walks. It's very pretty here. How are you all doing? There's a children's party this afternoon.

With warm greetings and kisses, and please also give my regards to Miss Martha [their housekeeper],

Yours, Renate XXXX

This afternoon there was a children's party. We had a really nice time playing. I won all the games and received a prize. I won the potato race and the trip to Jerusalem. Afterwards, people threw peas in the grass and we had to pick them up. I picked up 98. That was the most.

Greetings, Renate xxx

Erica, age eight, was not to be outdone by Renate. Erica wrote to her grandparents to keep them apprised of her adventures:

Dear grandma and grandpa!

We arrived well but starting in Basel it was raining. In Heidelberg we met Aunt Clotilde and Aunt Paula. We went to the castle in the evening and went to bed at ten. In Bern we saw the bears. They stood on two legs and danced.

Last night was a torchlight procession and mother bought me a torch (flashlight), but Renate did not want one. We took a nap before dinner so we could stay up. We waited until the torchlight procession started and then walked with it. Illumination was on in front of all the big hotels. We walked through the whole village. Yesterday afternoon we climbed up a steep canyon. I am very good at mountaineering. Today we went to the Biberg.

---

151 The Bern bears were brown bears displayed in a zoo-like enclosure in Bern. The bears were well-known throughout Germany and were a major tourist attraction in Bern.

This afternoon was a children's party. A man told us what games to play. First, we played potato racing and Renate won. Afterwards, each child was allowed to perform, and we played the accordion. Then we sang a Shirley Temple song together. Then the man threw peas on the ground and whoever got the most was given a prize. Renate had the most. She had 98 and I had 95.

Many greetings also for Miss Marta.

Yours, Erika

The family stayed at the Hotel Bernerhof so the girls could attend a sports camp where they spent their days swimming and doing gymnastics. Renate was intent on perfecting her headstands, handstands, and back bends, while Erica cartwheeled nearby. The family continued to Interlaken, which was nestled in the valley below the famous Alpine peaks of the Jungfrau, Mönch, and Eiger. They enjoyed a day boating on the famous Blausee (Blue Lake), famed for its striking color caused by glacial silt deposits. Trude and Max encouraged the girls to eat bowls of whipped cream for dessert each night. Trude was convinced this was the way to have the girls add weight to their young, thin frames. They concluded the trip with a drive to Lake Maggiore in northern Italy and a boat ride to Isola Bella. The stunning Isola Bella Palazzo, with its magnificent gardens and statuary, was a beautiful coda to their trip. This vacation, with its beauty, fun, and peacefulness, was not to be repeated.

Taking vacations became more and more difficult for Germany's Jews. The Reich Ministry of the Interior issued regulations in the summer of 1937 restricting Jewish access to the spas that had long been favorite destinations for Germans: "Jews were to have separate accommodations as far as possible, and restrictions could be imposed as to when and where Jews were allowed in drinking halls and bath-houses.[152] Jews could be banned entirely from spa gardens, restaurants and sports fields."[153] The Ichenhäusers were fortunate to have

---

152 *Jewish Daily Life* at 338.

153 *Jewish Daily Life* at 338.

traveled to Switzerland and Luxembourg where there were no such restrictions.

Not content with the discriminatory legislation and regulations issued by the Reichstag and Hitler's cabinet ministers, German municipalities enacted further restrictions on Jewish life. Many cities banned Jews from public parks, while others required that Jews use "Jews-only" park benches.[154] Even the sylvan Stadtwald, formerly a green oasis in the city, was now unwelcoming. Jews stopped going to concerts and museums, as they knew they were not welcome. Jews who had led active social and cultural lives no longer left their homes as they could not endure the hateful gaze of their Aryan countrymen. Jews abandoned going to cultural events because, in the words of Marta Appel, she "could not bear to be among people who hated me so much."[155]

On November 27, 1937, the Jewish Art Community of Cologne conducted a student music and gymnastics performance in the Gemeindehaus (community hall). Given the restrictions barring Jews from Germany's public life, virtually all cultural activities for Jews had to be conducted through Jewish organizations. The program included music by Schumann, Vivaldi, and Mendelssohn, along with an accordion group. Renate and Erika did not play accordion, notwithstanding their lessons; perhaps Renate put her foot down in protest and refused. Instead, they were in the Tanzgruppe, which performed a tap dance (Stepptanz) to "Good Cranes" by H.E. Stein.

Germany's Jews tried to carry on notwithstanding the crushing burdens the regime had imposed on them. By the end of 1937, tens of thousands of Jewish "professionals and civil servants, actors, musicians, and journalists had lost their jobs."[156] Many employers fired Jews under pressure from the S.A.'s brown-shirted storm troopers. Thousands of small Jewish businesses collapsed under the pressure of boycotts and violence. Under duress, many Jews sold their businesses

154 *Jewish Daily Life* at 336.

155 *Jewish Daily Life* at 339.

156 *War Against the Jews* at 96.

to Aryan purchasers for a fraction of the businesses' true value.[157] The viciously anti-Semitic newspaper "Der Stürmer" engaged in a campaign of intimidation by publishing the names and photographs of people who dared to patronize Jewish businesses. In Munich, the city government ordered that stores not owned by Jews must post signs identifying the businesses as "Aryan-owned" to try to ensure that shoppers did not inadvertently patronize a Jewish vendor.

In response to the worsening crisis, Jewish schools changed their curricula. By this time, it was clear to most Jews that they had to leave Germany. Schools began to address that reality by providing courses to prepare students for new lives in other countries. "Cologne's Jewish schools intensified instruction in Hebrew and English, and initiated training programs in carpentry, needlework, childcare, home economics, and agriculture, to prepare young Jews for emigration. Not surprisingly, interest in Zionism and membership in Zionist youth movements increased significantly."[158]

Meanwhile, the world at large was devolving into chaos. Japan, which had invaded Manchuria in 1932, surrounded and attacked the city of Nanjing in December 1937. Japanese troops killed hundreds of thousands of Chinese and committed mass rapes throughout the city. The Spanish civil war was raging with Germany providing arms and air support to Franco's forces. Providing weapons to Franco's Fascists was quite convenient for the Nazi regime as it allowed Hitler test German arms in combat before Hitler put them to use on Germany's behalf. Franco's forces were laying siege to Madrid; furious fighting was underway in Toledo and other Spanish cities. Although Hitler claimed after Germany reoccupied the Rhineland that he had no further territorial aspirations in Europe, Germany nevertheless continued its massive rearmament program. As 1937 drew to a close, the end of life as the Ichenhäusers knew it was at hand.

---

157 *War Against the Jews* at 96.

158 *Pogrom Night* at xxiv.

LIFE BECAME MORE AND
MORE UNBEARABLE

T HE NAZIS WERE INTENT ON EXERCISING EVER GREATER
control over the German populace. They did so by expanding
the regime's ability to arrest and sequester anyone whom it regarded
as a threat. The Minister of the Interior issued a decree on January
25, 1938, expanding the definition of "protective custody" so that
it applied to "persons whose behavior endangers the existence and
security of the Volk and the State."[159] This gave the police virtually
unfettered discretion to arrest anyone under the pretext of the individual posing a risk to the Volk or State. This opened the door wide,
to the extent it was not already fully open, for mass arrests and incar-
ceration of thousands of Germans in the expanding gulag of Nazi
concentration camps.

Alfred Klieforth, the United States Consul General in Cologne,
was paying close attention to political developments in Germany. He
authored a report entitled "Gossip Regarding an Austrian Putsch"
which he sent to Prentiss Gilbert, the interim Chargé d'Affaires at
the American Embassy in Berlin:

> As of possible interest to the Embassy, I have the honor to
> report that in local S.S. circles there is circulating a lot of
> braggadocio talk regarding a new attempt inspired by Goering
> and von Papen to seize Austria. The S.S. say that the job is

---

159 *War Against the Jews* at 98.

up to them, that the SA failed when they had their chance, that the legal forces of Germany, especially the Army, cannot be utilized for this purpose, and that Goering's designation as Hitler's successor needs only this crowning act and that Goering has the silent consent of all whom it may concern. The incorporation of Austria in the Third Reich is regarded in Party circles here as definitive as was the remilitarization of the Rhineland. Mussolini's objection to the scheme, it is argued, will be overcome in the course of time, while the objections of other nations can be brushed aside without any thought.

The Austrian Legion units in this part of Germany, the nearest one is at Bad Godesburg, Hitler's favorite habitat in the Rhineland, are still intact and impatient for "the day."

Very respectfully yours,

A.W. Klieforth, American Consul General (A.W. Klieforth letter to the U.S. Embassy in Berlin, January 26, 1938.)

Hitler's plan to seize Austria was obviously no secret to the United States, which did little, if anything, to head it off. Most Americans felt they had done their duty during WWI; they had no interest in getting involved in another "European adventure," regardless of how dangerous Germany had become and notwithstanding how despicably it was treating its Jewish citizens.

On Feb. 20, 1938, Hitler demanded the right of self-determination for the millions of ethnic Germans living in Austria and Czechoslovakia. "Chancellor Hitler in a militant speech to the Reichstag yesterday made a strong point of the right of self-determination for the 10M Germans in Austria and Czechoslovakia. He indicated force must be used in the end to break the status quo. He promised to go ahead with plans to enlarge the [German] army."[160] Austria had some seven million residents of German descent and Czechoslovakia had roughly three million. Anthony Eden, the British Foreign Secretary, resigned from the British Cabinet over Prime Minister Neville Chamberlain's policy of seeking accommodations with Hitler over the fate of Germans living in Czechoslovakia and Austria.

---

160   *The New York Times*, Feb. 21, 1938 p. 1.

Max's mother Emma Dülken Ichenhäuser died on February 23, 1938, eight days after suffering a stroke: "Today my beloved wife, our loyal mother and grandmother Mrs. Emma Ichenhäuser, née Dülken, passed away at the age of seventy-eight and a happy marriage in the 56th year. She was a heart full of love, a soul of goodness, a spirit of the purest disposition and the noblest willingness to help. On behalf of the bereaved relatives: David Ichenhäuser, Köln-Braunsfeld, Aachener Str. 409, February 23, 1938. The funeral will take place on Sunday, February 27, 1938, at 3:00 in the afternoon, in Bocklemünd." (Emma Ichenhäuser's obituary, printed on Feb. 25, 1938, in the Jüdisches Gemeindeblatt für Rheinland und Westfalen [Jewish Municipality Gazette for the Rhineland and Westphalia].) Max's father David continued to live in his and Emma's apartment. However, it remained to be seen how well he could live alone. This created another layer of anxiety for Max and Trude in addition to their concern due to the increasing political and economic turmoil.

On March 12, 1938, when Renate was ten years old and Erica not quite nine, the Nazis annexed Austria in an invasion known as the Anschluss ("connection"). Hitler had been threatening Austria for months over the conditions purportedly suffered by Germans living in Austria. He claimed the Germans were victims of violence the Austrian regime had failed to address. However, the reality was that Austria's Nazi party was fomenting disturbances and instigating violence as part of a coordinated effort with Hitler to create a pretext for Germany's demands to Austria and, ultimately, for German intervention.

"Under threats of force from Berlin, Chancellor Kurt Schuschnigg of Austria yielded last evening and resigned in dramatic circumstances. The Nazis, with Herr Arthur Seyss-Inquart, Interior Minister in the Schuschnigg Cabinet, as Chancellor, are in power."[161] Schuschnigg resigned in the face of the Nazis' threats to invade Austria if their demands were not met. Seyss-Inquart's first act as Austria's puppet Chancellor was to cable Hitler and ask him to send German troops to Austria to "help maintain law and order." Fifty thousand German troops, including infantry, cavalry, artillery,

---

161 *The New York Times*, March 12, 1938, p. 1.

motorized divisions, air force units and engineers, which Hitler had massed on the Austrian border for an invasion that was a foregone conclusion, poured across the border on March 12 and seized the entire country. "Nazi mobs took possession of Vienna and raided the Jewish quarter. The Swastika was flown over public buildings..."[162] Hitler set a referendum in Austria for April 10 to confirm the population's desire to unite Austria with Germany. The vote, whether it should be trusted or not, was overwhelmingly in favor of the union.

Austria's Nazis quickly ran amok. They forced Jews to clean sidewalks and street gutters. Storm troopers and crowds jeered at the Jews while they worked. The Nazis forced Jews to clean public latrines, while the security forces jailed tens of thousands of Jews and stole their victims' possessions.[163]

An additional consequence of the Anschluss was that Nazi military forces now surrounded Czechoslovakia on three sides. This made Czechoslovakia's defensive posture almost impossible to sustain, with dire consequences. Austria, as a practical matter, was no more. Czechoslovakia would soon find itself in the fire.

The Nazis allowed Sigmund Freud, the famed Jewish psychotherapist who lived in Vienna, to leave Austria in June 1938. However, "after the Nazis had impounded part of his possessions and imposed the emigration tax on Freud, they demanded his signature on a declaration to the effect that he had not been ill-treated. Freud dutifully signed the declaration and added in a classic turn of phrase: 'I can most highly recommend the Gestapo to everyone...'"[164]

Notwithstanding Hitler's claims that he had no further territorial ambitions in Europe after reoccupying the Rhineland, he began to reveal his true intentions with his seizure of Austria in the Anschluss. His ambitions included not only occupying what had been traditionally German territory, but now, by threats of overwhelming violence, he revealed that his goals included seizing territory, in fact, entire nations that had never been part of Germany. He

---

162 *The New York Times*, March 12, 1938, p. 1.

163 *Rise and Fall* at 351.

164 *Nazi Germany and the Jews*, Friedlander at 87.

did so under the gossamer thin pretext of seeking to protect ethnic Germans living in those territories and nations.

The handwriting on the wall, which Trude had seen and understood years earlier, was now visible and undeniable to Max as well. Max wrote in his journal that "life became more and more unbearable—in terms of both our personal and economic situation...We decided to emigrate to the USA." (Max's Green Diary.) The time had come to leave Germany.

Max and Trude moved forward with their efforts to emigrate. They sought advice from Consul Klieforth, who wrote to Max on March 12, 1938, the day of the Anschluss:

> My dear Dr. Ichenhäuser:
>
> With reference to your inquiry as to the medical examinations in the United States I beg to advise you to apply direct to the State Medical Board of the State of [whatever state Max might choose], addressed to the capital of the respective State, as the State Medical Board, Albany, New York, or Harrisburg, Pennsylvania. I am sorry to find that I have no information at hand as to the nature of the examinations in the different states.
>
> Mrs. Klieforth and I learned of your intended departure from Cologne, where you have been established as a practicing physician for a good many years, with much regret. Please accept our cordial thanks for your past services. You have taken care of Mrs. Klieforth, my two sons, as well as of me, ever since my arrival in Cologne in September 1935. You have also taken care of Vice Consul Wright and Mrs. Wright of my office for a period of seven years. We have been able at all times to rely upon your professional care as well as upon your personal advice, which we appreciate deeply.
>
> Please accept my best wishes for the future, and if at any time I can personally be of assistance to you, do not hesitate to inform me.
>
> Mrs. Klieforth joins me in sending you and Mrs. Ischenhauser (sic) my best regards,
>
> Very sincerely yours,
>
> A.W. Klieforth, American Consul General

Little did Consul Klieforth suspect that his offer of assistance would soon be called upon.

The regime continued apace with its efforts to crush Germany's Jewish community. On March 28, 1938, the Reichstag abolished the legally recognized status of the Jewish communities in Germany. This deprived those communities of the funding the state had previously provided to all religious communities. The Reichstag also required Jewish organizations to identify themselves in the State Register of Associations. This list would make it easier for the SS to seize assets, arrest the organizations' members and officers, and, ultimately, shut down every Jewish organization within the borders of the Reich.

The regime continued to find new ways to punish Jews and, in effect, make them internal exiles. There seemed to be no end to the invidious decrees and regulations that sought to steal Jewish livelihoods and assets, as well as instill fear into anyone who might be the least bit sympathetic to Germany's Jews. On April 22, Goering issued a decree that any German who tried to hide Jewish ownership of a business would be fined or imprisoned.[165] Now, not only Jewish business owners, but also any non-Jew who deigned to help Jews retain ownership of their businesses, were at risk.

On April 26, the regime enacted legislation known as the "Decree Regarding the Reporting of Jewish Property." This edict required that by June 30, 1938, every Jew had to register and assess all domestic and foreign property with a value in excess of 5000 RM (approximately $2,000) except for personal and household items.[166] By requiring registration of property, the regime sent a message to Germany's Jews that the Nazis now had a handy resource to help them identify and expropriate Jewish assets whenever the regime so desired.

The Nazis began making mass arrests of Jews in May 1938; they sent most of the detainees to Dachau outside of Munich. The Camp Commandant ordered the prisoners already there to sew Stars

---

165 *War Against the Jews* at 96.

166 *War Against the Jews* at 96.

of David on uniforms in anticipation of receiving new inmates who would need to be readily identifiable as Jews.

Hitler visited Munich in early June. While there, he ordered the destruction of the city's Great Synagogue, which was one of Munich's most well-known landmarks. He directed the synagogue be razed "because it was situated in close proximity to the German Artisans' House." The Führer apparently felt the presence of the large, elaborate synagogue detracted from the Artisans' House. The destruction of the synagogue began the day after Hitler issued his order; it was to be completed by July 8, "German Art Day."[167] Members of the congregation worked through the night to remove the synagogue's Torahs, prayer books, and other ritual items before demolition began the next day. The city reimbursed the Jewish community for a fraction of the value of the synagogue. For good measure, the city also destroyed the neighboring Jewish community building. The regime was as thorough as it was odious.

This act of religious and cultural violence was followed in short order by the destruction of synagogues in Nuremberg and Dortmund. The SS arrested 1500 Jews on trumped up charges and sent them to concentration camps for political enemies of the regime. While the SS soon released the prisoners, it did so on the condition they emigrate immediately. The campaign to cleanse Germany of Jews began to accelerate.

The United States' visa regulations required that applicants obtain a certificate of good conduct from local police:

> To Mrs. Max Ichenhäuser, Gertrude nee Moses born on 3 March 1901 in the district of Köln, is officially certified that she was registered with the city in the period from birth to today at Aachenerstrasse 412. In addition, police records do not show that she has committed any crimes.
>
> On behalf of the Chief of Police. (Criminal Record Notice from the Cologne Police Department, July 7, 1938.)

Trude was working doggedly to collect the items the family

---

167 www.yadvashem.org.

needed to secure visas to the United States. She had obtained the required certificate attesting she did not have a criminal record that might otherwise impede her efforts to emigrate.

Max and Trude began obtaining the affidavits they needed to secure visas. "My cousin, Gretel (Oberlander) Titche, in Monroe (Louisiana) and my friend and patient, U.S. Consul General Klieforth, provided affidavits, which came into our possession in July." (Max's Green Diary.) Max and Trude also obtained an affidavit from a Dr. Miron Silberstein in New York. (It is not known if Dr. Silberstein was a friend, family member, or professional colleague of Max.) The support affidavits were required to list the affiant's dependents, state the affiant's income, and provide the value of all real estate the affiant owned. The regulations required that the affiant state:

> I am willing and able to receive, maintain, support and be responsible for the alien(s) mentioned above while they remain in the United States and hereby assume such obligations, guaranteeing that none of them will at any time become a burden on the United States or any State, County, City, Village or Municipality of the United States; and that any who are under sixteen years of age will be sent to a day school at least until they are sixteen years old and will not be put to work unsuited to their years.

> That the above-mentioned relatives are in good health and physical condition and are mentally sound, to the best of my knowledge and belief.

> That I am and always have been a law-abiding resident and have not at any time been threatened with or arrested for any crime or misdemeanor, that I do not belong to nor am I in anywise connected with any group or organization whose principles are contrary to organized government, nor do the above mentioned relatives, to the best of my knowledge and belief, belong to any such organization, nor have they ever been convicted of any crime involving moral turpitude.

> Deponent further states: That this affidavit is made by him for the purpose of inducing the American Consul to issue visas to the above-mentioned relatives and the immigration Authorities to admit said relatives into the United States.

The United States was intent on refusing admission to anyone who might become a "public charge" or take jobs from U.S. citizens while the nation was still recovering from the Depression. The Immigration Act of 1882 provided that immigrants who could not support themselves were not appropriate for admission to the United States. The same exclusionary language was in the Immigration Act of 1891. United States' immigration policy also sought to exclude anyone who might be a Communist or anarchist.

The Johnson-Reed immigration bill enacted in 1924 provided for annual immigration to the United States of 164,667 people; this constituted two percent of each Caucasian nationality represented in the United States' population in 1890. The formula was intended to "maintain our standard of living, to sustain our institutions for the care of the socially inadequate, to preserve our basic political institutions, and 'to preserve the basic stream of our population.'"[168] The "basic stream of our population" formula was intended to keep the United States overwhelmingly Christian and Caucasian, and even then, allow immigration primarily from only certain Christian and Caucasian nations.

However, the economic concerns purportedly underlying the public charge restriction lacked a factual basis. The American Jewish Congress had data showing that Jews who came to the United States from Nazi Germany were not unskilled laborers who competed with American citizens for jobs, but rather were professionals whose skills were needed and whose presence actually expanded employment opportunities for American citizens.[169] Unfortunately, this data had no impact on U.S. policy.

"With unemployment rampant in the United States throughout the 1930s, no one who depended upon finding a job on arrival was allowed entry."[170] However, Nazi legislation prevented Jews from taking most of their assets with them when they emigrated. As a

---

168 No Haven for the Oppressed: United States Policy Toward Jewish Refugees, 1938-1945, Saul Friedman, Wayne State University Press 1973, at p. 21.

169 *No Haven* at 47.

170 *Flight from the Reich: Refugee Jews*, 1933-1946, Debórah Dwork and Robert Jan van Pelt, W.W. Norton & Co., (2009) at 144.

result, almost all would-be Jewish emigrants would need to look for work upon arriving in the United States or they would have to be able to rely upon support from friends and family in the United States if they were to have any hope of being approved for visas. Jews could not bring money with them when they emigrated, but the United States prohibited them from trying to support themselves through work when they arrived in that nation. As a result, obtaining "support affidavits" was the only way prospective immigrants could satisfy U.S. visa requirements. Even this was only possible for would-be emigrants who were lucky enough to know someone in the United States who was willing and able to support them. "There was a tragic element of truth in the statement circulating among Europe's Jews in 1938 that the world was made up of two kinds of countries: the kind where Jews could not live and the kind where Jews could not enter."[171]

In 1938, U.S. immigration policy allowed the State Department to issue 27,370 visas per year for Germans and Austrians. However, by June 30, 1938, nearly 140,000 Germans were on the German quota waiting list for United States immigration visas.[172] By September 1938, the waiting list was up to 220,000 German applicants; by 1939-41, the list had increased to 300,000.[173] The U.S. quota meant it would take eleven years to admit those on the list, assuming no more Germans applied. It soon became clear that wait was far too long. Death was in a hurry in Europe.

The Jewish Community Bulletin for Rhineland and Westphalia published an article on June 17, 1938, offering practical advice to prospective immigrants to the United States so they could decide what items to take with them and what they should leave behind. The article advised they could take "removal goods" (home furnishings) with them, as long as they were not intended for resale. "The immigrants must bring a list of all items to be imported as removal goods and for the purpose of customs clearance and duty-free imports...

---

171   *No Haven* at 56.

172   *The Holocaust Encyclopedia, United States and the Refugee Crisis*, 1938-1941.

173   *Id.*

The immigrant declares this list in duplicate and submits an affidavit at the bottom of the list that the objects therein mentioned were his property and will be transferred to the USA in order to be used by himself in the USA for residential purposes. It is useful if the immigrant has his signature certified by the police district responsible for his previous place of residence."

The article reported that apartments in New York were expensive and small, but larger, more affordable apartments could be found at "inland places." Immigrants should not bring large furniture with them; they did not need to bring wardrobes to hold clothing because American apartments had built-in closets. "Grand pianos and upright pianos are also duty-free, as are all technical and medical instruments if they are used to practice the profession of the immigrant concerned...It is customary in New York in the summer to provide furniture with covers, so that it is protected from the effects of heat and moisture and also any vermin."

"Table linen, bedclothes and underwear, if they have been newly purchased, must be thoroughly washed and, if possible, embroidered with a monogram so that the customs officer can see that it is for personal use and not for further sale." Since winter in the United States was regarded as more severe than in Germany, and summers were considered to be quite hot, "it is advisable to bring warm underwear, wool clothing, overshoes, rubber shoes, umbrellas, warm Ulster coats, light silk raincoats or water-proof raincoats for rainy summer days." Men's summer suits were worth bringing, but without linings. "The gentlemen wear straw hats here in summer." Further, men's "so-called knickerbockers" were not worn in the U.S. Men's shirts "should be in a style to be worn with a jacket with attached collars."

On July 6, further Reich regulations set forth a list of commercial activities in which Jews were no longer allowed to engage, including providing credit information and serving as real estate brokers.[174] The regime blocked all Jewish bank accounts. Max noted in his diary that he and Trude had been required to fill out an Estate Declaration of Assets and their bank accounts had been blocked. (Max's Green Diary.)

---

174 *Nazi Germany and the Jews* at 100.

In July, Trudy and the girls took the train to Amsterdam to visit the Emanuels. Max joined them towards the end of their visit and traveled home with them. "On the return trip, German officials took away our passports." (Max's Green Diary.) In the short term, this meant they could no longer travel outside Germany. What it meant long term, if they were able to secure the necessary permits and visas to emigrate, was not clear. What was clear was that with the loss of their passports, the Nazi noose around them was tightening. Avenues of escape continued to narrow and disappear.

On July 23, 1938, the Ministry of the Interior issued a decree requiring that all Jews apply for identification cards by year end. Jews were required to carry the cards at all times and present them on demand.[175]

In July 1938, President Roosevelt called for an international forum to discuss Jewish emigration from Germany. Thirty-two nations convened in Evian, France, to discuss the plight of Jewish refugees. While Roosevelt called for the forum, the U.S. expressions of concern and its call for action were shams. The United States had admitted a total of only 27,000 Jews in the five years from January 1933 to June 1938.[176] This meant the United States admitted only *2400 Jewish refugees annually* in the years between Hitler's ascent to power and the catastrophe of Kristallnacht. Even worse, "Between 1933 and 1945 the United States took in only 132,000 Jewish refugees, only ten percent of the quota allowed by law."[177] If the United States had done nothing more than admit the allowable quota of German immigrants during that time frame, it could have saved an additional 1,188,000 souls, the vast majority of whom would have been Jews who instead ended up in death camps or whom the Nazis murdered in other ways and at other locations.

"The invitation to the conference clearly stated that 'no country would be expected to receive a greater number of emigrants than is

---

175 *Nazi Germany and the Jews* at 99; War Against the Jews at 100.

176 *Jewish Immigrants of the Nazi Period in the U.S.A.,* Ed. Herbert Strauss, Pub. K.G. Saur, p. xx Table I.

177 *Gilder Lerhman Institute of American History—Immigration Policy During WWII.*

permitted by its existing legislation.'"[178] In other words, no country was expected to do anything beyond what it was already doing, which universally was orders of magnitude less than the crisis demanded.

In light of the U.S. position, it was no surprise that the participating nations, with the sole exception of the Dominican Republic, did not make any changes to their immigration laws; nor did they agree to accept refugees. As put by a Newsweek correspondent attending the conference: "Chairman Myron C. Taylor, former U.S. Steel head, opened the proceedings: 'The time has come when governments…must act and act promptly.' Most governments represented acted promptly by slamming their doors against Jewish refugees."[179]

> Over the years, most target countries closed their borders to refugees from Germany by arguing that they could not absorb any more immigrants. The Swiss slogan was typical of this: "The boat is full!" A whole series of countries introduced quotas for immigrants. This also applied to Palestine, where the British mandate authorities even reduced the existing quotas.[180]

Shanghai, which was under international administration, was the only destination for which an immigrant did not need a visa or other certificate for entry.[181] Some 18,000 Jews were able to find refuge in Shanghai, which at the time was under Japanese occupation.

And so, in an extraordinary display of irony salted with shame, and although many nations who attended the conference recognized Jews' desperate need to flee Germany, and now Austria as well, the assembled representatives dried their crocodile tears, shrugged their uncaring shoulders, and left the Evian conference without taking any action to help. Nations of the world pretended to care, but their actions, or more to the point their inaction, showed they most assuredly did not.

---

178   *Gilder Lerhman Institute of American history—Immigration Policy During WWII.*

179   *Paper Walls: America and the Refugee Crisis* 1938-1941, David S. Wyman [New York, 1985], p. 50.

180   *Germans No More* at 172.

181   *Germans No More* at 172.

"On July 25 the fourth supplementary decree to the Reich citizenship law put an end to Jewish medical practice in Germany. The licenses of Jewish physicians were withdrawn as of September 30, 1938."[182] The decree went on to provide that those Jews who formerly were "physicians" and who had received authorization to continue treating Jewish patients could no longer refer to themselves as physicians, but rather could only describe themselves as "caretakers of the sick."[183]

The U.S. Consulate in Stuttgart, located at 19a N. Königstrasse, was responsible for processing German requests for visas to the United States. "On August 3, we went to the U.S. Consulate in Stuttgart and registered to emigrate. Consul Klieforth had given me a letter of recommendation to give to his colleague in Stuttgart. This colleague received us immediately and spoke with us for three quarters of an hour but told us that we would have to wait one year." (Max's Green Diary.)

Max and Trude had planned to continue traveling from Stuttgart for a few days of vacation. However, an unwelcome surprise arrived when, on August 4, Max read in the newspaper that, because of the Fourth Supplementary Decree, his practice would be permanently closed as of September 30, 1938. (Max's Green Diary.) "On September 30, 1938, all Jewish doctors in Germany lost their license to practice."[184] The regulations revoking the right of Jewish physicians to provide care to patients with medical insurance was crippling for the vast majority of Jewish doctors.[185] Insurance plans were by far the greatest source of patient care and remuneration to physicians. In less than two months, Max would have no way to support his family.

Given the destruction of Max's practice and the freezing of his and Trude's bank accounts, not to mention the increasing street violence against Jews, a year-long wait for visas to the United States

---

182 *Nazi Germany and the Jews* at 100.

183 *Nazi Germany and the Jews* at 100.

184 *Germans No More* at 18.

185 *Jewish Daily Life* at 311.

seemed like an eternity to the Ichenhäusers. But the cupboard was bare of alternatives. The Ichenhäusers had to find ways to cope with the fact that they had no physical security, no financial security, and, so far, no way out.

The Stuttgart Consulate followed Max and Trude's visit with a letter of instruction:

> To: Dr. Max Ichenhäuser
>
> Köln-Braunsfeld Aachenerstrasse 412
>
> You are registered under the number 8298 Aug. 3, 1938, in the waiting list of visa applicants and should communicate any change of address promptly.
>
> If satisfactory evidence of your financial support in America is on file here, and if it is your turn, a summons will be sent to you for formal application. The summons will be sent approximately four weeks before the examination date.
>
> For all communications please state your waiting number. (U.S. Consular letter to Max, August 8, 1938.)

And so, the visa process dragged on with neither U.S. consular officers, nor the Ichenhäusers, knowing how much or how little time the family had left to get out of Germany.

The regime continued to attack its Jewish subjects. "On August 17, 1938, the Law Regarding Changes of Family Names and Given Names was issued providing that, as of January 1, 1939, all male Jews must assume the given name of Israel and all female Jews the name of Sarah.[186] Jews were forbidden to take as given names any [names] other than specifically designated 'Jewish' given names, as listed in an appendix to the decree."[187] The purpose of these decrees was to ensure that the SS, Gestapo, and any other interested authorities could readily identify Jews if the Jews' given names did not "sound Jewish."

Goering stated the objective of Nazi policy: "The Jewish question must now be grasped in every way possible, for they [Jews] must

---

186 *War Against the Jews* at 97-98.

187 *War Against the Jews* at 98.

be removed from the economy." All Jewish shops were ordered to close by December 31, 1938. Having been barred from professions and trades, Jews were now also prohibited from operating even the humblest store in order to sell a bar of soap, a spool of thread, or an apple to earn a few Reichsmarks. Sixty percent of the Jewish population had earned its living as owners of stores or other businesses. Now, that sixty percent had no means of support and no prospect of being hired by anyone. The Regime's intent was to make life so intolerable for Jews that they would leave by any means and go to any destination. In this way, Jews would "self-cleanse" Germany of its Jewish population. Germany's anti-Jewish policies could be summed up as identification, segregation, expropriation, concentration, emigration, or expulsion.[188]

On September 27, 1938, Hitler signed the Fifth Supplementary Decree to the Citizenship Law, this time prohibiting all Jewish attorneys from practicing law.[189] Jewish attorneys who up to then had fallen within WWI-related exemptions to the decree barring attorneys from practicing law, were now banned from the profession. Jews could no longer represent clients and most assuredly no Aryan lawyer would risk his reputation and livelihood by representing a Jew. Jews had already lost virtually all of their legal rights, but this completed their disenfranchisement from the German legal system.

As per the Nazi decree, September 30, 1938, was the last day of Max's medical practice. Since Max no longer suffered the distraction of seeing patients, he spent his days studying English at a furious pace to prepare for the medical certification boards he would need to take if the family were able to make its way to the United States.

The Reich's Law on Passports of Jews, issued on October 5, 1938, required Jews to hand in their passports for foreign travel; they were to be reissued with a large "J" printed on them designating the passport holder as a Jew.[190] Further, only those Jews who were about to emigrate would receive new passports. The passport law was one

---

188 *Nazi Germany and the Jews* at 157.

189 *Nazi Germany and the Jews* at 100.

190 *War Against the Jews* at 98.

more step in the regime's program to ensure it could readily identify Jews, be it by compelling them to take a "Jewish name" or requiring that their identification cards and passports identify them as Jews. By seizing their passports, the Nazis made Jews prisoners in Germany since they could not cross its borders to enter another country without passports.

Max and Trude decided to take classes in massage therapy. Perhaps they took the training to find a way to generate income, however little it might be, while waiting to emigrate since Max could no longer practice medicine. For Trude, being a massage therapist might give her a way to make money should they emigrate and need income while Max was taking the certification boards and building a practice. Their massage training included theoretical principles of anatomy, as well as practical massage training. Dr. Ernst Mayer, an orthopedic specialist at the Cologne Orthopedic Therapy Center and X-Ray Institute, provided a recommendation attesting to Trude's training:

> Mrs. Ichenhäuser above all had the opportunity to take the theoretical and practical massage skills I had taught her and to apply them to a large number of patients independently. I taught her specific hand techniques which she has mastered perfectly.

> I repeated the theoretical subjects several times in the course of her training and Mrs. Ichenhäuser has a solid understanding of them.

> Mrs. Ichenhäuser has mastered massage perfectly—both from a theoretical and a practical standpoint. As a result, I can highly recommend her in every way. (Certificate/Letter of Recommendation, Dr. Ernst Mayer and Dr. Med. Koppel, Sept. 30, 1938.)

Trude also took a course in "modern skincare." Her certificate of completion stated she demonstrated "very good theoretical and practical knowledge." (Testimonial of Completion, Method Academy Cedib Paris, Sept. 28, 1938.) Perhaps Trude and Max thought that, having been trained in massage and skin care, they could find clients in Cologne by offering some of the services the city's Jews had long enjoyed at Germany's spas before the Nazis barred Jews from visiting spas. Whether anyone could afford their services given the destruction of much of the wealth and income of Germany's Jews was another matter.

And so Max and Trude prepared, worried, and waited.

I Would Not Like to be
a Jew in Germany

O N September 15, 1938, British Foreign Secretary Neville Chamberlin flew to Germany to confer with Hitler in Berchtesgaden, a small town in the Bavarian Alps near the Austrian border. Chamberlain's trip was prompted by Hitler's demands that Czechoslovakia allow Germany to occupy and annex the Czech territory known as the Sudetenland in order to "protect" the three million ethnic Germans living there. Left unsaid was the fact that Nazi sympathizers instigated the disturbances in the Sudetenland from which those German-Czech citizens purportedly needed protection. Hitler's demand was part of a carefully coordinated plot to generate "troubles" which would serve as a pretext for Hitler's demands to Czechoslovakia. This was a frightening echo of Hitler's conduct prior to seizing Austria in the Anschluss. Hitler had issued an order to the Wehrmacht as far back as May 1938 to prepare to invade Czechoslovakia on October 1, which, in the end, was only two weeks after Chamberlin flew to Berchtesgaden. Hitler's order in May revealed that his plan, from the outset, was to invade Czechoslovakia after his sympathizers created a pretext for German forces to enter that country.

Chamberlin met with Hitler on September 16, 1938. The Czech government had declared martial law in the Sudetenland due to the breakdown in order caused by the Nazi mobs. On the same day as Chamberlain's meeting with Hitler, the Czech Cabinet ordered the arrest of Konrad Henlein, the leader of the Sudeten Germans, as a traitor. The Czech government announced the order after Herr Henlein issued a proclamation declaring that the Sudeten Germans wanted a union with Germany.[191] Henlein promptly fled to Germany.

Britain feebly tried to rise to the occasion. On September 27, it pledged to come to Czechoslovakia's aid if Germany attacked it. However, in a head-spinning move, Britain also guaranteed the surrender of the Sudeten areas to Germany if Hitler "kept the door open" for peace.[192] This was a promise without substance. Hitler could agree to "keep the door open," even by only the smallest crack, but then slam it shut once he had achieved his goals in Czechoslovakia. Chamberlain was prepared to carve up Czechoslovakia for something that was neither concrete nor, in any event, enforceable.

In a speech at the Sportspalast in Berlin, Hitler declared that "If the Sudeten territories were ceded, this would be the last territorial demand Germany would make in Europe."[193] However, he also declared that if the Sudetenland were not given to the Reich, Germany would take it by force. Despite Hitler having reoccupied the Rhineland and annexed Austria, and despite Hitler's previous proclamations that Germany would make no further territorial demands in Europe, Chamberlain believed, or perhaps only desperately hoped, Hitler would honor an agreement regarding Czechoslovakia if Hitler was given what he demanded, which was nothing less than the dismemberment of Czechoslovakia.

Chamberlain, in the final act of British appeasement for which he became infamous, offered the Sudetenland to Germany if Germany would refrain from war. In response, Hitler called for a four-power conference with Mussolini, Chamberlain, and French Prime Minister Daladier to try to resolve the German-manufactured "Czech crisis." The Conference took place on September 29 in Munich *without a Czech representative being allowed to participate* in the discussions that

---

191   *The New York Times*, September 16, 1938, p. 1.

192   *The New York Times*, September 27, 1938, p. 1.

193   *The New York Times*, Sept. 27, 1938, p. 1.

would determine the future of Czechoslovakia. The conference took place one day after Hitler declared that Germany would mobilize its armed forces and two days before the date on which Hitler had said Germany would invade Czechoslovakia. Chamberlain shamefully agreed to allow Hitler to occupy the Sudetenland in exchange for "peace in our time." Two days later, on October 1, 1938, Hitler's troops marched into the Sudetenland.

Britain's decision to acquiesce to Hitler's demands had the practical effect of destroying Czechoslovakia. That country not only lost a large portion of its territory, but also lost 3.5 million Czech citizens. The Sudetenland contained 70% of Czechoslovakia's iron and steel production and 70% of its electrical generating capacity. Czechoslovakia also lost two-thirds of its coal production, more than three-quarters of its cement production, and the majority of its chemical production.[194] The western territory the country ceded constituted the only favorable geographic lines of defense for Czechoslovakia by virtue of the area's mountainous territory and the fortifications Czechoslovakia had constructed there. As a result, once the Sudetenland fell into the hands of the German army, the remainder of Czechoslovakia was essentially defenseless. Without firing a shot, Hitler had now occupied the Rhineland, annexed Austria, and occupied a large portion of Czechoslovakia, with the remainder of the latter country helpless in the face of whatever further demands Hitler might make. The German populace was, by and large, delirious with joy at Hitler's resuscitation of German pride and their country's taking "its rightful place" among nations.

In a further cause for international concern, Germany abruptly ordered all of its merchant vessels to return to Germany immediately from ports around the world. The vessels complied without providing any explanation to shippers or passengers; the shipping lines simply cancelled passenger trips and left cargo sitting on docks given the haste of their departure. Many observers believed the order was an effort to get Germany's commercial fleet into home waters to

---

194 *Rise and Fall* at 422.

avoid having the fleet seized by Germany's foes as happened during World War I.[195]

The pressure of daily life for Jews in Germany was becoming unbearable. Jews were barred from professions, had been removed from public office, and had lost their right to vote. Jews could not operate stores or use public parks. Jewish children were assaulted on their way to school. Brown-shirted S.A. mobs were destroying synagogues. Erica left home one morning and found the word "Juden" scrawled on their front door. In the face of all this, the Ichenhäusers faced a one year wait before the United States would admit them to the country.

On October 27, 1938, a seventeen-year-old Jewish Polish student named Hershl Grynszpan, whose parents the Nazis had deported from Germany to Poland in an early act of ethnic cleansing, shot and killed a German official. In reprisal, on November 9, 1938, the Nazis organized and carried out pogroms throughout Germany that came to be known as Kristallnacht ("Crystal Night"). The name Kristallnacht was inspired by the piles of broken window glass strewn on streets throughout Germany after Nazi-incited mobs attacked and ransacked Jewish homes, businesses, and synagogues.[196]

Throughout Germany, at the behest of the SS and the direction of Joseph Goebbels, mobs looted Jewish businesses, smashed the windows of Jewish homes and stores, and destroyed synagogues. The rioters burned and desecrated prayer books, synagogue furnishings, and Torah scrolls. Police stood by and did nothing. Over the course of the night, Nazi rioters destroyed more than 1,000 synagogues and Jewish-community buildings in Germany and Austria. They destroyed seven thousand Jewish businesses.

---

195 *The New York Times*, Sept. 29, 1938.

196 Some refer to the night of the anti-Jewish riots as the "Night of Broken Glass" so as not to romanticize the horrific events by using the word crystal. Others refer to the night of destruction, beatings, and arrests as "Pogrom Night" since the events constituted a pogrom. This text refers to the pogrom that took place over the course of November 9–10, 1938, as Kristallnacht since that term is the most common usage for the event.

> An uncontrollable lust for destruction and humiliation of the victims drove the squads roaming the cities. "Organized parties moved through Cologne from one Jewish apartment to another," the Swiss consul reported. "The families were either ordered to leave the apartment or they had to stand in a corner of a room while the contents were hurled from the windows. Gramophones, sewing machines, and typewriters tumbled down into the streets. One of my colleagues even saw a piano thrown out of a second-floor window."[197]

Mobs pulled Jews from their homes and businesses and beat them. Jews unfortunate enough to be out that evening were threatened and mugged. The only reason the SS-led mobs did not burn down every Jewish-owned structure they could identify was because some Jewish homes and businesses abutted non-Jewish businesses and homes. The government feared that arson attacks on those Jewish properties might spread to the Aryan-owned buildings. Therefore, those Jewish-owned structures were not torched. Fire department personnel showed up at the sites where many Jewish buildings were burning. They stood by, their faces lit by the orange glow from the fires, and watched as long as no Aryan-owned structures were at risk.

> On that memorable day of November 10 we were hunted like animals. After the Gestapo repeatedly came to my girlfriend's flat to make inspections, the fourth time around we fled through the garden and onto the street. Since we didn't look particularly Jewish we thought we would be safest in the crowd. Upon reaching the train station I tried to find a way to get to my mother. I was still hoping that she had been spared all these things. She lived with an old uncle, and I reached her on the telephone. She answered the phone in a deeply agitated voice. I stepped out of the public telephone booth and what did I see? Two civilians were arresting a Jew who happened to be standing next to my husband in the public terminal hall. I thought they were going to arrest my husband too, and so with the presence

---

197 *Nazi Germany and the Jews* at 116, citing Gauye, Imboden, and Bourgeois, Documents Diplomatiques Suisse, at 1020.

of mind that danger often brings I spoke to my husband in English, loudly and firmly. We hastily disappeared into the crowd.[198]

The next day, the Gestapo arrested thirty thousand Jewish men and sent them to concentration camps.[199] This represented nearly ten percent of all Jews still in Germany. Many of those arrested were sent to Buchenwald in central Germany, some were sent to Sachsenhausen in northwestern Germany, while nearly thirteen thousand were sent to Dachau.

Erica left the house the morning after Kristallnacht to meet the students with whom she went to school each day. The children were surprised to see the display windows of Jewish stores had been smashed and the merchandise strewn in the streets. Upon arriving at school, their teachers told them there would be no school that day. Instead, the children were to return home right away.

Two days after Kristallnacht, on November 11, 1938, the Reich ordered the Reichvertretung (Germany's Jewish governing body) to shut down. The SS arrested the Reichvertretung officials and other Jewish functionaries and sent them to concentration camps.

In an act so craven it defies belief, on November 12, 1938, Goering issued a "Decree on the Penalty Payment by Jews who Are German Subjects" which levied a fine of one billion Reichsmarks on Germany's Jewish communities because of the "hostile attitude of Jewry toward the German Volk and Reich."[200] The penalty was equivalent to the value of twenty percent of all Jewish property in Germany.[201] The regime had already confiscated some two billion Reichsmarks from Germany's Jews. These two levies constituted a penalty equal to sixty percent of all assets owned by German Jews. It is worth noting that the decree referred to Germany's Jews not as citizens, but rather as "subjects." They were a group to be ruled; per the

---

198   *Germans No More* at 173.

199   *Germans No More* at 148.

200   *War Against the Jews* at 103-4.

201   *War Against the Jews* at 103.

dictates of the Nuremberg laws, they were not part of the German body politic.

The justification the regime offered for the billion Reichsmark fine was that the Jewish victims should pay the costs the Reich purportedly incurred in connection with the Kristallnacht riots. That is to say, Jews had to pay the costs associated with the destruction of their property during riots which the Reich had instigated and stage-managed. The Reich also ordered that insurance payments for damaged Jewish property were to be paid to the government. German Jews lost their homes, businesses, and places of worship. They were denied insurance payments for those losses and were forced to pay an enormous financial penalty to the government. All this for the privilege of having government-led mobs destroy their homes, livelihoods, and synagogues.

As Goering had previously made clear: "The Jewish question must now be grasped in every way possible, for they must be removed from the economy." On November 14, the Reichstag barred Jews from attending theaters and concerts.[202] On November 15, the regime issued the "Decree on Eliminating the Jews from German Economic Life." This decree barred Jews from patronizing retail stores and mail order firms, serving as craftsmen, selling any goods or services, being a member of a cooperative, or serving as the executive or manager of any business.[203]

Up to this point, many Jews had "voluntarily" sold their businesses to non-Jewish Germans, that is, they sold "voluntarily" in the face of SS intimidation of the Jewish business owners and their customers. The SS relied, at least in part, on none too subtle threats of violence. The resulting boycotts had inexorably destroyed the Jewish businesses. After November 15, 1938, such "voluntary" transfers became compulsory, which was nothing more than unashamedly stating out loud what was, as a practical matter, already the case. All Jewish-owned businesses had to be sold to Aryans. These forced sales meant most businesses were "sold" for less than ten percent of their

---

202   *The Holocaust Encyclopedia*, "The Night of Broken Glass."

203   *War Against the Jews*, Dawidowicz at 103.

value. The order also meant that, by the end of 1938, Germany's Jews would be fully, finally, and without exception eliminated from the German economy.

Nor were Jewish children spared. On November 15, the Ministry of Education decreed that, to the extent any Jewish children were still in German public schools, they were banned "once and for all;" those still in non-Jewish schools were to be expelled.[204] Most Jewish children had already abandoned attending public schools, which were no longer safe for them, and enrolled in Jewish schools. "The experience of Jewish children on the streets and in school had long driven them toward Jewish schools. Abuse and harassment on the way to school, already observed in the latter years of the Weimar Republic, intensified up to the start of the deportations."[205] Jewish children had "internalized the 'principle of remaining inconspicuous'" in order to avoid being seen and set upon by Nazi thugs or schoolchildren who mimicked the horrific conduct of their elders.[206] Jewish children walked to and from school with their eyes down, striving to be invisible, hoping to get to school and then home again without being seen and set upon.

On November 19, the regime issued a decree that Jews were to be excluded from Germany's general welfare system. Jews now were not only barred from virtually any means of earning a living, but they were also excluded from the welfare system that might otherwise have provided financial aid to those unable to work.

Kristallnacht was a final, undeniable wake-up call for many German Jews. Even those who had fervently believed Nazism was a phase that would pass, as well as those who thought their belief in their Germanness and generations of living in Germany somehow would allow them to maintain a semblance of life in Germany, now realized they needed to get out. For most, their belated epiphany was too late. It was now almost impossible to obtain visas to enter other countries. Their decision to persevere had sealed their fates.

---

204   *Jewish Daily Life* at 296; *Nazi Germany and the Jews* at 121.

205   *Jewish Daily Life* at 296-97.

206   *Jewish Daily Life* at 297.

On December 3, the Reich revoked Jewish driver's licenses.[207] On December 20, the Reich Labor Exchange and Unemployment Insurance Board issued a decree that all unemployed Jews who were fit and able to work were required to register for compulsory labor.[208] Thus began the onset of Jewish slave labor in the service of the Reich.

While several hundred thousand Jews were still in Germany, they were no longer part of Germany. The Nazis had officially ended their social, cultural, and economic lives. The Nazis' effort to literally end their lives would be next on the Reich's agenda. As Hermann Goering declared in hideous understatement on November 12, 1938: "I would not wish to be a Jew in Germany."

---

207 *Nazi Germany and the Jews* at 122.

208 *Nazi Germany and the Jews* at 138.

Come with Us

On the morning of November 10, 1938, the day after Kristallnacht, the SS pounded on the door of 412 Aachnerstrasse and arrested Max without any explanation. They simply said: "Come with us!" Renate and Erica were bewildered by their father's arrest; they did not know what to make of it. Trude and her parents, however, knew full well what this might mean. At midday, the SS transported Max and other Jewish men to the prison in Brauweiler, a village a few miles west of Cologne. After five days, the prisoners, who had not been allowed to communicate with their families, were transported to Dachau, an already infamous concentration camp.

Shortly after coming to power, the Nazis, with SS chief Heinrich Himmler in charge, established the Dachau concentration camp on March 20, 1933, near the town of Dachau, which was situated on the Amper River roughly fifteen kilometers northwest of Munich. The regime constructed the prison and labor camp on the grounds of an abandoned munitions factory. Himmler presided over the opening of Dachau, a camp that ultimately saw over 32,000 documented deaths, with thousands more deaths no doubt unrecorded.

As the Nazis' first Konzentrationslager (concentration camp or "KZ"), Dachau was originally intended for political prisoners, but later was expanded to include Jewish prisoners and others. Dachau, as well as Auschwitz and Theresienstadt, bore the infamous logo "Arbeit macht frei" ("Work will make you free") over the entrance.

"The building which housed the main operations of the camp had the slogan: 'There is one road to freedom. Its milestones are: Obedience, zeal, honesty, order, cleanliness, temperance, truth, sense of sacrifice and love for the Fatherland.'"[209] While the Gestapo was responsible for arresting individuals who became prisoners at Dachau, the SS was responsible for guarding the camp as well as inflicting abuse and torture upon the inmates. The Nazis eventually added crematoria to dispose of the bodies of the tens of thousands of prisoners whom they killed at Dachau. When the Allies liberated the camp on April 26, 1945, some 67,000 prisoners were still interned there.

The regime had enacted "Protective Custody" regulations in 1933 which, in effect, gave it the right to arrest virtually anyone at any time. The initial regulation provided: "Protective Custody is a coercive measure of the Secret State Police to protect the State against subversive activity and may be applied to persons whose behavior endangers the existence and security of the people and the State." The regulation was later revised such that in 1937 it provided: "Protective Custody is to be regarded as a most stringent measure to teach "Volksgenossen" [members of the Volk] who deliberately ignore their duties towards the community or endanger state security that they must submit themselves to the national interest and respect state discipline."

While Dachau originally housed regime opponents who were classified as "political," by 1937 it housed four main groups of prisoners: "Politicals, Racials, Criminals and Anti-socials."[210] "Racials" included Jews, whom the Nazis regarded as a race rather than adherents to a religion. The camp was secured by seven guard towers armed with machine guns that faced inward and had a view of the entire camp.[211] The Politicals were by far the largest group of prisoners. Many fell within the category of "NN"—short for "Nacht und Nebel"—which meant night and fog. "This phrase was applied

---

209 *Dachau—The Official History 1933-1945*, Paul Berben, Norfolk Press (1975) at p. 4.

210 *Dachau—The Official History* at 10.

211 *Dachau—The Official History* at 9.

to Politicals who disappeared [from their homes] as into the night and fog."[212]

Trude knew what Max's arrest meant not only for their family, but what it might also portend for their Jewish friends. She immediately telephoned a surgeon friend of Max's who had two boys the same ages as Renate and Erica in order to warn him. She was too late; the SS had already arrested him.

Trude hastily packed small bags for the girls and put Renate and Erica in the family's Opel automobile. Although it was unusual for women to drive, Trude knew this was no time for adhering to convention. She had already bucked tradition by going to college, so driving was hardly something she feared or was willing to forego in a crisis. She drove quickly through Cologne to pick up their friend's sons.

Trude drove the children out of the city and, she hoped, away from the Gestapo. What went through her mind as she drove through the city? Perhaps she thought she should drive straight to Holland and try to cross the border to get out of Germany. Maybe she should try to save the children and herself while hoping that Max and his colleague somehow would be released and could join them. But she had to consider whether the border police would detain her and the girls since they did not have passports, which might result in all of them being arrested to await who knew what fate. Or perhaps she debated with herself whether she should hide the girls and try to get Max released, but in doing so risk having all of them detained and imprisoned.

How was she able to drive in these fraught circumstances? Perhaps the fear and adrenalin coursing through her caused her foot to involuntarily press down harder on the gas pedal as the instinct to flee kicked in. Maybe she was able to control her emotions and maintain a steady speed despite her knuckles turning white from her iron grip on the wheel. Perhaps the Opel's speed fluctuated as Trude's thoughts raced and her emotions oscillated between fight and flight. All this likely coursed through her mind while she sought shelter for her daughters and the other children and thought about how to save her husband.

---

212 *Dachau—The Official History* at 12.

Trude sought refuge for the children with the Hartmann-Schmidts, who were non-Jewish friends of Trude and Max. (Unfortunately, at the time this book was written no one in the Ichenhäuser family knew the Hartmann-Schmidts' first names, nor has extensive research discovered their full identities.) The Hartmann-Schmidts were the same ages as Max and Trude but did not have children. They had vacationed with Max and Trude in Italy a few years earlier. Mr. Hartmann-Schmidt had lost an eye in WWI; he had a glass eye that he generally covered with an eye patch. The Hartmann-Schmidts, at great risk to themselves, agreed to hide the four children in their attic. If they were found hiding Jews, the Gestapo likely would have executed them on the spot.

Renate and Erica did not know what to make of the situation. Trude told them to stay in the attic and be quiet so as not to reveal their hiding place. This was extremely important since, as the Hartmann-Schmidts did not have children of their own, the sound of children in their house might arouse suspicion among their neighbors. The Hartmann-Schmidts brought meals to the children and comforted them, all the while trying to keep up the appearance of life as usual.

To Erica, it seemed as if they were playing a glorified game of hide and seek. Unbeknownst to her, there would be a grim price to pay if they were found. Renate tried to keep Erica and the boys occupied. Since she loved to draw, Renate used paper and pencils to help the children pass the time in a way that would not create noise and put them at risk. Renate, by then ten years old, understood enough to realize their lives had taken a bad turn. Having been chased through the streets by children throwing rocks and screaming epithets at her, having seen the wreckage of Kristallnacht, and having witnessed her father being arrested, Renate knew their lives were in jeopardy, even if she did not understand why.

While the children were hiding, Trude set herself to getting Max released. Since Max was the house physician to the American and British consuls in Cologne, Trude decided they were the people to whom she would turn. Her first stop was the U.S. Consulate.

ALFRED KLIEFORTH

A LFRED WILLIAM KLIEFOTH ENTERED THE WORLD ON October 10, 1889, in the tiny town of Mayville, Wisconsin, northwest of Milwaukee. (In 1935, Kliefoth changed his surname to Klieforth; that is the spelling that will be used for the balance of this narrative.) As a child, Klieforth enjoyed reading and art. While in high school, he taught grade school in a one-room schoolhouse near the town of Theresa, Wisconsin. He walked five miles to and from the school each day until one of his older sisters purchased a bicycle for him to use.

Klieforth was the first member of his family to graduate from college; he earned a bachelor's degree in 1913 from the University of Wisconsin. While in college, he tutored foreign students, including quite a few students from China which allowed him to develop a working knowledge of Chinese. Klieforth's tutoring of Chinese students also spurred in him a desire to see the world.

One year after graduating college, Klieforth took the United States Foreign Service examination. He did well and joined the Service. His first posting was in Torneo, Finland, where he served as a passport control officer. The Foreign Service sent Klieforth to Stockholm for his next posting.

After a short stint in Stockholm, the Service assigned Klieforth to serve as the Assistant Military Attaché at the United States Embassy in Petrograd (originally St. Petersburg), which at the time was Russia's capital and second largest city. Modeled upon European capitals, Petrograd was full of magnificent palaces and elaborate public buildings situated on broad boulevards and streets surrounding large public squares. When Czar Peter the 1st founded the city in 1703, he named it St. Petersburg. However, after the onset of WWI, Russian officials changed the city's name to Petrograd ("Peter's city" in Russian) to eliminate the German ending of "burg."[213]

Klieforth had a decent knowledge of Karl Marx's writings. He also spoke a smattering of Russian. He used these tools to try to understand what was occurring in Russia and help him provide insightful reports to the State Department in Washington. As a member of the consular staff, Klieforth came to know members of the Czar's court. On December 31, 1916, he attended the last New Year's Eve Party that Czar Nicholas II held in his glittering palace in Petrograd. Three months later, on March 15, 1917, Nicholas abdicated. The Bolsheviks soon imprisoned Nicholas and his family and executed all of them on July 17, 1918.

Klieforth attended lectures and speeches Lenin and Trotsky gave in Petrograd during the tumult of 1917 and the terror and famine which followed. "Walking from his offices in Petrograd to lunch, he [Klieforth] had to step over the bodies of the starved dead. He saw the starved living who would dart out of alleyways and fall upon a horse shot down in street fighting [to carve it up for food] ..." The Russian revolution was in full ferment. Klieforth was a reserve officer in the United States Army. Given the disturbances that followed the revolution, he was called to active duty as a Lieutenant while in Petrograd.

While stationed in Petrograd, Klieforth met Barbara Leslie. Barbara was the daughter of Russian General Alexander Leslie, who was of Scottish descent. General Leslie was stationed in Petrograd as an advisor to the Russian Army to help modernize the Czar's military. Klieforth and Barbara soon became a couple. Barbara had been close to Czarina Alexandra Feodorovna and acted as an informal "lady-in-waiting" to the czarina.

213 *World Book Encyclopedia*, "St. Petersburg." In 1922, the city was named Leningrad. Decades later, a 1991 plebiscite resulted in changing the city's name back to St. Petersburg.

The dangers the revolution created, along with the ensuing civil war and widespread lawlessness, became so grave that the United States decided to evacuate the "American colony" in Petrograd. The risk of arrest or attack by a multitude of armies, militias, and bandits was such that there were few safe routes out of Russia. It was impossible to evacuate by the shortest route to western Europe because World War I was still raging. Instead, the United States Embassy in Petrograd concluded that the only feasible evacuation route was eastward by train across Russia's vast expanse. The route the train was to follow would traverse European Russia, Siberia, past northern Manchuria, and terminate at Vladivostok on the Russian Pacific coast, where the refugees would be evacuated by ship to their native lands.

It fell to Lieutenant Klieforth to organize the evacuation of American citizens from Petrograd. But first, he had to determine how to save Barbara Leslie, to whom he was engaged. The solution he settled upon was to arrange a hasty wedding on February 20, 1918, so that Barbara was eligible, as Klieforth's wife, to participate in the American evacuation.

Years later, Klieforth wrote:

> Shortly after we were married on Feb. 20, 1918, the American Colony in Petrograd, now Leningrad, was ordered to evacuate Russia. A refugee train was quickly organized, a locomotive from here, a sleeping car from there and a most precious dining and kitchen car, and other cars. We left Petrograd for Vladivostok Siberia and there an American ship was to pick us up. I was the military officer in charge of the train. We organized a working crew, all work except that of technical engine and train business, was done by ourselves. We had American journalists on board, and they compiled this daily sheet.

The "daily sheet" to which Klieforth referred was a newsletter several passengers prepared twice each day to keep the passengers advised of important issues. As the military officer in charge of the train, Klieforth organized crews to handle various aspects of the trip. This was particularly important since the train did not have any

Russian staff other than the engine crew. By the time the train left Petrograd on September 25, 1918, the "Trans-Siberian Get-Away Train," as it came to be known by its passengers, was comprised of seven passenger cars, a dining car, and two baggage cars.

Klieforth decided to use Russian nomenclature for the work crews and, accordingly, designated them commissaries. A triumvirate of three "Chief Commissaries" was in charge of the train: Judge Jim Bailey, "Efficiency" Doc Huntington, and Torneo Al (Lieutenant Klieforth). Klieforth was known as "Torneo Al" based upon his posting in Torneo, Finland. The other commissaries included Finance, Kushits (food supplies), Kitchen Mechanics, Baggage, Archives, Tovarisch Commissary, and an Information Commissary denominated as the "Commissary of as good information as you got in Petrograd." Tovarisch is Russian for comrade; it is unclear what duties the Tovarisch commissary was charged to carry out.

George Sokolsky served as the Information Commissar on the Get-Away Express. Sokolsky had arrived in Russia in 1916 to work as a reporter for a British-owned newspaper—"The Russian Daily News." Sokolsky got to know the Bolshevik leaders Kerensky, Trotsky, and Lenin. While Sokolsky was initially politically left leaning, after seeing the violent and often murderous excesses that took place after the revolution, he became highly critical of the Bolsheviks. Taking offense at Sokolsky's critiques, Lenin and Trotsky "suggested" Sokolsky literally get on the next train out of town, which turned out to be the Get-Away Express.

"The Russian Daily News—Trans-Siberian Edition" was the broadsheet which the Information Commissar posted in the dining car twice a day to keep the passengers apprised of international news, work assignments, and other concerns. The bulletin was "Free to Good People." The first edition, posted on February 25, 1918, identified Klieforth and Barbara as newlyweds. The "News" asked Torneo Al if he knew a good joke, to which Klieforth replied; "Yes, I'm on my honeymoon." The News noted the train left Petrograd a minute and a half late according to the American schedule and two hours ahead of time according to "Tovarischchi (comrade) time."

The News explained to the Get-Away passengers what they

needed to do in order to have a safe evacuation: "Guards are to be appointed by Chief Commissary Klieforth to watch the baggage car, to get off at every station and to give proper alarm" whenever tovarishchi (comrades) attempted to board the train. Conditions in Russia were so bad and lawlessness was so rampant that there was an extremely high risk Russian military personnel and civilians would try to board the train in order to reach what they hoped would be less dangerous parts of the country.

Klieforth and the other Chief Commissars needed to figure out how to address medical needs of the passengers that might arise during their journey. The News asked that "All persons having in their possession medical supplies will kindly give an inventory of the stuff to the Commissary of Medical Supplies—Mrs. Long."

Klieforth's management of the train was made particularly challenging because the evacuees included members of the Chinese and Japanese missions in Petrograd and dozens of their citizens (thirty Chinese nationals and forty Japanese nationals, including the Japanese Ambassador), in addition to fifty-four Americans. Per the February 25 afternoon News: "Running a car [train] of 124 persons, of six nationalities and thirty employees, all eating at the same time, and meetings of the Commissaries held in English, Russian, French, Japanese and Chinese requires business organization and a reasonable office space and quiet. Tovarishchi are requested to keep out of the Smolny [administrative office in the dining car] except on business." The News' editorial staff prepared Japanese and Chinese translations of the paper to ensure everyone on board was kept informed.

Klieforth also needed to address provisioning for the long trip. The News issued a request: "California Ted—Commissary of Food Supplies would be happy to receive inventories of food supplies in the possession of all persons who have not turned their provisions into the pool. Don't get scared. He won't commandeer your stuff..." The food commissary was soon open for business offering corned beef, pork and beans (Boston style), peas, butter, jam, sardines, canned fruit (cherries, peaches, apples, and pears), cocoa, maple syrup, and more. Cocoa and sardines were at the high end of the price list, while peas and corn were apparently not much in demand if price was an accurate indicator of interest. If needed, "Lynn in Coupe 2 of Car 1843 has a corkscrew and can opener." The Commissaries established a dining schedule to avoid having all of the passengers try to eat at the same time, as well as to allow better preparation of food for the different national tastes on board.

As to the situation in Russia, the News' February 25th bulletin reported: "No news from the erstwhile front. Trotsky has probably made peace and the Red Guards are about to be demobilized. Hard luck for them at 20 roubles (sic) a day. We hope to get some Pravda news every day." The February 25th afternoon edition reported that: "First night of sailing went off allright (sic). Only one stowaway reported. He got on at the back end of the train, climbed on the roof, was discovered by our stalwart guards and kicked off the train." By day's end the train was some 329 versts (218 miles) east of Petrograd.

Perhaps the most critical issue Klieforth had to deal with was holding onto the train's steam engine. Locomotives were in short supply in Russia. Klieforth faced the possibility at every stop that some faction or purported representative of the government would seize the locomotive and leave the passengers stranded. Convincing station managers, local police, militias, and tovarishchi that the Get-Away should be allowed to pass took every bit of Klieforth's negotiating skills.

The News did its best to boost the passengers' spirits. It started a contest to rename the daily bulletins—"A can of fruit will be given the winner." The Commissary of Information advocated against shaving: "SHAVING ON THIS TRAIN IS PROHIBITED. IN SIBERIA A REAL FELLER WEARS WHISKERS" (Full caps in the original, perhaps to be "heard" over the sound of the train's steam engine chugging through the countryside.) Beards might provide some additional warmth for the hirsute men since temperatures in the depths of the Russian winter were dipping well below zero.

Klieforth and the other chief Commissars warned passengers they were forbidden to speak to any of the tovarishchi who hung around the stations at which the train stopped for water, coal, and provisions. The Commissars were concerned that one of their passengers might say something that would spark an incident with the many armed factions roaming throughout Russia. Those in charge of the train were adamant about avoiding contact that might result in any of those factions seizing the train and its passengers. Anyone who failed to obey the Commissars' instructions in this regard was to be put off the train at the next station.

The train continued east from Petrograd to Vologda where it arrived only seventeen hours behind schedule. The Information Commissar took it in stride: "Cheer up fellows the worst is yet to come." Vologda, some 400 miles east of Petrograd, was a good stop for the passengers since food was one-third cheaper than in Petrograd. The restaurant in the station had soup, ham, cold meats, and fish for sale. Meanwhile, Klieforth had his hands full maintaining security as tovarishchi continued to try to force their way on board to steal supplies or flee the areas where the train stopped.

The February 27 morning broadsheet advised passengers of the latest news: "All the People's Commissaries have been arrested in Petrograd. No Government is in control. The Germans are advancing in the direction of Petrograd and also other points. It is believed that they will reach the capital in less than a week. We have reason to believe the above information is correct. Our train Nachalnik [nachalnik means chief in Russian, presumably this was a reference to the train's conductor or engineer] had it [the news] by telegraph. In all probability Anarchy is rampant. As all messages from the (United States) Embassy have been directed to a point further East, we know nothing of the ambassador's plans."

To help pass time, the Commissary of Entertainment arranged card games, dominoes, poker, chess, and outdoor games at stops which allowed for such, subject to the approval of the "Dictatura" (the chief commissaries). Two passengers with fiddles played in the dining car, while passenger Jim Paramore was reputed to be "a fine singer of Hawaiian songs."

From Vologda, the Get-Away train continued to Viatka (Vyatka), some 1,150 versts (909 miles) east of Petrograd. While Viatka had good supplies of food for the passengers to purchase, the town was seething with anarchy, so the train quickly departed. The passengers apparently did not miss much as a result of the short stop since the chief tourist attraction in Viatka was a museum of "domestic industry products." The next stretch of the trip would be through Russia's vast pine forests. The steam train chugged eastward to Vereschagino, roughly 1,092 miles east of Petrograd, from which it continued to Perm, some 1,159 miles east of Petrograd.

On March 1, six days into the evacuation, dramatic changes occurred onboard the Get-Away train. The U.S. Ambassador sent a telegram to Klieforth instructing the staff of the U.S. Embassy and Consulate to disembark in Perm and remain there for further orders. The "unofficial" American passengers were to continue eastward with the Japanese and Chinese contingents. The Japanese Ambassador would be in charge of the train due to his rank. Understandably, the "unofficial" Americans were concerned about their safety if Lieutenant Klieforth were no longer on board to protect them. They eventually voted to make Harbin, China, the terminus of the trip, rather than continue to Vladivostok.

A partial newsletter stated that the U.S. Ambassador instructed the official U.S. contingent to remain at Vereschagino under Klieforth's supervision. The Embassy next instructed Klieforth to go to Archangel, above the Arctic Circle on the White Sea, not far from Murmansk in northeastern Russia. The U.S. ambassador and his staff met the Klieforth contingent in Vologda. There, they tried to arrange for a train to take all of them to Archangel. The Soviet government wanted to force the Americans to go to Moscow. The Soviets were afraid the Americans were going to leave the country from Archangel, which the Germans might take as a sign the Allies were abandoning the Soviets. The U.S. ambassador stressed that the Americans had no intention of leaving Russia. The Soviets, somewhat mollified, provided a locomotive to take the contingent to Archangel, where they arrived on August 9. The Get-Away train had been fraught with danger. Nevertheless Klieforth, with no more firepower than a few sidearms, was able to coordinate the safe evacuation of 124 passengers of various nationalities through a vast nation torn apart by civil war. They passed through lawless expanses in which obtaining provisions and maintaining security were challenging at best.

While in Archangel, Klieforth and Barbara had a son, Alexander

Alfred Klieforth, on December 31, 1918. The Foreign Service eventually evacuated Klieforth, Barbara, and Alexander. The Service next posted Klieforth to France and England for short periods before reassigning him to Washington, D.C., from 1920-1924. While in Washington, Klieforth worked for the State Department as an economic expert on Russia and Poland. In 1927, Barbara gave birth to their second son, Leslie ("Les"). Klieforth's next duty station was in Riga, the capital of Latvia, where he served with the American Legation from 1928 to 1929.

In 1929, the Service assigned Klieforth to the American Embassy in Berlin:

> Back in Berlin in 1929 he resumed political work, one of a group analyzing events and assembling information for the guidance of his government. As the most junior of the political staff in this foremost "window" of Europe, Mr. Klieforth was assigned the last half dozen of the 30 political parties contending in postwar Germany. One of these, seemingly a lunatic fringe of politics, was the National Socialist Party. He [Klieforth] read Mein Kampf and talked many times with Hitler, Goering, and Hess, seeking clarifications of the policy and theories Hitler set down in his book. Mr. Klieforth's knowledge of German was then almost perfect and he covered virtually all the public speeches of the Nazi bigwigs and kept an eye on the man a U.S. newspaper called "this little politician who dresses and parades like a Boy Scout leader gone crazy. (Commentary from Klieforth Family History.)

In 1933, the Foreign Service transferred Klieforth to Vienna, where he served until 1935 as the Secretary of the American Legation. Klieforth's next station was in Cologne in 1935, where he served as the U.S. Consul General until 1941. Klieforth had a first-hand view of the increasing Nazi belligerence towards its neighbors and the increasingly cruel National Socialist campaign against Germany's Jews.

This was the man whom Max Ichenhäuser had come to know as a patient and to whom Trude now turned.

All That Mattered Now
Was Getting Out

T RUDE DROVE TO THE UNITED STATES EMBASSY AT 21 Kaiser Friedrich Embankment and told the receptionist that she needed to speak with Consul Klieforth right away. Trude told Klieforth that Max had been arrested and that she needed Klieforth's help to get him released. After meeting with Klieforth, Trude drove to the British consulate at 80 Hohenzollernring to speak with the British Consul General. She told him "you have to get us papers to get to out of Germany so that I can get my husband released!" In 1938, the Nazis were allowing Jews to leave the country if they were not being held on specific charges and as long as they obtained the papers necessary to emigrate to another country. For Trude to argue to the SS that Max should be released, she had to able to prove the family could leave Germany immediately upon his release. Visas would literally be their tickets out of Germany and harm's way.

Klieforth wrote a letter to Max stating: "In view of the information received from the United States concerning your application, the Consulate is now ready to grant you a visa." (Klieforth letter to Max, Nov. 17, 1938.) The letter was technically accurate in that the U.S. was "willing" to issue a visa to Max, but arguably stretched the facts in that Max would have to wait for his and his family's U.S. quota numbers to come up before they could get the visas that they needed to enter the United States. However, that distinction was not worth a moment's consideration given Max's dire predicament. Trude took the letter to the Gestapo to plead for Max's release.

Klieforth also interceded directly by telling German authorities they should release Max because his patients needed him. The Reich had decreed that all Jewish physicians had to shutter their practices, but for the moment the SS apparently did not fixate on that. They may have concluded it was better to release this Jew to tend Jewish patients rather than face the possibility that an Aryan physician might have to care for Jews.

Many of the men whom the SS arrested after Kristallnacht and whom the SS imprisoned in Dachau were released over the next several months, but only after both "voluntarily donating" the bulk of their assets to the Reich and by pledging to emigrate immediately upon being released.[214] Those who were not released were eventually sent to death camps in the east.[215] The fact of the matter was Max and Trude were ready and willing to emigrate. The regime had already compelled Max and Trude to pay twenty percent of the family's assets to the Reich. Whether it was due to Klieforth's "visa" letter to Max, Kleiforth's comments regarding Max's practice and patients, or the ransom/immediate emigration policy, the SS released Max on November 26. While the immediate crisis had been averted, it might be only a matter of time before it was repeated. The Ichenhäusers had to get out of Germany.

However, the family still needed to find a country that would admit them while they waited for their United States visas. Trude and Max had no desire to test the limits of what the SS would consider "immediate" while they waited for as long as a year for their United States quota number to come up. That is where the British consul came in. He provided transit visas which would allow the family to enter Britain on a temporary basis as long as they did not try to settle in Britain permanently. Kathleen Goff's family rose to the occasion by advising the British consulate that they would take responsibility for the Ichenhäusers while the family was in Britain;

---

214 *Dachau—The Official History* at p. 13.

215 *Dachau—The Official History* at p. 13.

such an undertaking was a prerequisite to obtaining even a transit visa. But for the serendipity of Max being a physician, having had two foreign consuls as patients, and the Ichenhäusers having hired a British nanny whose family had a heart of gold, the outcome of Max's arrest might have been very different.

Trude and the girls received a postcard from Dachau dated November 25. The postcard read:

> My dear ones,
>
> I am healthy and hope you are as well. I can buy everything I need here. If you want to send me money, don't forget to include my date of birth, block and room number on the transfer notice. Many greetings to all friends and relatives. Letter follows.
>
> Loving greetings and kisses,
>
> From your Max

It is difficult to believe Max sent this card. The handwriting does not resemble the beautiful script in Max's WWI diary. If indeed Max wrote it, he likely did so under duress. Dachau's existence as a concentration camp for political prisoners was well-known among the German populace. A saying had developed to the effect of "Lieber herrgott, mach mich stumm, das ich nicht nach Dachau komm"—"Dear God, make me silent, that I may not come to Dachau."

Max had been arrested without explanation and without being allowed to bring anything with him. After being held incommunicado for five days in a prison in Cologne, the Gestapo had sent him to Dachau. Yet Max purportedly wrote this note making it sound as if he were at a summer camp or business conference and needed money to buy cigarettes or snacks at the canteen. Family records do not contain the follow-on letter referred to in the postcard, if in fact one was sent. Max never spoke to Renate and Erica about his time in Dachau.

After Kristallnacht and the mass detention of Jewish men, the world was a different place for those Jews still in Germany. "When the men were discharged [from detention] they found the world had totally changed: 'There was no Jewish life anymore. There was nothing but a crowd of frightened and hunted people.' All that mattered now was getting out."[216]

---

216 *Jewish Daily Life* at 354.

WE ARE GLAD TO BE IN
A FREE COUNTRY

As the family prepared to leave Cologne, Renate received a final report card from the Jewish Reform Gymnasium. Her assessment included evaluations of good in Torah, Biblical history, and Jewish history. She was also evaluated as good in German, natural sciences, singing, and needlework. Her strongest skills earned evaluations of very good in English, geography, physical exercise, and freehand drawing, the latter talent likely inherited from Max. Renate's "Record of Conduct" stated: "Renate Ichenhäuser, born March 7, 1928 at Köln, attended the above facility (Jewish Reformrealgymnasium) from April 1, 1938 to December 1938, during which time her conduct was praiseworthy. She leaves the facility to emigrate to England." (Reformrealgymnasium Certificate, Dec. 21, 1938.)

The Reich had already compelled Max to make a payment to the government of twenty percent of the family's assets, in addition to other payments the Reich had levied, so the family's financial resources were dwindling rapidly. The regime required that Max and Trude fill out a "Flight Tax Form" to be approved by the Currency Station in Cologne, which approval they obtained on December 20, 1938. The form, characterized as a "Clearance Certificate," was to be sent to the Senior Finance President at the Cologne Currency Station. The Certificate was valid only until January 31, 1939, so the family had to act quickly before it expired. The form stated that Max and Trude had "at present no balance of taxes, surcharges, penalties, fees and costs" owed. It further stated that the capital requested to be taken abroad was a personal asset, there were no tax concerns against the transfer of personal property, and "a suspicion of capital flight does not exist." However, immigrants could take only a portion of their assets with them, while the assets left behind were treated as a "blocked account."[217] Before Germany finally halted all emigration, "Jews could exchange their money for foreign currency (which they needed in order to pay for ship passage and to use in their new homelands) through the Deutsche Golddiskontbank at a loss of ninety-two to ninety-four percent."[218]

In early December the family received interim visas to leave for England. They wasted no time winding up their affairs, making arrangements for their parents, and packing what little they could take with them. They booked train tickets from Cologne to Amsterdam to depart on January 15, 1939. They could not drive because the Reich had revoked Jews' drivers' licenses and motor vehicle registration papers as of December 3, 1938.[219]

The scene at the train station in Cologne was chaotic as hundreds of Jews crowded the station to board trains leaving Germany. The scene was blurry for many as they viewed it through eyes brimming with tears. Trembling lips and twitching chins tried to find the right words to say. Comfort proved elusive as the life of every person on the platform was turning on a seminal inflection point. The air was thick with a roiling mix of anxiety, desperation, and heartbreak. Guilt over leaving loved ones permeated those fortunate enough to be departing. Those who were unable to leave were crushed by the departures of their loved ones; they were also filled with terror at what awaited them if they could not get out. Hysteria, relief, and fear percolated through the crowd. Several of Max and Trude's friends and Trude's parents Sigmund and Martha came to see the family

---

217 *Jewish Daily Life* at 356.

218 *Jewish Daily Life* at 356.

219 *Jewish Daily Life* at 337-38.

off. They all wept, knowing they likely would never see one another again. Renate was ten and Erica was nine.

As related by one who escaped:

> Now came an unspeakably difficult day, the day we had to bid farewell to my mother! How terrible, how ghastly to leave this seventy-four-year-old woman behind in a country that offered no security! My mother had enough to live on, but for how much longer? And I, her only child, was about to leave her. She had lost her other two children through death—her son was killed in the war and the other, a daughter, died at a young age. And now I was leaving her, too. It was a fate that cried out to heaven.[220]

While Trude and Max would spare no effort to get Sigmund and Martha out of Germany, it takes no stretch of the imagination to believe they harbored similar feelings of anguish and guilt.

By 1938, the Nazi currency controls allowed individuals to take only very small sums, approximately twenty-five dollars, when they left Germany. This restriction was still in effect in January 1939 when the Ichenhäusers prepared to depart. Assuming the family got safely across the border to Holland, the money Max had smuggled there would provide at least some funds they could use to establish a new life.

Grief and hope washed over them as the train left the station and slowly traversed the 133 miles from Cologne to Amsterdam. Their knuckles were white, their lips were pressed tightly together, and they could scarcely breathe when the train reached the Dutch border. Safety was near, but not yet secured. The border crossing went smoothly. Their eyes welled with tears as they left Germany and their family behind.

Cousin Walter Emanuel met them at Amsterdam's huge Central Station. The Ichenhäusers stayed with Walter and his wife Chelly at their home on Albrecht Durerstraat. The Emanuels lived in a neighborhood southwest of central Amsterdam, not far from the Vondelpark, Holland's largest and most popular park. The Emanuels

---

220 *Germans No More* at 179.

had a daughter the same age as Renate, so the three girls likely took advantage of the Vondelpark's bike paths, walkways, and play areas while the Ichenhäusers waited to leave for England.

The family had left Germany with only a few bags. While they were relieved to be out of Germany, the week they spent in Amsterdam was nevertheless nerve-wracking. The city was merely a way station for them. Given Max's narrow escape from the Gestapo, the family was anxious to put more distance between themselves and Germany. Every day so close to the Nazi regime kept them on edge. Having spent years preparing for this passage by smuggling funds, studying English, and pleading for visa papers, not to mention the disaster they narrowly avoided by prying Max from the Gestapo's grip, they were close to the next stage of their lives, but were not quite there yet.

Trude wrote to the Goffs from Amsterdam on Jan. 17, 1939:

> Dear Mrs. Goff:
>
> We are so happy to tell you that we arrived here safely. Although we have lost our home and left our parents behind us we are glad to be in a free country and to breathe freely. We intend to leave Holland on Saturday 21st at night and arrive in London on Sunday morning. If it is convenient to you we should bring the children to you in the course of the afternoon. I do not know which arrangements you have made with Mrs. Paynter, that's why I only write to you and put everything into your hands. If there is anything to tell us, please drop us a line to my address here: Ichenhäuser c/o Mrs. Emmanuel, Amsterdam, Albrecht Dürerstratt 9. I am downright thankful to you. Kindest regards to your husband, your children, Mrs. Paynter and to yourself.
>
> Yours very sincerely,
>
> T. Ichenhäuser

The Ichenhäusers had left behind their home and the rubble of Max's medical practice. They had left Max's father David, Trude's parents Sigmund and Emma, and Max's brother Ernst. While they had lost much, they had gained, at least it seemed, a future.

Shelter from the Storm

WALTER REGINALD GOFF WAS BORN IN 1890 IN COBRIDGE, a neighborhood of the city of Stoke-on-Trent in Staffordshire County in central England. Walter was an engineer and draftsman by trade who could repair almost anything mechanical or electrical.

Dorothy Massey was born in 1887 in Church Gressley, a tiny village in the southern portion of Derbyshire County, in England's East Midlands region. Derbyshire was primarily rolling hills; part of England's Peak National Park was within its borders. Dorothy was part of an enormous family of seventeen children.

Dorothy and Walter met as teenagers at a party. They were married in London in 1911 with two strangers as witnesses. Walter was twenty-one and Dorothy was twenty-four. They were devoted to one another. As devout Catholics, they attended Sunday mass every week.

Dorothy and Walter had four children: Kathleen in 1912; Bernard in 1914; Dorothy in 1920; and Josephine in 1926. In 1934, the Goffs moved into a home at 72 College Road in Harrow Weald, Middlesex, England. The owners had named the house Tenby after a lovely seaside town in Wales. Weald is an Old English word for woodland. Harrow Weald was a tiny village northwest of London, close to the villages of Bushey Heath, Stanmore, Wealdstone, Headstone, and Hatch End.

The Goffs' home had a sitting room in the back with French doors that opened to the garden behind the house. The garden contained pear and plum trees, a small plot of vegetables, and a bit of lawn. Dorothy grew nasturtiums every summer that she trained to grow up the rear wall of the house. Walter and Dorothy kept deck chairs in the garden where they sat and enjoyed the occasional warm days when the sun broke through the clouds over Britain. The front of the house contained the dining room and Walter and Dorothy's bedroom. There were two bedrooms in the back for the children. The bath and toilet were in separate rooms upstairs with a gas "geyser" for hot water over the tub. The Goffs were not well off, but they were kind, generous, and valued family. While they had no obligation to do so, they decided to help the Ichenhäusers in their time of need by taking Erica and Renate into their home for what might be as long as a year.

Garden Respite

The Ichenhäusers left Amsterdam for England on January 22, 1939, arriving in Harwich, a seaside town in Essex County on England's southeastern coast. They initially stayed in London with Trude's cousins Hans and Leni Rothschild. Anxious to provide some semblance of normalcy for Renate and Erica, and since the girls knew Walter and Dorothy Goff from having visited in 1936, Trude and Max readily accepted the Goffs' offer to let Renate and Erica stay with them. Hans took the girls to the Goffs' home in Harrow Weald, which was a one-hour ride from London on the Bakerloo tube line.

Max and Trude spent the next two weeks in a boarding house on London's Northend Road. They then moved to 214 Byron Road in Wealdstone to be closer to the Goffs. In June of 1939, they moved again, this time to 44 The Avenue in Harrow Weald. Max and Trude next rented a room from Mrs. Cambourne Paynter at 2 Hibbet Road in Harrow Weald. Mrs. Paynter's home was close enough to the Goffs that Renate and Erica could easily stop by to see their parents after school each day. Max and Trude later moved to 7 Woodcroft Avenue in Stanmore. All the while, Max immersed himself in studying "medical" English to prepare for the licensing examinations he would have to take in the United States.

The Ichenhäusers were not the only German refugees in London. Max and Trude were able to visit with the Rothschilds, Jupp and Aenne Merfel, Dr. and Mrs. Lechner, Lutz and Trude Ratzenstein,

Emil and Luise Tietz, the Paguters, and the Vaices. Seeing familiar faces, as well as being able to share concerns and speak German, were great comforts to Max and Trude as the newly minted refugees tried to plot a path for their new lives.

Roast Joint and Tarts

Dorothy Goff had her hands full feeding what had once again become a full house—Dorothy and Walter, Josephine and Dorothy (Kathleen and Bernard had long ago left the house), and Renate and Erica. Renate and Erica shared a room with Josephine, while Dorothy had the other children's bedroom to herself.

To run her daily errands, Dorothy left the house at 72 College Road and crossed the street. She headed left up to the High Street and then turned right to the row of stores where she did her shopping. She worked her way through the butcher, fishmonger, and greengrocer buying just enough for the day's needs. Dorothy limited her purchases in part because she had to carry her purchases home. Perhaps more importantly, she bought limited quantities because there were no refrigerators at the time. As a result, Dorothy purchased small quantities to try to ensure the family would be able to eat what she bought before anything went bad. Instead of a refrigerator, Dorothy had a larder about the size of a walk-in cupboard. The larder was outfitted with shelves from floor to ceiling. The shelf situated at waist height was wider than the others; it was made of marble to help keep foods cool.

Dorothy used fly nets to cover plates of food and jugs in the larder. The higher shelves held preserves, jams, pickles, bottled fruit, and the like. The larder floor was tiled. On the floor in one corner, Dorothy kept milk bottles in a basin of water; the water helped keep the milk cool. Dorothy occasionally salted an earthenware jar of runner beans to preserve them. A variety of vendors delivered foods to the home, including the milkman who made his rounds every day except Sunday. A baker with a huge basket of breads likewise made daily rounds through the neighborhood.

Every day, Dorothy prepared a hot breakfast for the family, a hot meal at midday, and tea in the late afternoon. The Goffs always had grilled bacon and tomatoes for breakfast, sometimes with sausages—at least they had sausages before the war began and rationing was implemented. Breakfast included toast, which Dorothy buttered in the kitchen before serving it, offering homemade marmalade as well. The family used the toast to soak up the "dip," that is, the fat that had been rendered out of the bacon. During winter, porridge was frequently on the breakfast menu. The family said grace before and after every meal.

Black tea was the breakfast beverage; coffee was nowhere to be seen. Walter drank his tea plain, while the others took theirs with milk or cream poured from a small pitcher on the table. Oatcakes, which were commonplace at breakfast, could be made two ways. One type originated in Scotland; these were crisp cakes about three inches across that one could purchase in most any market. Less common were the Staffordshire oatcakes that Dorothy made. Her oatcakes, which her family considered a treat, were soft and roughly nine inches across, about the size of a large pancake.

For the main meal of the day on Sundays, the practice in England was to have a "roast joint." A joint was a large piece of meat, usually containing a bone, that was cooked in one piece. Most often, the joint was beef, served with Yorkshire pudding, but sometimes the joint was lamb or mutton. Dorothy served mutton with a delicious home-made onion sauce. Sometimes she prepared pork with stuffing and applesauce for the Sunday lunch. What was left of the joint would be eaten cold on Monday and as far into the week as it would last. When the family got down to the last remnants, Dorothy would chop up the remaining bits of the joint and make them into a shepherd's pie or something similar.

It was extraordinary how Dorothy made food last through the

better part of the week without refrigeration. Chicken was expensive and rarely on the menu. The Goffs, being observant Catholics, ate fish on Fridays. During the week, once the joint had been exhausted, the family typically had sausages or chops for the noon meal. Dorothy occasionally made a savory stew that she sometimes paired with dumplings. She often served mashed parsnips with butter as a "veg" or brussels sprouts from the Goffs' vegetable patch.

The noon meal always included pudding (which much later came to be known as dessert). Pudding was usually something simple, such as apple pie or stewed fruit. Dorothy often made blancmange, a sweet dessert made with milk or cream and sugar, for the children. She thickened it with gelatin, cornstarch, or Irish moss (a type of seaweed that was processed into a powder and used for its thickening properties). Another choice for pudding was treacle tart. The tart was comprised of a pastry base that was covered with golden syrup and breadcrumbs or sometimes sprinkled with crushed corn flakes. If children were at the meal, Dorothy occasionally served a jelly (Jell-O) for pudding.

Afternoon tea, taken at five o'clock, was the last meal of the day. The foundation for tea was bread and butter with homemade jam, followed by cake. The children had to eat some bread and butter if they wanted cake; there was no going directly to the sweet stuff. Jelly was also sometimes a treat at tea; Dorothy typically served it with blancmange. Milk came in a jug. Jam was served in pots with special spoons, never from the jar.

The preparation of tea was subject to great ritual, although tea was in short supply once the war began. Dorothy purchased loose tea; the shop assistant weighed it and put it into bags made from sugar paper. At home, the tea was kept in a tea caddy, which was typically a nice wooden box or tin. When it came time to brew tea, Dorothy first warmed the pot, then measured out the tea with a shallow, round spoon. The "recipe" called for one spoon of tea for the pot and an additional spoonful for each person who was going to have some. Once the tea had steeped, milk was poured into the teacup. The tea was then poured into the teacups through a strainer which caught the leaves. There was also a "slop bowl" on the table into which the family poured any dregs that had slipped from the pot into the teacups before a second serving of tea was poured into the cups. Although tea was the last meal of the day, Dorothy typically brought the children a cup of milk and a biscuit (cookie) at bedtime to tide them over until morning.

Dorothy was, by all accounts, a good cook. She baked bread every week and frequently made egg custards for Walter, who suffered from a stomach ulcer. Dorothy also made damson jam using fruit from a damson tree in their garden. The damsons Dorothy used were small, dark red plums with a distinctive, somewhat astringent taste. Dorothy also bottled pears from the garden. Once the war began, the United States, Britain, Canada, and Australia encouraged their citizens to dig up their lawns and plant Victory Gardens to grow as much produce as they could. The Goffs did just that.

Dorothy came from the Potteries, on the Staffordshire/Derbyshire border in England's East Midlands region. She prepared some foods using regional recipes. Two of her specialties were Trentham and Bakewell tarts. Bakewell tarts originated in the picturesque town of Bakewell in the Derbyshire Peak District. The Bakewell tart was an easy-to-prepare, open-face tart made with plain flour, butter, water, jam, eggs, and almonds. The result was a tart with a fruit jam center and almonds sprinkled on top, good to be served for pudding or with afternoon tea. The Trentham tart was a sweet pastry filled with strawberry preserves and thick custard, topped with toasted coconut, and served with thick cream. Dorothy also made a tasty, rich, fruit cake for special occasions.

Walter bought his first car in 1939—a 1937 Ford 8. The Ford served the family well, making its way from Walter to Josephine and then to Kathleen. The family called the car "Jimmy" since its license plate was GME829. Walter was able to use Jimmy until 1943. Petrol and tires were rationed during the war, so Walter rarely used Jimmy over the next two years. He kept Jimmy in the garage, rolling him out only occasionally to take the family for picnics on Sundays and bank holidays. One such outing was to Bushey Heath, just north of Wealdstone, which had a lovely park with lawns on which the children played and trees with low branches suitable for climbing.

Since Trude had studied art history in college, the Ichenhäusers' weekend outings frequently included visits to England's many museums. During evenings at the Goffs' home the girls—Dorothy, Josephine, Renate, and Erica—sometimes took a deck of cards and played Racing Demon, which the Goffs called "Stop." Racing Demon was a game in which players raced to the conclusion by trying to get rid of their cards as quickly as possible. The game was played without the players taking turns in what was a sort of card free-for-all. The Goffs' house soon began to feel like a home away from home.

School in Harrow Weald

S INCE THE GOFFS WERE DEVOUT CATHOLICS, THEIR CHIL-
dren attended Catholic schools. The Goffs met with the administrators at the Sacred Heart High School in Wealdstone and explained
the Ichenhäusers' situation. Sacred Heart was a tuition school run by
the Sisters of Our Lady of the Missions. The student body was half
Catholic and half Anglican. While denominated a "high school," it
also had a junior school for children ages four to ten. At age eleven
students typically moved to the senior section. The students wore
uniforms, sometimes referred to as "gymslips," comprised of white,
long-sleeved blouses and navy-blue jumpers. The Sisters generously
agreed to let Renate and Erica attend without paying tuition.

It was a bit of an odd situation in that these young, Jewish
refugees were required to attend catechism classes. Renate sat and listened dutifully. However, she was not swayed into thinking of herself
as Catholic, nor did she regard the catechism classes as an effort to
convert her and Erica. She felt that she and Erica were well-accepted
by the other girls at school. Erica's recollection was that half the students went to Bible study instead of catechism and that is what she
and Renate did.

No surprise, the curriculum included a great deal of English
history. Erica got to the point at which she could recite the names of
England's queens and kings in chronological order, no small feat for
a child only nine years old.

Sacred Heart was a ten-minute walk from the Goffs' home.

Each school day began with an all-school assembly during which the students stood with their classmates while they listened to announcements. The girls then sang a few hymns, after which the school played a march, and the girls strode single file in time to the music to their classrooms. Years later, at age eighty-seven, Erica could still hum the tune "Country Garden" to which they left the assembly.

Lunch at Sacred Heart school was a hearty affair, just as the mid-day meal at home was the main meal of the day. Typical school "dinners" had two courses, the main course being variously sausage and mash, liver, shepherd's pie, corned beef, and, of course, fish or fish fingers on Fridays. The second course—the pudding—was typically rice pudding, crumble, treacle stodge (steamed sponge cake with golden syrup), semolina (a sweet dessert made from semolina and milk), or custard with stewed plums. Of course, the girls said grace before lunch.

The Ichenhäusers had found a warm and hospitable refuge while they bided their time waiting for the visas that would allow them to enter the United States. Words could not adequately convey their gratitude to the Goffs, a family who opened their home and upended their lives to host two young girls and provide emotional support and assistance to the girls' parents. The Goffs were quiet, generous, unassuming heroes.

LET'S HOPE ONE DAY
THE TIME COMES

WHILE MAX, TRUDE, AND THE GIRLS HAD ESCAPED, Ernst, Max's father David, and Trude's parents Sigmund and Martha remained stranded in Germany.

Grandma Martha and Grandpa Sigmund did their best to deal with the heartache of being separated from their daughter, son-in-law, and granddaughters:

> My good Renate, sweet little Eri!
>
> You've now been gone for over two weeks. My beloved children, I think about you so much and it makes me happy that you are with your beloved Kathleen's parents and sisters. I know that you are in good hands, which is a tremendous relief for me. That means that dad and mom can do what they need to do without being disturbed by you. How nice that you can help out a bit [at the Goffs]. I know how much fun it was when you were simply around and kept me company in the kitchen... Dearest Eri, your little [stuffed] dogs will go along [in the shipping container] and will be glad to see you again. They are sitting up there [in your room] all by themselves and are sad. They couldn't possibly understand that you simply had to leave.
>
> Today, Fritz and Herbert also left Hamburg on the steamer. They were very happy about the fact that they would be seeing their father again soon. I gave Fritz as a memento a compass and to Herbert a magnifying glass for the stamps, etc....It's very

quiet at our place, as you might imagine, but let's hope that one day the time does indeed come when we can be together again. The little picture with the fireplace made me very happy, firstly, because you dear Renate, made it and, secondly, because I see how you keep warm in England. Mom and Dad [Trude and Max] complain a lot about the cold. We are very spoiled by our heating. Today the sun looks magnificent and is already shining through the window. It's probably even warmer in England. I certainly hope so for you.

How is school? Are you still on vacation? Your English skills will improve, which is the most important thing at the moment. Last week, Miss Conrad visited me. We spoke of you very affectionately. She would also very much like to go to England. She has friends who could take care of her, but she cannot get in. With all the pain of separation, how good it is that you are away—that we don't have to relive how they [the Gestapo] picked up your good father.

I wanted to send you a little package, but mother writes that you have enough of everything, so I'm instead sending the little package to your parents who probably have more of an appetite for it. They will share some with you…

My good children, I will now close this letter. Grandpa will take the letter to the post office and visit Grandpa Ichenhäuser on the way. Please say hello to Mr. and Mrs. Goff for me and give Dorothy and Josephine a little kiss. Heartfelt kisses to both of you.

Yours,

Grandma

My dear Renate, My dear little Eri!

The little kisses you sent me made me very happy. I preferred the little kisses you gave me [when you were] here…Hopefully you have adjusted well to your new surroundings. I think that you will soon be in a good school and then you'll also be closer to your parents. Write again soon. Greetings to the Goffs and to you two.

Many kisses from your grandpa who loves you very much.

Grandpa (Martha and Sigmund letter to Max, Trude, and the girls, January 31, 1939.)

Max attempted to make sure that Trude's parents were provided for. He wrote to his bank in Cologne instructing it to continue paying the monthly allowance he had established for Sigmund and Martha. Communication with the bank was difficult, but Max persisted. If he and Trude could not be with their parents, Max could at least try to make sure their parents had enough money to meet their needs.

Martha wrote again in advance of Renate's birthday:

My dear, good little Renate!

This is the first time that we cannot spend your birthday together with you and that we can only be there with you in our precious thoughts. My dear child, from the first day you were born, the only thing you have given me is joy. I don't recall a single memory of you giving me cause to be angry with you. On the contrary, you have been my sunshine, and it is with profound love that I think of you, my good child. Stay healthy and hopefully we will see each other again. I can't give you anything. First of all, you have everything, and secondly, I did not know yet to whom to give the [tennis] racket, but it will come. I gave a man something yummy [for you] and he will give it to your parents when he meets them. Save some of it, because a time may come when I can no longer send anything—at least that's what people are saying! Your dear little letter made me very happy and so did the one little Eri [Erica] sent; I was proud of you when I read it. Your writing is so expressive and full of character. If you continue like that, you will find your path in life, and you will only make your parents and us happy.

So, in school you are doing well, and the kids are nice to you. It's great that you are in a class at school that's actually too advanced for you and that you can keep up—and on top of it in a foreign language in another country. Liese and Lore [cousins] are also in England now—maybe you will see each other. That would be a lot easier if counting every penny wasn't such a necessity… If there's anything else you'd like, please write to me. In the meantime, I also send Puck; [Puck was the protagonist in a series of children's books. It was also the title of the series.] the good man only had two copies. The enclosed card came from the Daily Mail [a British newspaper]. Plump Ernst gave me a box of Sprengel for you—don't forget to say thank you...

I wish you, dear child, a happy birthday. Sending warm greetings and kisses to you and little Eri.

Grandma (Martha Letter to Renate, March 5, 1939.)

"Plump Ernst" was not Uncle Ernst since he was slim; the reference to Sprengels was to Sprengel chocolates, a well-known brand of German chocolate that is still available today.

In the midst of the green refuge of the village of Harrow Weald, the Ichenhäusers had found shelter from the storm in Germany. However, their relief at having escaped was greatly tempered by worries about their family members who were desperate to get out, but who so far had been unable to find a way.

1939 — THE WAR BEGINS IN EARNEST

IN JANUARY 1939, THE NAZIS SUPPLEMENTED THE CITIZEN-ship law to prohibit Jews from being pharmacists, dentists, and veterinarians. On April 30, 1939, Germany lifted its rent control laws as to Jewish residents. Yet the nations of the world, including Great Britain and the United States, refused to increase or assist Jewish emigration and, in some cases, sought to impede Jewish emigration:

> In the spring of 1939, Great Britain, increasingly worried by the pro-Axis shift in the Arab world—a trend with possibly dire consequences for Britain in case of war—reneged on its commitments and for all practical purposes closed the doors of Palestine to Jewish immigration. And, after slightly liberalizing its immigration policy in 1937, the United States did not even fill the quotas for Germany and Austria in 1938. In July 1939 the Wagner-Rogers Child Refugee Bill, which would have allowed twenty thousand Jewish refugee children to enter the country, was not passed by the Senate, and, at the same time, despite all entreaties, the 936 hapless Jewish emigrants from Germany who had sailed on the soon-to-be-notorious St. Louis, after being denied entry to Cuba, their destination, were not admitted into the United States.[221]

In a colossal failure of leadership and demonstrating a staggering lack of empathy, President Roosevelt did not take a position on the Wagner-Rogers Child Refugee bill. The bill never even reached

---

221 *Nazi Germany and the Jews*, Saul Friedlander, at 128.

a vote in Congress; it died in committee because anti-immigrant sentiment was so strong. Opponents of the legislation argued that admitting refugee children would take jobs away from American children.[222] The concern was not that adult Jewish immigrants might take work from American adults, but rather that Jewish children might displace American children who, in any event, should be in school and not working. It seemed that not even Jewish children could find a safe haven in the United States.

> Those in power in the State Department insisted on enforcing the nation's immigration laws as strictly as possible. Breckinridge Long, the State Department officer responsible for issuing visas, was deeply anti-Semitic. He was determined to limit immigration and used the State Department's power to create a number of barriers that made it almost impossible for refugees to seek asylum in the United States.[223]

Apparently, Mr. Long had never visited the Statue of Liberty or otherwise read the words of Emily Lazarus's moving poem affixed to the statue's base. Nor did he seem familiar with that portion of the Constitution guaranteeing freedom of religion and equal protection under the law. As a result, twenty thousand Jewish children who might have been admitted to the United States and been saved, instead, were sent to death camps where the Nazis murdered them.

Britain was accepting only five hundred emigrants a week; it refused to take more. The British ambassador in Washington offered the U.S. State Department one half of the British immigration quota (65,000 per year) to be filled with emigrants from Germany and Austria; the State Department flatly refused.

Britain compounded the deadly effect of its policies limiting Jewish emigration to Britain by issuing its infamous "White Paper" in April 1939 restricting Jewish emigration to Palestine. Britain was anxious to avoid inflaming Arab anti-Jewish sentiment that it feared would ensue if Britain allowed Jews to immigrate to Palestine.

---

222 *The Holocaust Encyclopedia*, United States and the Refugee Crisis, 1938-1941.

223 WWW.FACINGHISTORY.ORG/DEFYING-NAZIS/AMERICA-AND-HOLOCAUST.

Britain was anxious to curry Arab favor to help maintain the British military position in the Mediterranean. Britain wanted to secure safe transit of British shipping through the Suez Canal should Britain find itself at war with Germany. In furtherance of this objective, over the next five years, during the height of the War and while the Nazis were slaughtering millions of Jews, Britain allowed only 75,000 Jews to enter Palestine.

By 1939, only one safe haven remained open to German Jews and that was Japanese-controlled Shanghai. Shanghai did not require visas for entry to the city. Ultimately, eighteen thousand Jews reached safety in Shanghai, albeit in a land exceedingly foreign to them.

The United States continued to keep its doors almost entirely closed to Jewish refugees.

> "The free admission of aliens into the United States on the basis of their allegations that they were suffering from racial, religious or political persecutions in their own countries would be almost sure to lead to delicate and hazardous diplomatic situations which would not be in the public interest," Undersecretary of State and flaming anti-Semite Sumner Welles declared in 1939.[224]

That purported public interest, which was barely hidden by the flimsy fig leaf Welles' phrasing sought to provide, was to maintain the racial and religious composition of the United States as it was prior to WWII. In 1938, the United States had immigration quotas limiting the number of people it would accept from each nationality already present in the U.S. The objective was to maintain the makeup of the United States as it existed first in 1921 and then in 1927, except for immigrants from Japan and China who were subject to more severe limits. These restrictions made German-Jewish emigration to the United States problematic since there were so few spots to be had relative to the number of Jews seeking to flee Germany. Under-Secretary Welles desperately wanted to avoid diluting the country's "racial and religious composition" with "aliens" who were different from those people already in the United States. This thinking was, if

---

224 *Flight from The Reich* at 144.

truth be told, not much different from the Nazi ideology specifying who could be members of the German "Volk."

The State Department was so rife with anti-Semitism that, in 1943, officials there prevented reports describing the Nazis' mass murders of Jews from reaching the United States. The State Department was anxious to avoid disclosing information that might increase pressure to help Europe's Jews, let alone admit those Jews to the United States.

Anti-Jewish sentiment and political discourse in Britain were not much better. As put by British Home Secretary Sir Samuel Hoare, "it would be necessary for the Home Office to discriminate very carefully as to the type of refugee who could be admitted to this country. If a flood of the wrong type of immigrants were allowed in there might be a serious danger of anti-Semitic feeling being aroused in this country. The last thing we wanted here," he concluded, "was the creation of a Jewish problem."[225] It was shocking to hear British politicians echo Nazi rhetoric with respect to potentially having a "Jewish problem." Rather than focus on the humanitarian issue of saving lives or trying to educate reactionary elements in Britain to be more tolerant, Britain by and large opted to wave off desperate Jews trying to find refuge. They were, apparently, the "wrong type of immigrants."

Britain eventually relaxed its rules at least enough to allow "trans-migrants" such as the Ichenhäusers to enter the country temporarily. Trans-migrants were immigrants who had credible proof they would be able to emigrate from Britain to another country within two years. If an immigrant had an American quota number valid for immigration in 1940 or 1941, the immigrant could enter Britain. However, the restrictive U.S. immigration policies that only grudgingly granted visas meant this exception was of limited value.

Notwithstanding Britain's restrictive immigration policy, thousands of Jewish children were able to escape Germany by means of the "Kindertransport." The Kindertransport was organized to get Jewish children out of harm's way. "The British government allowed Jewish aid organizations to arrange the immigration of children

---

225 *Flight from the Reich* at 148.

under seventeen and have them cared for by English foster parents. In total, the 'Kindertransports' saved close to 10,000 Jewish children from Germany, Austria, Czechoslovakia, and Poland. Many of the children never saw their parents again."[226] As for those children who did not get out, it has been estimated that the Nazis murdered between one and one and one-half million Jewish children during the Holocaust.[227]

Lene and Max Berlin were cousins on Trude's side of the family. Max Berlin was born in Rommerskirchen, northwest of Cologne, on March 16, 1887. Like David and Emma Ichenhäuser's sons, Max served in the German army during WWI. He came from an observant family and adhered to Orthodox practices. After the war, Max married Helene Voos, who tragically died giving birth to their daughter, Lisselotte, on March 1, 1924.

Several years later, Max married another Helene, that being Helene ("Lene") Roesberg, who also was from Rommerskirchen. They had a son, Gerhard Robert, on February 14, 1930. Max owned a stationery store in Cologne on Rubenstrasse, while Lene ran their household at 49 Mastrichstrasse and cared for Lisselotte and Gerhard.

By the end of 1938, Max and Lene knew their family had no future in Germany. Max was active in the Kindertransport; he and Lene eventually concluded they had to use the Kindertransport to get Lisselotte and Gerhard out of Germany while hoping that Lene and Max could find a way to join them. Lene's mother had dementia, and she and Max were reticent to leave her alone in Germany, and so they stayed. Gerhard was nine and Lisselotte (who went by Liesel) was fifteen when they left Cologne on August 24, 1939, aboard what was the last Kindertransport to leave Germany.

The Kindertransport placed Gerhard and Liesel with the Malones, an Irish Catholic family who lived at 20 Woodstock Road in the Redland neighborhood of Bristol, a city west of London near Britain's Atlantic coast. The Malones lived on a tree-lined street

---

226 *Jewish Daily Life* at 355.

227 *The Holocaust Encyclopedia*; United States Holocaust Memorial Museum, "Life in the Shadows: Hidden Children and the Holocaust, the Plight of Jewish Children."

in a two-story, field-stone home with bay windows and a peaked roof. Lene frequently wrote to Gerhard and Liesel urging them to behave, help around the house, and reminding Gerhard to wash his hands and trim his fingernails. Lene was happy to read Liesel's letters reporting that Liesel was washing and ironing her own laundry so as to spare Mrs. Malone from that additional chore.

Lisselotte attended and completed "Finishing School" in England. However, her classmates made fun of her name, calling her "Lies-a-lot." As a result, Lisselotte decided to change her name and go by Elizabeth. Upon completing her schooling, Elizabeth worked as a seamstress and later took an industrial "Rosie the Riveter" job. Life in England had additional challenges for Elizabeth. Upon turning seventeen, the British security forces required that she live in an internment camp. Apparently, the British felt that Elizabeth, as an adult, might be a security risk. Perhaps they worried that with her parents still in Germany, the Nazis might threaten harm to Max and Lene if Elizabeth did not commit espionage for the Germans. For the balance of the war, Elizabeth spent nights in the camp, but she was allowed to leave during the day to work and help look after Gerhard. Somehow, Elizabeth was able to ensure that Gerhard received a Jewish education and even arranged for him to be bar mitzvah in 1943 at the Park Row Synagogue in Bristol.

Meanwhile, the Reich continued to tighten the screws on those Jews still in Germany. On February 21, 1939, the Reich issued an edict seizing even more Jewish property than it had already taken through the forced Aryanization program. The "Decree Concerning the Surrender of Precious Metals and Stones in Jewish Ownership" required Jews to turn over to the authorities all gold, silver, diamonds, and other valuables without compensation.[228] A failure to do so would, if discovered, in all likelihood lead to immediate execution.

While the Ichenhäusers bided their time in England, the Continent slid further towards war. "On March 15, 1939, the Wehrmacht occupied the remainder of Czechoslovakia. As a practical matter, Czechoslovakia had now ceased to exist. Slovakia became a German-satellite; the Czech states of Bohemia and

---

228 *Holocaust Encyclopedia*, Anti-Semitic Legislation 1933-1939.

Moravia were turned into a protectorate of the Reich."[229] France and Britain, who had guaranteed the independence of what remained of Czechoslovakia—after they had betrayed that nation by forcing it to cede the Sudetenland to Germany—did nothing.

German now controlled territory on three sides of Poland: East Prussia to the north; Germany to the west; and Slovakia along Poland's southwestern border. Poland's military situation and its ability to defend itself were now in a posture frighteningly similar to that which led to the demise of Czechoslovakia, which Germany had surrounded on three sides before it occupied and dismembered the Czech nation.

In April 1939, Hitler announced that Germany was abrogating the German-Polish non-aggression pact of 1934, the Anglo-German Naval Agreement of 1935 (which placed limits on the size and composition of the German navy), and the Anglo-German Consultative Pact to which Hitler and Chamberlain had agreed in September of 1938. Hitler demanded that the Reich be allowed take control of the free city of Danzig (known as Gdansk in Polish) which was wedged between the Polish Corridor to the west and East Prussia to the east.

The dispute over Danzig and the Polish corridor stemmed from the aftermath of WWI. Poland had ceased to exist as an independent nation in 1795. It had been the victim of three successive partitions by Russia, Germany, and Austria in which each of those nations took chunks of Polish territory until no independent Polish state remained. After WWI, the Allies reestablished an independent Poland as part of the Treaty of Versailles. The Poles insisted and the victorious Allies agreed that, for Poland to be economically viable, it needed access to the Baltic Sea. The Allies decided the way to accomplish that was to give Poland a corridor of territory to the sea across land that had been part of Germany. This had the consequence of separating the German state of East Prussia from the rest of Germany. The Treaty of Versailles also made the formerly German city of Danzig an independent, "free" city governed under the auspices of the League of Nations.

Hitler demanded that Poland grant Germany a corridor fifteen

---

229 *Nazi Germany and the Jews* at 131.

and one-half miles-wide to run from Germany through Poland to Danzig and East Prussia. This was part of Hitler's drive to reunite all German territory and ethnic Germans within the borders of the Third Reich, as well as his desire to obtain Lebensraum ("living space") for the Reich to the east of Germany. This Lebensraum was, in Hitler's psychotic worldview, necessary for the economic health of the German nation. Poland flatly refused his demands. In May, Hitler again insisted that Poland grant Germany a corridor to Danzig. Poland again refused. Tensions escalated to the point that Poland began deploying much of its one million men under arms toward the German-Polish border.

In the face of Hitler's saber-rattling, as well as being belatedly sobered by Hitler's seizure of Austria and Czechoslovakia, Britain and France pledged to defend Poland if Germany attacked and the Poles resisted. Whether this offer of protection was worth more than the guarantees Britain and France had given to Czechoslovakia remained to be seen.

In May, Italy and Germany signed the military alliance that came to be known as the "Pact of Steel." Mussolini, hoping for glory by entering into the alliance, tied his fate and that of his country to Hitler. The pompous, preening Duce would pay dearly for his decision.

On August 24, 1939, to the shock and dismay of Britain and France, Germany and Russia signed a ten-year non-aggression pact. The pact provided Hitler the comfort of knowing that, if and when he attacked Western Europe, he did not need to worry about Russia attacking Germany from the east, which would have forced Germany to fight a two-front war. Hitler was, at least in the short term, anxious to avoid such a predicament and the enormous military jeopardy it would present to Germany. Russia and Germany also entered into secret protocols whereby Hitler would invade Poland from the west and Russia in turn would occupy Poland from the east. Stalin took a page from Hitler's playbook by using purported danger to Russian citizens in Poland as an excuse to seize Polish territory. Hitler hoped that Russian intervention would deflect from Germany at least some of the international outrage he anticipated would result from Germany's attack on the Poles.

Hitler rebuffed London's efforts to avoid war. He calculated that Britain's and France's pledges to protect Polish independence would turn out to be of no consequence, as had been the case with their warnings to Hitler regarding Czechoslovakia. However, Britain and France began mobilizing their armed forces by calling up reservists. They also began positioning men and material to be ready for action should Germany attack Poland and Britain and France have to act on their guarantees. "In effect, Herr Hitler told the (British) ambassador that Britain had no business in Eastern Europe and that her guarantee of Poland merely encourages Polish resistance to German demands, therefore it was up to Britain to persuade the Poles to yield or face the consequences."[230]

In a pre-ordained outcome and notwithstanding Hitler's spurious claims of having tried to avoid conflict, on Sept. 1, 1939, Germany attacked Poland based on fraudulent German claims that Poland had violated the border. Hitler shamelessly fulminated: "Germans in Poland are persecuted with a blood terror and are driven from their homes. The series of border violations, which are unbearable for a great power, prove that the Poles no longer are willing to respect the German frontier. In order to put an end to this frantic activity, no other means is left to me now than to meet force with force."[231] None of this was true. Nevertheless, Hitler launched a massive blitzkrieg that sent one and a half million German soldiers, supported by tanks, artillery, and aircraft, pouring eastward across the Polish border. The Wehrmacht launched attacks towards Warsaw from the north, south, and west.

On September 3, Britain and France fulfilled their pledges to Poland by declaring war on Germany. Undaunted, Hitler continued his onslaught against the Poles. Chamberlain called on the British Empire to join in the fight against the Nazis while Britain and France mobilized. Chamberlain appointed Winston Churchill to be

---

230   *The New York Times*, August 24, 1938, p. 1.

231   *The New York Times*, September 1, 1939, p. 1.

the First Lord of the Admiralty, which made Churchill the Cabinet Minister in charge of Britain's Navy.

Germany swiftly brought the war to Britain when, on Sept. 4, a German U-boat torpedoed and sank the British passenger liner Athenia 200 miles west of the Hebrides Islands off Scotland's western coast. Of the 1400 passengers, which included 292 Americans and many British children who were being sent to Canada for safety during the conflict, 112 died. Britain responded by announcing a naval blockade of Germany. The British used their enormous deep-water fleet to seal off German shipping from the Baltic, North, and Mediterranean Seas. Hitler's bloodless conquests were behind him; only bloodbaths lay ahead. World War II had begun.

On Sept. 17, 1939, barely two weeks after Germany had invaded Poland, Soviet troops invaded pursuant to the secret protocols Hitler and Stalin had signed. Russia claimed it invaded "to protect its own interests and to protect the White Russians and Ukrainian minorities" in Poland. Britain hastily set up convoys for its merchant ships in the Atlantic after U-boats sank twenty-one British vessels in the first two weeks of the war. The Poles put up fierce resistance, but their largely obsolete military, which included cavalry, was no match for the Nazi onslaught. On September 27, after barely four weeks of combat, Poland surrendered.

Now that war had begun, Britain began evacuating children from its large cities to protect them from the Nazi aerial bombing the government expected. "The greatest movement of population at short notice in the history of Great Britain is under way. It is an evacuation, under government order, of little children, invalids, women and old men from congested areas. From London, Birmingham, Manchester, Liverpool, Edinburgh, Glasgow and 23 other cities the great exodus is going on as this dispatch is being written. The numbers are stupendous. More than 3,000,000 of these helpless beings are being taken out of danger of German bombs."[232]

Max and Trude watched the events unfolding on the continent with alarm. Although they were in a state of limbo in Britain, they seemed momentarily immune from the conflict as daily life in Britain

232 *The New York Times*, September 1, 1939, p. 1.

continued without major disruption. "On September 30, 1939, the World War broke out. It brought blackouts, registration, trial and restrictions for aliens. Life [in England], however, went on quite normally." (Max's Green Diary.) However, their family in Cologne was not immune from the conflict and there was little Max and Trude could do for them.

As the war began and through its early months, Germany took further punitive actions against its Jewish population. On September 1, 1939, the Reich announced a curfew prohibiting Jews from leaving their homes after 8:00 p.m. during the winter and 9:00 p.m. in the summer.[233] Jews were forbidden to own radios.[234] On September 20, police began confiscating radios, leaving Jews with few ways to learn what was happening in connection with the war and in other regards. New regulations barred Jews from using public transportation. Once Allied bombing began, Jews were forbidden to use public air raid shelters.

On December 7, the regime reduced food rations for Jews to a level far below those allotted to the general populace. "Even before the start of the war, butter, eggs and oils were rationed."[235] However, Jews were soon subjected to even more dire food ration discrimination:

> As of 1940-41, they no longer received rice, legumes, canned vegetables, coffee, tea, cocoa, artificial honey, sweets, fruit, poultry, game or smoked foods. The only vegetables they could buy were rutabagas, cabbage and beets. In 1942, other products were added to the list of foods not available to Jews, including meat and meat products, eggs, wheat products, whole milk, and even "fresh skimmed milk," a product invented by the Nazis. If they received any food packages from abroad, the contents were subtracted from the allotted ration.[236]

Further, Jews were limited to shopping only at certain stores,

---

233 *Jewish Daily Life* at 360.

234 *Jewish Daily Life* at 360.

235 *Jewish Daily Life* at 281.

236 *Jewish Daily Life* at 281.

"meaning that as of mid-1941, hour-long 'shopping marches' often became necessary."[237] Jews were allowed to shop only during a one to one-and-a-half-hour time frame, usually late in the day when most stores had already sold out of their goods.[238] Hunger, in addition to hate, now permeated the lives of those Jews still in Germany.

---

237 *Jewish Daily Life* at 281.

238 *Jewish Daily Life* at 282.

Martha and Sigmund Moses at their 25th
wedding anniversary celebration, 1925

Trude, February 1925

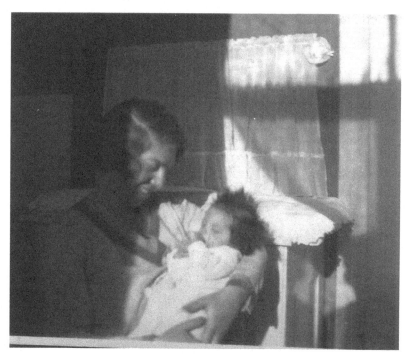

Renate is born March 7, 1928

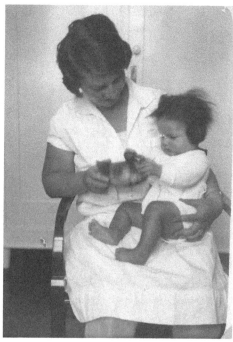

Trude and Renate, July 1928

Renate in her pram, summer 1928

Trude at the Gornergrat, Switzerland, July 1928

Max and Trude at the Gornergrat, July 1928, with
the Matterhorn in the background

Max hiking in the Riffelalp, July 1928

Max and Trude take a break while hiking in the Alps, July 1928

Max and Renate, December 1928

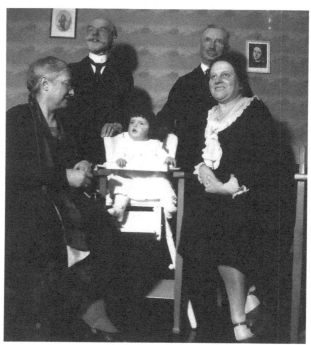

Renate with (L-R) Emma and David Ichenhäuser
and Sigmund and Martha Moses

Martha and Sigmund Moses take Renate for
a walk in the Stadtwald, June 1929

Emma and David Ichenhäuser take Renate
for a walk, December 1929

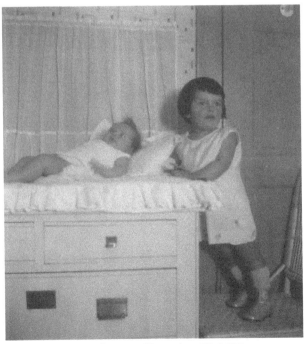

Erica is born on November 25, 1929,
seen here with Renate in 1930

Erica, Trude, Renate, and Max, June 1930

Renate, Erica, and grandmother Emma
Ichenhauser, December 1930

David and Emma Ichenhäuser with Max, summer 1930

Max standing alongside Lake St. Moritz, summer 1931

Trude with her alpenstock, summer 1931

Max and Trude hiking in the Rosegtal near St. Moritz, July 1931

The Ichenhäusers' new home at 412 Aachenerstrasse, July 1932. The open corner in the upper left was the rooftop garden and play area

Renate and Erica in front of the family home with the sign for Max's medical practice behind them

Erica and Renate dressed for Karnival, spring 1933

Renate and Erica with Sigmund and Martha Moses, July 1933

Renate, Max, and Erica, summer 1933, the year Hitler came to power

Renate and Erica riding their scooters in the Stadtwald, summer 1933

Male alles bunt an. Betrachte dir das Bild ganz genau, damit du nachher sagen kannst, was alles darauf ist.

A page from one of Renate's elementary school workbooks. "Paint everything colorful; take a close look at the picture so that you can tell afterwards what is on it."

PFLANZEN	TIERE	DINGE
BAUM	HASE	GIESSKANNE
TULPE	EICHORN	HAMMER
BLATTER	STORCH	TINTE
KAKTUS	KAMEL	BALL
PILZ	MAUS	KRUG

MALE DIE BILDER BUNT AN UND SCHREIBE ALLES IN DAS RICHTIGE KÄSTCHEN.

A page from one of Renate's elementary school workbooks. "Color in the pictures and write everything in the correct box" (plant, animals, things)

Renate, age six, leaves for school, April 14, 1934

The Ichenhäusers take a road trip to Manderscheid
in central Germany, summer 1934

Emma and David Ichenhäuser, Sigmund and Martha
Moses, Renate and Erica at a party to celebrate David's 80th
birthday and Sigmund's 75th birthday, September 1934

Kathleen Goff joins the family, seen here with Trude and the girls
blowing bubbles on the roof of the family home in June 1935

Erica, Kathleen, and Renate, 1935

Kathleen sings while Renate and Erica row on a lake
in the Stadtwald, August 18, 1935

Renate, Trude, and Erica boating in the Stadtwald, August 18, 1935

Kathleen and the girls dressed for
Karnival, February 24, 1936

Max, unknown man, Kathleen, Renate,
and Erica on a picnic, May 24, 1936

Renate (age eight) and Erica (age six), 1936

The girls visit the Goff family in England. (L-R) Erica (age six), Joan (a friend of the Goffs), Kathleen, Josephine Goff, Dorothy Goff, and Renate (age eight), July 26, 1936

Renate and Erica help load cheese onto a barge at the cheese market in Alkmaar, Holland, August 1936

Renate and Erica at the beach in Holland, August 1936

Max, Trude, Renate, and Erica at the beach in Holland, August 1936

The girls are bronzed from the sun, August 1936

Renate, Max, and Erica, 1937

Sigbert and Edith Wachs with Max and the girls, 1937

Visiting Kathleen in Italy, where she went to work after the Nuremberg laws forced her to leave the Ichenhäusers' home. Photo taken at Lake Maggiore, 1937

Renate with her dreaded
accordion, October 1937

Erica, Max, Renate, and David Ichenhäuser, spring
1938. This is the last photograph of David

Trude's passport photo taken in the summer of
1938 in anticipation of leaving Germany

Max's passport photo, summer 1938

Renate's passport photograph taken in the
summer of 1938 when she was ten

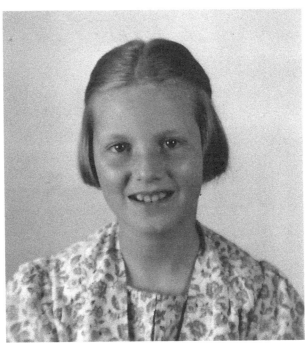

Erica's passport photograph, summer
of 1938, when she was eight

Dachau 25. XI. 38

Meine Lieben. Ich bin gesund, was ich auch von Euch hoffe. Hier kann ich mir alles kaufen. Wenn Ihr mir Geld schicken wollt, dann auf der Postanweisung mein Geburtsdatum, Block und Stube nicht vergessen. Viele Grüße an alle Bekannte und Verwandte. Mich holt. Herzliche Grüße und Küsse Euer Max.

post card from Dad from
concentration camp

The Nov. 25, 1938, postcard Max purportedly sent from Dachau after having been arrested the day after Kristallnacht, with a notation at the bottom that Renate made many years later

Passport cover

Max's Passport December '38 p. 2-3

Max's Passport December '38 p. 4-5

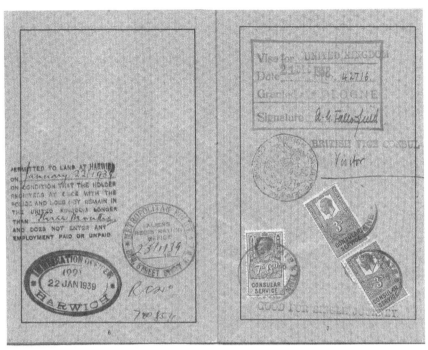

Max's Passport December '38 p. 6-7

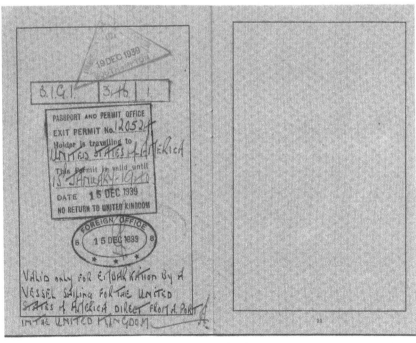

Max's Passport December '38 p. 10-11

Trude's Passport December '38 p.2-3

Trude's Passport December '38 p. 6-7

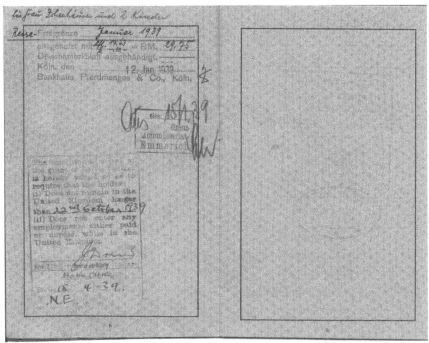

Trude's Passport December '38 p. 8-9

Trude's Passport December '38 p. 10-11

Hilde, Carl, Rolf, and Marianne Spiers

The December 21, 1938 "Notice Regarding Leaving" that Renate's school issued stating that Renate was a praiseworthy student and was leaving to emigrate to England

Amsterdam, the 17th of January.

Dear Mrs. Goff,

We are so happy to tell you that we arrived here safely. Although we have lost our home and left our parents behind us we are glad to be in a free country and to breathe freely. We intend to leave Holland on Saturday 21th at night and arrive in London on Sunday morning. If it is convenient to you we shall bring the children to you in the course of the afternoon. I do not know which arrangements you have made with Mrs. Paynter, that's why I only write to you and put everything into your hands. If there is something to tell us, please drop me a line to my adress here: Schönhäuser c/o. Mrs. Remanuel, Amsterdam, Albrecht Dürerstraat 9. I am downright thankful to you. Kindest regards to your husband, your children, Mrs. Paynter and to yourself yours very sincerely

T. Schönhäuser.

Trude's January 17, 1939, note (in perfect English),
to the Goffs telling them the family had escaped
from Germany and was in Amsterdam

31. Januar 1939.

Meine gute Renate, süßes Evilein!

Nun seid Ihr schon über 2 Wochen weg, meine geliebten Kinder wie viel denke ich an Euch, + bin ich nur froh, daß Ihr bei den Eltern + Schwestern von Euret so geliebten Kathleen seid. Ich weiß, daß Ihr gut aufgehoben seid, + ist das eine große Beruhigung für mich. Dadurch können Vati + Mutti alle Wege machen, ohne daß sie durch Euch gestört werden. Wie schön, daß Ihr etwas helfen könnt, ich weiß doch, wieviel Spaß es macht, wenn Ihr nur in der Küche so selbständig tüten könntet. Nun sind wir dabei alles vorzubereiten, weil übermorgen der Lift gepackt wird. Liebes Evilein, Deine Hundchen werden mitgehen + werden sich auf ein Wiedersehen mit Dir freuen. Sie sitzen so allein da oben + sind traurig, sie können ja nicht begreifen, daß Ihr weg mußtet. Auch Fritz + Herbert sind heute auf den Dampfer in Hamburg gegangen, sie freuen sich sehr ihren Vater bald wiederzusehen. Ich gab Fritz zum Andenken

The first page of Martha Moses's January 31, 1939 letter to Max, Trude, and the girls; this is the first letter Martha wrote to them after the family had left for England

Trude and Max, Mrs. Dorothy and Raymond Goff, Erica, Josephine
Goff, and Renate in Harrow Weald, England, 1939

Josephine Goff, Renate, and Erica (Renate and Erica sporting their newly-permed-hair) making snowmen (or snow somethings) in England, 1939

Holland-America Line. t.s.s. **VOLENDAM**. 15434 tons register - 25620 tons displacement

Holland-America Lines' Volendam, the ship the Ichenhäusers took from Southhampton to New York in December 1939

Renate, Erica, and a new friend aboard the Volendam

HOLLAND-AMERICA LINE

R.M.S. *Volendam*,
Dec. 28th 1939.

Dear all of you,
As the sea is fairly calm to-day, and as it is too cold to stay on deck I will write to you. Now I will tell you about our journey.

We left Waterloo at 8 p.m. and went to the station where we met our friends. We reached Southhampton in two hours and had to stand for ages for passport control and as it was not very warm our feet were nearly falling off. Then we went aboard a little steamer which took us to this big liner, because it did not came into the docks. We sailed next morning at about six. The weather was fine and sunny and we could see the English coast very well. We also saw the coast-guards, they were aeroplanes on the water for quite a long way.

First page of Renate's December 28, 1939,
letter to the Goffs from aboard the Volendam

The last page of Renate's December 28, 1939, letter to the Goffs from aboard the Volendam, with her sketches of the ship, a map showing the ship's location, and Renate's Dutch doll

To d Schönhausen and family from

Klieforth family photograph sent to Max on
January 2, 1939. L-R: Alexander, Leslie (seated)
Consul A.W. Klieforth, and Barbara Klieforth

A. W. Klieforth and family, in appreciation. Cologne. Jan. 2. 1939.

Back of the Klieforth family photograph sent to Max on January 2, 1939

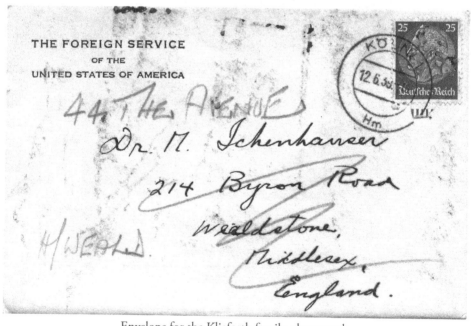

Envelope for the Klieforth family photograph

Dear Dr. Schenhausen

Thanks for your
letter of recent date. I
have hopes of seeing
you in London on
June 4th or 5th. if I can
get away. If so. I'll
let you know.
With my best
wishes to all of you. I am
Your very sincerely.
Klieforth

May 22. 1939

Klieforth note to Max, May 22, 1939

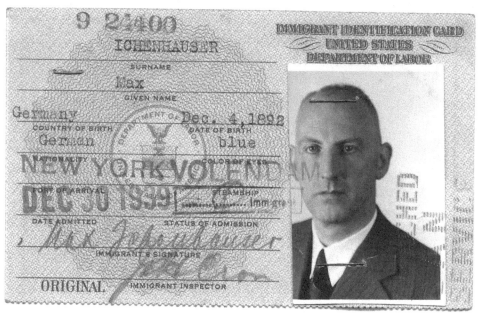

Max's U.S. Immigration ID Card December '39

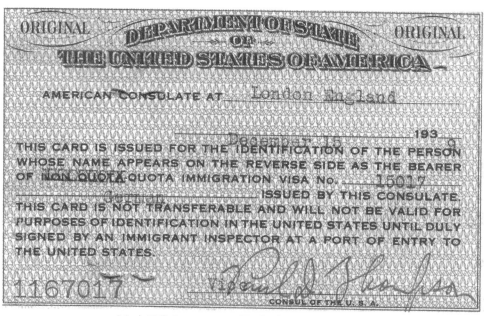

Max's U.S. Immigration ID Card December '39 p.2

KATHLEEN THE CODEBREAKER

KATHLEEN WAS WORKING IN CAPRI, ITALY, IN 1939 WHEN news came that war had broken out. She immediately returned to Britain. Because of her excellent German, she went to work as a secretary for an Austrian who managed a silk mill in Jedburgh in the Scottish borderlands. The mill manufactured the silk thread used to manufacture parachutes. However, the British soon interned the manager as a security risk, which left Kathleen unemployed.

Kathleen got on her bicycle and pedaled south from Scotland to volunteer for the Women's Auxiliary Air Force (the "WAAF"). The WAAF's most significant activities included working at radar stations to help direct air traffic and plot air routes in operations rooms—including during the Battle of Britain, the seminal air battle of the war. Other WAAF responsibilities included packing parachutes, performing aircraft maintenance, operating transport, handling communications operations, codes and ciphers, and conducting intelligence activities. The women who joined the WAAF (they were referred to as "WAAFs") were trained at West Drayton, Harrogate, Bridgnorth, Innsworth, and Wilmslow.[239]

Because of her fluency in German, Kathleen was assigned to the Y Service, made up of a group of WAAFs who listened to German pilots' radio transmissions. The WAAFs took down and translated everything the pilots said. The Royal Air Force ("RAF") did not designate the WAAFs as code breakers; the WAAFs passed their transcriptions to code breakers at Bletchley Park. It was the codebreakers at Bletchley Park who ultimately broke Germany's top secret "Enigma" code, which in turn informed crucial strategic decisions the Allies made over the course of the war.

Nevertheless, by listening to the Luftwaffe pilots' transmissions, plotting the pilots' actions, and comparing certain German words with certain outcomes, the WAAFs were able to decipher a great deal of the German radio traffic. This decoding was extraordinarily helpful to the British air defenses in deciding how to respond to German air attacks. The WAAF intelligence about how many German fighters and bombers were approaching, from what direction, at what altitude, and what their targets might be affected RAF decisions such as how many fighters to send up to meet impending bomber attacks, from what direction and altitude the RAF fighters should approach, and to alert anti-aircraft batteries in the areas towards which the Luftwaffe was headed. The WAAF decoding also helped Britain plan offensive sorties since they could largely understand what German air defenders were planning to do.

Since Kathleen was also fluent in Italian, the WAAF eventually transferred her to Cairo to monitor the Italian military's radio transmissions. When the Allies defeated the Italian army in North Africa and Italian forces were no longer active in the eastern Mediterranean, "Section Officer M.K. 'Rusty' Goff, an ex-Kingsdown WAAF who was experienced in both German and Italian air traffic," was transferred to the North African units of the WAAF and British forces further west in North Africa.[240] Kathleen was eventually sent "to work with the field unit sited at Ain Draham and later on the Cap Bon peninsula in Tunisia, where she would be the only woman in the team."[241] Ain Draham was in northwestern Tunisia, while the Cap Bon peninsula was on Tunisia's northeastern coast. In Tunisia, "Rusty" trained U.S. airmen regarding how to take down German transmissions for use by Allied code breakers and interpreters.

Kathleen's unit later moved without her to Sicily after the Allied invasion of the island. Kathleen was chagrined not to have been

---

240 *The Enemy Is Listening*, Aileen Clayton, Ballantine Books (1980), at 250.

241 *The Enemy Is Listening* at 256.

transferred there. "However, when the Italian naval vessels surrendered after the Armistice (with Italy), the energetic and irrepressible Rusty flew over, first to Taranto (on the northwestern edge of the "heel" of Italy's "boot") and then to Gibraltar, with our (the WAAF's) scientific officer, Eric Ackermann, to act as his interpreter when he examined the radar equipment on board the Italian warships."[242]

The WAAF eventually transferred Kathleen back to England, where her commanding officer assigned her the task of instructing U.S. service men on how to take down German transmissions while on aircraft flying missions over Germany. "When she had occasion to criticize the paucity of their logs during operational flights, she was challenged to do better herself. She took up the challenge, flying on a raid over Wilhelmshaven (on Germany's northern coast just west of Denmark). The logs that day were so good that Kingsdown control profusely praised them, while having no idea Rusty had prepared the logs since the American flight crew had smuggled her onto the plane for the mission.[243]

Kathleen's sister Dorothy also joined the WAAF. She worked at airfields driving the "tug" trucks that pulled aircraft out of their hangers and into position for takeoff. She was particularly proud to work with the Lancaster bombers, which became Britain's most successful and widely used bombers. The Lancasters carried a crew of seven, were equipped with eight Browning machine guns for defense, had a range of 1,660 miles, and could carry a bomb payload of 14,000 pounds. The Allied 1,000 bomber raid on Cologne was comprised of Lancaster bombers. It was an odd twist of fate that Dorothy helped position the bombers that attacked the home city of the Ichenhäuser family who only a few years earlier had stayed at Dorothy's family home.

---

242 *The Enemy Is Listening* at 315.

243 *The Enemy Is Listening* at 332.

THE ROTHSCHILDS IN LONDON

WITH HIS FAMILY SAFELY ENSCONCED IN LONDON, HANS David Rothschild put himself to work supporting the Allied war effort. Since Hans had worked in the metal fabrication industry in Germany, he was able to use his knowledge to help the RAF identify bombing targets to disrupt the Reich's ability to produce metal and fabricate metal products for the German war effort. Hans knew where all the steel mills and fabrication plants were located in Germany, as well as what they manufactured, so he was able to help the British pinpoint where they should send their bombers in order to have the maximum impact on the German military.

Hans and Leni's younger children, Anne and Peter, began to learn English. They eventually spoke a very "British" English in terms of their accent, idioms, and vocabulary. Hannah, their older daughter, enrolled in nursing school. Aanchen Simons, another cousin of Trude's, was also in London. Aanchen lived with the Rothschilds while she tried to get her husband, whom the Nazis had arrested in Germany, released from the concentration camp in which he was being held.

As war clouds gathered, Hans had an air raid shelter dug in their garden. It would protect them from bomb shrapnel but would not be of much use if they suffered a direct hit. Groundwater seeped into the shelter, so whenever they had to use it, they took turns operating a hand pump to keep water out.

In September 1938, when Hitler was threatening to invade

and dismember Czechoslovakia, residents of London, including Hans and Leni, were trying to decide whether they should evacuate their children to the countryside to get them out of harm's way in the event Hitler bombed London as a prelude to a Nazi invasion of England. Hans and Leni decided that Anne and Peter should evacuate with their classmates at the Woodstock School. Unfortunately, Anne sprained her ankle so badly that she could barely walk. As a result, she was quite worried she would not be able to leave with Peter. Nevertheless, Leni packed bags for them in the event they were instructed to leave over the next few days. Hannah was to stay in London with Hans and Leni.

One evening, Hans told the family that Chamberlain had gone to Munich in an effort to prevent war. By September 30, 1938, Chamberlain had negotiated the shameful pact pursuant to which Britain agreed that Hitler could occupy the Sudetenland portion of Czechoslovakia without resort to military force, resulting in the infamous "peace in our time" agreement. Anne wrote a school essay the next year in which she described these events: "By Oct. 30 it is all over. All of London is happy again. Peace, Peace! We knew there was not going to be a war."

Of course, the "peace" Chamberlain had secured did not hold. Anne described that turn of events in her essay: "Who asked if Hitler was going to stop marching? I? Never! There he has gone again threatening Poland. It's 1939." The British decided once again to evacuate children from London. This time, Anne and Peter were to be evacuated separately, since at that point they attended different schools.

Anne said goodbye to her family on August 31. She was to be evacuated from London the next day with her classmates. Anne was particularly upset to be leaving because Hannah's birthday was two days later. When Anne arrived at her school, she saw that many of the girls were teary-eyed. Anne resolved that she would not cry. She described the moment of departure in her essay: "Goodbye, goodbye see you soon. Come and visit me. Yes, I'll write often. Cheer up it's not so bad. Don't worry about me. I'll be alright, yes, I've got a hanky. Well, goodbye." Unfortunately, Hans and Leni would not be able to visit Anne. Germans were considered aliens and security risks and, therefore, were not allowed to travel within Britain.

Miss Potter, the headmistress of the school, did her best to encourage the girls. Even with her classmates for company, Anne was bereft at the thought of leaving her parents. She quickly wiped away the tear that rolled down her cheek. Anne was more than a little angry at Miss Potter's instruction to the girls not to cry: "'Hurry up girls! Cheer up girls!' Oh, that woman, I could kill her. Can't she be quiet once? She knows we are fighting against tears."

The girls arrived at London's Euston Station to wait for their train. Miss Potter suggested they sing, which helped lift their mood considerably. The ancient-looking train which was to take them away soon arrived. The girls clambered on board and they were off. To pass the time, they started singing "Ten green bottles are hanging on the wall." Ten Green Bottles was a popular children's song in Great Britain similar to "100 Bottles of Beer on the Wall" in the United States. The sole verse is repeated over and over, but each time with one fewer bottle as one bottle falls and breaks in each verse.

The train headed northwest from London along the West Coast Main Line. It eventually pulled into Watford Junction, roughly seventeen miles from Euston Station. A man at the station was selling Wall's ice cream. Wall's, founded in 1922, sold its popular ice cream throughout greater London by means of hundreds of tricycle vendors with placards reading "Stop Me and Buy One."

The girls were hungry by this point; seeing the Wall's vendor made them ravenous. Anne shared her sandwiches with a classmate who had forgotten her lunch. The train moved forward again as the girls wondered what their billets (assigned lodging) would be like. The train soon pulled into Berkhamsted Station where the class disembarked. Berkhamsted, a historic market town in Hertfordshire, was situated in England's Bulbourne Valley some twenty-six miles northwest of London.

The students boarded buses that drove past the school where they would attend class. The school was an ugly, grey building. The swimming pool was filthy, with worms and a dead bird floating on the surface. The girls were to attend class in the afternoon because local students would be attending in the morning.

Miss Potter assigned Anne to Shenstone Court for her billet, along with two classmates. A driver took them to their destination. As they approached Shenstone, their jaws dropped. Anne wrote: "How beautiful! It's not much smaller than Buckingham Palace." The owners of Shenstone Court were Lady Cooper and Sir Richard Cooper, both of whom were waiting on the driveway for their guests. They gave each girl a kiss and took them into the manor house. The three girls shared a large room with an adjacent bathroom. They were indeed lucky in their billet. The Cooper Baronetcy of Shenstone Court in Stafford County had been created in 1905 for agriculturalist Richard Powell Cooper. Although the manor house was stunning, the grounds were beautiful, and the girls' room was more than comfortable, loneliness began to set in. Anne missed Hans and Leni dreadfully.

Ultimately, ten girls and a teacher were billeted at Shenstone Court. The girls' tempers flared occasionally due to the stress and worry of being away from their families. Anne switched to billet with her classmate Hazel; they roomed in the gardener's cottage. Some nights they could hear the air raid sirens in London. When that happened, they raced to the manor's air raid shelter in their nightclothes. Lady Cooper joined them, with her hair done in pigtails for sleeping. Eventually, Lady Cooper's son gave them the all-clear to return to their rooms. The days and weeks passed as the girls went to class in the afternoon and enjoyed the gardens at Shenstone Court when they were not studying. They wrote to their parents in the evenings and fought the loneliness of being away from their families. But, at least for now, they were out of harm's way.

A New Life Begins

O N December 14, 1939, the Ichenhäusers' United States' quota number came up. Max immediately went to the U.S. consulate in London for his interview to, at long last, obtain entry visas. "On December 15, 1939, we finally got our visas for the USA. After a lot of running around, we were able to leave with the Volendam from Southampton on December 19. Fortunately, for our passage [to the United States], which we had paid for in Germany, was still valid." (Max's Green Diary.) After almost a year in England, the family's time to leave for the United States had come.

The Second World War had "officially" begun with Hitler's blitzkrieg attack on Poland on September 1, 1939. Notwithstanding Hitler's occupation of the Rhineland, annexation of Austria, and invasion and dismemberment of Czechoslovakia, all of which could have been considered acts of war, the "shooting war" began with Germany's invasion of Poland. Britain was now on a full war footing. Nighttime blackouts were in force. Aliens such as the Ichenhäusers were subject to registration requirements and at risk of being put on trial if they were found to be engaged in suspicious activity. Since the Ichenhäusers were living outside of London and not in areas targeted by the Luftwaffe's daily bombing raids, the war seemed less a threat as they prepared for the next stage of their journey to freedom and safety.

Renate and Erica withdrew from the Sacred Heart High School in Wealdstone. Renate's "Terminal Report" (it sounds grimmer than it was), which the Reverend Mother issued on December 20, 1939, stated: "Renate has given every satisfaction. She is a very promising pupil and should do well at her studies. We wish her every success." Before sailing, Trude took Renate and Erica to a beauty parlor to get "perms." Someone told Trude that most women in the United States had curly hair. Since Trude wanted the girls to fit in when they arrived at their new home, she had their straight, page-boy cuts replaced with curls.

The family secured passage on the SS Volendam, a Holland-America cruise ship, to sail from Southampton to New York. Holland-America's brochures described its ships as offering the "Luxury of The Spotless Fleet…at Economical Rates." The ship offered first class and tourist class. "Although it does not offer all the sumptuous luxury of Cabin Class, Tourist Class on Holland-America Line is considered ideal by knowing travelers who welcome the proverbial hospitality, the real comfort, the superb food and the wholesome travel companions that are customarily found on ships of the Spotless Fleet." Holland America's brochures did not explain what constituted wholesome companions or how Holland America screened for such. Nevertheless, the brochures declared the Line's ships were chosen by "thousands of students, teachers, college professors, business executives, young businessmen and women, authors, artists, and whole families."

The Volendam featured a Lounge, Dining Room, Smoking Room, and Veranda Café, all "decorated and furnished in a manner that would have been considered luxurious a generation ago." Most of the staterooms, for those who could afford them, offered hot and cold running water. In typical cruise line fashion, food was a central element of Holland America's appeal. Passengers could enjoy breakfast, mid-morning bullion, luncheon, tea, dinner, and a buffet supper, with each being a "delicious feast of its kind…served to you by polite, cheerful, English-speaking Dutch stewards."

A "luncheon" menu demonstrated the enormity of the dining offerings. Hors d'oeuvres included "Fresh Shrimp Salad, Norwegian Relishes, Iced Table Celery, Smoked Salmon, Julienne of Cucumber, Tomato and Clam Juice, and Spanish Green or Ripe Olives." If that was not sufficient, luncheon included three types of soup, two types of eggs, and two types of fish (mackerel and haddock). That was before passengers considered the entrée offerings of "American Pot Roast, Breaded Pork Chops Boulangere, Roast Rump of Beef with Gravy, Fricandeau of Veal Glacé and Braised Duckling with Peas," as well as steak, lamb chops, sausages, and lamb cutlets from the grill. Travelers could also tuck into side dishes of beans, cabbage, macaroni, rice, and five kinds of potatoes.

If a hot meal at mid-day did not suit passengers, the Volendam offered a cold buffet that had so many types of meat (seventeen!) that it might have made Henry the VIII blush and push back from the table. To top things off, diners could finish with salads, compotes, sweets (the apple strudel would have provided a taste of home), a selection of twelve cheeses (of course including Edam, Gouda, and Leiden, as well as French Roquefort and Camembert and British Stilton and Cheddar), and nine types of fruit, along with coffee or tea.

As to the ship itself, the Volendam, whose port of registry was Rotterdam, cut an impressive figure. She featured two huge smoke-stacks, known as funnels, that belched black smoke when she was underway. She had large yellow masts fore and aft and two decks above the water line. Her black hull was set off by the canary yellow funnels, both of which were decorated with two Kelly-green stripes divided by a band of white. The Volendam also bore a red stripe from stem to stern roughly ten feet below the top deck.

The firm of Harland & Wolff, Ltd. built the Volendam in Glasgow in 1922. The ship displaced 15,434 Gross Registered Tonnage and was outfitted with two double-reduction geared, Brown-Curtis steam turbines which generated 8000 shaft horse-power.[244] The Volendam utilized nine boilers to generate the steam needed to drive her turbines.

Holland America deployed the Volendam primarily on

---

244 Gross Registered Tonnage [GRT] was the volume of the space within a ship's hull and the enclosed spaces above the deck of a merchant ship which were available for cargo, stores, fuel, passengers, and crew. It was actually a measurement of volume, not weight. See, WWW.ECONOMICTIMES.COM.

trans-Atlantic routes. With a length of 575 feet (175.6 meters), a beam of 67.3 feet (22.4 meters) and a depth of 41.16 feet (13.7 meters), she had a top speed of 15 knots. Her fuel bunkers had a capacity of 3,569 tons of oil, which she burned at the rate of 102 tons per day. She was constructed of steel as a passenger ship with four full decks and six cargo holds. The Volendam was originally designed with a passenger capacity of 263 passengers in First class, 436 in Second class and 1200 in Third class, with a crew of 328.

The Ichenhäusers' voyage to the United States began by boarding a train at 8:00 in the evening at London's Waterloo Station on December 19, 1939, for the two-hour trip to the port of Southampton on Britain's south-central coast. Southampton's port was ten miles inland from the Atlantic. The Isle of Wight across from the inlet protected the harbor and vessels moored there from storms blowing in off the Atlantic. Upon arriving at Southampton, the Ichenhäusers lined up for passport control prior to boarding the ship tenders that ferried passengers to the Volendam for the ten-day crossing to New York. According to Renate, "we had to stand for ages for passport control and as it was not very warm our feet were nearly falling off. Then we went aboard a little steamer which took us to this big liner, because it did not come into the docks." (Renate letter to the Goffs, Dec. 28, 1939.)

The Cabin Class Manifest of "Alien Passengers" identified the family as:

> Max Ichenhäuser, age 47, doctor, nationality German, race or people—Hebrew, birthplace Cologne.
>
> Gertrude Ichenhäuser, age 38, housewife, nationality German, race or people—Hebrew, birthplace Cologne.
>
> Helga Renate Ichenhäuser, age 11, nationality German, race or people—Hebrew, birthplace Cologne; and,
>
> Margot E. Ichenhäuser, age 10, nationality German, race or people—Hebrew, birthplace Cologne.

Germany had mined British waters by the time the Volendam left Southampton on December 20. Trude did not let the girls sleep in their cabin the first two nights the ship was at sea. If the ship were to hit a mine, she did not want them sleeping below deck while Trude struggled to find them if the ship was in chaos and at risk of sinking. Therefore, she had the girls stay on deck with Trude the first several nights at sea. The girls wore heavy, grey coats to keep themselves warm from the chilly, North Atlantic air and brisk breezes that blew across the Volendam's decks.

This was all a great adventure to Renate. She had no sense of the danger they were facing during the crossing or the coming apocalypse that had led to their flight from Germany. Years later, Erica recalled that by the time they sailed the War had started, but as far as she could tell it had not affected them in England. She had no idea how close to disaster their Atlantic crossing would take them.

The Volendam had already had a taste of war. In September 1939, she had been put into service taking United States' citizens home from Europe as war threatened. On September 17, 1939, she responded to a distress call stemming from Germany's sinking of the British aircraft carrier HMS Courageous. She rescued many of the survivors. The Courageous had been on patrol off the coast of Ireland. Two of her escort destroyers had been dispatched to help a merchant ship that was under attack by German U-boats. As a result, the Courageous was only partially shielded from attack by her remaining two destroyers. As she turned into the wind to launch her aircraft for patrol, a U-boat, which apparently had been stalking her for hours, fired three torpedoes. Two struck Courageous in the bow. She sank in only twenty minutes with the loss of 519 crew members.

Renate recalled boarding the Volendam on the evening of December 20. The ship steamed westward at 6:00 a.m. the following morning on a sunny day that afforded an excellent view of the British coast. As the family stood on deck, they could see British coast guard planes patrolling the coast for quite a while as the ship left British waters. The next day, they saw a convoy of ten ships, including tankers, surrounded by cruisers and destroyers. The guns on the Naval vessels were clearly visible. As they began their voyage, evidence of the war was all around them.

Renate described the voyage in her letter to the Goffs:

We get lovely dinners here, for example oysters, pheasant, duckling and ice cream daily for supper and luncheon. Pineapple is one of the most common things. But sad to say, we were all of us so awfully seasick we could scarcely eat a thing for six days. On Monday night we had a frightful storm. In the dining room the dishes fell over and hardly anybody felt well enough to have turkey and plum-pudding. There is ever such a pretty Christmas tree and we each got a present of a Dutch doll. The ship did not get forward an inch all night and we thought it would go to pieces. It didn't luckily and in two days we will be in New York. I shall be glad as my inside is still a bit wobbly.

It did snow on Christmas but the snow melted. Yesterday it snowed again but not very thickly.

Love and kisses from Renate.

P.S. You will excuse my shaky writing but as I said I still feel a bit wobbly.

Renate ended her letter with drawings of the ship, pointing out where the family's cabins were located, along with a map showing the coast of New York and Newfoundland, and Renate's Dutch doll.

Max wrote in his diary that the crossing was stormy; he, too, noted they suffered from seasickness. Dramamine was not developed until 1949, so there may not have been much, if any, treatment for seasickness at the time.

The Volendam carried other Jewish émigrés seeking new lives. Renate and Erica befriended several children on the voyage, playing shuffleboard and board games with them to pass the time. After the family had endured ten stomach-churning days at sea, New York City appeared off the ship's bow. The family's third home in a third country in little over one year awaited. As Max wrote in his diary, "a new life begins."

They docked at Ellis Island on Dec. 30, 1939. (Max's Diary p. 27.) Walter and Gert Rothschild, who were also from Cologne and had emigrated to the United States, met them, and helped them work their way through customs. Trude and the girls waited in a huge hall packed with immigrants while Max went to register them. According to Erica, their last name was too difficult for people to pronounce, so the family decided to shorten it from Ichenhäuser to Houser. For consistency, this narrative will continue to refer to the family as the Ichenhausers, even though the family became the "Housers" upon entering the United States.

The United States Department of Labor required that all ships arriving at U.S. ports of call provide a manifest of alien passengers bound for the United States. The Manifest for the Volendam departing Southampton on December 19, 1939, identified Max (age 47) as a doctor, Trude (age 38) as a housewife, and the girls as students. The form stated Max could read English, but listed only German for Trude, Renate, and Erica, even though they could read, speak, and write English fluently. The form included a column asking for the immigrant's "Race or people;" the Ichenhäusers were identified as "Hebrew."

The family spent several days at the Hotel Monterey at Broadway and 94th Street on New York's Upper West Side, three blocks west of Central Park and two blocks from the Hudson River and the Henry Hudson Parkway. The Monterey's stationery boasted that every room had a bath and shower, and the hotel was "absolutely fireproof."[245] After several days at the Monterey, the family moved to a boarding house on Central Park West.

The Ichenhäusers used their time in New York to visit friends and relatives, most of whom were refugees like themselves. They visited with Paul and Lilli Caan, Dr. Rosental, Dr. Rosenfeld, Grete Schneller, Rudi and Henry Waller, the Sterns, and the Israels. They also visited with the Abrahams, Margot Cohen, and Sofie Abraham. These connections from their former home must have been of great comfort, both in terms of being able to obtain guidance on how to adapt to life in the United States, as well as letting the Ichenhäusers know they were not alone in facing their new and challenging situation.

Max wrote to the Ohio State Medical Board:

---

245 Fireproofing may have been sufficiently important to merit inclusion in advertising due to the Triangle Shirtwaist Factory Fire in Greenwich Village in 1911 in which 146 workers died. It was one of the deadliest industrial disasters in U.S. history.

After having arrived in the United States I beg to send you my credentials and a certified translation (of Max's medical training and certifications in Germany). The application I sent you about one year ago. May I send the still missing photo as soon as my luggage is in my hands. Owing to the war I was not able to send the papers earlier as they were not in my hands anymore. I beg to be admitted to the next examination in June.

Very truly yours,

Dr. Max Ichenhäuser

After ten days, Max got an urgent call from his cousin Leo Teitz in Cincinnati telling Max he needed to go to Columbus right away to take the state medical boards. Max immediately left for Cincinnati by train, arranging for a berth in a Pullman sleeping car. Leo met him at Cincinnati's mammoth Union Station a few miles north of the city's downtown. Max stayed with Leo until Trude, Renate, and Erica took the train to Cincinnati to join him one week later.

The family was fortunate to have reached the United States with only winter storms to deal with during the crossing. The route the Volendam had taken to New York was rife with danger as evidenced by the British naval vessels and patrol aircraft the family saw as they departed. The Volendam's last civilian voyage from Rotterdam took place a few months later in April 1940. She escaped the Netherlands before it was overrun by the Nazis in May 1940. The Dutch government then seized and chartered her to the British Ministry of War Transport, which put the Volendam into military service. She was assigned to the British Children's Overseas Reception Board as part of the British version of the "Kindertransport" program that was evacuating children from Britain to safe locations overseas, primarily to Canada.

On August 29, 1940, the Volendam sailed west from Liverpool as part of a convoy of thirty-three ships. Among her 879 passengers were 320 children with 271 adult escorts, plus 286 other passengers. On August 30, 1940, one day into her voyage and while the ships were steaming in the North Atlantic only a few hundred miles west of Northern Ireland, U-boats targeted the convoy. Submarine U-60 fired two torpedoes that struck the Volendam's Holds 1 and 2, causing massive flooding in the holds. The Volendam's captain gave the order to abandon ship even though the vessel was in rough seas. All aboard were able to evacuate safely into the ship's eighteen lifeboats except for one crew member, a Dutch purser, who was struck in the head by a swinging pulley and knocked unconscious. He fell into the churning sea and drowned. Other merchant vessels in the convoy quickly rescued the evacuees, who were returned to Greenock and other western Scottish ports on September 1.

Tugboats secured the Volendam. They towed her to the Isle of Bute where she was beached in the Firth of Forth. Temporary repairs were made there to keep the ship afloat. Tugs then towed her to Glasgow for final repairs. In Glasgow, repairmen discovered that only one of the two torpedoes fired at the Volendam had detonated. If the second torpedo had exploded, the ship likely would have sunk rapidly with a catastrophic loss of life. While in the repair dock, she was retrofitted to serve as a troop ship for the balance of the war, capable of carrying 2500 troops at a time. By the end of the conflict, the Volendam had carried 132,551 troops to and from various theaters of combat.

Several months after the torpedoing of the Volendam, some of the children who had been evacuated from the ship were placed on the SS City of Benares to escape the war. The Benares did not have the luck of the Volendam. A U-boat torpedoed the Benares causing heavy loss of life. The casualties included seventy-seven child evacuees. The loss of life was so horrific that it led England to stop relocating British children.

The Ichenhäuser family had experienced an extraordinary measure of good luck. They had secured Max's release from Dachau, escaped from Germany, and relocated to England to stay, albeit as refugees, among friends. They had secured passage to the United States, withstood seasickness and violent storms at sea, and reached New York without their ship having been attacked by U-boats. Time would tell if their luck would hold.

A New Home

O HIO WAS ONE OF THE FEW STATES THAT ALLOWED NON-United States citizens to take medical board certification examinations. The day after Max arrived in Cincinnati, he went to Columbus to register for the boards in June. Trude and the girls arrived in Cincinnati a week later. The family stayed with relatives for several days before they moved into a small apartment in a two-story, brick building at 538 Rockdale Avenue on January 23, 1940.

The two-room furnished apartment had one bedroom; Max's diary states that Renate and Erica slept there. Max and Trude slept on a convertible sofa in the living room. Erica's memory of the apartment differed from Max's. Her recollection many years later was the girls slept in a fold-out sofa-bed, while Max and Trude slept on a double bed that they stood upright in a closet during the day. Erica recalled they strung a blanket between the two beds in a one-room apartment so the girls could sleep while Max and Trude still had light in the evenings. Whoever was correct, their recollections agree they lived in a cramped apartment while they sought to get their bearings in Cincinnati.

Renate soon began seventh grade in Walnut Hills, while Erica attended sixth grade in Avondale. They were both placed ahead of the year in which they normally would have been in school, but with their mastery of English they were able to keep up. Unfortunately, the children at Walnut Hills had never seen an immigrant before. Renate's clothes did not match what the other students were wearing.

The result was cruel comments from Renate's classmates. Nevertheless, she eventually began to make friends and settle in.

Trude wrote to the Goffs to let them know how the family was faring. She thanked Mrs. Goff for a cookbook Dorothy had given to Trude. Trude wrote that she had made a recipe for "frighed [sic] onions" that had turned out quite well. Trude also asked about their former landlord Mrs. Paynter.

> I often think of you [Mrs. Goff] and imagine myself meeting you in Highstreet, doing my shopping and having a chat with both of you…I hope you all enjoy good health, inclusive Kathleen. Perhaps you could let her read this letter, as I cannot yet write to her. Please give my love to Mrs. Paynter and Mrs. Baker, and kindest regards to Father Osmund, Sister St. Paul and Reverend Mother. Lots of love to you both and Kathleen, Dorothy, Josephine, and do not forget to give my greetings to Bernard and Pearl.
>
> Yours ever,
>
> Gertrude Houser/Trude Ichenhäuser

Max added a few lines to Trude's letter:

> I only spent a week in N.Y. because I got an urgent letter to apply personally for examination over here. I, therefore, had to leave my family on the same day. I am busy with studies now and hope to reach my goal after several months. Then we have to find out [sic] a place for settling down. Please, remember me to all our friends over there. With kindest regards to all of you.
>
> Yours sincerely,
>
> (now) Max Houser

Max studied in a class for immigrant physicians at the Jewish Hospital in Cincinnati. The men in the class were from various cities in Germany, as well as Prague and Vienna. When Max was not studying, he and Trude often got together with the Behrs, Susskinds, and Goldsteins from Cologne, as well as the Lauters. They drew comfort from being able to share worries, concerns, and coping strategies with people from a common background who were facing similar challenges. Cincinnati had a sizable German-Jewish population, so the family stood a good chance of being able to find familiar foods in local stores and restaurants to ease their transition into life in Ohio.

Renate's first impression of their new home was how bitterly cold Cincinnati was. It was so cold during the winter of 1940 that the Ohio River froze over. Renate was astonished that people could walk across the river from Ohio to Kentucky. The girls wore knee socks to stay warm, but even so, their exposed knees were so cold that Renate and Erica burst into tears. From the peak of Mt. Adams overlooking the Ohio River, they could see downtown Cincinnati and across the river to Kentucky on the southern riverbank.

While the Ichenhäusers tried to establish themselves in their new home, the war in Europe worsened. On April 9, 1940, Germany invaded Denmark and attacked Oslo, the capital of Norway. Hitler claimed he invaded both countries to protect them from the Allies, who he claimed were planning to occupy them. In effect, he claimed he was invading those nations for their own good. While Denmark did not resist, Norway declared war on Germany and fought back. However, Norway's resistance was short-lived; after two months of fighting it, too, fell victim to the Nazis' latest blitzkrieg.

On May 10, barely one month after Hitler had attacked Denmark and Norway, Germany launched land and air attacks on Holland, Belgium, and Luxembourg. The Nazis used the same pretext they had offered to justify their invasions of Denmark and Norway; they claimed they were invading the Low Countries to protect them from an imminent Allied invasion. Germany attacked these three small countries notwithstanding the fact that Germany had repeatedly guaranteed their neutrality and borders. "Peace in our time" crumbled before the unprovoked and unjustifiable Nazi attacks on six European nations.

The German attacks across a front 175 miles long were disastrous for Britain's military position. Chamberlain lost a "division vote" in Parliament which was, in effect, a vote of no confidence in Chamberlain. Unable to form a broad-based government, Chamberlain advised King Edward to send for Winston Churchill and ask him to form a government. Churchill, who had characterized Chamberlain's appeasement of Hitler in Czechoslovakia as an unmitigated disaster for Britain, became prime minister. On May 13, Churchill gave one of his most memorable speeches, telling the British people "I have nothing to offer but blood, toil, tears, and sweat."

The Dutch resisted by sending their small air force to oppose the Luftwaffe. They opened dikes to flood the countryside and impede the Wehrmacht's progress on the ground. The Germans countered by dropping paratroopers inside Holland and bombing Schiphol airport, the Netherland's largest airfield, located just outside Amsterdam. The Dutch were no match for the massive and well-armed Wehrmacht; Holland surrendered on May 15 after only five days of fighting.

The Wehrmacht launched similar attacks on Belgium by bombing Brussels and Antwerp and dropping paratroopers. The Belgians resisted with anti-aircraft guns, artillery, and Belgium's small air force. Hitler continued to justify Germany's attacks under the pretext that it was invading the three small nations with overwhelming force in order to protect them from Allied invasion. He claimed the Allies planned to use those countries as bases from which they would invade Germany's industrial heartland, critical to its arms industry, in the Ruhr district just north of Cologne.[246]

By mid-May 1940, the Nazis' hail of destruction by air and massed ground attacks led by Panzer divisions allowed the Wehrmacht to blast through the Netherlands, Luxembourg, and much of Belgium. The Nazis swiftly took Brussels, the Belgian capital. The Belgian government decided to abandon the capital and retreat to Ostend on the North Sea coast. While the Belgians resisted, they, too, were no match for the Nazi blitzkrieg. Belgium surrendered on May 28, less than three weeks after the Nazi blitzkrieg began.

The Wehrmacht did not stop in the Low Countries. It continued to attack and soon breached the French border and pierced the key French defense fortifications, known as the Maginot line, along a sixty-mile front. Britain had dispatched an army, known as

---

246 *The New York Times*, May 10, 1940, p. 1.

the British Expeditionary Force, to France after the Nazis attacked Poland and the French and British had declared war against Germany. The war quickly took a frightening turn for France and Britain; it soon became nothing less than catastrophic. The British and French had rushed their armies north and east to meet what they thought would be the main German thrust towards France through northern Belgium, near the coast. However, the Wehrmacht attacked further south, surging westward into France, and then wheeling north to the French coast along the Strait of Dover. With this, the Nazis out-flanked and quickly surrounded the British and French armies at Dunkirk, just west of the French-Belgian border on the Strait. The German strategy cut off the British Expeditionary Force, and much of the French army, from the balance of French forces further to the west. While this encirclement was taking place, additional Panzer formations continued advancing to the west. German tanks soon crossed the River Aisne in northeastern France, putting them within sixty miles of Paris.[247]

The situation of the British Army, surrounded by the Wehrmacht at Dunkirk, was desperate:

> No one has yet come from that inferno in Flanders to describe the scene; doubtless it baffles the imagination. For the battle is being waged in the land, in the air, on the sea and under the sea. Every engine of death yet devised by man is in action and the fight never ceases day or night. Nor is it confined to the actual battlefield. All bases, all lines of communication are bombed continually on both sides, with the Germans concentrating a great effort on Dunkerque.[248]

Hitler then committed one of his worst blunders of the war. He ordered his Panzer divisions to stop advancing in order to let the Luftwaffe and Kriegsmarine (the German Navy) finish off the British and France forces trapped in the tiny enclave they occupied on the beach at Dunkirk. The British Admiralty quickly launched "Operation Dynamo," which was a desperate effort to save the

247 *The New York Times*, May 22, 1940, p. 1.

248 *The New York Times*, May 30, 1940, p. 1.

British forces. The operation called for hundreds of vessels, from large naval ships to tiny pleasure craft, to sail the twenty-one miles from Britain to Dunkirk to evacuate the British Expeditionary Force trapped there. It did not matter whether the ships and boats could carry five soldiers or five hundred, almost anything that could float was called into action. Many vessel owners simply set sail on their own across the Channel to try to save British servicemen. By the time the operation ended five days later on June 4, the motley flotilla had saved 338,000 British and French troops, virtually an entire army. While the troops were devastated and had suffered extensive casualties from fighting against an overwhelming foe, they would live to fight another day. Had Hitler allowed the Wehrmacht to quickly finish the job at Dunkirk, the loss in British lives and morale might well have dealt a fatal blow to the British war effort.

On June 4, Churchill gave what is widely regarded as the finest speech of his career, in which he urged the British to steel their nerves for the long struggle that lay ahead:

> We shall go on to the end. We shall fight in France, we shall fight on the seas and oceans, we shall fight with growing confidence and growing strength in the air, we shall defend our island, whatever the cost may be. We shall fight on the beaches, we shall fight on the landing grounds, we shall fight in the fields and in the streets, we shall fight in the hills; we shall never surrender.

Despite Churchill's call to arms, the war became more and more grim for the British. On June 10, the French government abandoned Paris. Italy belatedly fulfilled the terms of its pact with Germany and joined the war by attacking southern France. The Nazis occupied Paris on June 14. Battle-scarred Panzer tanks clanked through the City of Lights while jack-booted German troops marched down the Champs Elysée after passing under the Arc de Triomphe. The swastika flag flew from the Eiffel Tower. The City of Lights and joy passed into darkness and despair.

On June 14, the Germans opened the Auschwitz concentration camp in the southern Polish town of Oswiecim. This development did not make the wire services. It would take some time before Auschwitz grew into the death camp that became the site of the worst genocide the world has known.

After barely six weeks of combat, France surrendered and signed an armistice with Germany on June 22, 1940.[249] Hitler insisted the French sign the armistice in the forest of Compiegne in the same railcar and at the same location where the Allies had compelled Germany to sign the humiliating terms of surrender ending WWI. The armistice divided France into two zones. One was a "free" zone based in Vichy in southern France that was to be governed by French Field Marshall Petain; this came to be known as the Vichy regime. The other zone encompassed northern France and the French Atlantic coast; it was occupied and ruled by the Nazis.

Britain vowed to continue the fight, regardless of the French decision to concede and no matter how bleak the British military position appeared. As to the French, "The motto of the État Francais, *Travail, Famille, Patrie* [Work, Family, Fatherland], replaced that of the republic: *Liberté, Égalité, Fraternité*."[250] The Nazis now controlled virtually all of Western Europe.

Worse was soon to come for the beleaguered British. On July 10, barely three weeks after the French surrendered, the "Battle of Britain" began; it continued until October 31, 1940. Wave after wave of Luftwaffe fighters and bombers attacked Britain. They bombed military installations inland and along the coast, initially targeting armament factories and docks. The Germans bombed London and other cities without regard to military value to try to destroy the British resolve to continue fighting. The Luftwaffe was estimated to have 1100 bombers and more than 900 fighter planes to use in the bombing campaign, while Britain's RAF "could rarely muster more than 600 fighters."[251] People living in southwestern England, who could see the French coastline from the chalk cliffs of Dover, watched in horror as wave after wave of Luftwaffe aircraft flew overhead on

---

249 *The New York Times*, June 23, 1940, p. 1.

250 *Nazi Germany and the Jews* at 193.

251 *The Enemy Is Listening* at 27.

their daily bombing runs. They saw the contrails of fighter planes swirling in the sky, creating intricate traceries, as the RAF fighters attacked Luftwaffe bombers and the German fighter planes sent to protect them.

However, "By this time, the cryptographers at Bletchley were reading into the Luftwaffe's high-grade, machine-enciphered Enigma traffic and were producing what came to be known as Ultra intelligence."[252] With the benefit of Bletchley's code-breaking expertise, the code-breaking WAAFs, and the bravery and skill of the RAF pilots, Britain ultimately beat back the Luftwaffe and prevailed in the aerial war known as the Battle of Britain. With this, Britain repulsed the air attacks Hitler had unleashed as prelude to "Operation Lion"—the code name for the Nazis' planned invasion of Britain.

However, just as the RAF was winning the Battle of Britain and bringing an end to Germany's devastating daytime air raids, the Luftwaffe began a campaign of nightly bombing raids on Britain known as the Blitz. These attacks rained terror upon London night after night from September 1940 until mid-May 1941. The raids killed thousands of civilians and made hundreds of thousands homeless. London's underground "tube" stations were converted into bomb shelters where many Londoners slept each night. Even if the nighttime raids failed to lay the ground for an invasion of Britain, the Germans thought they would destroy British arms manufacturing, homes, and morale.

On September 27, 1940, Germany, Italy, and Japan signed the Tripartite Pact, forming the Axis Alliance. On October 3, 1940, the Vichy regime issued a law, the Statut des Juifs, abolishing the civil rights of Jews living in France. The Vichy regime, while nominally independent, elected to comply with the heinous Nazi ideology, rounding up Jews in France and turning them over to the Gestapo and SS who, in turn, sent France's Jews to the death camps.

The United States evacuated Consul Klieforth's family from Germany in September 1939 shortly after the war began. In an October 1940 letter to his son Alexander, Klieforth described what his life in Cologne was like:

---

252 *The Enemy Is Listening* at 31-32.

Life here is quite interesting but on the other hand very lonely. I see very few people and then always the same ones. Sitting alone in a darkened apartment is not my idea of spending a year's time in solitary confinement. If I have to be alone I would choose a different setting or traveling. Or living alone in a comfortable hut in an interesting forest, close to nature, shooting and fishing etc. is not a bad sort of life, but this kind of existence is neither human nor existing. Mother [Mrs. Klieforth] is afraid that I am not getting enough sleep. The contrary is the case. In the first place I have not more than an hour's work each day, although I have to sit around the office pretending to do work. This alone get's (sic) on my nerves in a very short time. Then the darkness. This business of groping around with a flashlight, then the quiet of the apartment and the early bed hours, is wearysome (sic). Since the fireworks [Allied bombing] now start as early as 9:45—and as the winter advances—at about 8:30, all visits have to be concluded about 30 minutes before the alarm [air raid alert]. If I have guests for bridge, they have to finish early and get home before the alarm. The "alert" period lasts two hours, but it may last five hours. One never knows. I stay in bed and have learned to sleep during the alert unless the noise is too loud or the shooting is too near, which happens every now and then. Likewise, I watch the stunt, now and then, especially when a British plane has been caught in the circles of search lights. Then the shooting is terrific and if the plane is driven over the center of the city I run behind a shelter. But since my return the planes work [target] the industrial plants of Leverkusen, Troisdorf and of the other suburbs near Cologne... So when you hear on the radio that the British dropped bombs on the factories of Cologne you know that does not mean the center of the city. Most of the damage done to the city since my arrival was done by the duds of the German anti-aircraft guns. One fell within hundred feet (sic) of the Consulate last week but only smashed windows of the adjoining homes but not those of the Consulate...When the shooting is near the noise is terrific. The houses tremble with the vibration and the noise is like the most awful thunder but stronger in volume. I don't think it is something that mother could stand for a long time. The fireworks in connection with an affair of this kind look and act just like fireworks only that they take place very high in the air. Very often the British drop flares from a terrific height at the same time, which light up the countryside for an area of about 25 miles in diameter.

Either people are terribly frightened and nervous or they are not. Even Katie our cook of whom I expected a complete collapse remains perfectly quiet. One never knows in advance how it will affect people. In most cases it is the reverse of what was expected. (Klieforth letter to Alexander Klieforth, October 7, 1940.)

Klieforth tried to stay occupied by reading *Reader's Digest, Time, Life*, and the *Saturday Evening Post*, but he missed having access to a library with literature. He was glad that Barbara, Alexander, and Les were safely in the United States. Long gone were the days when the Consulate entertained guests with menus such as Bertshok à la Russe (Russian style borscht), soufflé de mais aux champignons (mushroom soufflé), dinde rotis au riz (roast turkey with rice), glaces a la crème (ice cream), choux au fromage (cheese puffs), and melon glacé (frozen melon). Instead, Klieforth's life in Cologne was dominated by darkness, loneliness, and bombing raids.

Now, For You, the
Tide Has Turned

While Europe was now fully engulfed in flames, the members of the Ichenhäuser family worked to establish themselves in their new home. Max took the medical boards in Columbus on June 4-6, 1940. The examination was difficult, but Max felt he had done well. Four weeks later he learned he had passed. In the interim, Max had been investigating where he might open a practice. He learned that the Village of Deer Park, ten miles north of Cincinnati, with a population of roughly three thousand residents, did not have a doctor. Max concluded that Deer Park might be a good place for the family to settle and for Max to open a practice.

In June, Max was invited to meet James Stewart, the Mayor of Cincinnati. They were interviewed together for a radio program.[253] The interview resulted in Max securing a letter of recommendation from the Mayor:

> To Whom It May Concern:
>
> This letter will introduce Doctor Max Houser, who has been a resident of Cincinnati since his arrival in America the first of this year. He was a distinguished physician in Cologne, Germany, for sixteen years, and was the personal physician of the American Consul General in that city, as well as the Vice-Consul, and their families.

---

253 Research has not disclosed who arranged the interview or for what purpose.

Doctor Houser has recently passed the State medical examination in Ohio and is now visiting various places with the idea of picking a location for his permanent residence where he may practice his profession.

He is a man of character and attainments and I feel certain would make a valuable contribution to any community of which he may become a citizen.

I shall appreciate it very much if anyone to whom he may present this letter will give him considerate attention and advice.

Very sincerely,

James Garfield Stewart,

Mayor (Mayor James Stewart letter of recommendation, June 1940.)

Believing he would soon have the means to support his family, Max purchased a home in Deer Park at 4247 Amity Road where Amity came to a dead end at Galbraith Road. The neighborhood was populated largely by single-family homes set on streets lined with silver maples, pin oaks, and the occasional hickory or beech tree. Grey squirrels skittered across the lawn as they collected acorns to, well, squirrel them away for the winter. The Ichenhäusers' corner lot bordered a church on Amity Road and a single-family home on Galbraith.

Woodmont Dairy, just a few blocks away on Galbraith Road, was where the residents of Deer Park could purchase quarts of milk in glass bottles with cardboard stoppers. Woodmont also sold pint bottles of chocolate milk, just the right size for children. Renate and Erica each had a sweet tooth from growing up eating bowls of whipped cream, German and Belgian chocolate, and marzipan candies. No doubt they were excited when they learned of the proximity of cold bottles of chocolate milk. While residents could buy milk at the dairy, many families relied upon a milkman to deliver dairy products to their homes, where the milkman placed their orders of milk, butter, and cottage cheese in insulated boxes by the families' back doors.

The Ichenhäusers' new home had eight rooms. It would suffice quite well for both a comfortable home and medical office. The front yard, which faced Galbraith Road, had space for several flower beds, which Trude eventually filled with bright red canna lilies. Monarch, sulfur, and cabbage butterflies flitted around the house on warm days. The back yard had a lawn and a huge pin oak in the corner of the lot behind the detached, one-car garage. The lawn was large enough for the girls to play games and spray one another with a garden hose on hot summer days. The lawn also provided a place where the girls could lie in the sun on humid summer days to read *Life* magazine while listening to the radio and working on their tans. The family eventually dug up a portion of the back yard to plant a victory garden filled with tomato vines and runner string beans that twined their way up thin bamboo stakes. Beefsteak tomatoes and blue lake string beans made for wonderful summer salads and vegetables.

The side of the house facing Amity Road had a raised concrete patio on the ground level and a deck above the patio which the family could reach through French doors in the master bedroom. The patio made a perfect spot to sit in the shade on hot summer days and drink iced tea or lemonade while watching passersby. On warm evenings, the family could sit and watch fireflies' blinking yellow glow as the black insects with their yellow-edged wings floated across the yard on the evening breezes while cicadas buzzed in the trees.

The family moved in on August 24, 1940. Their lift-van shipping container arrived with the few furnishings and limited clothing they had been able to ship from Cologne. It was not much, but the items would suffice to make the house start to feel like a home, as well as provide a few reminders of the home they had left behind. Trude and Max had managed to save their bedroom set made of gleaming, curly maple. The wood's rich, gold grain glowed under the thick coat of varnish that protected it. The bedroom set included a glossy maple headboard and an armoire with a glass front. A green curtain on the inside of the armoire door shielded the contents from view. Additional furnishings included another headboard, a second armoire, and one chair.

They had also shipped several Persian rugs whose intricate

multi-colored patterns were enhanced by the home's hardwood floors. Trude had also shipped a glass-topped jewelry case the size of an end-table. The case had green velvet backing on the bottom; Trude used it to hold a comb, hairbrush, and the few items of jewelry she had managed to take with her. Trude and Max had also shipped a full-length mirror that swiveled forward and backward so they could adjust the angle of reflection. Their bathroom medicine cabinet contained a bottle of Trude's favorite perfume, 4711 Cologne with its gold and aquamarine filigree label, which served as a fragrant reminder of the life they had left behind.

Max received his medical license in late August. He opened his practice on September 6, 1940, on the ground floor of their home, advertised by a sign in the front yard stating "Max Houser, M.D." He also placed a notice in the local newspaper announcing his practice and offering office hours of 2-4 and 7-8, as well as by appointment. Max and Trude modified the home's ground floor to accommodate Max's practice. They divided the living room into two sections, one portion serving as a waiting room, while Max used the other, larger area as an examination and treatment room. The office contained an imposing wooden desk that was populated with numerous compartments for papers and writing materials. It also had a built-in leather blotter for use as a writing surface. Slowly, but surely, Max's practice began to grow.

Over the fireplace, Max and Trude hung a large oil painting of an elderly gentleman with a long grey beard, black hat, and dark clothing. Trude's father Sigmund once had a customer who needed a new suit but did not have cash to pay for it. The customer negotiated a barter with Sigmund in which the customer obtained a new suit in exchange for the oil painting. The painting, attributed to the Düsseldorf school, was reminiscent of some Dutch masters' paintings in terms of the dark pallet the artist had used. The painting occupied pride of place in the living room/treatment room.

Until Max's practice developed, the family had to survive on the limited savings they had been able to take when they left Germany, in addition to the money Max had smuggled into Holland. Much of those funds had been depleted paying their expenses during the year they spent in England, so their financial situation was a source of concern.

Once the family moved to Deer Park, Renate and Erica enrolled in the Deer Park elementary school across the street from their home. The girls could no longer attend the Walnut Hills and Avondale schools because they were too far away. This would be their fourth school in a third country in little over one year. The school tested them to determine in what grade level the girls should be placed. Erica and Renate tested well and were advanced beyond what their age would have called for. The girls had no difficulty with English given their time with Kathleen in Cologne and the year they spent in England. They spoke English fluently with, well, a bit of an English accent. Being placed one year ahead of her age cohort was not a problem for Renate and she made friends readily. However, Erica struggled socially at times since she was only eleven years old and was two years ahead of her age cohort. Nevertheless, she eventually made friends. She was particularly intrigued when a friend introduced her to Halloween and the concept of candy to be had merely by asking for it.

Trude made sure to check with the school to see how the girls were doing. A transcription of what appears to be an internal report in which a member of the faculty solicited information about Renate stated:

> Mrs. Houser is eager to know just what Renate's standing is. Their home life is beautifully organized in every detail and [Renate's] mother is with us to the nth degree—is also very appreciative in our interest in the child. She is to call me at 9:00 a.m. Thursday morning, so I shall appreciate whatever data you can give me.

> Answers:

> The English teacher: Renate is doing very well in English— in fact she made 100% in the last test on Courtship of Miles Standish. Her composition work is very good considering. The children report that she is very popular with other children. As far as I know everything is quite O.K.

The social teacher: I find Renate a very fine pupil. She is quite responsive, interested and attentive. The result is as would be expected—very fine work.

The Mathematics teacher: Renate is capable. She is not free my second bell, when I could help her individually—She has some obstacles—such as fundamentals etc. to overcome. I believe she will succeed.

Trude decided the girls should continue their music lessons. She signed them up for accordion lessons taught by Mr. Gene Lipka at the Wurlitzer music store in downtown Cincinnati. Franz Rudolph Wurlitzer, a German who had immigrated to the United States in 1856, founded the Wurlitzer Company. The company quickly became the largest purveyor of band instruments in the United States. It also manufactured the huge organs installed in movie theaters around the country, as well as the juke boxes found in bars, diners, and dance halls around the United States. To get to their lessons, the girls took a bus downtown from Deer Park. Since they did not want to carry their heavy instruments on the bus, they used one of the Wurlitzer store's accordions for their lessons. Mr. Lipka hand-copied the music for their new pieces while the girls played the assignments they had practiced that week.

Mr. Lipka convinced Renate and Erica to join a children's music club. The club held monthly meetings for its fifteen to twenty members. Several members of the group played solos at each meeting. All the students except Renate and Erica played piano or violin. When it was Erica's turn to perform, she played the Finale to the William Tell Overture. The girls also joined the Avondale school band. They even played the accordion in amateur hour shows on local radio stations. A photograph of them playing on WKRC Radio in Cincinnati shows Erica standing by as a page-turner, while Renate sat and played. Renate stared at the sheet music with what was either intense concentration or barely concealed distaste for the instrument and the entire undertaking.

Family life in Ohio was quite different from Germany. Renate and Erica were used to a very structured existence. Trude had planned and programmed everything for them in Cologne. In Germany, children were not asked for their opinions or desires. Nor did German parents typically discuss anything of substance with their children. Parents in Germany simply told their children what to do and that was the end of the matter. Life in the United States was far more relaxed. It was difficult for Trude to adjust to this free-flowing lifestyle.

Max Schiff, the President of Cincinnati's Jewish Community Center, wrote to Max to provide a membership card for Cincinnati's Jewish Center. The membership entitled Max to participate in the activities the Center offered. It also entitled him to join the Gate Club, whose members were German-Jewish immigrants who had settled in Cincinnati in the 1930s and 1940s. The JCC membership included a subscription to the American Israelite, Cincinnati's Jewish community newspaper. Mr. Schiff's letter of introduction suggested that Renate and Erica look into activities they might enjoy at the Jewish Community Center's Branch at 610 Forest Avenue in Cincinnati's Avondale neighborhood, which was not far from Deer Park.

Tante Ann wrote to Max and Trude in early September 1940. The letter does not state Tante Ann's full name; surviving family members do not know how she was related to the family. It may be that her use of "tante" was not meant to connote an actual relative, but rather was a term of endearment used among close friends. In either event, Tante Ann was a German Jewish refugee like the Ichenhäusers who had made her way to Britain. British security services had taken her husband into custody as an alien and potential security risk:

September 2, 1940
105 Westbourne Terrace
London, Paddington

Dear Friends:

Thanks a lot for your very cheerful and kind letter. My congratulations for your settling-down. Now for you the tide has turned and you are looking forward to a new life—all the best to you.

I don't know whether you learned that the male refugees have been interned 10 weeks ago. My husband too. You can imagine how I feel. But there is hope that he may be released one day and so I am carrying on and in the meantime trying to be permitted to see him once....Let us hope he will be back soon and forget all about it, but I must confess it is the most dreadful experience of my life: the police was a bit of the Gestapo; I did not hear for four weeks where my husband was (in the meantime the Arandora Star had been sunk) and no God could or would tell me. But I beg you most urgently: don't tell a word to your mother! Because my mother still thinks we are together and you can imagine what a shock it would be for her to learn that I have been left behind all by myself in a foreign country where I went only to be with him.

Apart from that there are [sic] not many news. I think you read about the [air] raids. You get accustomed to it and it is not bad at all. Anyway, the Nazis won't get us down this way, that is pretty sure. I think you and I have more reason to be worried about the Cologne area than about London. It is a silly world, isn't it? But on the other hand, I think, the harder they try the sooner it will be over and the miracle will happen that England wins in the end after the defeat of all her allies. Wishing—wishing!...

Give my love to your parents and mine, and all the best to you.

With kindest regards,

Tante Ann

The SS Arandora Star was a British passenger ship operated by the Blue Star Line. At the outset of the war, Britain requisitioned her to use as a troop transport. In late June 1940, the British used her to transport Italian and German civilian internees, as well as German prisoners of war, from Britain to Canada in order to remove them from the theater of war in England. The British wanted to eliminate the chance that the internees might escape and act as German agents trying to disrupt the British home front.

In late June 1940, the Arandora departed from Liverpool with, among hundreds of other passengers, 479 interned male German refugees. The ship was bound for Newfoundland; the internees and prisoners were to be sent to internment camps in Canada. On July

2, the Arandora was sailing alone when the German U-boat U-47 torpedoed her. The torpedo struck the engine room killing the entire engine crew and destroying the Arandora's turbines and generators. She sank quickly resulting in 805 casualties. One survivor described the scene:

> I could see hundreds of men clinging to the ship. They were like ants and then the ship went up at one end and slid rapidly down, taking the men with her...Many men had broken their necks jumping or diving into the water. Others injured themselves by landing on drifting wreckage and floating debris near the sinking ship.[254]

Tante Ann was no doubt frantic with worry that her husband was one of the interned refugees aboard the Arandora when it went down because the press reported news of the sinking and loss of life, along with a general description of the categories of men aboard. She had no knowledge as to whether her husband was one of them. One can only wonder whether, if the Ichenhäusers had stayed in England longer, Max might have been included in the sweep of internees and been sent to his death aboard the Arandora. It would not be a stretch to say Max had cheated death once again.

The Nazis continued to isolate Germany's Jews. No aspect of daily life was too small to escape the Reich's oppression. As an example, on July 19, 1940 the Nazis seized all telephones owned by Jews, further isolating the remnant Jewish population in Germany from the outside world and from one another.

By September 1940, Max's practice was developing, although he was not feeling quite up to par. The girls were settling into school. Trude maintained the books for Max as she had done in Cologne. She ran the household, albeit on her own, without the help of her mother, a cook, and the maid they had employed in Germany. Life was different and challenging, but the four of them were free and safe. It seemed that, at long last, they had established a new life and could look to the future.

---

254 Sergeant Norman Price, Wikipedia, The SS Arandora Star.

THIS QUIET, BEAUTIFUL
PIECE OF LAND

IN JULY 1940, LENI ROTHSCHILD VISITED HER YOUNGER daughter Anne at Shenstone Court to share a secret. The family was going to emigrate to Ecuador. Leni was there to take Anne back to London to prepare for the trip. With the onset of the war, the British viewed all Germans in England with suspicion and concern that they might be German agents. When Hans and Leni learned they might be interned, they decided to leave England. Hans had been warned about possible internment through his work helping the RAF identify German targets for British bombing runs. Hans and Leni did not want to risk having their family separated from one another, which led them to the decision to emigrate yet again.

Ecuador and Brazil were two of the few countries willing to accept Jews in 1940. Since Brazil had a large German community, which the Rothschilds feared would be hostile to them, they decided to emigrate to Ecuador. Anne had never heard of Ecuador; she was somewhat in disbelief they were going to South America. Anne had grown very fond of Lady Cooper, as she and Sir Richard had been very kind to the girls billeted at Shenstone, so Anne was sad to leave them.

Nevertheless, in the end, Anne was happy to return to London, even with evidence of the war all around. She saw many houses had been reduced to rubble by German bombing. During the blitz, Anne and her friends would sometimes jump from one pile of rubble to another, playing a sort of mountain-climbing game. Frequent German air raids disrupted daily life and drove the city's residents into bomb shelters. At night, the Rothschilds watched searchlights crisscross the sky looking for German aircraft. The shafts of light looked like the arms of giant, drunken metronomes sweeping back and forth in search of the correct tempo. The family cheered when they saw a German plane plummeting to earth, a victim of the British anti-aircraft batteries.

The Rothschilds obtained visas from the Ecuadorian embassy and prepared to leave Britain. They took the train to Liverpool, their port of departure. Anne saw the burnt hulks of vessels resting on the floor of Liverpool's harbor, casualties of German air raids. The family boarded the sea-green ocean liner Orbita for the voyage. The Orbita was one of the last passenger ships to leave Britain. The Harland & Wolff firm had built the vessel in Belfast for the Pacific Steam Navigation Company. With one large funnel amidships, she was sixty-seven feet across and 550 feet long. The Orbita joined other ships in a convoy for a portion of the voyage since U-boat wolf packs were lurking in British waters searching for Allied shipping to attack. Anne wrote in her school essay that she was confident the Germans would not sink their ship.

After three weeks at sea on a route that took them through the Panama Canal and along the western coast of South America, they reached Ecuador. Anne wrote: "Hurrah, hurrah! Salinas, what a harbor, but better than I expected." The city of Guayaquil was Ecuador's main port. However, it could not accommodate large ships. Instead, ocean liners like the Orbita had to moor offshore. Small boats picked up the passengers and took them to the towns of La Libertad and Salinas, the latter being a fishing village on Ecuador's southwest coast. Both towns were situated on a peninsula that jutted into the Pacific Ocean. As they came ashore, Anne was relieved at how quiet it was. There were no guns sticking out of thickets, nor were military planes patrolling overhead. Anne wrote: "I am going to love this country, this beautiful, quiet piece of land!"

The Rothschilds and other Jewish immigrants aboard the Orbita boarded a railway car that took them to Guayaquil. When the Rothschilds arrived in Guayaquil, they were met with quite a hubbub. Word had gotten out that "the Rothschilds" were coming. While it was true the Rothschilds were coming, Hans and Leni had to inform the Ecuadorians who came to meet them that, unfortunately, they were not "those" Rothschilds.

The Rothschilds nevertheless were taken to the offices of *El Universo*, the biggest newspaper in Guayaquil, for an interview. Along the way they saw workers spreading cocoa beans on tarps in the streets to dry them in the sun. They rode past the Metropolitano, the best hotel in town, whose cooks stood in the street watching the new arrivals.

From Guayaquil, the family boarded a train for the twelve-hour trip to Quito, Ecuador's capital. Located 167 miles northeast of Guayaquil, Quito is in the Andes mountains at an altitude of 9,000 feet. The climate there was far different from steamy, tropical Guayaquil and far more familiar to the new residents. In Guayaquil, they feared contracting malaria, typhoid fever, dysentery, amoebas, and hepatitis. In Quito, the refugees could be spared from at least some tropical diseases, although many still became ill from other diseases and suffered from altitude-related hardships.

The trip to Quito was quite an eye-opener for the Rothschilds. They saw local indigenous vendors along the route offering the passengers roasted cuys (guinea pigs) to eat. During the journey, the refugees noticed that local people rode on the roof of the train. They also noticed the humble bamboo huts in which many locals lived. Notwithstanding the strange scenes around them and the sense of loss they felt for all they had left behind, they were relieved to know they were away from the war and the air raids in London.

Upon arriving in Quito, the Rothschilds initially stayed in a hotel. They were met by the Chilean consul in Quito, who had heard that "the Rothschilds" were in town. He soon joined the ranks of other disappointed Ecuadorians who had been hoping to meet the "real" Rothschilds.

Quito was very different from what the family and the other Jewish refugees were accustomed to in Europe. Located in Pichincha province, Quito is surrounded by snow-capped mountains, volcanos, and verdant valleys. It was a rough and underdeveloped city, but even with a small income, the refugees could live relatively comfortably. Ecuador had virtually no industry and precious little commerce other than exporting agricultural crops, so there were many opportunities for the emigrants to pursue.

By this time, Hannah was nineteen, Anne was thirteen, and Peter was ten. Anne was sorry to have left England and her friends, but it was time to make a new life, yet again, in another country. Having learned English, they now had to learn Spanish and become accustomed to Ecuadorian practices and mores. The family was resilient, as were many of the refugees. Further, as far as Anne could tell, they were well received in Ecuador. The Ecuadorians were friendly and the family was gradually able to integrate into Ecuadorian society. Anne and Peter attended the American school known as the Colegio Americano. It was staffed by American, British, and Ecuadorian teachers. The school day featured a two-hour lunch break, so Anne and Peter went home to eat and still had quite a bit of time to play before returning to class.

Galo Plaza, who became Ecuador's president from 1948 to 1952, encouraged Hans Rothschild to go into agriculture, because the country's economy was mainly agricultural. That being the case, Galo could not understand why Hans would want to do anything else. However, Hans had been in the metal fabrication business in Germany, so he decided to do what he knew and pursue business in that field.

In 1941, Hans established a small metal-fabrication factory, which he named "Atu," on Necochea Street in the outskirts of Quito. He started out by making metal milk cans and pots. Hans eventually expanded Atu's product line to include bicycles; he purchased the parts and assembled the bicycles for sale. Later, he began manufacturing metal office furniture and fireproof safe deposit boxes. Many years later, after returning to Ecuador from attending Alfred University in New York State, Peter added a division named Electro Motor that manufactured small engines. Hannah worked with Hans; she could be seen on the shop floor assisting with the manufacture of their products. Later she moved into the office to handle administrative tasks.

Ecuador's government wanted European immigration to help develop the country and settle unpopulated or under-populated parts of the country. Ecuador issued visas requiring refugees to work only in agriculture and industry. They were not allowed to work in commerce, although many immigrants took chances by ignoring this requirement and opening shops or selling merchandise door to door. Until 1944, when the law was repealed, refugees still had to get official approval to work in fields other than industry or farming.

Since Ecuador was undeveloped, there were many opportunities for Jewish immigrants with an entrepreneurial spirit. Some, like Hans, started new industries. Some opened small lodging places for other refugees. Others started to bake and sell cakes and then expanded to a variety of foods. Some sold whatever wares might fill local needs, both as peddlers and by opening shops.

Even when they could make a living, some of the immigrants suffered from depression; they mourned the loss of loved ones in Europe and felt displaced in this strange new land which bore no resemblance to the world they had left behind. However, neither Leni nor Hans rued leaving Germany; they were thankful they had managed to escape.

Ecuador offered a wide assortment of fruits, both tropical and those grown in the Andes, for the refugees to eat, but the fruit always had to be disinfected before being eaten. The Rothschilds had bananas at every meal. There were bananas with yellow skin and those with purple skin with pinkish flesh, and very sweet, tiny bananas called oritos. Hans and Leni almost never ate bananas; they looked down on them as a humble and unpalatable fruit. Hannah, Anne, and Peter were, at least with respect to bananas, less discriminating and enjoyed eating the many varieties available to them.

The family also ate plantain, which they sliced and fried in butter, since plantains cannot be eaten raw. They also had papaya and other local fruits such as the oval-shaped chirimoya, or custard apple, which has green skin and white, creamy, sweet flesh. The family had lots of avocados for their kitchen which they plucked from trees by their home. They also ate a type of cactus called paxo.

The refugees had to be careful to boil their water. Leni and

Hannah, notwithstanding the lush local produce, tried hard to recreate familiar German dishes. They cooked sauerbraten with sweet and sour red cabbage, along with special potato balls. They made matzo ball soup, but they made it the German way using matzo, almonds, and eggs. Another favorite dish they prepared was oxtail soup. The German foods on their menu were rich and included a lot of cream. They never cooked with oil, they used only cream and butter. Another classic German dish they made was "Himmel und Erde," the apple and potato dish whose name was adopted by the social club at which Max and Trude had met.

Leni did not cook from recipes. She belonged to the "handful of this and pinch of that" school of cooking. Anne eventually wrote down many of Leni's recipes in a mixture of Spanish and English. The family made no pretense of being Kosher, although it is not known if this was due to the lack of a shochet (ritual slaughterer) who could prepare Kosher meat or because they were Reform Jews who did not observe Kashrut.

Leni and Hannah also baked all kinds of German pastries. Leni was the master baker of the family, making many kinds of cookies, as well as a chocolate roll similar to a babka. Leni also made "berliners," the famous jelly-filled, German donuts. She always kept a cupboard full of chocolate for the children. Leni also started a sewing circle of Jewish women to make items for Allied soldiers. Through her efforts, the family came to know the British ambassador in Quito.

Once Hans' business was up and running and he had established a steady income, Hans and Leni built a home that became the center of their lives. Their house in Quito's La Mariscal neighborhood was large for Quito. The house had three bedrooms, two baths, a large kitchen, a living room, dining room, second floor balcony, a lovely garden, and quarters for a live-in maid. The maid left the home on Saturdays and returned to work on Monday mornings. They furnished the home with their Bauhaus style furniture from Germany.

Hannah married Gunter Engel, a German Jew who had emigrated to Ecuador. They held the ceremony at the British Embassy on September 16, 1944. The British Ambassador was happy to let them use the Embassy given the work Leni and her sewing circle were doing for Allied troops. Gunter's family had owned a successful drapery business in Dortmund. Gunter and his family had seen the coming storm and fled to Czechoslovakia after Hitler came to power. When that country proved to no longer be a haven, they obtained visas to emigrate to Ecuador.

Anne fell in love with and married Gerhard Anker, who was some twenty years her senior. Anne's parents were initially opposed to the marriage due to the age difference, but they eventually relented and allowed the marriage to go forward. Anne and Gerhard were married on September 2, 1945, also at the British Embassy. Anne and Gerhard (who later used the name Gerardo to meld further into Ecuadorian society) lived next door to Hans and Leni. Hans set up a clothesline between the balconies of their homes so they could reel messages and items to one another on the line.

The Rothschilds were a very close family. On Saturdays they participated in Jewish activities. Sundays were family days. They spent all of their holidays together. Anne often wrote plays which the children presented to the family. The children played in the gardens at their homes and in the streets. There were several movie theaters in town which the family frequently attended. Occasionally, they went to the ballet. Quito had a few nightspots where residents could go for diversion and a night out. Some Jewish residents started a delicatessen, but beyond that, Quito did not offer much by way of commercial entertainment. Anne and Leni were also voracious readers.

Virtually no one in the Jewish community traveled abroad. When they needed to take time out from their daily lives, many refugees, including the Rothschilds, traveled to Baños, a charming resort town with mineral-rich hot springs. Several Jewish immigrants established pensiones (lodgings with meals) for the visitors. Located seventy-four miles south of Quito in the foothills of the Tungurahua volcano, Baños is the last town in the mountain region and served as a gateway to the Amazon jungle and towns in the Amazon river basin.

The Rothschilds' lives centered around Quito's Jewish community, which by the 1940s had several thousand members. Hans was president of the community and at one point was president of the

Bnai Brith (a Jewish service organization) in Quito. Hans was also one of the founders, along with other members of the Jewish community, of a savings and loan association that lent money to immigrants who needed funds to establish businesses.

In the mid-1940s, Quito's Jewish community established a social club, youth club, sports club, and synagogue. However, they had no rabbi; lay leaders conducted religious services. Ecuador's Jewish communities were primarily devoted to social and cultural pursuits; they were far less focused on the synagogue and Jewish ritual.

The immigrants built a community center in the heart of Quito known as the Asociacion de Beneficencia Israelita. The center served as a religious community as well as a cultural and charitable association. It housed an Orthodox synagogue: men prayed on the ground floor while women prayed in the balcony. The Asociacion was the heart of Jewish life in Quito; most significant events took place there. The community also established a funerary society and a small, gated cemetery in Quito.

The Asociacion had a social hall which served as the venue for weddings, bar mitzvahs, and performances. The community occasionally held "Colorful Evenings" at which members of the community performed humorous vignettes. Others sang or played musical instruments. The community formed a library and members addressed educational issues concerning their children. The Asociacion provided financial assistance and other aid to those in need. It also served as a forum for adjudicating disputes which the disputants did not want to take outside the Jewish community. All in all, the several thousand Jews in Quito constructed a rich life which met many of their needs. They developed a sense they had a real home, replete with friends, familiar activities, and a community in this strange, quiet, beautiful piece of land.

GRASPING AT STRAWS

MAX AND TRUDE CONTACTED AS MANY RELATIVES AND acquaintances as they could to help Ernst, Martha, and Sigmund. Grete Oberlander Titche, one of Martha's cousins, had emigrated to the United States on September 19, 1934. Grete and Martha were Oberlanders by birth; Trude's mother and Grete's grandfather were siblings. Grete and her husband Leon Titche settled in Monroe, Louisiana, a small city in the northern part of the state about an hour east of Shreveport. Leon was a doctor at the Vaughan/Wright/Bendel Medical Clinic situated at the intersection of St. John and Oak Streets in Monroe. Max wrote to the Titches to ask if they could provide immigration affidavits and money to help Martha and Sigmund.

Leon responded that "The affidavits were mailed yesterday afternoon and you should have them today." (Leon Titche letter to Max, December 12, 1940.) Leon wrote he needed to know how much money was needed, for what purpose, and for how long. The funds Max requested were to pay for passage on whatever shipping line Ernst, Martha, and Sigmund could secure a guaranteed place.

After Leon forwarded the support affidavits to Max in December 1940, Leon and Grete relocated to Biloxi, Mississippi. Grete executed an additional support affidavit in Biloxi on June 14, 1941. The affidavit provided that Grete would provide financial support for her cousins Martha Oberlander Moses and Sigmund Moses if the United States issued visas allowing them to emigrate. "Affiant further specifically states that this affidavit is made by her for the purpose of inducing the American Consul to issue visas to the above-mentioned relatives and the Immigration Authorities to admit said relatives into the United States." Grete's affidavit stated that she, thirty-one years old, had been born in Germany and became a naturalized United States' citizen in Monroe on October 6, 1938. Grete declared that she was a housekeeper with little income, but her husband Leon was a medical officer employed by the Veterans' Administration.

Even though Max had been able to obtain support affidavits from Grete, formidable obstacles remained. He and Trude still had to find funds to pay for ocean passage, book confirmed passage, and find a way for Ernst, Sigmund, and Martha to get from Cologne to a port of departure. With Europe nearly two years into the war by the time Grete prepared her July 1941 affidavit, getting from Cologne to a port for passage was virtually impossible. Notwithstanding the odds stacked against them, Max and Trude persevered.

Max tried to make sure Trude's parents were provided for. In January 1941, he instructed his bank in Cologne to continue paying the monthly allowance he had established for Sigmund and Martha. He also sent food packages to Martha and Sigmund, with the help of Rudy Waller in New York, through a company that offered "food packages in great variety." It was anyone's guess whether such packages would reach the intended recipients, would be seized by Nazi customs officers, or whether the Reich would reduce Martha's and Sigmund's food rations to the extent of any care packages they received. By this time, Sigmund and Martha were no longer living in the family home on Aachenerstrasse, as they had been forcibly relocated to a home at 2a Lortzingstrasse.

Max and Trude doggedly continued their efforts. The task was difficult and frustrating. They attempted to enlist the support of Consul Klieforth, but there were limits to what he could do:

My Dear Dr. Houser:

I received your letter of December 3, 1940 and was glad to hear from you. Unfortunately, there is nothing that I can do about the immigration visas of your brother and parents-in-law, as it is not the practice of the Consulate at Stuttgart to state in advance of the investigation of the applicants the amount of bond required under the affidavits. It is possible, however, that you can obtain the information you desire from the Bureau of Immigration, Department of Justice, Washington, D.C.

With my regards and best wishes to you and your family, I am,

A.W. Klieforth, American Consul General. (Klieforth letter to Max, January 14, 1941.)

Ernst stayed in constant contact with Max regarding his efforts to obtain visas:

It is said that individual numbers over 29,000 that have particularly good guarantees are obtaining their AC certificates. Now I'd like to ask you, Max, to send me an affidavit; state in it how you will support me, that I can live with you and eat with you and that you will supply me with $5 or $10 pocket money weekly, or however much is feasible for conditions there. It is said to be better to make up the affidavit in this form...Here there are currently lectures on America, which have met with great interest and which I have also attended... (Ernst letter to Max and Trude, Feb. 18, 1941.)

Ernst noted from Max's letters that it seemed his practice was growing slowly, but steadily. Ernst also commented: "Dear Trude, you are a competent doctor's wife in that after a mere description you came up with the right diagnosis, whereas two physicians after seeing (the patient) gave incorrect diagnoses. Your praise was rightly earned."

The day after Ernst wrote to Max, the American consulate in Stuttgart wrote to Ernst:

To the holder of Registration number 27209:

This is to inform you that the documents you have submitted for review are conditionally considered to be sufficient and that your matter may be considered immediately, provided that quota numbers are still available, as soon as you can provide evidence that you will be able to travel to the United States if you have been issued a visa. The ability to travel to the United States is not just that you are able to leave Germany, but also about being able to access ocean passage and reach the port of embarkation. In view of the current limited availability of ships passages, the deposit of a sufficient amount for your ocean passage cannot be regarded as conclusive evidence of the possibility of traveling to the United States.

Once you have made firm travel arrangements, you should provide documentary evidence of such so that you can be invited to appear at the consulate for visa application.

The American Consul General. (U.S. Consular letter to Ernst, Feb. 19, 1941.)

Ernst had finally obtained Consular approval of the documents he had submitted in support of his visa application. Now, if only he could obtain proof of confirmed transportation to the United States and evidence that he had the ability to reach the port of departure, he would be eligible to have the Consulate schedule his interview. If the interview were satisfactory, he would at long last obtain a visa. However, finding a ship and booking confirmed passage while the world was at war proved, unsurprisingly, to be extraordinarily difficult. With Europe engulfed in war and the Reich in control of much of the continent, time for Ernst, Sigmund, and Martha to escape was running out.

Ernst wrote to Max two days later: "This morning I was overjoyed to receive my AC certificate from the consulate in Stuttgart, that is, the information that my sponsors' guarantees are sufficient and my summons to appear may follow as soon as I can show a reservation for my ship passage." Ernst explained that a reservation on a vessel was not enough; rather, he had to have a confirmed berth on a ship. He asked Max to help him secure a berth out of Lisbon, which was one of the last ports in Europe still operational for civilian transport. Ernst hoped to accomplish this by means of payment to the American Jewish Joint Distribution Committee, commonly referred to as the "Joint," after which Ernst could respond to the consulate. The Joint was the largest nonpolitical organization committed to helping Jews in need and distress around the world. Ernst concluded his letter: "I hope to see you in a not too distant future." (Ernst letter to Max, Feb. 21, 1941.)

The Joint's Committee on Refugee Aid in Europe acknowledged Max's letter of February 24, 1941, that had enclosed two checks to the Joint, one for $400 and one for $2.00, the former for Ernst's transportation and the latter for the cost of telegraph cables. (February 26, 1941 letter to Max from Irwin Rosen, Secretary of the Committee on Refugee Aid in Europe of the American Jewish Joint Distribution Committee.) The Joint wrote it would cable confirmation of the deposit to the Hilfsverein in Cologne, which in turn would forward the information to the American Consulate as proof of Ernst's ability to travel to the United States.

Unfortunately, the next, crucial steps were maddeningly difficult. Ernst learned he could not secure a berth through the Joint. Instead, he had to make payment for a berth directly to the shipping line. He wrote to Max that he needed him to authorize the Committee to pay $320 from Ernst's $400 deposit to American Export Lines in New York. American Export Lines would, in theory, inform its Lisbon branch of the payment, which in turn would wire confirmation to the Lindemann Travel Agency in Cologne. The Export Line would also provide the date of Ernst's travel and the name of the ship on which he had a confirmed berth. Once the Lindemann Agency had the details regarding the ship and date on which Ernst had confirmed passage, it would issue a certificate to Ernst that he could send to the United States consulate in Stuttgart. The consulate would then issue a summons for Ernst to appear for an interview to obtain his visa. Notwithstanding the many hoops through which he was trying to jump, Ernst kept up a brave front: "For now, lots of greetings and kisses to you all. Your Ernst." (Ernst letter to Max, Feb. 27, 1941.)

Ernst Oberlander, a cousin of Martha's, wrote to Max, Trude, and the girls in March 1941 to wish Renate a happy birthday. (Ernst Oberlander letter to Max and Trude, Feb. 28, 1941.) He recounted how Sigmund and Martha had been quite ill. Martha had suffered a bad case of the flu as well as "heart spasms." After she had been in bed for two and one-half weeks, Sigmund fell ill, which was challenging for him because by that time he was eighty years old.

Mr. Oberlander reported that Max's colleague Dr. Hugo Zade stopped by frequently to tend to Martha and Sigmund. They refused Dr. Zade's recommendation that they go to the hospital to recuperate, even though their coughing was so severe they kept one another up all night such that neither of them could get any rest. They eventually recovered, but only after Martha had been ill for four weeks. Mr. Oberlander mentioned that "he and mother" had obtained their AC certificates from Stuttgart, but Olga Oberlander had not. She needed to have her United States guarantor intervene in order to obtain her visa. He noted that cousin Lore was still not in the United States, even though she had her visa. "Let's hope that someday we will all be together in the U.S." Many members of the Ichenhäuser and Moses' extended families were struggling to get out of Germany and running into the same bureaucratic hurdles as those that Ernst, Sigmund, and Martha were trying to overcome.

The Joint wrote to Max advising that since his funds had been "committed to the Hilfsverein in Koeln (sic) by our cable confirmation" the Joint could act only upon the Hilfsverein's instructions. The Joint noted it had deposited $320 with American Export Lines for the cost of Ernst's ocean passage. (Joint Letter to Max, March 10, 1941.) The unending back and forth between and among the interested parties and agencies, with no discernable progress, was maddening.

Meanwhile, Trude's parents wrote to the family; their longing and despair were palpable:

> My dear children!
>
> My thoughts are with you much of the time; through your detailed letters I feel I am actually with you...In our minds we are already making the big trip [to join you]. Everywhere soldiers are arming themselves. Everyone is preparing themselves to flee to their children. I am eager to receive news from Stuttgart; what's difficult is booking the passage...Everyone is grasping

at straws. How wonderful it makes me feel when Renate says: "When grandma comes"—this means she's still thinking about me...

Love and kisses to all four of you,

Mother and Oma (Martha letter to Trude and Max, March 14, 1941.)

Ernst wrote to the family the same day:

My dears!

Today I have let Father write first because he now wants to have his noon sleep. In the meantime, we received your letters from February 26 and March 10 and hope that more will arrive soon. In my emigration matter I have heard nothing more; it is supposed to take a long time until the American Export Lines allocates ship passage from Lisbon. I cabled to you on February 27 again as follows: "Allow Joint to transfer $320 of four hundred dollars deposited to American Export Lines, wire confirmation to Lisbon. Lisbon is to telegraph travel agency Lindemann. This relates to the following: in the past, the shipping companies have allocated ship's passage when the money for the passage has been deposited with the Joint, they no longer do this now, but demand that the money be deposited with them. That's why the money has to be transferred from the Joint to the American Export Lines, maybe you'll be able to arrange a confirmed ship's passage there, it does not have to be on the American Export Lines, it can also be a different line, be it American or Spanish or Portuguese. Should you be successful with that, I would have to have telegraphic confirmation of that. The appointment to go to Stuttgart you get only if you can prove a fixed ship's passage and I would like to come in this quota year if possible. (Ernst letter to Trude and Max, March 14, 1941.)

Ernst's inability to procure confirmed ship's passage was the only thing preventing him from emigrating. There was a very real possibility that, for lack of a berth, he would lose his life.

Ernst also wrote to Renate and Erica:

Dear Erica! To win the first prize, we sincerely congratulate you and are happy about [your] success. We hope that you can win quite a few prizes, first and others, as well as you dear Renate; maybe you have also won a gold watch or an otherwise nice prize. I would be glad if I could look at your prizes. Keep it up, best regards and kisses,

Your Uncle Ernst (Ernst letter to Max and Trude, March 14, 1941.)

Nine days later, Ernst wired Max that the support affidavits for Trude's parents had arrived. He asked Max to pay the parents' passage from Lisbon to New York. (Ernst wire to Max, March 23, 1941.) Trude's parents still did not have their AC certificates from the consulate in Stuttgart; apparently the United States had put new visa procedures in place. All was not well regarding Ernst's immigration. Ernst noted Max's recent letter to the effect that the Joint had postponed Ernst's passage until July. Ernst asked whether that meant the Joint would only start allotting spots again in July, or if it wanted to give him passage in July? If the latter, he was not concerned, as there were no berths available before July. As to booking passage, "Whether it is better to pay into the Joint or the shipping company can only be judged by the situation, which may change daily." (Ernst letter to Max, March-April 1941.)

As further evidence of the chaos that had engulfed the emigration process, W.T. Schaefer, Assistant Passenger Traffic Manager for American Export Lines, wrote to Max: "We have your letter of March 11, 1941 and note what you say. Apparently, the moneys you paid to the American Jewish Joint Distribution Committee was forwarded (sic) directly to our office in Lisbon and was not cleared through us. We suggest that you get in touch with them." (Letter to Max from American Export Lines, March 17, 1941.)

The confusion was further evidenced by a contemporaneous letter to Max from Irwin Rosen, Secretary of the Joint Committee on Refugee Aid in Europe:

Please be advised that we have not received any word from the Hilfsverein in Koeln (sic) in reply to our cable for authorization to make refund to you. However, the American Export Lines has discontinued the policy of accepting deposits for passage due to the fact that they are booked until the end of June. Therefore, we believe it would be to the advantage of the above named [Ernst] if the funds you deposited with us were left in our possession, and we are today taking the liberty of cabling instructions to the Hilfsverein to disregard our cable requesting authorization to make refund. It would be well for you to advise your brother of our action in the matter. (American Joint Distribution Committee letter to Max, March 18, 1941.)

Sigmund and Martha wrote to Max and Trude in late March. Sigmund, at age 83, was having trouble with his vision, but he could read typewritten letters. Regarding their efforts to emigrate, they wrote: "In any case, we are making as much effort as possible to obtain passage. But you read newspapers also [and therefore understand the obstacles they faced trying to leave Germany]." (Martha and Sigmund letter to Trude and Max, March 27, 1941.)[255]

Ernst penned a lengthy addendum to Sigmund's letter, which said, in part: "You write already of my coming over there and I anticipated that event with pleasure, but unfortunately it is still far off. My joy at receiving the AC document quickly turned to vinegar: there are no places on ships."

Ernst explained:

The Joint at present has no openings; that is why I wanted to transfer the money to the American Export Lines. But the Joint only does this upon the order of the local agency; then comes the blocking of the Export Lines, which, according to the local travel agencies, will not accept any money for passage until July. There are hundreds of others in the same situation as I. Stuttgart [the U.S. consulate] showers AC documents [on people] and

---

255 It should be noted that, according to Renate, Max corresponded with his father David and David wrote to Max. Max's letters to his father were lost in the war, as were Trude's letters to her parents. As to David's letters to Max, it is not known what happened to them. It may be that Max did not save such correspondence, as opposed to Trude, who did.

yet there are no ship berths to be had. If the Joint does not see to it that passenger ships come to Lisbon so that passages become available, then everything is in vain. (Ernst letter to Max, March 27, 1941.)

Ernst went on to note that American Export Lines was no longer accepting deposits for passage; as a result, that line was no longer available to provide passage from Lisbon. Ernst explained this was why he was asking Max to send funds to Hapag (Hamburg-America Line) in the hope of obtaining passage on one of its ships. He pleaded that Max "Do therefore whatever you can to make the entire Jewish community aware and active so that the Joint will get ship berths, possible by chartering entire ships. It also affects the parents [Sigmund and Martha] whose passage money also was not accepted because of the ban at the Export Lines." Ernst noted the registration numbers the consulate in Stuttgart was working on were in the 10,000 range; Ernst's number was 27,209—"still a long way off"—and the parents' number was 27,551. Ernst's frustration was as undeniable as it was understandable:

A cable from you to Stuttgart isn't necessary and will not help, since one is summoned only when one can prove a definite place on a ship. On the other hand, the visa becomes invalid after four months. There is talk here of a new bill that would make immigration to the U.S. easier. But what good is that, even if it were true, when one can't travel. (Ernst letter to Max, March 27, 1941.)

Hamburg American Lines wrote to Max to explain it was unable to make bookings for a definite date. Rather, bookings had to be left to its European organization, "which will always try to arrange for the earliest possible departure." (Hamburg American Line—North German Lloyd letter to Max, March 28, 1941.) However, Hamburg American refused to provide any guarantees. The approximate cost of passage as of March 1941 was $400 per person via Spain or Portugal and $600 via Siberia/Japan. Hamburg American did not provide suggestions on how Ernst might get from Germany to Spain, Portugal, Siberia, or Japan in order to board a ship in any of those countries.

While Max was working with Ernst to obtain visas and book transit, Trude was mining family relationships to obtain help. She wrote to Walter Rothschild to enlist his assistance. Walter's sister, Meta Rothschild Lissauer, was a cousin of Trude's who had attended university and obtained a doctorate, a true rarity for women. Meta and her husband Meno Lissauer lived in New York, where Meno had established a scrap metal company—Associated Metals & Minerals Corporation. Meno wrote to tell Trude that his brother-in-law Walter had suffered a nervous breakdown due to the stress he was suffering in trying to get family out of Germany. Meno wrote they were leaving no stone unturned in their efforts to help Ernst. However, "currently there is no passage because the shipping lines to the U.S. have been fully booked for months already, and the American consulates in Europe do not issue visas, as I was personally informed in writing by the consul in Stuttgart." (Meno Lissauer letter to Trude, March 31, 1941.)

As to Martha and Sigmund: "The above statements apply also to your question regarding passage for your parents. I am still try-ing, through negotiation with a travel agency with which we have good connections, to have some sort of reservation accepted, so that at such time as the prohibition is lifted a booking may be speedily obtained."

It seemed there was no end to the demands and changing reg-ulations affecting immigration to the United States. In April, Ernst wrote to Max to report that the Consulate in Stuttgart had found fault with Max's application for Sigmund's and Martha's visas. The then current requirements for American sponsors for immigrants provided:

1) Your American Sponsor should present proof of income.

    A.   If he is an employee, [he needs] a notarized statement from his employer confirming the amount of his income, how long he has been employed by his current employer and whether his position is considered a permanent one.

B. If he is self-employed, [he needs] a report from a well-known American credit agency, a trust company or similar institute. This report should describe both his income and his assets.

C. The sponsor should present a certified true copy of the original of his latest Federal Income Tax Return. Such copies are issued on demand by the tax authorities (Bureau of Internal Revenue, Department of the Treasury, Washington, D.C.). If the sponsor has not presented a Federal income tax return and cannot fulfill the conditions under items 1A and B, he should have a credible third party, such as a tax auditor (certified public accountant), give a notarized statement concerning his income and assets.

2) Your sponsor should present proof of asset value.

A. A certified statement by an authorized bank official showing his available funds/credit balance. This statement should simultaneously show since when he has had this account as well as when and how he had made individual sizable deposits.

B. A statement issued by his insurance company regarding the cash-in value of his insurance policies.

C. A certified property statement by a bank or authorized real estate broker regarding his assets and the current market value of his securities. (Excerpt from Form KG.811.11.)

Max needed to comply more fully with the financial provisions to show he would provide for the applicants on a "fairly indefinite basis" before Sigmund and Martha could obtain visas.

Ernst wrote that he and Trude's parents had received a letter from Max and Trude with photographs of Renate and Erica. "Your daughters have become big girls who will make their own way. Have they in the meantime worked capably and again won a prize?" A physician friend had commented to Ernst that the best advertisements Max could have for his skill as a physician were his daughters, given how bright, pretty, and healthy they were. Ernst also commented regarding Trude's efforts to earn money: "$20 for an embroidery, dear Trude, is a decent sum and a very nice side-income." While Max's practice grew slowly, Trude was trying to earn money by taking advantage of her childhood training with needle and thread at Sigmund's fabric and menswear business. As to the primary issue at hand, however, she and Max could feel Ernst's despair: "Obtaining a place on a ship is a long, difficult, and nerve-wracking matter. When one thinks one has progressed, one still has nothing." (Ernst letter to Max and Trude, April 12, 1941.)

While the Ichenhäusers continued their efforts, the war spread further across Europe. On April 6, 1941, Germany invaded Yugoslavia and Greece. Hitler claimed he invaded Yugoslavia after it signed a treaty with Russia that Hitler claimed was an attempt to encircle Germany. He attacked Greece claiming the British planned a landing there in order to attack "Germany's interests" from a base in southern Europe. The Luftwaffe bombed the Yugoslav capital of Belgrade into rubble in retribution for the Yugoslav refusal to promptly agree to German occupation of the country. A week later, on April 13, the Yugoslav army surrendered. Meanwhile, the RAF continued its massive bombing raids against Germany. The raids included huge incendiary bombing runs against Hamburg, which was Germany's second largest port and one of the Reich's main centers for constructing U-boats.

Ernst wrote several weeks later further describing how difficult it was to work with the several immigration agencies since each had its own procedures and requirements. He experienced similar frustration dealing with the shipping companies and the U.S. Consulate.

> Payment to the Joint is being recommended by the Agency; that the Joint in its management would make so much difficulty and cause red tape in its bureaucratic operation, more than the local agency, was not known here, especially not to me. There seems to be another factor come into play: up to Feb. 19, as soon as the money was paid to them, the Joint obtained immediately a booking at the ship's office for the person concerned, but since Feb. 19 this procedure is not in operation, why, no one knows.

It is rumored that the Joint had differences with the shipping line; perhaps over there you might find out more about it. If that were true, it would be very sad, that such differences should be carried on the back of the emigrants. Not to be disputed is the fact that the agency has messed up a lot, but the Joint also; unfortunately, one can't do without both of them.

***

The telegram of March 23 referred to a payment to the Export Lines, however, at that time the latter was not accepting money anymore, and this fact was not known here. Moreover, the Export Lines is not booked solid up to July, but instead will not accept money until July; they are booked solid up to February of next year and possibly even longer; at least for February they already have bookings. Why the Lines don't make use of their business connections and send other ships is incredible.

***

I had another appointment at the agency yesterday since I received a letter from the Hapag, which is now handling my case, to turn the booking over to a Lisbon office, so I could immediately inquire about this. The agency agreed and therefore I have authorized it and hope that the matter will proceed and I will have something definite. In our last letter I wrote you about a telegram in which you were to get a refund and pay it to the Hapag; after 10 days I was informed that because of new regulations this telegram was never sent. Now you see how time is lost and nothing can be done about it.

To obtain a booking before the money is in the hands of the shipping line or the travel agency is impossible. The lines here are so overrun that they don't have to operate any differently. The summons to Stuttgart does not follow when the money for passage is available, but only when one has a definite booking space; the travel agency gives out a voucher that must be sent to Stuttgart, then the summons follows. (Ernst letter to Max and Trude, April 22, 1941.)

Despite the frustration they felt and what seemed like running in circles, the family had no choice but to pursue every possibility in case one, finally, might work. As Sigmund wrote: "In spite of the time slot given (at the Consulate), frequently he (Ernst) has to wait two hours before it's his turn. Until now nothing has come of all the visits…There are always delays and no progress." (Sigmund letter to Trude and Max, April 22, 1941.)

Nevertheless, Trude and Max continued to write to friends, family members, and other contacts to try to secure passage for Ernst, Sigmund, and Martha. Roadblocks persisted. Meno Lissauer wrote to Trude:

> My dear Mrs. Houser:
>
> As much as I am moved by your lines of April 21, I am sorry that at present I can't tell anything but what I have already written to you.
>
> Passage is not available at this time. If you hear something else from another side, then it is only passage on obscure or at least unreliable shipping lines. One can't rely on booking such a passage. The danger of losing a paid-for passage that one can't use in time, is very great, and there have been sad experiences along this line. Be assured that I would help you if I knew a way; but right now, there is none.
>
> I hope your husband is on the way to recovery.
>
> Meno Lissauer (Meno Lissauer letter to Trude, April 24, 1941.)

Max had not been feeling up to par for a while, hence Meno's comment.

The Joint wrote to Max and expressed little optimism about being able to bring Trude's parents to the United States:

> May we point out to you that accommodations are very scarce and all boats are heavily booked up for months to come. Aside from that no Portuguese transit visas are being issued for the time being. Should you want to make a deposit in favor of your parents, we are ready to accept your funds, however, we cannot predict just when a booking will be made on either of the lines communicating between Lisbon and New York.

We regret that we are unable to give you a more favorable reply. (Letter from the Joint Distribution Committee to Max, April 30, 1941.)

Max tried to obtain help from another cousin, Walter Rothschild, who outlined the difficulties Trude was facing in securing passage from Lisbon for Ernst:

> I received your letter of May 8. You are giving me a hard nut to crack. The payment to Hapag follows this procedure: they receive dollars and compensate the Portuguese line in German Reichsmarks. I would not assume that this is to be recommended, because what one hears about the Portuguese line is not exactly gratifying. By way of proof I am enclosing a letter I received from Switzerland, but I ask you to return it to me eventually. If you want to take this chance, I can't deter you, but it could happen that your brother arrives in Lisbon with a ticket in his pocket but is not allowed to board the ship. It has happened frequently that the same ticket is sold numerous times, at ever higher prices. A valid booking can be obtained in Lisbon, but it depends on whether you are the highest bidder. With your limited means, you shouldn't be so eager to take this chance, so I advise you not to do it. But you must decide yourself. (Walter Rothschild letter to Max, May 15, 1941.)

As to Trude's parents, Walter went onto explain that, according to his experience, the United States' consulate demanded an affidavit from a non-relative showing, not just promising, so many dollars are available to support the applicant, with $2,000 being the amount the consulate suggested. The funds were to be deposited in a bank and would be returned to the depositor when the family members arrive, at which time they would receive monthly payments from the deposit. Walter was unable to provide the deposit. "Furthermore, there is the circumstance that a 'foolproof' passage can't be booked in a foreseeable time. Therefore, what good is a deposit if you can't get your parents out. I am sorry that I have to give you such unpleasant information, but what good are kind words if the situation does not conform?" (Walter Rothschild letter to Trude, May 15, 1941.)

As to Max having been ill, Walter wrote: "I am happy that Max is well again; my inquiries among my physician friends lead me to believe that Max can reach old age with his anemia and can continue with his practice. I hope that this information is true and that the hospital stay was only an alarm, just as my hospital stay was." (Walter Rothschild letter to Trude, May 15, 1941.) Family records do not contain information about Max's condition. However, based on Walter's letter, Max apparently had been diagnosed with anemia. The fact that Max had been hospitalized was reason enough for Trude to be deeply concerned.

A series of Allied air raids on Cologne in the spring of 1941 had a dramatic impact on the city's housing stock. The Allies sent 262 air raids to strike Cologne over the course of the war. Cologne's answer to the Allied bombing and resultant destruction of the city's housing stock was to seize homes occupied by Jews and provide them to Aryan residents. The city issued an order that Aryan-owned homes with Jewish residents and a number of Jewish-owned homes should be cleansed of their Jewish residents. Aryans whose homes had been destroyed were to move into those homes. The State, the city of Cologne, members of the S.A. and SS, and Jews' Aryan neighbors all seized and occupied Jewish-owned homes.

To make it easier for the SS and Gestapo to locate Cologne's Jews, in May and June 1941 the SS began to concentrate the city's remaining Jews in "Jewish houses" known as "Judenhäuser." These were not ghettos, but rather were specific buildings in which only Jews were housed.[256]

Cologne's municipal government also established the so-called "Judenlager Müngersdorf" ("Jewish camp") in 1941 in Fort V and the surrounding Müngersdorf district. The Fort and Judenlager were located on Cologne's west side in the Lindenthal district, adjacent to Braunsfeld where the Ichenhäusers' family home was located. In the 1870's, the Prussians constructed a ring of fortresses around Cologne. The fort located in Müngersdorf, built in 1874-76, was designated Fort V as part of Cologne's outer fortress ring.

After WWI and as part of the demilitarization of the Rhineland, Germany dismantled the fortresses. However, it left some of the

---

256 *Pogrom Night* at xxvi.

barracks intact. To address the impact of the Allied bombing raids, Cologne used the barracks and former prison at Fort V to house Jews whom the city had evicted from their homes. To add insult to injury, having been forced out of their homes, the city compelled the Jewish community to bear the cost of building the additional, unheated barracks needed to house the forcibly relocated Jews. The SS transferred Jews living in Judenhäuser to the barracks at Fort V.

The Jewish residents forced from their homes lived in the Müngersdorf camp until the SS deported them to concentration camps beginning in 1942. Once deportations began, and since most Jews knew what awaited them in the camps, many Jews in Müngersdorf committed suicide. Taking their own lives was, in a heart-breaking manner, a way in which they could control their destinies. These suicides echoed the decision of the Jews on Masada to take their own lives rather than let the Romans capture them and force them to serve as slaves. Since the Nazis used many Jewish concentration camp inmates as slave labor, the comparison is apt.

The SS sent Jews from the Müngersdorf camp, the Judenhäuser, and Jews who had taken refuge in the Rhineland Lodge, to the Theresienstadt ghetto, which served as little more than a way station before the SS sent prisoners held there to the death camps. Many Jews from Müngersdorf were sent directly to death camps in the east. At times, up to 2500 Jews were kept in the barracks behind Fort V prior to deportation. "Between October 1941 and October 1944, approximately 11,000 Jewish people were sent to the ghettoes or extermination camps from Cologne…"[257] Immediately prior to deportation, Jewish victims were sent to the Fair Hall in Cologne-Deutz on the eastern side of the Rhine; the Hall served as a pre-transport detention camp. The transports left from the underground portion of the Köln Messe/Deutz Station. The SS sent its victims to Lodz, Theresienstadt, Riga, Lublin, and other ghettoes and camps in eastern Europe from where they were eventually sent to death camps.

The U.S. Consulate in Stuttgart wrote to Ernst:

To the owner of the registration number 27209

---

257 *Pogrom Night* at xxvi.

Herewith you are informed that the documents you submitted for examination are conditionally deemed sufficient, and that your affair can be considered immediately, on the condition that quota numbers are still available, as soon as it can be shown that you are in a position to travel to the United States if a visa is furnished. The possibility to travel to the United States depends not only on your being in a position to leave Germany, but also that you can obtain ocean passage and reach the port of departure. Considering the currently limited ship passage available, the deposit of a sufficient amount for ocean passage cannot be considered conclusive evidence for the possibility of a trip to the United States.

As soon as you have completed preparation for travel, you should submit documentary proof so that you may receive a summons to appear at the consulate office. (Undated, unsigned letter from the United States consulate to Ernst based on his registration number.)

While Ernst was no doubt pleased to receive this letter, it set forth conditions that were then and would continue to be impossible for him to fulfill, including paying the high costs of emigrating, securing a confirmed berth for ocean passage, and finding a way to travel to a port of departure.

However, Ernst had no alternative but to keep trying. He continued to keep Max apprised of his efforts. Ernst authorized the Hapag of Essen (a city north of Cologne) to use the money he had deposited with the Joint to secure a booking, but only if the Hapag could confirm definite passage for him. Ernst noted the local travel agencies in Germany were all working with Portuguese shipping lines. Ernst continued to be frustrated that the Joint did not charter ships to evacuate Jewish emigrants.

Ernst wrote that he was not going to be able to visit the agencies and the consulate in Stuttgart as frequently as he had been because "tomorrow I begin working in a furniture factory from 7 a.m. to 6 p.m." (Ernst letter to Max and Trude, June 6, 1941.) It is likely this employment was not elective, but rather was part of the forced labor program to which Germany subjected its remaining Jews. Private employers had long before stopped employing Jews due to the employers' anti-Semitism and their fear of retribution if they were seen employing Jews. However, with most Aryan men serving in the armed services, Germany needed people to work in civilian jobs. As a result, the Reich overcame its aversion to Jews, but only insofar as they could be put to productive use in service to the Reich. "Starting in the fall of 1940, all Jews could ultimately be mustered for forced labor. The age limit, especially in Berlin, was raised to 65 for men and 60 for women."[258]

Trude, Erica, and Renate wrote often to Martha, Sigmund, and Ernst in an effort to keep their spirits up. In an undated letter, likely from 1941 or 1942, Renate wrote:

> Dear Grandma, Dear Grandpa, Dear Uncle Ernst,
>
> Last week, I became the art editor of our school's yearbook. That's a very high position to hold and I'm very proud of it. I'm the youngest of all the kids, who are mainly 15-16 years old (Renate was 13-14). At the moment, I do quite a bit of drawing at home. On Saturdays, we always take a drawing class at the art museum. I really enjoy it.
>
> Otherwise, there's nothing new at school. I always go to my clubs and really like going. Two days ago, all the clubs were photographed for the yearbook. A picture of every club will appear in the yearbook. Once a week, I play netball [similar to basketball] after school. It's my favorite game and I'm really good at it now—at least better than a lot of other kids.
>
> I gave Eri a skirt for her birthday. Mrs. Behr had given it to me and it was bit too small and I only wore it three times—that's why I gave it to Erica.
>
> Otherwise, I don't have anything to report. I hope that you are all doing well and that we soon get mail [from you]. Many warm greetings and kisses.
>
> Yours,
>
> Renate

While these letters no doubt warmed Sigmund, Martha, and

---

258 *Jewish Daily Life* at 360.

Ernst's hearts, they were also painful reminders of what they were missing while trapped in Germany. Each letter was a source of both comfort and agony.

For the Love of Their
Fellow Man

T HE ICHENHÄUSERS WERE, OF COURSE, NOT THE ONLY PEO-
ple desperately trying to get out of Germany. Trude was trying
to help other Jews as well. One person from whom she sought assistance was Lionel Friedmann of Friedmann & Co. Realtors in New
York:

> Dear Mrs. Hauser (sic):
>
> I hasten to answer your letter of the 27th and to assure you I have
> been and am willing to do anything possible to help Clotilde
> Hahn and Edith and Sigbert Wachs to come to America [Edith
> was a cousin of Trude's and Clothilde was a long-time friend]. In
> fact, I have received several letters from them and have written
> and cabled them, but it would seem they have not received my
> communications.
>
> I have also been to New York to try to arrange to have their
> money transferred to me so that it would not be impounded,
> and in this connection am enclosing copies of several letters
> which you will find self-explanatory.
>
> You say you do not know what member of the Friedmann
> family I am, and I might explain that Clotilde's father was my
> father's brother.

I might add that I have also been to Washington to see if I can get special permission to bring them over here under some visitors' quota, but as yet have no word from Washington on this. At my request the State Department has cabled to the consul in Marseille to see what can be done, but we have had no reply to date.

I will gladly have the supplemental affidavits made out promptly, and in accordance with your request will send them to you to be attached to the papers you are sending.

Very truly yours,

Lionel Friedmann (Lionel Friedmann letter to Trude, Jan. 29, 1941.)

Edith and Sigmund had sent a telegram to Trude on January 26 asking Trude to obtain "moral affidavits" for them and send them to Lionel at his Rittenhouse Square address in Philadelphia.

On February 11, 1941, Trude sent a packet via registered mail to Edith and Sigbert Wachs at 6 Boulevard St. Michel in the village of Condom, near the northern edge of the Gers department in France, northwest of Toulouse, in an area that was under Vichy control. Most likely the packet contained support affidavits for Edith and Sigbert.

Mr. Friedmann wrote to Trude on February 13 advising her that the National City Bank of New York had applied to the U.S. State Department for permission to transfer the Wachs' funds to Lionel. In the meantime, he had received a cable from Sigbert Wachs to the effect that Lionel should pay 15,000 Uruguayan piastres to the National Republic Bank in Montevideo as security for Clothilde and Edith. Based on this request, Lionel believed the Wachses and Sigberts had secured permission to travel and had confirmed arrangements to travel to Uruguay. Therefore, he wanted instructions from Trude as to whether he should continue his efforts with the State Department to try to gain entry for them to the United States.

In May, Lionel wrote to Trude once more: "We have been doing all that is possible to try to get the Wachs family admitted here or to Uruguay, but the Government has refused to grant a permit for the transfer of Sigbert's funds from the Bank in New York to me and has also refused to grant a permit for the transfer of the necessary funds to Uruguay. I am in constant communication with the bank and am still working on this, but it does not look favorable. I sent the moral and political affidavit directly to the consul in Marseille some time ago. As for the financial affidavit, I regret to say that the Marseille consul will not accept any more from me as I have so many on file with him already. (Lionel Friedmann letter to Trude, May 5, 1941.)

Dr. Hugo Zade was a medical colleague of Max's. Dr. Zade was the first pediatrician in the town of Langenfeld, roughly fifteen miles north of Cologne. In 1935, S.A. thugs forced Langenfeld's residents to boycott Dr. Zade by "urging" them, in a way that only armed hooligans can "urge," to see other doctors. Dr. Zade soon lost his medical license and the right to attend patients at the Richrath hospital in Langenfeld because of the Nazi edicts prohibiting Jewish physicians from practicing medicine. As a result, Dr. Zade was financially ruined.

Dr. Zade, his wife Marta, and their adult daughter Ursula left Langenfeld in 1937 and moved to Cologne. There, he worked at the Jewish hospital, the Asyl.[259] That is most likely where he came to know Max. Dr. Zade wrote to Max regarding Max's father David, Sigmund, and Martha, as well as in connection with Dr. Zade's efforts to escape:

Dear Colleague:

Sans Gêne [a French phrase meaning "without shame"]—I'll get right down to it! In the last letter that you sent to me directly and in which you thank me for providing medical care to your father and parents-in-law, you wrote among other things: "Please expect me to always be at your disposal if you need my advice or actions. I haven't heard anything from my relatives concerning your plans; I'd be interested in knowing what your plans are." Up to now, we've had no plans, could make no plans, because

---

259 The Asylum, or Asyl, was the vernacular name for the "Israelite Asylum" as the Jewish Hospital was known in Cologne. The Nazis prohibited the Asyl from accepting non-Jewish patients in 1936. They later closed it altogether and deported its patients. Their destination, no doubt, was the death camps.

our America [quota] number, which we'd requested years ago just in case and in case there'd be a miracle, would come up— in terms of human counting abilities—in the year 1943 at the earliest. But a little while ago, there was an announcement that the number of immigrants to be accepted had been increased so much that even by the end of this very year all numbers up to 30,000 should be called up in Stuttgart. Our numbers— meaning ours and that of our daughter—are somewhere in the vicinity of 29,500; this means that we could be called up in December of this year unless events occur that would prompt the U.S. to renege on their commitment. Apart from this number, however, we do not possess any papers that would facilitate our entry into this hospitable country [the United States]. No one belonging to our two families has emigrated in years or decades; all of them lived, as far as I can see looking back, in Germany for generations, and no one felt compelled to leave this country. That such a clinging to the home soil wasn't very useful in light of the current situation is something that could not be foreseen—that's something for which I cannot begrudge my ancestors and relatives. It's likely that they were as attached to this country, its language and its culture, as I still am to this day. So, this is our current situation, and therefore it prompts us to ask the following simple questions: "How could we acquire an affidavit for our numbers?"—because the number has actionable value only in conjunction with a solid affidavit. To put it simply and directly—I am aware that I am saying something grand in a casual manner—could you help us acquire such a document? Do you know of any people who, for the love of their fellow man, would be willing to provide us with such a solid affidavit? And—if this isn't possible for all three of us—at least for our daughter?

Because the mail is taking such a long time going back and forth, I want to give you the necessary data just in case:

I, Hugo Zade, Dr. med., born in Berlin on December 13, 1880, after finishing high school at the Berlin Humanistic Gymnasium, [a German college prep school] pursued university studies at Berlin and Konigsberg, and graduated in April 1905 at Konigsberg, receiving my medical Staatsexamen degree, and then in May 1905 got my medical license as a Doctor of Medicine; I was a general practitioner for 32 years in the country in Immigrath, after that in Cologne, with an interruption from October 1, 1938 through November 22, 1939—during which period I, too, had to stop working in light of the general annulment of the approbation [licensure] of all Jewish physicians—from that point on, I was given permission once more to provide treatment to Jewish patients. Over the years, I have authored a number of scientific works on pediatric care as well as on general illnesses (pathologies), some of these were quite voluminous; almost all of them can be found in the medical archives. I could thus work anywhere as a practitioner of medicine or as a research assistant.

Dr. Zade went on to describe his wife and daughter:

My wife, Mrs. Marta Zade, nee Flatauer, born in Konigsberg on October 22, 1883, graduated from a high[er] school for girls and finished business school; after that, she studied for 8 semesters at the Public Academy for Fine Arts in Konigsberg and now she is an artist specializing in painting, etching, and arts and crafts doing commercial graphics and posters, etc.[260]

My daughter Ursula Zade, born in Immigrath on March 11, 1912, went to elementary school in Immigrath, than attended intermediate school in Langenfeld, then the Realgymnasium for girls in Düsseldorf, completed her Abitur exam at 18 years old, studied medicine in Cologne, Konigsberg and Düsseldorf, finished her Staatsexamen with a final grade of "Good" in December 1935 in Düsseldorf, and has for the past 5 years been working in Internal Medicine at the Asylum, meaning she thus has more than served all the hours that are demanded of medical professionals specializing in Internal Medicine.[261] Of course, she is also proficient in all the required laboratory activities, blood cell counts, blood sugar levels, electrocardiography, all the

---

260 Dr. Zade's reference to a "higher school" for girls is to a 19th century German Tochterschule (usually referred to as Hohere Tochterschule). This "higher" school for girls was equivalent to the Gymnasium (which was originally only for boys), except that the Tochterschule lacked the final three years that were college preparatory.

261 The 19th century German Rektoratsschule was an intermediate school chiefly in rural areas preparing students for the college-preparatory Gymnasium. The German Realgymnasium was a school squeezed in between the Intermediate School (late Realschule) and the pre-academic Gymnasium. The Arbitur is the German final exam at the end of studies at the Gymnasium.

chemical exams of bodily fluids, determining residual nitrogen levels, basic metabolic rates, etc. She's also utterly confident when doing autopsies and interpreting post-mortem findings...

Dr. Zade reported regarding his visits with and treatment of Max's father David. He wrote he had finally gotten a handle on David's heart arrhythmia. "Thus, in spite of his bad hearing which he got used to a long time ago, the old man is a lively, happy and limber old guy." And, as many physicians experience with patients, "I now know better than to try and tell him to rest and stay in bed. As soon as the weather allows it, he goes out for a walk—be it on his own in the garden, be it in the street accompanied by his brother." Dr. Zade wrote that he usually saw David once a week, more if needed.

He also reported on his visits with Trude's parents. He was treating Sigmund for high blood pressure. Dr. Zade noted that Sigmund and Martha frequently went to see David. Sigmund enjoyed taking one to two-hour walks through the town forest. "It's amazing how happy he is and quite fast too when he's reading big and good books, he's especially fond of high-quality history books. I quite frequently take the time to chat with him about his readings and I can see again and again how deeply he knows what these books are about, and at times he has some very critical ideas about them."

Well, now you're up to date. If you can do something for us I would be very grateful to you, as would be my wife and daughter.

I was very happy to hear that your practice is slowly but surely establishing itself. I had foretold this outcome to your parents-in-law when I heard you quite reasonably set up your practice not in the big city but in a small town on the outskirts of a big city. I do not doubt that this progress is going to continue; to make a living after all, it's not necessary to have a large number of patients, and the freedom to be one's own master as a physician and only obey one's own clean conscience is, in my opinion, a boon for which no price to pay is too high.

For now, best wishes to you two and to your children, in case they still remember me; and my family joins me and sends you the same but adds to the wish of a further "Vivat, crescat, floreat!"[262]

Yours,

Hugo Zade (Dr. Zade letter to Max, Feb. 2, 1941.)

Unfortunately, Max was no more able to help Dr. Zade and his family escape than Max was able to arrange for Ernst, Sigmund, and Martha to leave Germany. The Zade family would need to look elsewhere for help if they were to escape.[263]

---

262 A Latin phrase meaning "Live, grow, flourish."

263 Dr. Zade's son Hans Peter, age thirty-one, who had been living in Berlin, managed to escape. He emigrated to England in 1938.

OLD PEOPLE WITH
CHILDREN'S FACES

A S THE NAZIS SETTLED UPON AND IMPLEMENTED THE Final Solution, Jewish efforts to flee Germany continued running into roadblocks. The Transmigration Bureau circulated a June 11, 1941, notice that encapsulated the difficulties emigrants faced and the frustrations they experienced. The Bureau wrote that it was pleased to forward a booklet to potential immigrants describing the services, policies, and operating procedures of the Joint Distribution Committee's Transmigration Bureau. However, the Bureau cautioned that "Changing conditions affecting emigration and transportation procedures are of frequent occurrence. You will therefore understand that statements contained in the booklet may be outdated in a short time." Thus, the Bureau welcomed readers to study the pamphlet when attempting to arrange for friends and family to escape Germany, while simultaneously acknowledging that the pamphlet could be out of date at any moment and, therefore, useless.

Trude wrote to Walter and Meno Lissauer once more:

> Today, we read in the *Aufbau* newspaper that the Joint chartered a Portuguese steamboat, which is scheduled to leave Lisbon for the first time on June 12 and repeat this trip in the coming months. We are interested in sharing this information with you just so you know, because it might be possible to secure passages for my brother-in-law and my parents. As I already mentioned,

the Joint received payment in March for my brother Ernst's passage and it [the Joint] still has the money. (Trude letter to Walter and Meno Lissauer, June 16, 1941.)

The *Aufbau* was a German-language newspaper printed in the United States for the German Jewish refugee community there. Trude went on to note that she had received a letter from her parents telling her they had to take three relatives into their home "until everything is okay with their house again." The last portion of Trude's letter is missing. The surviving portion ends with: "reading between the lines…" Reading between the lines, likely explanations for the problem at the relatives' home were: (1) the home had been requisitioned by the regime to provide shelter for non-Jews in order to replace housing destroyed by Allied bombing; (2) the home had been damaged and rendered uninhabitable by Allied bombing; or, (3) it was no longer safe for the relatives to stay in their home by virtue of them being Jewish.

Trude also cabled the Joint to try to obtain passage: "Today we read in the paper that the Joint has chartered the Portuguese liner Moznijho. With reference to the passage paid in March '41 for my relative Ernst I., I beg you to secure passage for him at the earliest opportunity." (Trude cable to the Joint, June 16, 1941.)

The Joint replied by referring Max to the booklet it had recently sent to Trude: "Though the Hilfsverein are making every effort to secure passage for the earliest possible date, you will certainly understand that, in view of the extremely difficult situation, which has even aggravated recently (sic), it cannot be predicted just when they will be successful in each individual case." (Joint letter to Max, June 23, 1941.) The Joint went on to state there was nothing it could do; its only suggestion was that the prospective emigrant should be advised to keep in close touch with the Hilfsverein in Cologne in order to be kept aware of all developments.

While the author of the letter from the Joint did not say what had recently occurred to aggravate "the extremely difficult situation," the author may have had in mind the fact that on Sunday morning, June 22, 1941, the day before the Joint's letter to Max, Hitler launched his long-planned assault on the Soviets, which the Nazis code-named "Operation Barbarossa." This was the same day on which Napoleon had launched his ill-fated march towards Moscow in 1812 and one year to the day after France had surrendered to Hitler at Compiegne. The Wehrmacht attacked Russia across an enormous front six hundred miles long. Hitler had long planned to attack Russia, notwithstanding the non-aggression pact he and Stalin had signed two years earlier in August 1939. The attack stemmed in part from Hitler's belief that Germany needed "Lebensraum in the East." He believed the only way to obtain that Lebensraum was by conquest. The attack was also fueled by Hitler's disregard for the Slavs as a people and his belief that Germans were the superior race. Therefore, he believed Germany should occupy much of eastern Europe, including large portions of the Soviet Union.

By autumn 1941, Hitler was confident his forces had crushed the Soviets. The Wehrmacht had advanced nearly five hundred miles and Moscow lay less than two hundred miles further east. German troops were also advancing through the Baltic countries towards Leningrad. Hitler gave a speech in October claiming the Soviets had been crushed and Russia would never threaten the Reich again. However, events would soon prove Hitler's boast was premature.

The Wehrmacht's advances paved the way for Nazi mobile killing squads to follow. By the time 1941 came to a close, these squads had murdered almost one million Jewish men, women, and children in the east. In December 1941, the Nazis established the Chelmno death camp in Poland to formalize their killing operations, to be followed in short order by the establishment of more killing centers.

By the end of the war, the Nazis had slaughtered as many as 1.5 million Jewish children. The SS typically sent children to the gas chambers upon their arrival at the camps unless the children were old enough to be used in forced labor. Of Poland's nearly one million Jewish children before the war, roughly 5000 survived. As one child survivor put it, the survivors were "old people with children's faces, without a trace of joy, happiness, or childish innocence."[264]

The Nazis continued to press towards Moscow. Soon, they

---

264 www.ushmm.org/hidden-children/insideZ/.

were only forty miles away. However, by October the Russian rains, known as the "Rasputitza," began, turning the Russian dirt roads to mud. Virtually every Nazi vehicle became stuck in the mire, some sinking up to their axles. Soon after the rains, the bitter cold and snow came. The German troops did not have adequate winter gear. Their equipment began to freeze up. They also lacked adequate air cover. The Wehrmacht had taken the same route towards Moscow as Napoleon had taken. Hitler, while claiming to be a student of history, had either not learned or had forgotten the fate of Napoleon's army during the brutal Russian winter.

The Wehrmacht came within sight of the Kremlin from Moscow's suburbs in early December 1941, but that was as close as they came to capturing the Soviet capital. While the Wehrmacht made one last push to capture Moscow, its overextended supply lines and the bitter cold combined with stalwart Soviet resistance to end the Nazi advance. The Soviets unleashed an enormous counterattack, forcing the Wehrmacht to pull back. While the Soviets had not destroyed the Wehrmacht, they had stopped its advance and inflicted heavy losses on the Germans. For the first time since the war began, it appeared that perhaps the Nazis were not invincible.

Meanwhile, the Royal Air Force continued to launch punishing bombing raids on German seaports and air bases in France. The RAF also continued its bombing raids inside Germany, with the bombers' fighter escorts downing dozens of German fighter planes in the process. While the Germans continued to bomb London and much of southeastern Britain, the British were taking the war to the German heartland. The Reich was getting a taste of what it had seemed able to inflict, almost with impunity, on much of Europe.

It Is a Dreadful Fate We Have

In early July, one of Trude's friends, Toni C., wrote to Trude to wish her a happy birthday (Trude's birthday was July 3):

> But even though many miles and a vast ocean separate us, our thoughts are often with one another, we spent too great a part of our lives together to be separated now. I always see you before me as an able doctor's wife, an ambitious mother of talented daughters and competent homemaker, who puts her home in the center of her universe. Max can be lucky that fate gave him such a helpmate on the road to a new life. (Letter from Toni C. to Trude, July 6, 1941. No records have been found giving Toni C.'s full name, although several documents refer to a Toni Cohen.)

"You probably hear from your parents that Walter's mother committed suicide" as had two more of their women acquaintances. Toni passed along news of friends whose families had left for Sao Paulo and Switzerland. "About Hilde's [Hilde Spier] father, I have gone to a great deal of trouble to find out his last whereabouts, but strangely all avenues failed, even the Red Cross. Presumably he is dead, but we have no confirmation." Toni wrote she had taught one of their friends to play bridge. "[I]n today's time [bridge] is not to be underestimated as a past-time, to make the time go and to thwart thinking." (*Id.*) "All the flower gardens have been turned into victory gardens as one prepares for next winter, so that we must not

go hungry like the poor French, Belgians and like 9/10 of Europe."
Toni's reference to victory gardens suggests she had made her way to
Britain, Canada, or the United States.

Toni concluded her letter by ruminating on what the future
might hold: "One becomes a fatalist and takes things as they come.
There are so many worried 'angehorigen' [relatives] and life seems so
useless, that one has to wonder when someone complains, after all,
everything comes as come it must." Toni closed her letter: "And now
Trude, regards to your Max, the children and take a special greeting
for yourself from Dorotee and your old friend." Dorotee Cohen was
a friend of Max and Trude from Cologne.

On July 1, 1941, Sigmund and Martha were forcibly relocated from their room on Lortzingstrasse to 63 Rolandstrasse. The
new location was quite a distance from the former family home on
Aachenerstrasse. Their new "home" was in south-central Cologne, a
few blocks west of the Rhine. They tried to put the best face on their
situation:

> My beloved children!
>
> *We're done with the move; it's of course a huge adjustment for us.
> We have to summon all our willpower to be able to master this
> situation.* Because of my long illness, my nerves have been
> affected. *The nights are long; there's too much time to brood about
> everything.* How often I think of you, my sweet ones. Our wish
> to be with you again is always with us, whatever we do; and the
> thought that one of these days this may come to pass is what
> gives us strength to bear all this hardship. (Martha and Sigmund
> letter to Trude, July 6, 1941; emphasis in the original.)

Martha noted the State Department had issued new regulations for emigration and now everything had to be done through
Washington D.C. They were now living "with some nice people,"
but no one they had previously known. Nevertheless, having other
people nearby and being able to share their worries provided comfort: "During times of suffering, one's solidarity with others doubles,
that's tried and true."

Martha shared news about friends and relatives, all of whom

faced adversity of one kind or another, whether they were dashed hopes about emigrating, being forced from their homes, or being separated from loved ones. "We had a desperate report from Fritz and Adi; they believed they were several weeks away from their goal [emigrating], and now it's back to square one." Martha reported that other friends had a great scare at their house, and they were lucky to survive it with no more than a scare. The scare was likely an attack by S.A. brownshirts or an attempt by the Gestapo to arrest and deport Martha's friends. "Lene [Berlin] can't forget her beautiful garden; she is completely distraught; we can talk to her to give her courage, but no more than that, and all the while we're discouraged ourselves." As to the room where Martha and Sigmund now lived:

> In the winter, we'll have to make do with a stove to warm us up. The joy we used to feel about the garden and terrace [at the Ichenhäusers' home on Aachenerstrasse] is now reduced to only a memory; other people will now take walks there.

Martha noted that a friend had visited David Ichenhäuser and Ernst in the boardinghouse where they now lived. She had not visited them because it was difficult for her to leave the house. She expected to have a sink installed in their room the next day, which would improve their situation. They had a two-burner hot plate on which Martha prepared their meals. Martha and Sigmund still went out for lunch, although they were unsure how long they could continue to do so.

Martha concluded:

> I keep looking at the picture of your house; it looks so nice, we could sit comfortably on the veranda or terrace and be cozy together. The children won't be children anymore if we ever see them again...In my thoughts I hug and kiss all of you. Don't forsake us.

> Your Mother and Grandma

Sigmund added: "I can hardly write. It is a dreadful fate we have. I know what your situation is. It's a good thing that you're out of the fray. I will spare you the details of our misery. We must bite the bullet..." (Martha and Sigmund letter to Max and Trude, July 6, 1941.)

Sigmund and Martha wrote again a few days later. They were thrilled to have received letters from Trude and Max. They were especially delighted with photographs of the house in Deer Park and of Renate and Erica. "It's a tiny bit of compensation for everything that we have to do without." (Martha letter to Trude and Max, July 10, 1941.) They now had a clear idea of the family's situation. "The children look especially nice on the picture with the automobile. Now I know the entire family: cat, car, house and garden. Oh, if only we could enjoy this alongside you!" The cat was a stray, jet-black, green-eyed cat whom Renate and Erica had adopted and named Timmy.

Martha and Sigmund continued to adjust to life in the room into which they had been forced to relocate: "Gradually we are getting accustomed, though with difficulty. Thank God we can connect our wash basin, which is a plus. I received a hot plate from Ernst and Olga."

Martha reported that Dr. Zade regularly visited David Ichenhäuser. She also noted that, since Ernst had started working, they spoke with him less frequently. That was no surprise given that Ernst was working eleven-hour shifts, not including the time he spent going to and from the furniture factory.

Since the foreign consulates in Germany had closed, everything in connection with their efforts to emigrate had to be handled in the United States. "We seem to have arrived at a dead end and have to wait now until the political situation is cleared up...At present there is nothing one can do, but don't ignore any avenue that presents itself." Martha continued:

> It makes me happy what you write about the children. Renate looks sweet in the picture, Eri nice and unchanged. It is good that Renate is eating properly, that makes raising children much easier. How did the competition in the music hall go? How nice that the children thought of a watchband for me. Will we ever get that far [for me to receive it]? I doubt that we will achieve a reunion.

Martha was pleased to read about the girls' activities: "To read 50 books in a single year, that's a lot; not many children, Eri, can compete with you on that." She wrote that her mouth watered knowing the girls were picking berries during summer vacation. "I'm with you in my thoughts and I am totally in agreement and on board with the concluding sentences to your penultimate letter: 'Come soon.' Make certain that it'll become reality. Sending wishes and kisses to all four of you. As always, I remain your mother and grandma."

Sigmund added a few wistful lines: "My dear ones! We were very happy with the photos...Though I'm constantly in doubt as to whether we will ever get there [to join them], but it calms me down to know that you, being free human beings, can build something up there, if it's at all feasible...Are you able to imagine how we live? Love, Father."

Cousin Emil Teitz wrote to Max and Trude to bring them current regarding family news and to compare notes on emigration for those still in Germany. (Emil and his wife Luise had recently emigrated from Germany.) Max's anemia was still an issue: "First off, I wish from all my heart, dear Max, that you will soon return to good health and that you'll be completely restored. Our thoughts are with you during these times, and we would like to help you more than just take some of your letter writing chores off your hands. We were especially happy about your reports on the girls—and we will solemnly swear not to use the designation 'little' ever again." (Emile Teitz letter to Max and Trude, July 12, 1941.)

Emil noted the new U.S. emigration regulations requiring that each applicant provide two support affidavits. The applicant needed to provide precise personal data, in effect a biography, of the prospective immigrant. Furthermore, the people who provided support affidavits had to provide reference letters for themselves, written by two different U.S. citizens or legal immigrant aliens. The United States was insisting that potential immigrants provide references not only for themselves, but the people acting as references also needed to provide references. One could excuse potential immigrants if they felt like they had fallen down a rabbit hole and landed in a deadly wonderland.

For Ernst, the new regulations meant he needed to provide an affidavit in addition to the one Sophie Nathan (a cousin) had provided for him. Ernst also needed to provide a biography, which Emil suggested might best be provided by Max. "When you receive these forms, you'll be duly shocked because of all the things these people in Washington want to know, but these are problems that can be tackled." (Emile Teitz letter to Max and Trude, July 12, 1941.)

For Emil, the bigger problem was "Will Ernst be able to get a visa at all since he has such close relatives who are staying behind in Germany?" The U.S. State Department, well-known at the time for its anti-Semitism, had instructed consular officials to exercise extreme care when vetting visa applicants: "In view of the international situation, it is essential that all aliens seeking admission into the United States, including both immigrants and nonimmigrants be examined with the greatest care." As Ernst and many friends had made clear to Trude and Max, visa applicants were required to submit detailed information and "moral affidavits" attesting to their identities, good behavior, and financial wherewithal. However, the State Department now added another potentially disqualifying condition for visa applicants:

> Fears of infiltration and espionage led to additional restrictions on visa applicants. On June 5, 1941, diplomats abroad were cautioned that visas would soon be denied to applicants with close relatives remaining in German-occupied countries. American officials were concerned that unfriendly governments would use family members as hostages or bargaining chips to coerce immigrants to commit acts of sabotage or espionage.

> On July 1, 1941, the same day that the new "relatives' rule" went into effect, the State Department centralized all visa control in Washington. Visa applications were placed before an interdepartmental review committee consisting of representatives of the Visa Division, Immigration and Naturalization Service, FBI, Military Intelligence Division of the War Department, and the Navy Department's Office of Naval Intelligence. At this time, documentary requirements were also increased: applicants now needed two financial affidavits instead of one.

U.S. consulates in Nazi-occupied territory shut down in July 1941. For most Jewish refugees, the new paperwork combined with the lack of access to American diplomats ended their hope of immigration to the United States.[265]

The closure of U.S. consulates occurred just as the Nazis began to implement their program of systematic, mass murder of Jews in territories the Reich occupied during its invasion of Poland and the Soviet Union. President Roosevelt warned that Jewish refugees could become a threat to the United States due to family members being held hostage by the Nazis; the FBI warned Americans to be on guard. (*Id.*) Rather than take steps to help family members leave Germany, the United States instead adopted a rule that effectively condemned entire families to remain in Europe to be slaughtered. No one could get out if the entire family could not get out. This new regulation was, in effect, a death sentence for thousands of Jews.

Emil commented: "There's no one here who could tell how this new regulation will be implemented," whether strictly or with some leeway:

> If it's the first [strictly]; then almost no one will be able to get out anymore, since almost everyone leaves behind relatives who are close enough to be covered by the new regulation.—I have the same problem with my mother—even though she already has a passport and a Cuban visa and we're hoping that we'll soon be able to book her passage to Cuba. But what then? Will she be allowed to go on from Cuba to the U.S. since she's got a son and various siblings who are staying behind in Europe? That's how everyone has the same problem, and everyone has the same worries and despair. Still, there's nothing else to do but to fill out all the paperwork, to get the forms and to hope for the best. If it doesn't work out, then at least one has done one's duty. (Emil letter to Max and Trude, July 12, 1941.)

Emil enclosed a newspaper clipping which reported that, pursuant to the new emigration regulations, the American Consulate

---

265 WWW.ENCYLOPEDIA.USHMM.ORG/CONTENT/EN/ARTICLE/UNIT-ED-STATES-MIIMIGRATION-AND-REFUGEE-LAW-1921-1980.)

in Marseille had stopped issuing visas and instead was requiring the State Department in Washington D.C. to make the initial determination as to whether visas should be issued. Emil went on to recount Trude's efforts to help Edith and Sigbert Wachs and recite the litany of hurdles they faced trying to satisfy the pertinent regulations.

In closing, Emil wrote: "What you've told us about your loved ones in Cologne deeply concerns us. All of these personal discomforts and then the nightly bombing raids on top of all that. If only your parents and father [Ichenhäuser] could leave. We can imagine how you must feel. We can only hope that one day we will see our loved ones again."

Max had still not recovered from his anemia. In an undated letter, the content of which suggests it was from sometime during May to July 1941, Ernst wrote to Max:

> I was deeply stunned and upset to read about your illness. I hope that by now you have recovered and that business at your practice/doctor's office has picked up again and you have continued with your medical practice. As you desired, I have not told anyone about your illness. You write, the doctors blame it on nutrition, but how is that possible? You have been writing letters to us all this time with a typewriter, did you do that at the hospital, or did you have dear Trude typewrite for you even way back when?

Ernst's comment about Max's doctors believing his condition was due to diet suggest that Max was suffering from anemia and his diet was not providing sufficient iron. Ernst's comments about Max having been hospitalized reveals that by the middle of 1941 Max's condition was serious.

Ernst reported that the two grandfathers had recovered from their recent ailments and, while Martha was feeling better, she was recovering more slowly. Meanwhile, Ernst continued to struggle with the agencies to arrange for visas and ocean passage:

> My telegram telling the Joint to reimburse you so we can pay a deposit to Hapag was returned to me by the Aid Association (Hilfsverein) after ten days because, so they say, Joint regulations

didn't allow this. But now it's supposed to be possible to do this
again. But this is not the only thing the Joint screwed up for me
and for others. It seems that Joint regulations are changing all
the time. Just recently the Aid Association suggested that I do
something it had told me was impossible to do just four weeks
prior. (Ernst letter to Max, mid-1941.)

Ernst explained he continued to experience problems working
with the Joint Committee and the Aid Association. Each seemed
to contradict the other while the requirements to obtain visas were
constantly changing.

> The sad thing is that one needs both, otherwise one would tell
> them something different and much more than I already told
> them. A guarantee that one will get an early or a definite date
> no shipping company and no travel agency will give you, all
> of them do nothing until they have the money, and even then,
> there's nothing but waiting and hoping with our hearts in our
> mouths.

Unfortunately, Ernst had no choice but to work with both and
hope for the best. In closing, Ernst wrote "I wish you—if still necessary—a speedy recovery."

An undated letter fragment from Martha reiterated that
requests for visas had to be submitted in Washington. The applicant
was required to make his or her request in a special document along
with two affidavits. A commission would rule on the application. If
the decision were favorable, the Commission would notify the consulate. The consulate would then issue a summons for an interview
and medical examination of the applicant. The consulate would also
issue a quota number to the applicant. Granting of a visa would
follow when the quota number was reached in Washington and the
emigrant showed proof of a definite travel booking. However, it was
doubtful that, in any event, the United States could issue visas to
German applicants since Germany had ordered the closure of all
U.S. consulates in July 1941.

Martha wrote to Trude after returning home from a visit to
the Hartmann Travel Agency. It is not known whether this agency

was connected to the Hartmann-Schmidts, who had hidden Renate and Erica after Max's arrest. Since visa applications now had to be submitted in Washington, Martha was returning the forms for Trude and Max to handle. "They are making everything so difficult and, nevertheless, you will have to take care of it if we are ever to see one another again." (Martha letter to Trude and Max, July 15, 1941.)

Martha added that she and Sigmund tried to visit David Ichenhäuser, who now lived far away, but since the street cars kept breaking down it was difficult for them to get to his home. She and Sigmund were getting accustomed to their living situation. She prepared breakfast and dinner on their hot plate. Some of their friends were fortunate enough to have heat in their rooms. Some friends were emigrating to Cuba. "I am with you in spirit, best wishes to you my dear ones, say hi and give a kiss to the children, much love to you two, your mother." And so, Martha and Sigmund waited in their unheated room, cooked on their hot plate, and prayed for a deliverance that showed no signs of coming.

INFINITE DESPAIR

E MIL TEITZ WROTE TO TRUDE AND MAX REGARDING HIS efforts on Ernst's behalf:

> I assume you received my letter dated the 12th (of July). In the meantime, Sophie Nathan has written that she is at her summer residence and cannot do anything about the matter of the affidavit from there, so she is postponing everything until she gets back to New York. That means September. This is not a problem concerning Ernst as, unfortunately, it turns out that at this time it is impossible for people in Germany to obtain a visa for the U.S. That is, as long as the applicant is not able to enter a neutral country. As long as this is the case, the State Department will not process any applications, and they may not even be sending out any of the required forms. In other words, that option is closed.—For about $250 (à fonds perdue), one can get a Cuban visa here; this covers all the filing fees. If this interests you, I can give you a trustworthy address here in NY where we also obtained my Mother's visa for Cuba. $250 is relatively cheap; I had only recently found out that another source demanded $375. However, you need to know whether you can finance the passage from Spain to Havana to New York as well as the stay in Cuba. No one knows how long you will remain there; it depends on how quickly the State Department processes the application and on how they interpret the paragraph pertaining to relatives. (Letter from Emil Teitz to Trude and Max, July 18, 1941.)

Emil's reference to "à fonds perdu" meant non-repayable funds, as in money going into a black hole. Emil noted he had not been able to book passage for his mother. A draft letter from Max to the Joint Distribution Committee in New York stated the sad truth of the matter: "In March 1941 I sent you $400 to secure passage for my brother Ernst Ichenhäuser 409Aachenerstrasse, Cologne-Braunsfeld, Germany. I beg you to refund this money to me because there seems to be no possibility of his coming over for the time being." It was becoming clear that Ernst was not going to be able to get out and would have to meet his fate, whatever it might be, in Germany.

Carl and Hilde Spier wrote to Trude about their situation. Hilde Wolff, a childhood friend of Trude's, was born on June 18, 1901, in Cologne. Her father Bernard was a physician who specialized in internal and nervous diseases. Hilde's mother Selma died when Hilde was only three years old. Hilde studied languages and literature at the University of Cologne. She obtained her doctorate in philology (the study of language) in 1923, having written her thesis on "The Representation of the Child in German Poetry at the end of the 18th Century." She first worked as an editor at the magazine *Mode und Kultur* (style and culture). She then worked for several newspapers in Cologne reviewing plays. She eventually took a position at the *Kölnische Illustrierte Zeitung* (*Cologne Illustrated Newspaper*) as the editor of fashion and culture.

Hilde met Carl Ludwig Spier at a dance class in 1921; he was twenty and she was twenty-one.[266] Carl, the son of Rudolf and Emma Spier, was born on December 15, 1900, in North Rhine-Westphalia. Carl and Hilde soon fell in love. However, Hilde's father, a partner in the lithographic firm of Stollenwork & Spier, opposed them getting married because Carl was still studying economics at Cologne University. Seven years later, Hilde's father finally relented. In 1928, the year Renate was born, Hilde and Carl were married in Cologne. They set up their household at 1 Friedrichstrasse in the district of Porz on the east side of the Rhine roughly seven miles southeast of central Cologne.

---

266 (Return to Erfurt, Story of a Shattered Childhood: 1935-1945, by Olga Tarcali, CPL Editions, at p. 32.)

Carl was soon offered the position of manager at the Eduard Lingel shoe factory in the town of Erfurt in central Germany. The Lingel shoe brand was well-regarded throughout Germany, which made it an excellent opportunity for Carl. Hilde left her job at the newspaper to join Carl in Erfurt. While in Erfurt, they had two children, Marianne and Rolf, who were born in 1930 and 1932, respectively, making them a few years younger than Renate and Erica. The Spiers were an attractive family. Carl had a high forehead and dark, wavy hair. Hilde wore her hair relatively short and parted it on the left. Marianne and Rolf sometimes sported matching, double-breasted jackets. Marianne held her shoulder length hair in place with a barrette. Rolf kept his jaw firmly set, projecting an image of strength notwithstanding his youth.

The Spiers lived in a lovely, half-timbered home alongside a large park through which a small stream flowed.[267] Marianne and Rolf loved to play on the terrace at their home. Hilde, an avid photographer, constantly took pictures of them as they played on the patio and in the park. The Spiers felt they were as German as any non-Jewish German.[268] The Spiers were not religious; they observed only a few Jewish rituals and those largely as excuses for family gatherings. They were, to all appearances, fully assimilated.[269]

When the Nazis enacted the Nuremberg laws, the Spiers decided the time had come to leave Germany. They fled to Brussels on November 19, 1935, to join Hilde's half-brother Ernst Spier. They were able to ship many of their belongings to Brussels, including Marianne's prized rocking horse with its glistening black mane.[270] The Spiers were happy in Brussels. The house and garden where they lived were delightful. Marianne enjoyed her teachers and schoolmates. She filled a notebook with drawings of animals and insects and pasted in pressed flowers, bits of grass, and other items.[271]

---

267 *Return to Erfurt* at 31.

268 *Return to Erfurt* at 31.

269 *Return to Erfurt* at 31.

270 *Return to Erfurt* at 73.

271 *Return to Erfurt* at 79.

Marianne and Rolf quickly learned French, the dominant language in Belgium. Hilde was able to help them since she spoke French fluently without a trace of a German accent. Carl found work as a consultant in economics and industrial organization, in effect working as a marketing consultant. Carl and Hilde took daily walks in their home's garden and continued their strolls into the nearby Bois de Cambre (a park in Brussels on the edge of the Sonian Forest south of central Brussels).[272] The Bois featured promenades, an artificial boating lake, a velodrome, theater, and dairy.

While their lives in Brussels were good, the Spiers were not immune to developments in Germany. They listened to the news and gathered information from other Jewish émigrés in Brussels. They were careful to hide any concern from Marianne and Rolf. The one time they let their masks slip was when they learned that Hilde's first cousin and her husband had committed suicide rather than face what was coming in Germany.[273] Marianne could tell something was terribly wrong.

In the end, Brussels did not serve the Spiers well as a safe haven. The Luftwaffe bombed Brussels on May 10, 1940, as part of the Nazi blitzkrieg into Holland, Belgium, and Luxembourg. The Belgian police arrested Carl on May 12, 1940, because he was German. The police apparently did not consider what should have been the determinative fact that Carl, as a Jew, was unlikely to be a German sympathizer who would pose a threat to Belgium's defense.[274] The unthinking Belgian police initially sent Carl to the St. Gilles prison in Brussels. Once the Nazis had overrun Belgium, which occurred after only a few weeks of combat, the Belgians sent Carl to the Saint-Cyprien internment camp in southern France near the Pyrenees.

Hilde, Marianne, and Rolf fled towards France with friends who owned a car.[275] Marianne was ten and Rolf was eight. They crossed the Belgian border into France near Dunkirk, where chaos reigned.

---

272 *Return to Erfurt* at 75.

273 *Return to Erfurt* at 76.

274 *Return to Erfurt* at 80.

275 *Return to Erfurt* at 83.

The trapped British army was desperately trying to evacuate from the beach. Hilde, Marianne, Rolf, and their friends joined the massive civilian exodus towards southern France. The roads were jammed with refugees. Horses and mules with protruding ribs dragged overloaded carts. Many people walked; they carried or dragged with them what few possessions they were able to take. Many refugees jettisoned belongings along the way when exhaustion had overtaken them and they could summon only enough strength to carry themselves and their children. Some sold their few possessions for food and shelter as they fled the Nazi blitzkrieg. Drivers of the few cars on the road futilely honked their horns as they found themselves mired in the frightened mass of humanity.[276] The human river of sadness and fear slowly coursed its way southwest from Belgium and away from the Wehrmacht.

The Belgian police told Hilde and her friends that they, as "undesirable Jews," had to go to the Gurs internment camp in southwestern France near the Pyrenees. Upon arriving there, the Vichy authorities imprisoned them for three months, along with 4,000 other German Jews, as "enemy aliens." The French, like the Belgians, did not understand that Jews posed no threat to France. Perhaps endemic French anti-Semitism made the gendarmes only too happy to arrest Jews wherever they found them and regardless of where the Jews were from.

Conditions in the Gurs camp were appalling. The prisoners lived in large sheds on marshy ground; the sheds had neither heat nor water.[277] The inmates slept on thin mattresses infested with fleas. Hilde spent her days writing to everyone she could think of trying to find Carl. After two months, she learned he was interned in the Saint-Cyprien camp in the eastern Pyrenees on France's Mediterranean coast, just north of the border with Spain. In July 1940, the Vichy police allowed Hilde and the children to join Carl there.

Hilde wrote to friends:

---

276 *Return to Erfurt* at 85.

277 *Return to Erfurt* at 86.

This is a very hard time for us. Apart from the paltry [financial] resources which will only last a few months, we've lost everything: our beautiful home and everything we own. We have no clothes; I was only able to bring a small suitcase. We do see my husband and brother every day, but under difficult circumstances: each day, the women have to wait two hours in blazing sun to be let through. Eventually we can meet each other in a little square, without any shade to protect us, without anywhere to sit down, we have to stand, or lie on the ground.[278]

Hilde wrote further: "We feel so very powerless, abandoned, and alone. Infinite despair. Only visas from across the ocean can save us. And only if they come quickly! Our lives depend on it."[279]

The police moved Carl among several internment camps. The French eventually released him and allowed the Spiers to live with the Walter Mayer family in Cap-d'Ail, which was in unoccupied France on the Côte d'Azur just west of Monaco and northern Italy. Notwithstanding the terror which permeated their lives, the family occasionally found solace in nature: "June 18 was my mother's [Hilde's] birthday and, to celebrate it in a special way, she decided that we'd spend the night outside. We began by going to the beach to admire the sunset. It was an amazing sight we could have watched forever. When night came on, we got lost in a sky filled with stars, and such a clear beautiful moon."[280] As they stared at the night sky laced with stars, Hilde and Carl must have been dismayed to think that in a universe so vast, they were unable to find shelter in some tiny country or town where they might live in safety with their children.

Hilde and Carl wanted to emigrate to the United States. Like Ernst, Sigmund, and Martha, they faced endless roadblocks. As they toiled without progress, their fear and frustration mounted:

We were delighted with your letter of June 13, and fervently thank you for all your efforts to secure affidavits for us. We were already overjoyed when we received your news, but

---

278 *Return to Erfurt* at 87.

279 *Return to Erfurt* at 90.

280 *Return to Erfurt* at 91.

our disappointment, for which you are not to blame, was tremendous. In the meantime, we have tried in vain to get results at the consulate—in the past four weeks new regulations have been issued, by which *only* the State Department in Washington can decide who gets visas. (Carl Spier letter to Trude, July 27, 1941. Emphasis in the original.)

Carl wrote that his cousin, Jules Durham, had tried to help Carl and Hilde, in particular in connection with submitting the required affidavits. Carl was also trying to get his mother out of Germany. Carl worried that since he and Hilde were trying to get their family of four out, the demands from Washington for documentation were so great the Spiers were once again facing "a fiasco." He asked whether Trude had acquaintances who would submit affidavits in support of their visa applications. Carl was hoping that if the family submitted separate affidavits for each family member, instead of one affiant for all four, that would improve their chances of obtaining State Department approval. Carl was willing to take this approach even if all they could achieve was to get visas for Hilde, Marianne, and Rolf. "What we want to avoid under all circumstances, is that we must wait once again for months for answers from Washington, and then be told that the affidavits are inadequate."

Carl told Trude the family was staying at the home of Walter Mayer in Cap d'Ail. "How long we can stay together here doesn't only depend on the question of the prolonging of the [police] permission to stay, but also whether my sick leave will be extended, but most of all whether we have the means to keep going…As lovely as the natural setting here is, the uncertainty of the immediate future, not to mention the distant future, the sleepless nights and the constant pressure make one absolutely crazy…" Carl commented that he was under the care of a doctor and weighed only 58 kg fully dressed (127.6 pounds). He did not say whether his weight loss was due to illness, worry, or starvation rations in the internment camps. Carl added that Walter Mayer sent his regards to Trude and Max. Walter's mother had died several weeks previously; Carl suspected she had committed suicide. "Hopefully, Peter [Trude's pet name for Max], is completely well again, naturally we did not discuss [this] with anyone."

In closing, Carl wrote:

> We wonder whether our children can once again grow up in a country where they are not hampered by nationalism or race or both?
>
> Always your Carl (Carl Spier letter to Trude, July 27, 1941.)

Hilde was near a breaking point:

> I personally have no hope in this matter anymore. I am so tired of the battle and only the desperate thoughts of the children pull me back to reality…I worry about Carl's physical condition. The only thing he is able to do is to lie down, but it is impossible to keep him nourished as he ought to be. You can imagine how worrisome this is…Hopefully, Max has recovered, please write soon about it. We wish him a quick recovery with all our hearts…And now I congratulate you on your exemplary children—it must be a real pleasure to be with them! About ours, Carl already wrote to you. Here there is no use to have either talent or industry, they are always judged only average and alone. Everything one wanted to spare them, now they must endure doubly. And one must be silent and watch—even there…I can't write any more, Trude. You know how very grateful I am for all your efforts. I wish you continued success with all my heart, for you and yours, with best regards to all and a kiss for you.
>
> Your Hilde (Hilde Spier letter to Trude, July 27, 1941.)

The Spiers were in one of the most beautiful locations in the world, with the blue Mediterranean on side and the glories of Provence on the other, but they could hardly enjoy any of it while they were consumed with dread for themselves and their children. They were running out of money, options, and hope.

IT IS NOT BELIEVED THAT ANY
USEFUL PURPOSE WOULD BE SERVED

O N AUGUST 2, 1941, THE STATE DEPARTMENT WROTE TO Max:

In reply to your letter of July 11, 1941, regarding the visa cases of your parents and brother-in-law now residing in Germany, I have to inform you that no consular action may be taken in this case at present because there are no American consular offices operating in the district under reference.

In the event that the alien or aliens in whom you are interested proceed to a territory in which they may appear at an American consulate, you should notify the Department immediately in order that appropriate advice may be given regarding your further procedure; or, if you have any definite grounds for believing that these aliens have reasonable expectation of being able to proceed at an early date to a district where American consular visa offices are available, you may wish to communicate any facts in this connection for the consideration of the Department.

In the absence of reasonable expectation of such departure by the alien or aliens in whom you are interested, it is not believed that any useful purpose will be served by further correspondence in this matter.

Very truly yours,

A.M. Warren, Chief, Visa Division.

No useful purpose would be served…How could Max and Trude square those words with their desperate efforts to save Max's brother and Trude's parents? They could not stop trying, no matter how futile their efforts might be.

The State Department wrote to Max once again regarding Ernst, Martha, and Sigmund and declared yet again it would further consider Max's requests if he provided details regarding the prospective emigrants:

> You are advised however, that in the event the alien or aliens in whom you are interested reside in Germany, Italy, or in a territory occupied by Germany or Italy, no action may be taken in this because there are no American Consular offices operating in such territory.
>
> If the persons or person in whom you are interested are able to proceed to a territory in which they may appear at an American consulate, you should notify the Department immediately in order that appropriate advice may be given regarding your further procedure. Before taking action the Department should be furnished with some definite evidence that the alien or aliens concerned will be able to obtain permission to leave the country in which they are now residing and to enter some other country where the visa application will be executed. Otherwise it is not believed that any useful purpose will be served by further correspondence in this matter. (State Department letter to Max, August 12, 1941.)

For all practical purposes, the Ichenhäusers had reached the end of the road in their efforts to get Ernst, Martha, and Sigmund out of Germany. The United States consulates in Germany were closed, which meant there was no place for the three applicants to go for visa interviews and to obtain visas even if the United States were willing to issue them. It was likewise impossible to secure ocean passage, proof of which was a condition to obtaining a visa. There was no prospect of getting from Germany to a port of call, be it Lisbon, Marseille, or anyplace else in Europe, let alone Siberia or Japan. For Jews in Germany, emigration was a desperate, impossible dream. All that remained was their nightmare.

There Is Still Someone
Who Worries About Us

Despite the State Department's letters telling them there was no point in continuing to seek visas, Max and Trude refused to give up. Johanna Sinn, a representative of the Cincinnati Committee for Refugees, wrote to Trude on August 5, 1941, to confirm a telephone conversation between the two of them. On behalf of the Committee, Mrs. Sinn offered to assist Trude with her efforts to get an affidavit from "signers" in Biloxi. Mrs. Sinn offered to contact the affiants or the nearest agency to recruit it to work with the affiants. She also sent a questionnaire for Trude to fill out which might be helpful in procuring affidavits.

Trude already had an affidavit from Grete Oberlander Titche, one of Trude's cousins. Obtaining affidavits was not the problem, unless new regulations made the existing affidavits inadequate. The problems were finding the money to pay the cost of transit, securing confirmed passage on a ship to the United States, and getting the immigrants to a port of departure. As to each of those obstacles, there appeared to be no solution.

Max was now bedridden. Trude had her hands full caring for Max and the girls, but she nevertheless found time to provide financial support for relatives in Germany. She authorized the Pferdmenges Bank in Cologne to send her uncle Fritz Israel Oberlander in Frankfurt-am-Main a payment of 300 RM out of Trude's frozen German bank account. She also instructed the bank to pay her parents 200 RM monthly from the account. If Trude could not take money out of Germany, she could at least try to put it to good use in Germany.

Martha was thrilled to receive Trude's letters. "[A]s always, we were very happy about that, since it gives us proof that in this big, far-flung world there is still someone who worries about us, who is still even interested in us. We are feeling so deserted, so helpless." (Martha letter to Max and Trude, Aug. 5, 1941.)

Martha tried to put the best light on their situation. After a "hard start," they were settling into their living quarters. The residents were friendly and willing to help one another. Their room was comfortable, "as long as the longing for home and these dark moods don't take hold of us." They now had running water in their room, which was a comfort and made life easier. They did not have heat, but they hoped to get a space heater before autumn arrived. They went out to eat several times a week; otherwise, Martha cooked on the hot plate in their room. "So, don't let your hair turn gray with worry. If we survive all of this safely and soundly, we'll have a happy reunion one of these days—despite all the difficulties we don't think we'll be able to master at the moment." (Martha letter to Trude and Max, Aug. 5, 1941.)

Ernst and David Ichenhäuser were living at a boarding house at 23 Venloerstrasse in Cologne. Unfortunately, David's room was not pleasant. However, there were several armchairs in the dining room where he could sit comfortably to pass the time. David and Ernst enjoyed the food in the boarding house, which helped ease their discomfort a bit.

In the midst of the challenges Martha and Sigmund were facing, Martha still found time to console Renate and Erica on the death of their cat. Timmy had ventured onto busy Galbraith Road where he met an untimely end. Martha was pleased to learn Erica was doing well in her science class and that she was interested in zoology. Martha shared news about friends and family. She and Sigmund had received photographs of the Stommlers (Aunt Hannchen's family). She reported they, too, had no expectation of getting out of Germany. "Dear children, don't worry about us, we'll be able to manage if only we remain healthy." Martha closed her letter: "Enough for today! Many wishes and kisses to all four of you from your Mother."

Sigmund added a few lines to Martha's letter: "My dear ones: I can tell from the letter we received yesterday that you are in the know [presumably about Martha's and Sigmund's situation]. We have furnished our room as comfortably as possible: blue sofa, two blue armchairs, a small round table—that all makes for a cozy corner...On the issue of leaving the country: It looks very bad...Don't worry about us. Stay healthy and positive...Best wishes to all of you, Father." (Sigmund and Martha letter to Trude and Max, August 5, 1941.)

Emil Teitz wrote to Max and Trude regarding his efforts to help friends and family. His mother had left Germany and was on her way to Cuba, although Cuba was not her preferred destination. While he hoped to get his mother to the United States if the State Department did not make things more difficult and "screw this up for us," he was thrilled he had gotten her as far away from Germany as she was at that point.

Emil described how bad the news was regarding emigration:

> The local organizations and agencies are telling us nothing can be done right now for emigrants waiting to leave Germany. However, they're saying there's still hope for those who were close to getting a visa because possibilities will be created for them soon. How this is supposed to be done, I can only infer, thinking that they'll be able to take persons concerned to Spain or Portugal. I assume you can get information on all these items from the local organizations over there, too. As for the various forms, I haven't had any luck. HIAS [Hebrew Immigrant Aid Society] and the National Council are holding on to them tight, though they do process the affidavits if you go there with the documents ready at hand. Washington didn't react at all when I requested forms for my mother. Acquaintances of mine sent their son to Washington and he only got a form after he put up a great fight. I am very sorry I can't give you better news....
>
> All of this is a battle that people over there cannot even imagine. And yet, the fact remains that there are sad reports that indeed we can't simply ignore. What you told us about our loved ones

is truly very depressing. Let's just hope the loved ones will get through this struggle, and they surely will as long as there is hope. (Emil Teitz letter to Trude and Max, August 6, 1941.)

Since hope was all they had left, hope was what they would cling to. Time would tell whether Emil's hope was justified.

Ernst continued to report to Trude and Max about his unceasing efforts to emigrate, but he also wrote about other matters. He was sorry to hear about Timmy's death: "In the last picture he looked so cute and had such beautiful green eyes, at that time he was still small. Perhaps you can get a new Timmy." (Ernst letter to Trude and Max, August 11, 1941.) Given Erica's interest in animals, he wondered whether she might become a zoologist or operate a "silver fox farm," as Ernst had heard such farms were very lucrative.

Ernst noted the newspaper in Cologne had printed the new emigration regulations, the same as those he had previously forwarded. They included the details for affidavits and the requirement that each affiant submit statements from two "moral" witnesses, that is, individuals attesting to the affiants' good character.

Some of their male acquaintances resided in the boarding house where Ernst and David lived, one of whom was a tablemate of Ernst's at mealtime. Some men were living four to a room. David and Ernst shared a room, but since Ernst worked during the day and David often sat in an armchair in the dining room, they were able to tolerate being roommates. One thing that had not changed was their prospects to emigrate, which were gone.

We Can't Change our Destiny

MARTHA WROTE A FEW DAYS LATER FROM THEIR ROOM AT 63 Rolandstrasse:

> Today with great joy we received your letter from July. The photo of the kids is especially nice. It helps us picture how much Renate has grown up; she looks like a little teenager in this one. It's really visible how tall she has become but being away from you for two and a half years is a long time. Eri is the same, though she has grown taller too. You, dear Max, didn't get any younger, even though you now have more free time than you'd like. I hope that in September your practice will start to get busy again now that you have weathered the first year. (Martha letter to Trude and Max, August 13, 1941.)

Martha and Sigmund did not know that Max was ill, which no doubt accounted for his aged appearance in the photograph. Martha tried to offer comfort regarding her and Sigmund's situation:

> Don't worry about us. There's nothing you can do to change our fate. Your imagination is painting a darker picture of our situation than things are in actual reality. After a hard time getting used to this at first, we are now content. We have a nice room, are staying with people who want to help, are pretending that we're living in a hotel where you also live in one room for weeks at a time. In the evenings, we all get together, that is, whoever wants to; otherwise, I play games with father. (Martha letter to Trude and Max, August 13, 1941.)

Martha provided news about friends and family. "All of them have surrendered to their fate and are wishing for nothing but to be left in peace…" And so, "my darlings, let me give all four of you a hug, thinking of you, Mother and Grandma."

Sigmund, as usual, added a few lines:" My dear ones! Renate looks spectacular in that photo! She has grown up so much. I don't recognize her anymore. Erika has not changed at all—her letter made me feel so proud." Sigmund added:

> We are healthy and hope you are too. Dr. Zade is coming by on Saturday evening to see us. He's not coming by for medical reasons. We are always happy about the letters from the children. As for leaving the country: It looks very bad. When will you send us a picture of yourself dear Trude?
>
> Best wishes,
>
> Father

Martha wrote a few days later. She and Sigmund had finally been able to visit David and Ernst. Martha noted that Max and Trude's most recent letter had taken only eleven days to reach them. "Taking a closer look, we saw that it came directly from Lisbon—without going through censorship; that's why it was so quick." She responded regarding comments Trude had made in a recent letter:

> You don't have to say you're sorry for not being able to do anything for us at this time. It's a question of money, and because you over there are not a Croesus,[281] it's not possible for us to go via Cuba. We have to be patient, like so many parents, and wait until the war is over—which will be the case one of these days. If we stay healthy until that date, then hopefully nothing will interfere with our being united. (Martha letter to Trude and Max, August 17, 1941.)

Indeed, money was tight in Cincinnati. The family had little capital after a year in England and in light of the Nazis having

---

281 Croesus was a king of Lydia, in ancient Greece, who was renowned for his wealth.

blocked their bank accounts in Germany. What little money they had went towards paying the mortgage on their home and their other bills. Max's illness cut into the time he could devote to his practice, reducing their income. Max and Trude simply did not have the means to pay what, for them, was the enormous cost for their parents and Ernst to emigrate to Cuba. In the end, the lack of money was a moot point since they could not obtain visas, get to a point of departure, and secure ocean passage.

To try to put Trude's mind at rest, Martha provided details about her and Sigmund's living situation. They had been able to fit their bedroom furniture from Aachenerstrasse into their room; the exception was their chest of drawers, which they had to put elsewhere in the building. They had a washstand, two small tables, an electric hot plate, and the blue sofa with armchairs from the Aachenerstrasse living room. Martha cooked on the gas stove in the building, so they typically ate at home incurring very little expense. Outside their room, Martha had a white cabinet with boards from the old pantry; she used that to store her dishes and "Kolonial ware." ("Kolonial ware" were items imported to Germany from outside of Europe.) Martha kept her brooms in a closet, while she stowed her shoebox and cleaning materials in a built-in cabinet. She also had an area where she kept items in a communal storage locker.

Martha offered the names of people whom Trude might contact to help them emigrate. "Everyone is grasping at straws, but so few wish to help." Many people continued to try to go to Cuba, although it was more expensive than going to the United States. Further, one could travel to Portugal only if one had secured passage on a ship. If an applicant could prove he or she had confirmed passage, only then, at the last moment, would a transit visa be issued. "Nothing else to report. Stay well, don't worry about us, whatever will be will be, we can't change our destiny. For our beloved Renate and Erilein love and kisses, also to you both." (Martha letter to Trude and Max, August 17, 1941.)

Ernst wrote to Max and Trude the next day to update them regarding his efforts. "In the main, I am writing to inform you that today I have tasked the Relief Society here that the Joint refund the [shipping] deposit to you; since the latter, in the view of the Hilfsverein, can do nothing for the time being…It is hoped that it will open up other countries such as Cuba, but these are still vague hopes for the time being." Ernst explained that he and father Ichenhäuser were moving to another room in their boarding house. Their new room would be very small and cramped, "but at least [it is] a self-contained room and no walk-through room." He enjoyed the photographs Max and Trude had sent and commented how Renate had become a young lady. (Ernst letter to Trude and Max, August 17, 1941.)

Martha continued her correspondence a week later. "We've really gotten used to this place. The only thing we hope for is to be able to stay here in peace until we are able to see you again." (Martha letter to Trude and Max, August 25, 1941.) Martha heard that the cost of going to Cuba had dropped, but since the consulates in Germany had closed that was of little benefit to them.

In the meantime, Martha and Sigmund typically ate at home since they enjoyed Martha's cooking more than restaurant food. Dr. Zade continued to visit and check on their health. Martha saw from a recent photograph that Renate had, indeed, grown into a young lady. "We're happy that they [Renate and Erica] like it wherever they go, that they are happy and get to grow up as free people…My loved ones, I hope to hear from you again soon. I send my warmest greetings and kisses to all four of you, in faithful memory, your mother." Sigmund added a short postscript in which he advised he was healthy and commented how "Mother's cooking is indeed better than restaurant food." (Martha letter to Max and Trude, Aug. 25, 1941.)

Ernst soon wrote again regarding the latest on emigration:

> In order to emigrate, you need to do the following: You need to contact Washington and based on the AC certificate that was issued to me by the consulate in Stuttgart, you need to ask Washington to send my visa to the U.S. Consulate in Madrid. Please also ask the consulate to immediately notify me when the visa arrives. Because of this visa, the aid organization will help me get a visa for Spain. I would pick up the U.S. visa in Madrid. (Ernst letter to Trude and Max, August 26, 1941.)

In September 1941, the German government blocked bank accounts holding 60 million Reichsmarks that the Jewish community had collected and earmarked for emigration assistance. While Germany wished to be free of its Jews, it nevertheless was preventing them from leaving by freezing the community's funds. Foreign consulates were closed, so there were no visas to be had. Proof of ship's passage was required to emigrate, but shipping lines were not booking passage. One had to offer evidence of access to a port of departure, but there was no way to get from Germany to such a port, be it in Portugal, Spain, China, Japan, or Siberia. The only things not in short supply for Germany's Jews were hunger, despair, and dread.

In early September, Martha wrote that "[o]nly your interest in us gives us the strength to keep going. It is regrettable that we can't come to you, it's hard to understand that entry into a country has so many obstacles...You know what's going on, since in this century every news is disseminated over the entire world by radio. We must wait patiently for whatever will happen. We thank God that you two and the dear children again have a home." (Martha letter to Trude and Max of September 1, 1941.)

On a more mundane note, Martha reported there were now "all kinds of beans available" and the new potatoes were good. She and Sigmund were planning to take a walk in the nearby public garden. Fall had arrived and temperatures had begun to cool. She reported their dentist was still in his old residence, but he had little to do since all his patients had left—voluntarily or otherwise. Lene and Max Berlin had visited a few days prior. They were trying to have Hans Rothschild, who had emigrated to Ecuador, "claim them" so they could emigrate there. Martha was happy that Erica and Renate were developing so well. She asked if there was a way to see the newspaper that had printed one of Renate's sketches. (The newspaper had printed Renate's sketch on a weekly children's page.) "Be well, let things continue to go well with you, and be greeted and kissed by your mother and grandmother. (Martha letter to Trude and Max, September 1, 1941.)

Sigmund added a few lines: "I will only add my greetings. I can't write you happily, and about troubles I don't want to write. We get along well with the neighbors in our building. Otherwise, we hope that our destiny will improve."

THERE IS NO ONE TO CELEBRATE WITH

O N SEPTEMBER 1, 1941, THE GERMAN POLICE ISSUED A decree requiring that all Jews over six years old wear a yellow Star of David on the left side of their chest clothing with the word "Juden" inscribed on it.[282] Germany already required that Jews take the name of Sara or Moses, have a "J" stamped on their passports, and use only approved "Jewish" surnames. While the first several requirements were not obvious to passersby on the street, the order requiring a yellow star labeled "Juden" would make Jews obvious to one and all. Now, any Jew courageous, foolhardy, or desperate enough to venture outside his or her home was a readily identifiable target.

On September 11, the police issued a decree disbanding the Kulturbund. To a great extent, this was a formality. Most of the Kulturbund's activities had already been prohibited or rendered moot since the combination of the curfew for Jews and Jewish fears of being attacked if they ventured out made it difficult for the Kulturbund to stage cultural events. The police seized Jewish musicians' instruments and distributed them to the S.A. and SS. "In

---

282 *War Against the Jews* at 375; *The Holocaust Encyclopedia*, "The Jewish Badge During the Nazi Era."

Germany the last remains of authorized Jewish cultural activity had been snuffed out."[283]

Luise and Emil Teitz stayed in touch with Max and Trude from their home in New York:

> It's already several weeks since we last heard from you. In the meantime, we had a visit from Leo (Teitz) and Erich (Ashkenazy), who had much to tell us, unfortunately some of it unpleasant and sad. But everyone has a load of sorrows to carry. I hope with all my heart that your load will not be too heavy and hope that for your loved ones abroad a way will soon be found. A direct emigration is at present impossible, and I really don't know what the agency in Berlin and the local organization here can bring about. Hopes to be raised that cannot be fulfilled. Emigration over [to] Cuba is again possible, but, unfortunately, it's a matter of money that only a few can afford.
>
> Going into a new year [Rosh Hashanah], we express best wishes for all our loved ones, and this time most especially for you. We feel, along with you, the enormous worry that's on your shoulders, and we can do nothing but pray and hope. (Luise and Emil Teitz letter to Max and Trude, Sept. 7, 1941.)

Emil was also trying to help the Wachs family escape. He thought they had a reasonable chance because, since they were living in unoccupied France, they could go to the U.S. Consulate in Marseille for visa processing.

Martha and Sigmund continued to dote on news about Renate and Erica:

> We received your letter of Aug. 18, on Sept. 6, and were quite delighted with the news about the children and with their letters. The newspaper clipping about the honors of dear Renate I read with great interest and admired the drawing. It is really marvelous the way the children have developed; they not only have practical talents, but also artistic ones. We would hope and wish that life will go more smoothly for them than ours has, already since the World War. What success did they have this week with accordion playing? Poet and Peasant and William

---

283 *Nazi Germany and the Jews* at 255.

Tell overtures are lovely pieces and are recognized by everyone, which is an advantage. I would guess that they have adjusted well to school after the long vacation. They are attending Deer Park school for a year already, how the time flies! And we are still sitting here, without any prospects of joining you. But everyone else has the same situation, and that is a very small comfort. The only thing that might achieve some results, would be if your friend K. [Consul Klieforth] would apply to Washington, I hear that a personal application to Washington is very helpful... So please leave no stone unturned, our most fervent wish is to be able to join you. (Martha letter to Max and Trude, Sept. 8, 1941.)

Martha noted that several friends had booked passage in October, but their plans had collapsed. She wrote that Lene Berlin likewise had no prospects, as it cost $500 to go to Ecuador, but she had no way to obtain the money. Sigmund added a few lines inquiring about the girls' musical performance at a Cincinnati church and lamenting that he could not send them an accordion from Germany. Martha and Sigmund now lived at Zugweg, a few steps from Bonnerstrasse. They were soon going to have to move again, likely due either to the Reich's efforts to concentrate Jews in specific locations or because the Reich, once again, had decided their home was needed for Aryans who had been displaced from their homes by Allied bombing.

Martha added a nervous comment: "You wrote nothing about yourselves, that is not a good sign for me." Martha's maternal antennae were tingling; she sensed something was amiss.

One week later, Sigmund wrote to advise that Martha had come down with shingles affecting the left side of her face and her left eye. Her condition was extremely painful. Sigmund was pleased to have learned from Trude that a local newspaper had published one of Erica's poems, but he needed Trude to translate it into German. He closed with a heart-wrenching note: "Thanks a lot for your birthday wishes. There is no one to celebrate with." (Sigmund letter to Trude and Max, September 14, 1941.)

Ernst continued to get the run around as a result of the

contradictory policies and regulations that various countries had put into place:

> In the meantime, we received your letter of August 26, for your efforts I thank you, hopefully they will have results, and hopefully the lady at the agency is correct with her "hopeful"—I am not as hopeful as she is, evidently, she does not know the attitude of the American government, who refuse their help to those people who need it the most and who have first claim to it. Cuba, according to the newest information I am able to get, costs $900 and $400 for the journey, altogether $1300, from which $650 is held back.
>
> The Americans say they will not issue a visa if one is not in an interim country, the interim countries say they will not issue a visa if one does not have an American visa—so how does one get into an interim country? You write about my calm and lassitude, it is not so, but what can one do? (Ernst letter to Trude and Max, Sept. 16, 1941.)

Ernst continued running in circles trying to recover the funds they had deposited for Ernst's ship passage:

> I already wrote to you that the Joint has advised through the Aid Association here that the payment to you be returned. The Payment was sent by telegram. Your reproaches to the Joint are unfortunately quite correct, you can tell them from me, that it is the rottenest organization that has ever been on this earth, as is the Aid Association here.

Ernst was pleased with a poem Erica had written; he took great pride in both girls. "They will both soon be well known personalities if they are often in the papers. You wrote earlier that children wear nail polish so young, therein America has far surpassed Europe." Ernst, like Martha and Sigmund, allowed himself to be transported, if only for a few moments in his mind's eye, to another country, a place where cats, poems, and nail polish were the order of the day and air raids, hunger, and despair were not.

DISASTER

THE DAY AFTER ERNST WROTE HIS LETTER, DISASTER STRUCK half a world away. On Sept. 17, 1941, Max died. He was forty-eight years old. Max had been ill for almost a year. By autumn 1941, he had been bedridden for several months. His physicians eventually determined he was suffering from leukemia. Anemia is a symptom commonly associated, at least today, with leukemia. It is also frequently attributed to dietary deficiencies, which explains Ernst's comment months earlier inquiring about Max's nutrition. Max's doctors at the Jewish Hospital in Cincinnati hospitalized him for several weeks before sending him home. They told Max he could check into the hospital as an outpatient every Friday and they would transfuse him for whatever benefit that might provide. Trude dutifully drove Max to the Jewish Hospital every Friday. However, there was no cure for leukemia.

Max had been released from Dachau and avoided arrest when smuggling money into Holland. He had managed to get his family out of Germany and into the United States, enjoying the good fortune of a safe crossing of the Atlantic, notwithstanding the fact that U-boat wolfpacks were stalking Allied shipping. He had found a home for his family and been certified to practice medicine in a new country with a different language. Having survived and accomplished all this, fate visited from out of the blue and struck him down with leukemia.

Trude published Max's obituary in the *Aufbau* newspaper:

On the 17th of September 1941 my dearest husband, our unforgettable father

Max Houser, M.D. (formerly of Cologne)

Gone from us at the age of forty-eight years after months of illness.

In deepest pain:

Trude Houser, born Moses

Renate and Erica Houser.

Deer Park—Cincinnati, Ohio, 4247 Amity Road.

Renate was thirteen and Erica was twelve when Max died. Max Ichenhäuser—doctor, hiker, poet, artist, kayaker, traveler, WWI combat veteran, and, most importantly, son, brother, husband, and father—was gone.

My God, What Does that Mean?

On September 29, 1941, over the course of a single day, the Germany army slaughtered 33,700 Jews from Kiev in the Babi Yar ravine. Kiev was, at the time, within the Soviet Union. The Nazis, upon capturing Kiev, posted notices for the city's Jews to assemble to be transported for resettlement. Instead of being resettled, they were marched to the Babi Yar ravine outside the city where they were machine-gunned to death. It was and remains one of the largest massacres ever.

On October 1, 1941, Germany forbade all emigration. The Reich wanted to make Germany Judenrein, yet it was refusing to let its remaining Jews leave. It had excluded Jews from the economy and prevented them from earning a living, which meant the Reich needed to provide at least starvation rations to them. Yet, it now prevented them from emigrating which would have alleviated that burden. Instead, in October, the regime reduced food rations to the Jewish populace even further and restricted shipment of food parcels to them. Even if someone else was paying, the Reich was not going to allow its Jews to be fed. They would stay and starve—unless and until the Reich devised, as it soon did, other ways to resolve the purported burdens Germany's remaining Jews imposed on the Volk.

Martha was gradually recovering from her bout with shingles. Not knowing the severity of Max's illness, let alone that it had just claimed his life, she wrote to Trude and Max:

My darling, so-far-away-children,

When one is sick, one feels the aloneness much more. I only have one wish, to be able to be with you. It is so sad, this separation, everyone consoles me that they bear the same fate. But nevertheless, this weakness that I have makes it impossible for me to do anything. Anna, Katy, and Lene supply us with meals, we have no worries about that, but with the cleaning woman things don't work out, and I am getting someone new on Monday, who will also cook for us. The shingles are gone outwardly, but the pain persists, and consequently I can only get some sleep with a sleeping pill; my appetite is also not great.

But we were overjoyed when your letter of September 3 arrived, we waited for it for two weeks. The snapshot of the children is adorable, also their words made me very happy. Please, God should keep you and the children well, so that one day we can be reunited. I only want peace, peace, and once again, peace. (Martha letter to Trude and Max, Oct. 1, 1941.)

Notwithstanding the restrictive rations the Reich allotted to Jews, Lene was able to bring food to Sigmund and Martha. Trude's cousin Otto Roesberg (one of Lene's brothers) had sold his farm in Rommerskirchen to a family by the name of Trippen. He asked the Trippens to look after his siblings by giving them food from the farm after Otto emigrated to the United States.

Otto's property was not truly a farm as such since Otto was a cattle dealer. His type of farm was referred to as a "Hof." Otto purchased cattle in northern Germany, brought them to the Hof, and resold the cattle to local farmers. Along with his cattle trade, Otto maintained a vegetable garden at the farm. The garden was the source of the food the Trippens shared with Max and Lene and that Max and Lene, in turn, shared with Sigmund and Martha. Since Jews were given only half the rations Aryan Germans received, the food was a godsend. The Trippens would meet Max and Lene at the railroad station in Ehrenfeld or take the streetcar from Bocklemünd to a predesignated meeting spot. They typically were able to provide potatoes, pork, eggs, flour, sugar, and a bottle of milk. They also included a note with the location for their next meeting place. They made their meetings as clandestine as possible to avoid trouble with the Gestapo. The Trippens would surely be arrested if the police discovered they were providing food to Jews.

Martha noted that Sigmund had recently celebrated his birthday. Ernst, Tante Hannchen (a relative of Sigmund's), and Lene Berlin joined them for the occasion. Martha echoed Sigmund's comment from two weeks earlier about not having anyone with whom to celebrate: "Never in our lives was there a sadder birthday."

Sigmund added a postscript. He had developed Parkinson's which made it difficult for him to write and made reading his handwriting quite a challenge. He wrote that he tried to keep himself busy in the house, but it was becoming ever more difficult. He was pleased to hear about Renate and Erica. He noted that Martha was feeling better, so that was good, even though "she had little appetite."

Martha wrote again a few days later, still not knowing about Max. She hoped she soon would be able to take over the household duties from the woman whom she and Sigmund had hired to help while Martha was sick. Martha recounted the futile efforts of friends who had tried to arrange passage to Cuba. A family they knew had sold their house to fund their emigration; the proceeds were not even enough to pay for their ocean passage, reflecting both the high cost of passage and the pathetically low prices Jews received on what were essentially forced sales. The purchasers had taken advantage of the family's desperation to negotiate paying a mere pittance for the home. "But for only the hope, the people grasp at every straw. Here in the apartment house are only elderly people, who have children over there or abroad." (Martha letter to Trude and Max, Oct. 6, 1941.) Martha also commented: "The little poem of Erica's is darling, how did she come up with it? And that she adopted a stray kitten, gives me even more pleasure…"

"The main topic of conversation here is always the loved ones across the ocean and all our longing is for them. The reasons you will be able to understand, but it is no life for us, always in fear and apprehension…Enough for today, I love you and kiss you all four." Sigmund added a note that while Martha was gradually recuperating, her health had deteriorated much faster than the pace of her recovery. "We do not experience anything good; we have to take it as it comes…We are pleased with your letters but missed Max's in the last one. Stay well with your children and loving regards. Your father." It seemed that Sigmund's parental antennae were starting to vibrate along with Martha's.

By mid-October, Ernst had broken the news of Max's illness to Trude's parents:

> Just now Ernst brought your letter, dear Trude, of September 19. I must admit we got quite a shock, you dear Max, are ill, my god what does that mean? I don't know what to say. The far distance, how can one decide what is going on when one is not right there? I hope to God, dear Max, that you will soon be well again, perhaps when it gets cooler it will influence your well-being. Now new worries about you—but the hope of a reunion with you lets us endure a great deal. (Martha letter to Trude and Max, October 11, 1941.)

Martha continued:

> The last time [in Trude's last letter] we already missed your writing, dear Max, and in today's letter there was also nothing. So, one feels the connection and the fast ties that bind us even doubly in sorrow. My shingles is behind me, just that I must still recover from it. About the conditions here, I needn't write to you, you are informed [by news reports]. In one's wildest dreams one could not imagine and think about what has befallen us. Dear Max, my greatest worry now is firstly your health. My dear Trude, you are a brave soul, who can do more than I can, and I am convinced that you are doing everything to nurse Max back to health…Oh God, what worries I have for you!

Martha wrote that cousin Lene Berlin was soon going to leave for Cuba. Her departure would be a tremendous loss for Martha and Sigmund, as Lene visited them frequently and helped Martha when she was ill. Martha "kvelled" (a Yiddish term meaning to brim with pride, typically over a child's accomplishments) over the fact that "Renatelein won a 1st prize of $75 is really something, I am really amazed. How thrilled she must be." Martha wrote that Miss Frankel,

Renate's former teacher, had died; "she just wasn't able to cope with life." Unspoken was the implication that Miss Frankel had joined the ranks of the many Jews who, in desperation and in a last act to control their fates, had committed suicide.

Martha continued:

> Now my dears, I will finish. It is bedtime, but I wanted to write immediately. That you live so alone you will feel, if only you at least had some relatives! Nothing is certain in this world, but the fact that the vast ocean separates us we must, like so many other parents, endure and bear, and hope for better times. For you, dear Max, my heartfelt wishes for your recovery, and for you, dear Trude, the strength to do everything that is required of you, it is truly too much. The dear children will be by your side faithfully, Renate is after all, already a big sensible girl. My utmost hugs and kisses as always, your true and worried mother. (Martha letter to Trude and Max, October 11, 1941.)

Sigmund added several lines of concern: "That Max is ill has really upset us terribly, I hope that in the three weeks that the letter was on its way, he will have improved, which we will hear in the next eight days. We are very uneasy about it, is Max in bed or is he able to practice? If Max cannot endure the climate there, is it possible for you to go to another locale? Your health is the most important thing. I congratulate Renate that she met with such success. Perhaps she will study art later on. Now we only await good news from you."

Martha and Sigmund did not yet know their hopes were to be dashed. What the SS did not do in Dachau and the U-boats did not accomplish in the Atlantic, the leukemia did. Nearly three years after Kristallnacht and less than two years after arriving in the United States, Max was dead.

ALL WORDS ARE IN VAIN

ERNST WROTE TO TRUDE:

The day before yesterday [October 10, 1941] I received your letter with the terrible news. We were aware that dear Max did not write anything on your last letter to us, but we never thought of the worst possibility. I can't tell you how this news affected me and how my heart aches. I just can't grasp that your dear Peter, my beloved brother, had to leave us so soon. To inform the parents of this is the worst and bitterest task to befall me. But you are right, I must remain strong, as you have been, and will carry it out as soon as it is possible. I can imagine how dreadful you feel and how unutterably sad you feel, and also, how much you suffered seeing the unavoidable coming and not being able to delay it. I would like to offer you so many words of comfort but faced with this all words are in vain; only one thing I can say to you, may you find comfort in your children and in the memory of the years you shared. I admire you in that you are so strong, and I know that you will remain so. It relieves me somewhat that you don't have financial problems and I hope that good friends will stand by you.

I am saddened that my emigration was not successful, so that I could be with you at this time and work for you. Can nothing be done about Cuba? That would enable me to come to you? Perhaps someone can still be softened to provide the required sum? (Ernst letter to Trude, Oct. 12, 1941.)

Ernst laid out additional information he had learned regarding emigrating to Cuba and then to the United States, *if* he could obtain a Cuban visa, *and* confirm passage, *and* get to a Spanish port. "I am sending this letter only today because I wanted to show the dear parents first the other letter about Max's illness. Lene Berlin was coincidentally there, also Dr. Zade. Naturally they were very upset and we had trouble calming them down." Ernst closed: "Regards to Renate and Erica, stay strong for your children. My thoughts are always with you."

As Ernst explained, he did not immediately tell Trude's parents about Max's death, as they first had to process the news that he was ill. Thus, Martha, still not knowing Max had died, wrote to Trude that "My thoughts are with you more than ever before." (Martha letter to Trude and Max, October 20, 1941.) She worried about Max and how, with Martha being so far away, she could not give advice about what he might do to regain his health. She hoped perhaps the cooler weather of autumn might help. "In the past two letters, I missed seeing your [Max's] greeting."

As to her and Sigmund's situation, Martha had recovered enough from shingles that she could cook again. Ernst visited them frequently. She marveled at how Trude could manage everything that was on her plate. She wrote, not knowing the irony of her words, that "It can only be because things have gotten a lot easier." Martha observed that she had only a single room to take care of; however, since she and Sigmund were in it all the time, it got dirty quickly. "You get used to not having your own home. You get by with the bare necessities, but a room [one room] is often more work, because you do everything in it." (Martha letter to Max and Trude, October 20, 1941.)

Martha wrote that friends had received permission to emigrate to Santo Domingo in the Dominican Republic. But the friends had not yet left and "you know how everything falls apart at the last minute." Other friends thought they had confirmed plans to get out, only to have their plans put on hold time and again. "Dr. Z. said goodbye to us…I was really sorry to see him go; he wasn't just a doctor to me but a friend as well." She did not say where Dr. Zade was going. Martha was thrilled to read about the $75 prize Renate had won. "The children make us really happy. We only have one wish: that we can enjoy their company in person. Every day of being alone is torture for us." Martha added: "Today I have only one wish, that Max regains his health. If possible, he should spend some time in another climate. Surely money can be borrowed for that...Hopefully good news before long."

Sigmund added a postscript: "My dear ones! Today, I have only one wish: that Max is well again soon...We are very worried. We hope to receive good news from you soon."

As to Dr. Zade having stopped in to say goodbye, he did not say goodbye because he and his family were emigrating; their attempts to emigrate had been unsuccessful. On October 21, 1941, the Nazis deported Dr. Zade, his wife Marta, and his daughter Ursula to the Lodz ghetto in Poland, some seventy-five miles southwest of Warsaw. There, Dr. Zade worked in the ghetto's medical department, such as it was. In 1944, the Nazis deported the Zades to Auschwitz, where the Nazis murdered them in the gas chambers.

Dr. Zade, a pediatrician who served patients in Langenfeld-Immigrath and Cologne for thirty-two years and who was an author of numerous scientific works on pediatric care and general illnesses, was sixty-four when the Nazis murdered him.

Marta Zade, who had a business degree, who had studied at the Public Academy for Fine Arts and become an artist creating paint-ings, etchings, sculptures, and commercial graphics, was sixty-one when the Nazis murdered her.

Ursula Zade, a skilled young physician who specialized in inter-nal medicine, was thirty-two when the Nazis murdered her.

Ernst finally broke the news to Sigmund and Martha:

Dear Trude:

The day before yesterday I received your sad letter dated September 25 and yesterday afternoon Lene and I went to visit your parents to deliver the bad news. It was really hard for both of us. Of course, your parents were very upset by it, especially your dear mother, who still hadn't fully recovered from her last illness. She was, however, feeling a lot better and can do some of the errands on her own. Despite the situation, they decided to stay strong, especially in their hope for a future reunion. They are very affected by the fact that many of their friends have left Cologne, but we hope that your dear parents will soon recover.

I haven't said anything to my dear father yet. I'd like to keep it a secret from him for as long as possible, which is easier for us, since we live in a pension [boardinghouse]. Nonetheless, the others [friends and acquaintances] all know about it now, and some of them already knew about before I said anything. (Ernst letter to Trude, October 23, 1941.)

It is not known whether the departures of friends from Cologne to which Ernst referred were voluntary departures through emigration or, far more likely, were deportations to camps. With Europe ablaze, emigration was impossible. There were no ships on which to secure berths, there was no way to travel to points of departure, and there were few sources from which to obtain the funds needed to emigrate. Sigmund and Martha's friends who had "left" at this point likely shared common destinations—the death camps in the east.

We Have to Endure Such Endless Sorrow

T HE DAY AFTER ERNST broke the dreadful news, Martha wrote to Trude:

My darling dear Trude:

I was deeply shocked by the sad news, which Ernst brought me yesterday afternoon. Although we knew from your last letters that our dear Max was ill, we could not even think of the worst. He was such a strong, vibrant, still-young man, and to have suddenly succumbed to a terminal illness! My dear Trude— what can I say to you? I can only speak with your own words— you lost the best husband, the children the best father, and we the best son-in-law. How often he worried about us, a child of our own could not have been kinder to us.

We were so happy to know that you were out [of Germany] and you and the children had found a home again after so much travel, and now that has been destroyed. I imagined how lovely our eventual reunification would be and hoped at least that you could all go out together and I would look after the house, as I loved to do in Braunsfeld. Now everything has changed. If I could at least be with you, so that I could relieve you of some of the work, so that you could do what needs to be done. But the world is so horrible, the ocean lies between us, and mankind forbids that we can be together.

Dear Trude, how strong you are, to have kept everything secret and spare us four weeks of worry. Max only brought us joy, we were so proud of him, his death is the first grief he has ever brought us. Now I realize what the reason was that you never wrote about the office. I didn't want to ask and to hurt you. What will become of you and the children now, I can't say from here, nor can I offer advice...

I hope and pray that the whole family will not abandon you, until you can support yourself. How sad it all is and how wonderful it might have been. All the toil and work to pass the exams [Max's medical certification boards] for nothing. Poor dear Max had to suffer so. How strong and how brave you were, that you were able to hide it from him, the severity of his illness. Dear Trude, be glad that you don't have my nature, I buckle with the least little thing. And yet there is trouble here, I can't write about it today, but will tell you about it in my next letter. Most of our friends are gone, but for now we are still here. But life is hard! But with it all, I can't get it through my head that our dear Max is no more. What will his old patients say when they hear of it? I could imagine everything, but not this. He was only ill once when he came into our family and now his death. That patients loved him I can understand, especially if you compare him with others, whom I came to know after you left.

Lene came with Ernst. I opened the door for him and when I saw their "downcast" expressions, I knew at once what it meant. Lene was like a guardian angel, if she could only stay with us until their departure. Ernst also lost his anchor; he had hoped to find a home with his brother. What fate has spared Mother Ichenhäuser! [Max's mother Emma had died in 1938.] How dreadful when parents have to see their children die before they do! Dear Trude, you have wonderful children, they will be a great comfort to you, but years will pass that will be tough for you.

How happily I hear only good about Renate and Eri, may they stay healthy to make us all happy. But most important, dear Trude, do not overstrain yourself, take care of your own health, you are after all _our_ whole life. Be assured that we feel deeply with you, and we know what you have lost. Ernst wants to spare his father as long as possible. I greet and kiss you and the children most dearly with greatest love and faith.

Your mother (Martha letter to Trude, October 23, 1941; emphasis in the original.)

Sigmund's Parkinson's was causing severe hand tremors and, as a result, his handwriting suffered greatly. Nevertheless, he added a few lines to Martha's letter:

Dear Trude, dear children,

Fate has hit us so hard. That Max was a good son to us you know Trude better than I can articulate. Life does not do right. I just hope that you can cope with it Trude and I hope that you will have much joy from the children. Unfortunately, I can't help or advise you. If only we could be together—we have to endure such endless sorrow.

Love, Father

Endless sorrow ravaged the Ichenhäusers on both sides of the globe. Only fate knew if this would be the last of their sorrows.

How You Must Have Suffered

H ILDE SPIER WROTE TO TRUDE TO OFFER HER CONDO-
lences:

> My dear, dear Trude:
>
> If only I knew what I could say to you. Your letter shattered me
> deeply. In spite of your news reports of May, I never dreamed
> that it would come to such an end. Poor, poor Peter...I can
> only hope and wish that the care of your wonderful girls, and
> the girls themselves, can help a little to overcome your grief. I'm
> very happy to know that Walter Rothschild and Wilhelm Kahn
> are trying to assist you. Let us know soon how you are managing
> and how you expect to arrange your life. I cannot rest until
> I know. As Carl rightfully wrote: If only one could help one
> another in these cruel times. How gladly I would do for you,
> as you would for me, but one can only watch and always take
> leave again—so difficult has life become. I always look at the
> snapshot you sent; Max already looks frighteningly wretched
> in it. How you must have suffered, having to watch. But the
> children are adorable. Renate is pretty as a picture and quite like
> your mother. Erica is a new, small Trude Moses. (Hilde Spier
> letter to Trude, October 25, 1941.)

Hilde expressed concern about Trude's parents:

> We also feel so dreadfully sorry for them. Why have all these
> poor old people, who are left behind, deserved such a fate? I
> no longer mourn for my parents; they are well off. Only the

uncertainty, or rather, the knowledge that father somewhere, somehow, alone, deserted, without friends somehow perished, that is a torment and hard for me.

In closing, Hilde offered words of consolation and encouragement:

Yes, and this I must still tell you, that in your terrible grief you still think of us, that we will never forget! Know then, that our thoughts are with you, dearest, and in old friendships, much more so and more meaningfully than this irrational and confused letter can tell you. Be brave and courageous Trude, for your children's sake. And write to us again soon about everything. I embrace you, and remain with a thousand fond regards, in old cordial friendship,

Your Hilde

Hilde's comment regarding her parents suggests not only that they had died but she believed they were better off being dead than to continue living in a world that was treating the elderly as the Nazis were.

Carl also wrote to express his condolences:

My Dear Trude:

We are devastated to learn from your letter, which arrived today, of the dreadful blow that fate has dealt you. Our words of sympathy can never be a comfort to you, and we admire you, how bravely you are arranging your future for your children. Do you have financial worries momentarily dear Trude, and what can we do for you? How hard the loneliness must be for you, even if your children are of great support...We feel so far away from you, doubly so because we feel so hopeless, and yet we want by deed to demonstrate how much we feel for you and somehow want to help. We, too, ask ourselves the question why this wonderful man who was so great in all regards was torn from his family; why he had to suffer so. We can find no answers. Hopefully you will find in the love of your children and in their future, some small consolation. I say small consolation, because no one on earth can fill the void of this terrible loss.

But that in your pain, you can still think about our fears and concerns, is the finest example of our friendship, and exceeds what in another case someone might have done, and which I am not sure that I would be capable of. We don't know how we can ever thank you, and therefore we want to show you by deed, how closely we feel related to you. So, if I respond to certain points in your dear letter, I do so because, even in your sorrow, you are concerned about us. So be thanked for everything. (Carl Spier letter to Trude, October 25, 1941.)

Carl went on to discuss the responsibilities of those who submit affidavits in support of prospective immigrants, how his assets that had been frozen might be used to pay for ocean passage, and other issues related to his efforts to get Hilde, Marianne, Rolf, and himself out of France:

I had thought of the possibility of an affidavit sponsor to be found for Hilde, and another one for the children. It is more important to me to know that Hilde and the children are safe, than for myself. I can't bring myself to leave Hilde and the children in Europe and to come there (even if this is just theoretical.) But if a sponsor for me could be found within your circle of acquaintances, then perhaps something could be found for Hilde and the children through my cousin Jule's efforts. People are of the opinion that one cannot leave a wife and children alone in Europe, rather "zugänglich" as today, where they say that all of us here in Europe must escape our common fate.[284]

But we won't talk about us any longer, what comes will come as it must. Our thoughts, our sympathy, are with you. Write soon.

Always your Carl

Alfred Klieforth wrote to Trude to express his and his wife's shock at learning of Max's death and to offer their condolences:

---

284 "Zugänglich" means accessible in German. Its meaning as Carl used it is not clear.

Dear Mrs. Houser:

Mrs. Klieforth and I were shocked to receive the news of the death of your husband and we hasten to extend to you and your children our deepest sympathy. As you know I was very fond of your husband and regarded him with much respect. And now the struggle for the support of your family as well as yourself falls entirely upon your shoulders.

***

With my best wishes to you and your children, in which Mrs. Klieforth and the boys join me, I am

Yours very sincerely,

A.W. Klieforth. (Alfred Klieforth letter to Trude, October 25, 1941.)

And so, Trude, at age forty, after barely two years in the United States, had lost her husband. While trying to save the lives of her parents, brother-in-law, and close friends, she had to find a way to support herself and her daughters and not lose her mind in grief and fear. She was resourceful and strong, but she was facing more than any person should have to bear.

THE GREAT SORROW ALL AROUND

ERNST CONTINUED HIS DESPERATE EFFORTS TO ESCAPE. HE wrote to Rudi Waller about trying to book passage with the Hartmann travel agency. Unfortunately, communication was proving difficult due to misaddressed letters and other delays. "I gather from all this that you are troubling yourself for my emigration via Cuba, and I thank you heartily. I beg you to do anything you can to enable me to emigrate, even if you have to put out money. Not only will I be eternally thankful, but it is of course understood that any expense will be considered a loan which will certainly be paid back. I would so much like to go to Trude, to help her build up a new existence for herself and the children." (Ernst letter to Rudi Waller, October 26, 1941.) However, since Germany had halted Jewish emigration, any further departures would be to the east. For Ernst, the door to emigration had fully and finally closed, whether he realized it or not.

Martha wrote to Trude:

My beloved good Trude:

Our thoughts are always with you my darlings, but since Wednesday I can only think about your tragic fate. Day and night, I can't shake the idea that our dear Max is no more, that you and the children are all alone in the world. It hit us like a bolt out of the blue, he was so wonderful to you and that was our joy...If only I could be with you and the so-loved children during your bereavement, but it can't be so, fate has decreed otherwise. (Martha letter to Trude, Oct. 27, 1941.)

However, the loss of Max was not the only issue weighing heavily on Martha's mind:

And on top of that, the great sorrow all around to take farewell or go silently knowing one will never see each other again.

Martha was referring to the decision Germany's Jews were facing regarding whether to say goodbye to friends and family before being deported to the east or simply to leave without comment. By this time, Jews knew what awaited them if they were deported. That is why the question of whether to say goodbye was so excruciating—they would never again see those to whom they were saying goodbye.

Martha continued:

And yet one is more closely connected than ever before because of this tragedy. Our circle knew even before we did what tidings awaited us, there are always connections which report such things. But it [Max's death] hit us hard, so very hard, all plans for the future destroyed. We always believed that we could live quietly with you in our declining years, to share in your luck and the development of the children. Poor Max, you are no more!

At night I repeat the words of your letter, which wanted to shield us, you were too considerate; you know your parents, you know how they suffer, knowing that their only child must bear such tragedy. It is a comfort to me, that you have good friends who are concerned about you, but they are not always there, and you are alone with the children.

When I sit down at the table with father, I think how you are missing your good Peter. How deeply saddened he would have been had he known that he would have to leave you in a strange land alone. He, who always only worried about his family and only lived for his loved ones. I am, of course, wondering how everything will play out, what you are thinking of doing. The best thing would be if you find another physician who would continue the practice, pay rent and service charges, at least the children would still have their home when they return from school and would find their mother there. Such a sad shadow to fall across their youth.

On November 25, Erica will be twelve years old, this time there will be no birthday [party]. Exactly as in November '38 [after Kristallnacht], when we were also so sad. Since that time, we have not found peace. For us the thought that you are across the ocean was always a comfort, we thought of the separation as good fortune. I am such a sensitive person, always feeling things more deeply than many others. Your Ernst is so dear, he comes here daily, he was also hard hit—always believing he would find a home with his brother. How everything will turn out, the future must show us. (Martha letter to Trude, October 27, 1941.)

Martha went on to tell Trude about people who had come by to offer condolences. She appreciated the gestures of support, but each visit reopened the wound. Ernst had not yet told David Ichenhäuser about Max because there was so much excitement and upset in their boarding house regarding the ongoing deportations. Ernst wanted to spare him further anguish for as long as possible.

Martha brought her letter to a close:

I have nothing to write, but the urge to speak to you, dear Trude, makes me write this letter. If you can no longer write every week, whether to save time or postage, we won't be angry. We have full understanding for it. For you, dear Erilein, I wish with all my heart the best in your new life year, stay well. My good Renatelein, always be good to your Mummy, as you always have been. I hug and kiss you most heartily with much worry about you,

Your mother and Grandma.

My dears—I still cannot grasp it, that Max is no longer. It is too hard. What do you plan to do dear Trude?

Sigmund

The sign on Trude and Max's front lawn announcing Max's

practice would soon be removed. Trude needed to decide what to do with Max's office and his medical equipment on the ground floor. She also had to figure out how she could keep the three of them financially afloat. Reminders of Max were everywhere, as were many questions regarding what the future held for Trude, Renate, and Erica.

I Dread the Street

MARTHA WROTE TO TRUDE ONE WEEK LATER; SHE WAS still trying to process the fact of Max's death:

> My thoughts have always been with you, but I can't think about <u>anything</u> else, day and night, but you my dear ones. It all happened so quickly I still can't comprehend it that you, dear Trude, are now on your own with the children, that your beloved husband, our dear Max, is no longer with us…Your fate is a hard one; we are deeply shocked along with you, since our whole lives were solely dedicated to the well-being of our child and how we also worry about the welfare of our beloved granddaughters. Hopefully, everything can be arranged in such a way that you can hold onto your home, until the time that we can join you and that would free you up. Above all things, stay <u>healthy</u>, because now you have the exclusive responsibility concerning the children. Don't take on too much because the last few months were hard, very hard for you, dear child. In spite of all the work, you've written to us regularly and put on a false front to conceal your heavy burden from us; you were successful in this, but now it takes a hold of me a thousand-fold. All the while there is so much suffering around us. It's our old age now that protects us. (Martha letter to Trude, November 3, 1941; emphasis in the original.)

Martha's reference to their age protecting them was because the Nazis did not initially deport elderly Jews to the death camps. That was an omission which they would reverse soon enough. Martha wrote about friends who thought they had arrangements in place to emigrate, only to have their plans collapse at the last moment, leaving the friends devastated. There were new regulations making emigration more difficult. For Ernst, there seemed to be no possibility of emigration, even to Cuba. Martha wrote that Lene and Max Berlin could not leave; they had been on the verge of leaving but the new regulations stopped them. "Lene is inconsolable." Martha reported that many older people were alone; younger family members had managed to escape or, perhaps, had already been deported. "Help from America has come too late for everyone."

Martha wrote how thankful she was to have Sigmund with her:

> [b]ut father is always around; he's so touchingly affectionate, wants to help me with everything, in spite of his eighty-two years. It's a good thing that we are together, and that father enjoys himself. He eats and sleeps well, especially when I do the cooking; he goes shopping in the neighborhood; I don't go out, though not because I can't, but because I dread the street, the people. Now, my dear Trude, I want to come to a close. The letter is just a sign for you that we're still alive. I fervently greet you and the children.

> Always your Mother and Grandma. (Martha letter to Trude, November 3, 1941.)

Sigmund added a few lines to express his concerns:

> Dear Trude, dear children!

> I feel awful that we can't help you, that we're separated by a world. I still can't comprehend it and don't know what, dear Trude, you might be able to do to earn a living. I would love to give you everything we still own, but at this point this isn't possible. How are the children dealing with their fate? You aren't destitute, are you? I worry about you a lot. Write to us every week. Stay healthy and take on life as it is.

> Yours,

> Father

Ernst wrote to Trude a few days later. He asked whether things had worked out in connection with finding a doctor to rent Max's office. Ernst got Trude caught up regarding people who had left, as well as the heartbreak of others who thought they were on the verge of leaving only to have their plans fall through at the last minute. Now "everything's too late." He continued to keep the news of Max's death from his father. Ernst felt his father had suffered so much already, no doubt having Emma's and Heinrich's deaths in mind, that he did not want to compound his father's sorrow with the news of Max's passing. "Warm regards and kisses, also for the dear children, Your Ernst."

As if Max's death were not enough to bear, Trude had to go to New York for surgery, while the girls stayed with friends in Cincinnati. Fate seemed intent on not giving Trude any respite.

THERE IS NO TIME TO THINK

Martha wrote a few days later and echoed Ernst's comments about how people they knew who had obtained visas for Cuba now could not leave—it was too late.

My dear Trude!

It's Sunday morning—how much did I enjoy writing to the both of you, but this letter is going to be really hard for me to write, since I can only address it to you alone, dear Trude. I feel for you and know you are handling it in a calm, collected manner, since you watched your good husband suffer so much. For us, of course, the news came from out of the blue.

With everything that happened, I was consoled by one thought: that the children are safe. Everyone is comforted by your energetic, efficient manner, but how much more beautiful it would have been if you could have continued sharing your skills and talents with your family. But we can't argue with fate. So many people are affected and, of course, for different reasons.

I am glad you are standing with both feet on the ground, and hopefully better days are heading your way too. The children are a comfort to you and for us too. Your last letter was so good for us to read; you had so many beautiful, good things to say about the children; they will support you in your life, even if it takes a little while. We had imagined the children to have had a different young life and you, too. After all, everything over

> there went according to plan, except that hadn't reckoned with the fact that Max might die. He was so worried about us. We had a real son in him.
>
> Father I. [Ichenhäuser] still doesn't know anything. He always asks about the mail, but we tell him that the mail has temporarily stopped. Ernst thinks he should be spared as long as possible. (Martha letter to Trude, November 9, 1941.)

Martha brought Trude up to date regarding the fate of friends and family. She reported that Lene and Max Berlin would not be able to leave—"They waited too long." She and Sigmund received many people who stopped by their room to offer condolences. They also received many letters to the same effect, "but neither provides any form of consolation; all it does is reopen the wound." As to the future in Cincinnati, Martha was happy Trude was planning to stay in the house. She wondered whether Trude could rent the medical office to a physician.

Martha waxed nostalgic:

> There's housework to be done even though we only have a single room—things never change. I'm comfortable using the heater stove. When I add coal in the evening and stack up the briquettes, I think of your room on Kamekerstrasse [where Trude, Sigmund, and Martha lived before Trude and Max were married]. Those were such blissful times! (Martha letter to Trude, November 9, 1941.)

"So, my dear Trude and dear Renate and Erica, I wish you all the best. Stay healthy and think of your mother and grandmother, who sends you her warmest greetings and kisses."

Rudi Waller, who had emigrated to New York and operated an import/export business, wrote to Trude: "We hope that you are all right and the children too, and that you are more settled after all your sorrow." He told Trude about his efforts to complete the papers to help Martha, Sigmund, and Ernst emigrate. He seemed to think there was reason to believe they might still get out; he asked Trude to take the next steps to complete the applications he had prepared. He hoped the three of them would be able to leave Germany soon "so

that they won't be in danger of being deported as so many others."
(Rudi Waller letter to Trude, Nov. 10, 1941.)

Trude also heard from friends in England. Mrs. Alice Chapman
wrote to Trude from Sticklepath Hill, in Barnstaple, North Devon:

> Dear Mrs. Houser:
>
> I hardly know how to write you after so long, but feel I must
> say how very sad Janet and I are to hear of your sad loss and
> to convey to you & Erica & Renate our sympathy in your
> suffering.
>
> We have been here for nearly a year, but often think of you, and
> Mrs. Goff always mentions news of you in her letters to me,
> and we were shocked to hear of the doctor's illness and death.
> Forgive me writing you. It must be very painful to you to receive
> letters of sympathy after you have suffered so much, but I would
> just like to say that we are your friends here in England and will
> do anything we can to help you. So if there is anything at any
> time that we can do to help either you or your dear little girls,
> please do not hesitate to let us know, and we shall be glad to do
> it. We are a long way from you but do not forget you and would
> be happy to have any of you with us now, and please God when
> this war is over we may someday meet again.
>
> Janet is at school here and I am working and praying for the
> day when we may return to our normal lives again. It is better
> to work hard all day, the time passes quickly and we do not
> have time to think so much. It is very lovely here and we have
> enjoyed the summer and days by the sea, but we look forward
> to returning to our friends and our homes soon.
>
> With love to Erica and Renate from Janet and myself and to
> yourself dear Mrs. Houser my wishes that the future may yet
> hold some happiness for you, in the sincere wish of,
>
> Yours very sincerely,
>
> (Mrs.) Alice M. Chapman.

Mrs. Chapman's references about returning to their homes suggests she and her daughter Janet had been evacuated and were living
in the British countryside, out of range of German bombing. The

Chapmans' family home was at 82 College Road, six doors down the street from the Goffs in Harrow Weald, which is how the Chapmans had come to know Max, Trude, and the girls.

Martha wrote to Trude the following week:

> My loved ones, I'm with you in thought and only hope that you are doing well and that you are, above all, healthy…I'm very comforted by the fact that you, dear Trude, visited several doctors who reassured you that you are in good health. Don't use your strength to do anything more than your housekeeping tasks. You have to take doubly good care of yourself for your children's sake and ultimately also for our sake…We hope to see you again. When that will be, one cannot say. Hopefully, it will be soon! (Martha letter to Trude Nov. 16, 1941.)

As to the situation in Cologne, "Things are tragic wherever you look. It's lonely here. So many people are away [deported]…We have no choice but to accept our destiny and to bear the burdens that are being put on our shoulders…There's no time to think; just live through the day.

Martha noted their friends Fritz and Adi had written to them to say goodbye. "Help came too late for them." Martha noted they were no longer allowed to send wires abroad except in connection with emigration. She wrote that "Father's age protects us, but one can't help feeling for the others…Lots of love and kisses for our good children and for you my dear Trude." (Martha letter to Trude, November 16, 1941.) Martha and Sigmund watched as their friends and neighbors were deported to death camps. They understood that Sigmund's age protected them from such a fate, but for how much longer?

Martha was happy to know people were visiting Trude and offering support. She commented that her and Sigmund's address remained the same for the time being, implying they might be forced to move yet again. She was anxious to hear more about Renate and Erica: "I'm happy that the children are so unaffected by what happened—happy youth. Just let them enjoy themselves; memory is the only paradise we can't be expelled from."

WHAT SORROW I HAVE

B Y EARLY DECEMBER 1941, THE WEHRMACHT WAS WITHIN sight of Moscow. However, the Soviet army, which had been reeling ever since the initial Nazi onslaught, stiffened. The Nazis would advance no further. The Soviets launched a massive counterattack, forcing the Nazis to retreat. While the Soviets did not destroy the German army, the Wehrmacht had suffered a significant defeat. For the first time, it seemed that the Nazis could be beaten.

Early in the morning on Sunday, December 7, 1941, Japan attacked the United States' Pacific Fleet at anchor in Pearl Harbor. Trude, Renate, and Erica learned of the attack while listening to the radio at home that fateful Sunday morning. The United States declared war on Japan the next day. Japan's Axis allies, Germany and Italy, promptly declared war on the United States, bringing the United States fully into World War II. Roosevelt had not declared war on Italy and Germany at the same time the United States declared war on Japan because he wanted the Axis powers to "strike first" by declaring war on the United States. That way, he could tell the American public the United States was entering the war in Europe not on the initiative of the United States, but rather in response to declarations of war by the Axis powers. The United States would enter the war without the political restraints that had so far held it back. Hitler now faced the tremendous economic and military capacity of the United States that had contributed mightily to Germany's defeat in WWI.

On the same day the United States entered the war, Trude wrote to her parents. This letter is available because it was returned to Trude marked "Service Suspended." Once the United States entered the war, mail service to Germany ended, so Trude's letter was returned to her as undeliverable. The letter provides almost the only contemporaneous knowledge still available regarding what Trude was feeling and experiencing:

My dear, good parents,

Today is my day to write, and I will converse with you even though there is no letter to reply to. Your last letter was from Oct. 27. What all has happened in the meantime! There is always reason for alarm, particularly since my cable to the Hartmann Travel [agency] concerning Ernst remained unanswered. Is Ernst at Albert and Irma Karmers? Gertrude heard about the Isensteins. It is such a horrible world. I would much rather experience a little less world history and have a peaceful existence. Life is so short, one prefers to live it in peace. Now we are also at war; even though the Pacific is far away, it will influence our lives and our taxes. Events are quicker than us. How will the world look after the war? Will this letter even reach you? You cannot imagine how my thoughts go, what sorrow I have on your account, especially since I am not in a position to help you through my own efforts.

Don't worry about us. I will survive and am determined to keep the house, since through events over there I learned that in uncertain times real estate is the only value. Americans do not see this, they have no experience and want to advise me differently. But on this point, I am steadfast; I pay monthly as much as I would otherwise pay in rent, which then would be lost. By renting out one room our payment is less. The renter makes for hardly any work, is gone through the day and most evenings. I can't find a doctor for the office and have given up that plan; I sold the instruments and thus paid off my car. I can't be without a car, and once it is paid off it doesn't require much to maintain it. I earn as much as I would in employment, however it varies, sometimes more, sometimes less per week. The most I had was $18; that much Peter would sometimes earn in one day and didn't have to toil like I do. Poor Peter, on his birthday (Dec. 4) we three visited his grave and brought flowers, that is all I can do for him. The children were very serious, but I don't want them to be sad, their lives have enough unpleasantness. Therefore, from the cemetery we went to the museum, where they had an invitation to the opening of an exhibit of the works of the Saturday morning classes, with a subsequent tea. There were cookies for everyone, as much as one could eat. A class in drawing was introduced. One drawing of Renate's hangs in the junior museum since last week. Last week the children had state tests in school that are given in all Ohio schools. Eri was the best in all subjects, she even surpassed Renate by seven points in the English test, in which R. was the best among four classes in her school year. The questions are the same in five school years but must be answered according to age.

Sunday the Goldsteins [Curt and Kathryn Gonnard] were here with bride, sister-in-law, and niece. The niece was in Renate's class in Cincinnati and was happy to visit. Her mother told me that the children in Eri's class were glad when Eri moved to Deer Park, that they were rid of the competition. I must say, that hurt me, as nice as it is on the one hand. Poor child, she doesn't have it easy with schoolmates because of her capability. Kurt's bride is very intelligent, but homely, plump, and looks old compared to him, though they are the same age. I can't understand him; in comparison Marianne Emmerich was a fine girl. But this one is American and is employed, that seemed to clinch the matter.

It may be of interest to you what I am working on. Now, before Christmas, gift articles like writing table covers, calendars, paper containers, match boxes in chintz or leather; yesterday I had a leather bag with a knitted monogram, and endless decorative aprons. Gradually, I am adjusting to the work and do it more rapidly. For after Christmas, I have already looked around for something else. I will be taught at a furniture factory to make sofa covers, which everyone here has or needs, and which are made according to a pattern. This is supposed to bring in $18 for five days of eight hours [forty-five cents per hour]. Even though I must work, it doesn't go badly with me; I make my expenses and allow myself music lessons for the children.

Yesterday I had a letter from Anna, she is happy with the sister-in-law. She is exceptionally nice toward me, writes me regularly, I only wish that I could speak to her now and then. Gert sent Eri boots with ice skates from Anita, the same as Renate has.

But it isn't cold enough here; it is cold, but it doesn't freeze. I still wear socks and need stockings only when I go into town. Last week an American lady, also a doctor's wife, was here with me and did sewing with me. Such people have no idea what trouble is, they have never had any. The man is a surgeon, and they have a farm with cows and riding horses; the daughter rides in tournaments in New York. In spite of this, the woman sews everything for the family herself and gave me some advice.

How is Papa [Grandpa Ichenhäuser]? Does he know about Peter? Do you see him occasionally or can't you get together? How is Uncle Fritz and family? I haven't heard from him in ages. Did Aunt Hannchen go into the old age home? Where are Anna and Hella? Else, Frieda, George, and Inge wrote to me, but Ernst not [these are some of Trude's first cousins—children and grandchildren of Sigmund Moses' brother Karl]; evidently, he doesn't consider it necessary.

There is nothing I wish more than to have news from you soon. But no one [here] had mail, that comforts me somewhat. Stay healthy and brave.

Love and Kisses from your Trude (Trude letter to Martha and Sigmund, December 8, 1941.)

It is impossible to know, but not difficult to imagine, what may have gone through Trude's mind when her letter was returned as undeliverable. As she wrote in the first paragraph, she was filled with sorrow over her parents' predicament, yet she was helpless to resolve it. Maybe she maintained her mental balance by thinking her parents had moved to another location and her letter simply had not been forwarded. Perhaps she staked her hopes on the mail being disrupted due to the war, with her parents still fine, but beyond the reach of the postal service. Trude was a smart woman who likely could devise strategies to avoid thinking the worst. But when she paused from her stitching, or lay in bed at night, or at odd, quiet moments during the day, did dire thoughts creep into her mind? By now, the German immigrant community was aware of the suicides, murders, and deportations. Perhaps Trude's mind went to such dark places. But her iron will may have been such that she successfully compartmentalized her fears so she could function, hour by hour and day by day, and present a hopeful front to her daughters.

As to her financial situation, with Max gone, Trude had no choice but to find work. She started doing piece work as she described in her letter. She later took a job operating a sewing machine at a local garment factory. This was a huge change in lifestyle. In Cologne, Trude had lived in a large house with a maid, nanny, and her mother to help shop and cook while Trude worked in Max's office. Now, she had no husband, no help, and two daughters for whom she was the sole support.

Trude had never cooked in Cologne unless she wanted to; Martha and the cook took care of kitchen duties. Trude now not only had to work, but she also had to run all aspects of the household, including preparing meals. She prepared potatoes many ways; they were a staple. When Trude was young, in particular after WWI when the German economy was in a state of collapse, her family often had nothing to eat except potatoes. As a result, she had quite a repertoire when it came to this part of their diet. Trude served potatoes baked, mashed, escalloped, and pan-fried.

For breakfast, Trude often prepared thin, Swedish-style pancakes which the girls topped with lingonberry jam and confectioner's sugar. Sometimes Trude made apple pancakes with thin slices of tart apples in each pancake, sweetened further with maple syrup. Soft-boiled eggs, served in delicate egg cups, were often on the breakfast menu. Lunch was typically cold cuts, such as salami and hard cheese eaten on thinly sliced, dense, dark bread. For later in the day, Trude baked delicious, almond-based, double-layer sandwich cookies. She slathered currant jelly between two cookies, glazed the upper cookie with sugar icing, and placed half an almond on top for a visual accent. For dessert or to share with guests who came for coffee, Trude sometimes made a hazelnut cake with chocolate icing or an orange-almond cake covered with an orange-lemon glaze. With a dollop of whipped cream added for good measure, the flavors elicited memories of the konditorei in Cologne that the family had enjoyed so long ago.

Renate and Erica helped around the house as much as they

could. The house was heated by a coal furnace. When the girls returned home from school during the winter, they had to clean the ashes out of the furnace, add coal, and get the fire going so the house was warm by the time Trude arrived from work. Renate did the grocery shopping and the girls tried to get dinner ready so they could eat as soon as Trude arrived.

Trude wanted to send Renate and Erica to a Jewish Sunday school. However, the schools would not accept the girls since the family had not joined a congregation. In Germany, the state funded all religious institutions. In the United States, Trude faced a different cultural approach to synagogue membership. This was a problem, because while Trude wanted her daughters to be part of the Jewish community, she could not afford synagogue dues. Trude resented this obstacle to her efforts to give her daughters the life she wanted for them.

Trude's frustration boiled over one evening when she attended a meeting of one of the Jewish community's organizations. The leader of the meeting was teaching American songs to the recent arrivals, perhaps to help them learn English or thinking they would fit in better if they knew the songs. Trude told the group leader that she, and Max before he died, were desperate to get their relatives out of Germany and needed help to do so. Becoming conversant with American songs was not on her list of priorities. The combination of being excluded from local congregations and the lack of help with her most fervent need left her embittered. Her experiences led her to believe that religion was, more than anything, a source of conflict.

THE FINAL SOLUTION

B Y MARCH 1941, THE NAZIS HAD REACHED THE DECISION
to implement the "final solution." Top members of the
regime had already discussed the horrific premise which had long
been central to Hitler's ideology. However, it did not become official policy until the Wannsee Conference on Jan. 20, 1942. On
July 31, 1941, Hermann Goering gave written authorization to
SS-Obergruppenführer Reinhard Heydrich to prepare and submit a
plan for a "total solution of the Jewish question" in territories under
German control and to coordinate the participation of all government organizations that were to be involved in implementing the
solution.[285] The Wannsee Conference was the result of this directive.

Heydrich conducted the conference in the Berlin suburb of
Wannsee in a beige, sandstone, three-story villa with a small portico
in front set off by a circular garden and gravel driveway. The Nazi
leadership met to discuss how to solve Germany's "Jewish problem."
The regime had already deported hundreds of thousands of Jews to
concentration camps in the east. Nazi-instigated civilian pogroms
and the Wehrmacht had already murdered hundreds of thousands
of Jews in the territories Germany occupied. However, the National
Socialist regime concluded that a more systematic approach was
required in order to efficiently achieve its goal of a "Jew-free" Europe.
Another factor driving the decision to organize a formal "solution"

---

285 *War Against the Jews* at 136.

was the Nazis' need, after poor harvests in Germany in 1940 and 1941, to allocate food to the German army and Aryan populace. These allocations could only be made in sufficient quantities by eliminating "useless" mouths which the regime might otherwise need to feed. Jews were the leading category of mouths whose elimination would ease pressure on the food shortage the Reich was facing.

Reinhard Heydrich, director of the Reich's Main Security Office, arranged the conference, which included representatives from the Reich's Foreign Office, the Justice, Interior, and State ministries, and the SS. Heydrich explained the solution to the "problem" was to collect and send Europe's Jews to camps in occupied Poland where they would be killed.[286]

The initial plan allowed for a few exceptions—Jews over age sixty-five, Jews who had been seriously wounded in WWI, and Jews who had otherwise served with distinction in the War were to be spared.[287] Those Jews would be sent to a ghetto for the aged. Theresienstadt was the camp selected to "host" them. In the end, Theresienstadt served as nothing more than a way station for its prisoners before they, too, were deported to camps for annihilation, primarily in Auschwitz.[288] Heydrich told the attendees at Wannsee that while several government and military agencies would be involved in the rounding up and transporting of Jews from Germany and German-occupied territories, the SS would run the camps and handle the actual extermination.

And so, as if mass expulsion and murder were simply mundane government policies such as improving agricultural yields or managing industrial production, the systematic murder of millions of people became formal, if unwritten, government policy. A written order reflecting the policy has never been found because, although the Nazis generally were compulsive record-keepers, this was an area where they sought to avoid creating evidence and implicating

---

286 *The Wannsee Conference in the Development of the "Final Solution."* Peter Longeric (2000).

287 *War Against the Jews* at 137.

288 *War Against the Jews* at 137.

themselves in a policy that they knew was monstrous and criminal, but which they nevertheless were determined to pursue.

Commentary is Superfluous

In January 1942, Carl and Hilde Spier wrote to Trude. Carl and Hilde were continuing their efforts to emigrate to the United States, but the new regulations were making it even more difficult. "[I] do not know if under the new regulations it is possible to finalize the immigration, but we do not want to give up the hope to live once again in freedom and to see our children grow up." (Carl Spier letter to Trude, January 4, 1942.) Trude sent a telegram to the Spiers at St. Cyprien telling them she had been able to secure support affidavits for Carl and Hilde and had mailed them to Marseilles.

The difficulties of daily life continued to weigh heavily on the Spiers. The building in which they were living had been sold and they were not sure how long they could remain in it. They were not even sure how long Hilde and Carl would be able to stay together. "Many acquaintances have been forced into residence in tiny villages, others into work camps." Carl thanked Trude once again for her efforts to obtain support affidavits for their visa applications:

> Please also express our thanks to the affidavit donors, we will never forget you, that with all your own troubles, you still had the strength to help us. It hurts us so to read how hard you have to struggle, and we have great admiration for you." (Carl Spier letter to Trude, Jan. 4, 1942.)

Carl commended Trude's efforts to hold onto the house for Renate and Erica, but wondered whether moving to a larger city might provide more employment opportunities for Trude. He asked whether she might earn more making luxury piecework. He expressed his heartfelt desire to help Trude, but given their circumstances, Carl and Hilde were unable to do anything to assist her:

> Hilde and I are on our feet all day in long lines to obtain the most necessary things to eat, everything is rationed and so little that even with Hilde's cooking and stretching attempts, we are still hungry. Momentarily the ration per person per week: 2000 grams bread, 100 grams fat, butter, etc., about 500 grams vegetables, no potatoes, 150 grams meat. Commentary is superfluous.

These rations provided a weekly diet of barely four-and-one-half pounds of bread, one-quarter pound of fat/butter, one pound of vegetables, and roughly one-third of a pound of meat. One-third of a pound of meat is roughly equivalent to a single, thin hamburger patty for one person for an entire week. The butter/fat allocation was less than a single pat of butter per day. The vegetable ration was barely two ounces of vegetables per day, and that was made up almost entirely of rutabagas and parsnips. The bread ration allowed several slices per person per day, but it was of little nutritional benefit since the bread was made primarily with fillers and only a bit of grain, if any. The rations did not include any fruit, making them extremely vitamin deficient. These were, by any measure, starvation rations so devoid of nutrients as to deprive the recipients of the strength they needed for daily activities, as well as causing the onset of diseases associated with malnutrition.

Carl closed his letter by asking Trude if she would please send a snapshot of herself and the children. "And once again, dear Trude, and also the affidavit sponsors, our deepest thanks and many regards."

Hilde wrote to Trude the same day:

> My dear Trude:
>
> You didn't really think we could <u>not</u> thank you? I can only tell you that I wish and hope with all my strength that you will reap from your children all the friendship that you have shown us…

> We think of you often and how hard it is for you. I understand completely that you only want to live for the children now, but for their sake you have to think of yourself too, and not use yourself up. What you wrote about your uncles is dreadful. Sadly, also Eugenchen with both children is gone, also Otto and Else David, Linchen Klein, and countless others. Your parents can probably stay due to their age, just like my relatives, Kimmelstiehl's father, Max Goldburg's mother, etc. Have you any kind of news of them in the interim? We ourselves fear as before and after, the same fate, unless by some miracle our immigration works out. The children still go to school, are always the best in their classes and have lots of little friends. But naturally their opportunities are limited because one has no chance. (Hilde Spier letter to Trude, Jan. 4, 1942.)

She continued: "My father is missing; all inquiries are without results." Hilde spent much of her time sewing, making alterations, and patching garments, because "one can't buy anything." (Clothing was either not available or too expensive.) "We ourselves *hope*—that we can remain together, but each week it is more uncertain. Dear Trude, again our deepest thanks, and best regards also from the children and a kiss for you. Your Hilde." (Emphasis in the original.)

With the cessation of mail service after Pearl Harbor, information about David, Martha, and Sigmund became sketchy and intermittent. What little is known is that in January 1942, Martha and Sigmund were forced to move yet again. Sigmund was hospitalized for a while; the reason is not known. Upon being discharged, he and Martha moved into an old age home.

On March 24, the Nazis barred Jews from using public transportation; the only exception was for Jews who were able to obtain a special police permit. "Jews in the Reich are now forbidden to use railways, buses or other transportation facilities unless they are working in armament factories located more than ninety minutes walking time from their homes."[289] If Jews worked someplace far from their homes that required them to walk for well over an hour to get there, well, so be it.

On March 25, 1942, Sigmund died of arteriosclerosis in the

---

289 Jewish Telegraphic Agency, May 5, 1942.

Jewish hospital in Ehrenfeld, a district on Cologne's west side. He was eighty-three. Sigmund was buried in the Jewish cemetery in Bocklemünd, northwest of Ehrenfeld, in the outskirts of Cologne. Martha then moved—whether voluntarily or involuntarily is not known—to a small building at Rathenauplatz, roughly one-half mile south of the former family home on Aachenerstrasse.

In June 1942, the Reich barred Jews from owning electrical appliances.[290] Jews had to surrender all electric cooking devices and household appliances; they were also ordered to surrender cameras, binoculars, and bicycles.[291] This meant the end of the hot plate on which Martha had cooked their meals.

On September 2, the Ministry of Agriculture issued a directive that Jews would no longer receive rations of meat, milk, white bread, or tobacco products.[292]

Notwithstanding the stalled Nazi offensive against Moscow in December 1941, the war, by and large, had been going well for Germany. Rommel was sweeping from Libya eastward across north Africa towards Egypt. By late June 1942, Rommel and his famed Afrika Corps had captured the key British defense fortifications at Tobruk in eastern Libya and had advanced to within sixty-five miles of Alexandria and the Nile delta. If Rommel captured Alexandria, he could close the Suez Canal to British shipping and deprive the British of their lifeline to the British empire in Asia. German troops were also nearing Stalingrad. It seemed there was no stopping the Nazi onslaught across Europe. With huge amounts of Allied shipping being lost in the North Atlantic to U-boat attacks, it was difficult for the British to obtain the supplies and armaments the United States was willing to provide and that the British so desperately needed.

By the summer of 1942, German sources confirmed to the Allies that the Reich had instituted a program of systematic, mass murder. The program encompassed transporting Jews from all over Europe to death camps in Eastern Europe. Yet, the Allies did nothing to

---

290 *Jewish Daily Life* at 282.

291 *Nazi Germany and the Jews* at 303.

292 *Nazi Germany and the Jews* at 304.

intervene. They did not bomb the train lines leading to the camps or the stations from which trains departed transporting Jews to slaughter. Nor did the Allies bomb the camps to destroy the gas chambers and impede the mass murders. Simply put, the Allies did nothing to interdict the transport and slaughter of Europe's Jews.

By February 1942, Ernst was living in the barracks camp at Fort V in Müngersdorf. The SS notified Ernst that he was to be deported on June 12, 1942, on a train bound for Minsk, the capital of Belarus. Belarus, east of Germany, was wedged between Poland and Russia. Ernst knew full well that such trains went to the death camps, if, in fact, the trains arrived at the camps. Often, the trains stopped before they reached their destinations. The SS ordered the passengers out of the cars and into the woods, where the SS shot them and buried the bodies in mass graves. Knowing this, Ernst refused to go willingly to his death. He decided to take his chances by staying in Cologne and going into hiding. As Ernst suspected, the train he had been ordered to board did not go to Minsk. The train went on a detour and the SS murdered everyone on board.

Ernst went underground. He spent several days hiding in a home at 14 Mauritiuswall in western Cologne. A cigar trader by the name of Heinrich Mehlkopf had leased the house and was renting rooms to Jews—albeit illegally since by then Jews were allowed to live only in designated areas and buildings. Ernst then moved to Hohenzollernring 65 or 67 and rented a room from a Miss Neubert. In August, Ernst took the name Müller as cover and moved to 44 Brabanter Strasse, a building owned by the Pees family. Ernst occasionally returned to 14 Mauritiuswall to purchase food stamps from Jews who were hiding there.

In September 1942, an informant sent a "denunciation letter" to the Gestapo claiming that Jews were living illegally at 14 Mauritiuswall. Many Germans eagerly denounced Jews as well as anyone whom they suspected of aiding Jews. The denunciations sprang variously from anti-Semitism, a desire to curry favor with the authorities, or to strike at those whom they suspected of aiding Jews because of some other resentment or conflict. The Gestapo raided the Mauritiuswall house and found several Jews hiding there. The

Gestapo arrested them, and, under questioning, the victims admitted they were trading food stamps (ration coupons) on the black market. The regime considered this to be an "economic war crime." Jews had no legal way to obtain food stamps because the Reich had completely disenfranchised them from all aspects of the German economy and legal system, including all aspects of social welfare. Nevertheless, if Jews wanted food, they had to find a way to get food stamps. The black market was their only option, which meant that Jews were imprisoned for purchasing—not stealing—the food stamps they needed to survive.

Ernst returned to Mauritiuswall on October 12 to purchase more food stamps; he had been underground for four months by then. Unfortunately, the Gestapo raided the house that day and captured him. The Gestapo questioned Ernst and sent him to the local jail, Klingelpütz, where the authorities held him from October 12, 1942 to December 16, 1943.

On August 23, 1942, the battle of Stalingrad began. It was to be one of the seminal battles of the war. The German lines were dangerously over-extended as a result of having marched so far east so quickly. The Luftwaffe bases were too far back to allow it to provide effective air cover for the ground troops. Yet Hitler insisted on taking Stalingrad both because he regarded it as highly symbolic, as well as important to his efforts to seize nearby oil fields. The Soviets saw Stalingrad as one of the keys to their nation, as a result of which their resistance to the Nazi onslaught stiffened dramatically. The battle was joined and would continue for months.

The Vichy police arrested Carl and Hilde Spier on August 25, 1942. The police banged on the family's door at 4:00 a.m., allowing them one hour to prepare to leave.[293] They sent the Spiers to a camp for "foreign Jews" in Auvarre, near Nice. Families were split up upon arrival at the Auvarre barracks. Rumors circulated that they were going to be sent to the east. A sympathetic police officer told Hilde and Carl they should separate themselves from their children because "unaccompanied children," at least at that moment, were not being sent to the east. Hilde and Carl made the gut-wrenching

293 *Return to Erfurt* at 96.

decision to leave their children to try to save them. Hilde and Carl feigned illness—Carl by taking pills that sped up his heartbeat, Hilde by claiming she had bad kidneys.[294] The camp administrators hospitalized them, which allowed them to achieve the desired separation from their children. A local Jewish organization was able to retrieve Marianne and Rolf from the camp and take them to its headquarters nearby.[295]

Hilde, desperate to find someone to take custody of Marianne and Rolf, had written to her cousin Ilse Klein in Cologne. Ilse's husband, an Italian attorney, contacted his cousin Angelo Donati. Donati, an Italian diplomat, was a member of one of the most prominent Jewish families in the town of Modena, which was situated midway between Milan and Florence in Italy's Emilia-Romagna region. Donati's father, Salvatore, was a merchant. Donati's seven brothers included a banker, the head of an accounting firm, a professor of philosophy, and an industrialist. His cousins included a president of a university, a world-famous surgeon, and a lawyer who became a member of the Italian Parliament. Donati obtained a law degree and worked in the banking industry in Milan and Turin before fighting in WWI. After the war, he moved to Paris, where he founded a Franco-Italian bank, became president of the Italian Red Cross and the Italian Chamber of Commerce in Paris, and became the recipient of the French Legion of Honour and the Order of the Crown of Italy.[296]

In advance of the Nazis marching into Paris, Donati fled to southern France. When Italian troops, as part of the Axis powers, marched into southern France, Donati took responsibility for the fate of the Jews in the Italian-occupied zone of southern France. The Nazis did not suspect Donati was Jewish because of his Italian name. As a result, he was able to operate relatively freely. He was able to forestall deportation of the area's Jews for a while. However, the Vichy regime eventually capitulated to the Germans' demands and

---

294 *Return to Erfurt* at 97.

295 *Return to Erfurt* at 98.

296 *Return to Erfurt* at 103-104.

ordered the mayor of Nice to round up all foreign Jews in the Côte d'Azur. Donati nevertheless was able to help 2500 Jews escape from Nice to areas in southern France not yet under Nazi occupation.

Among the Jews whom Donati saved were Marianne and Rolf Spier. He secured the frightened children from the office where the local Jewish organization was holding them. Marianne had never met Donati. She was racked by doubt and worry, as she did not know where her parents were or what was to become of them, or what fate had in store for her and her brother. Now, a stranger had arrived saying she and her brother should go with him. Marianne was not sure whether she should trust him. However, she had a small address book in which her mother had written the names of friends and relatives who might be able to help them. Donati's name was in the book, which convinced Marianne it was safe for her and Rolf to go with him.

Donati left a message at the Auvarre hospital for Hilde and Carl telling them he had secured Marianne and Rolf and they would be safe in his care. The next day, on August 31, 1942, the Nazis deported Hilde and Carl from Nice to the Drancy detention camp, northeast of Paris in occupied France. They went to their fate knowing the heart-rending decision they had made to separate themselves from their children would likely save their children's lives.

The Drancy camp served as a collection and detention camp from which foreign Jews (Jews from another country who were in France) were deported to extermination camps. On September 2, 1942, the Nazis deported Hilde and Carl from Drancy to Auschwitz on Convoi No. 27. Hilde's name does not appear in any records at Auschwitz. The most likely explanation for this is that upon arriving on September 6, Hilde was selected for immediate murder and was sent directly to the gas chambers. The camp assigned Carl to forced labor. If Carl was not immediately aware of Hilde's fate as they disembarked the train and were assessed for fitness by the corrupt Nazi physicians who sorted new arrivals, he no doubt soon learned of it from other inmates who explained to him how Jews were "processed" and what the selection process meant.[297]

---

297   Fewer than 2,000 of the almost 65,000 Jews deported from Drancy to death

In November 1942, the Nazis decided to occupy all of Vichy France. From then until the Allied invasion and liberation of France, the Nazis were in control of the fate of all Jews whom the Vichy regime had not already rounded up and shipped north to the Reich for extermination. This would have included all of the Spier family had it not been for Donati's intercession.

Marianne and Rolf went to live with Donati in his apartment on the Promenade des Anglais in Nice. Marianne knew her parents had been sent to a camp, but she did not know where or what their fate was. Nevertheless, she and Rolf tried to live a normal life; they began school and started to learn Italian.

Donati was working on plans to help thousands of Jews interned in the Italian occupation zone in southern France escape to Palestine or north Africa. However, when the Italian King Victor Emmanuel III authorized an armistice with the Allies after Mussolini was overthrown in July 1943, Donati's plans collapsed. General Eisenhower publicly disclosed the armistice sooner than agreed and before Donati was able to complete plans to evacuate the Jews he had identified for rescue. When the Germans learned of the armistice, they invaded Italy on September 8, 1943, and occupied the entire country with the exception of the small foothold the Allies had secured during a landing in southern Italy.[298] The Italians could no longer protect Jews in their occupation zone. Suddenly, those Jews were at risk of deportation.

The Gestapo, by then, was on the lookout to arrest Donati. The Gestapo had finally realized that, notwithstanding his Italian name, Donati was Jewish. When the Gestapo also became aware of his efforts to save Jews, they were furious. However, by this time, Donati and the children were living in Florence. Donati soon fled to Switzerland for the remainder of the war. He arranged for his butler, Francesco Moraldo, to take Marianne and Rolf to Creppo, Moraldo's tiny hometown in Italy's Ligurian Alps. Moraldo hid the children there with his parents in a tiny stone cottage, with the

---

camps survived the Holocaust. (*The Holocaust Encyclopedia*, Drancy.)

298 *Return to Erfurt* at 113-14.

unspoken assistance of the other residents of the village, hoping to keep Marianne and Rolf safe from Nazi patrols roaming the area.

A FINAL FAREWELL

I N July 1942, Martha sent a message to Trude through the International Red Cross. The form by which the Red Cross transmitted the message was one used by the Central Agency for Prisoners of War. The application identified the sender as Mrs. Martha Sara Moses residing at Horst Wessel Platz 14 in Cologne. (After the war, Germany changed the name of the plaza back to Rathenauplatz and banned the singing of the "Horst Wessel Song.") Since Martha's given name did not include Sara, the inclusion of Sara was the result of the Nazi decree requiring all Jewish women to take the name Sara to make them readily identifiable as Jews. The intended recipient of Martha's message was listed as Mrs. Trude Houser at 4247 Trinity Road in Cincinnati. Trude's correct address was 4247 Amity Road. (Cincinnati eventually absorbed Deer Park and changed the Ichenhäusers' address to 4247 Galbraith Road.) The message, which the Red Cross form limited to twenty-five words, read:

> Faithfully thinking of you on your birthday today. I am healthy, hope you are too. Hedy has been released from long-term suffering. The people are always without information. Heartfelt kisses. Mother

Hedy was a family friend; family records do not disclose her last name. A few documents refer to a Hedy Wallerstein, but it is not known if this is the same Hedy. The available records also do not disclose whether Hedy's release from suffering was due to illness, suicide, or having been murdered by the Nazis. Although Martha sent the greeting on July 4, 1942, the American Red Cross, which was the conduit through which the International Red Cross forwarded communications, did not send the letter to Trude until November 19, 1942, a four-and-a-half-month delay. The Red Cross cover letter advised Trude that:

> If you wish to send a reply, will you please come into the Red Cross Chapter House, 2343 Auburn Ave., any day between 8:30 a.m. and 4:00 p.m., <u>bringing the enclosed message form with you</u>. It is important that you bring this form as the answer is placed on the reverse side. Due to censor regulations your reply must be placed on the form by us and must be in English, so please do not write on or deface the form in any way. (American Red Cross letter to Trude, November 19, 1942; emphasis in the original.)

Family records do not contain further communications from Ernst during the war. After the Gestapo captured Ernst on October 12, 1942, he was unable to write to Trude, even if postal service had still been operating. Trude had no idea what his fate was. What passed through her mind as weeks, months, and years went by with no word from Ernst? Having lost her husband, had she now lost his brother as well?

And what of Trude's father? Sigmund had passed away, although it is not known whether Trude learned during the war of his passing. Since Sigmund died after postal service had ended, any letters Martha tried to send would not have reached Trude. When Martha wrote her birthday greeting to Trude, she may have thought Trude was already aware of Sigmund's passing.

Family records evidence one further postcard from Martha. Martha's note is in the same format as the birthday wishes Martha sent to Trude in July 1942, so it is likely this second card came via the International Red Cross:

Sender—Martha Sara Moses
Receiver—Mrs. Trude Houser
Deer Park, Cincinnati, Ohio
4247 Amity Rd. USA

Message: Before my departure a final farewell. Indivisible in thoughts with you, hope for an eventual, healthy reunification. Travel with Lene, Max. Theresienstadt. Stay well.

Mother, Grandma.

According to Renate's translation, the note was in Martha's handwriting. This was the last message Martha sent before the Nazis deported her to Theresienstadt, where she arrived on September 25, 1942. She was deported with Lene and Max Berlin. There is nothing showing when Trude received the note. However, she may have received it within a few months of Martha's deportation assuming this card took roughly the same amount of time to arrive as did the previous card Martha sent via the Red Cross.

Theresienstadt ("Terezin" in Czech) was a "Potemkin village" concentration camp. The Nazis used it to defraud the international press and the International Red Cross. The Reich set up Theresienstadt to demonstrate how well the Nazis were purportedly treating Jews in their prison camps. This, of course, begs the question of how "well" anyone is being treated when arrested and incarcerated for no crime other than the religion into which the victim was born. The SS, which ran the camp, built a fake café, stores, a bank, and schools. When the Red Cross visited, its representatives were allowed to meet with select prisoners who knew what awaited them if they did not cooperate with the Nazis. Of course, the guards had told the interviewees precisely what they should say. The Red Cross was completely fooled.[299] "Ultimately, the Nazis intended to mask the extermination of European Jewry by presenting Theresienstadt as a model ghetto."[300]

The camp administration created ersatz "currency" for the prisoners to use as a way to show the camp was a place where prisoners

---

299 www.yadvashem.org/Theresienstadt.

300 WWW.YADVASHEM.ORG/THERESIENSTADT.

lived, shopped, and transacted business. The currency also served to give the impression the camp was an autonomous community. The fraudulent scrip featured a drawing of Moses holding tablets bearing the Ten Commandments. The scrip was denominated in crowns because Theresienstadt was in Czechoslovakia whose currency was denominated in crowns, not Reichsmarks as in Germany.

The truth is Theresienstadt was a concentration camp. It was not a death factory like other camps such as Auschwitz. Nevertheless, the Reich killed tens of thousands of Jews at Theresienstadt by starvation, lack of medical care resulting in deadly epidemics, and directly such as being shot. The Nazis initially built Theresienstadt to hold Jews from what had been Czechoslovakia. Later, the SS sent German Jews there as well, including many elderly Jews.

Conditions at the camp were horrific. The prisoners were starved. They lacked even the most basic hygiene facilities and medical care. Epidemics frequently swept through the camp. Thirty-three thousand Jews died there in addition to the nearly ninety thousand Jews whom the Nazis deported from Theresienstadt to death camps. Theresienstadt became a holding operation to which the Nazis sent Jews before sending them to death camps, most often Auschwitz and Treblinka, to be murdered.[301]

Martha's card must have devastated Trude. Up to that point, she knew from her parents' letters that they had suffered forced relocations, inadequate food, and illness. She knew they were fighting depression as they lost their home, Cologne was bombed into rubble, and friends and family disappeared by emigration and deportation. Nevertheless, Trude at least knew Sigmund and Martha were alive. Now, she could no longer have such confidence. The lack of any reference to Sigmund may have led her to conclude that her father was dead.

Perhaps Trude took comfort from the fact that Martha was deported with Lene and Max Berlin. At least Martha did not travel alone to the next stage of her fate. Martha was by then sixty-two and had suffered a number of health problems. Knowing that Martha had family accompany her to help ease this frightening transition may

---

301 www.yadvashem.org/Theresienstadt.

have helped Trude cope upon receiving the news. However, Trude knew Martha had been sent to a concentration camp and almost certainly knew about the death camps and what awaited inmates at Theresienstadt.

It is a wonder that Trude could do laundry, cook meals, and stitch clothing knowing what the postcard told her explicitly and implicitly. She likely had to fight off images of her mother crammed into a boxcar with hundreds of other unfortunate souls on their way to Theresienstadt. She no doubt anguished about where her mother might be sent next, in another boxcar crammed with victims, knowing it would most likely be to a place where death awaited.

Notwithstanding her comment about "hope for an eventual, healthy reunification," Martha was either prophetic or simply truthful when she wrote that the card was a "final farewell." Deportations to Theresienstadt and from there to a death camp was the fate for tens of thousands of inmates at Theresienstadt. Time would tell if such would be Martha's fate.

Lene and Max sent a message via the Red Cross to Lene's brother Otto, who had managed to emigrate to the United States in 1938. Otto lived on a dairy farm in Suffield, Connecticut. Lene and Max's message, truncated by the word limitations the Red Cross imposed, said:

> Had news from Liesel Paul. We healthy [sic]. Travel tomorrow to Theresienstadt. Keep our head high. Hope to see you again. Take care of Liesel and Gerhard. Helene and Max.

Lene and Max signed the devastating card on Sept. 16, 1942.[302] The reference to keeping their heads high suggests Max and Lene knew well what deportation meant for them and they were prepared to meet their fate. Their request that Otto take care of their children Liesel (Lisselotte/Elizabeth) and Gerhard likewise suggests Max and Lene knew that Otto was going to have to raise their children. And so, they courageously said goodbye. Max and Lene had a window

---

302 Lene's card said she and Max were to be deported on September 17. However, the Yad Vashem Names Database states that Max was deported to Theresienstadt on September 25, so their date of deportation was apparently delayed a week.

of opportunity when they might have escaped Germany. However, Lene's mother Antoinette "Netchen" Roesberg was suffering from dementia and they did not want to leave her. Eventually, their window of opportunity closed and their fate was sealed.

The SS arrested David Ichenhäuser on July 27, 1942. They deported him to Theresienstadt the next day on Transport III/2, Train Da 76. While in Theresienstadt, David lived in Room 118 of Building L211. He died there on August 9, 1942, within two weeks of having been arrested and deported. The Theresienstadt Medical Office listed heart disease ("myocardial cardiomyocytes") on David's death certificate as the cause of death. However, there is no reason to believe heart disease was the actual cause of death, as opposed to starvation, preventable or treatable disease for which no means of prevention or treatment were provided, or simply having been shot. The Yad Vashem Names' Archive states that David was murdered in Theresienstadt.

David Ichenhäuser—the dapper gentleman with the neatly trimmed beard and moustache, who was born in Fürth and lived his entire life in Germany, who worked as a lumber dealer and was the father of three sons who served in the German army—was eighty-eight years old when the Nazis murdered him.

And so, no one was left in Germany from the family whose lives had centered upon the home on Aachenerstrasse. Trude, Max, Renate, and Erica had emigrated, but Max was now dead. David, Emma, and Sigmund were dead. Martha had been deported to what would likely be her death. Ernst was somewhere, perhaps in forced labor, but Trude had no way of knowing that. All she knew was that she had lost contact with him after postal service ended when the United States entered the war. Whatever the reason, Ernst, too, was gone. As Martha had written about the family home in one of her letters: "Someone else will walk in the garden now."

A Family of Three

Without the income from Max's practice, money was tight. Trude, Renate, and Erica had to do financial triage. Trude decided the girls should finish high school in three years so they could graduate and go to work. At the same time, Trude considered college to be essential to their futures. In order to accelerate the girls' education and let them graduate in three years, the girls had to take five subjects each semester instead of four. In addition to her classwork, Erica decided to play French horn in the school band.

The three of them also decided Renate and Erica should earn money each summer to contribute to the family's support. In the summer of 1942, Renate, age fourteen, got a job two or three days a week helping a woman in the neighborhood who was expecting and needed help around the house. That meant Erica, age thirteen, was alone for much of the day, which was not to her liking. Erica knew the Regan Fruit Farm was not far down the road from their home. One day, she walked to the farm and asked the owners if they needed help picking fruit. They did and Erica spent the summer picking strawberries and raspberries for three cents a quart.

One of their relatives, Wilhelm Kahn in New York, sent Trude sixty dollars every month to help them get by. That made a huge difference after Max's death until Trude found work to keep the family afloat.

The Cincinnati Jewish Community sponsored Renate and Erica, as recent immigrants, to attend Camp Livingston, the Jewish community's sleep-away camp, for several weeks in the summer. The camp was ten miles northeast of Cincinnati along the Little Miami River near the village of Indian Hill. The camp offered sports, drama, canoeing, handicrafts, nature study, and photography. It had a swimming pool, along with tennis courts and campfire areas. The camp held informal services on Shabbat and served Kosher-style food in the mess hall, along with plastic pitchers of "bug juice" (a Kool-Aid type of drink). Meals were followed by a robust round of singing to demonstrate the campers' "ruach" (spirit). Scholarships were available for those who needed help to cover the cost of $7 per week. Since Trude frequently earned only $18 per week from her piecework, scholarships were the only way the girls could afford to attend.

Erica was captivated by the nature study classes, which mostly involved catching insects with a net, killing them with a few drops of formaldehyde in a jar, and mounting the insects on pins. When Erica was not threatening the local insect population, she played kickball and volleyball. Although she knew how to swim the breaststroke, she added the American crawl and backstroke to her aquatic repertoire. Renate loved Camp Livingston; she gravitated towards arts and crafts and activities where she could draw and paint. The girls spent the next two summers (1942-43) at Camp Livingston.

At home, the family's small victory garden came in handy once rationing began in the United States. Sugar was the first item to be rationed, then coffee. Eventually meat, lard, shortening, cheese, butter, margarine, canned foods, canned milk, jams and jellies, firewood, shoes, and coal were rationed. The family received ration books with stamps bearing pictures of an airplane, tank, aircraft carrier, ear of wheat, fruit, and more. The recipients used the stamps to purchase rationed items to the extent such items were available.

While Trude, Renate, and Erica were trying to make their way, the war continued to devastate much of Europe. On May 30, 1942, the Allies launched their first air raid that involved fully 1,000 bombers. The Allies' "Thousand Bomber" attack carried out on Cologne during the night of May 30-31 caused tens of thousands of Cologne's residents to become homeless. The Allies' hope was that the enormous scale of the raids would force Germany to surrender or, at the very least, substantially erode German morale. For these raids, the Allies used, for the first time, the "bomber stream" tactic which subsequently became common. The Allies' belief was that a huge number of aircraft flown in a tightly formed "stream" would overwhelm German defenses and reduce to a sustainable number the number of Allied aircraft lost during the raids. Over the course of the war, Allied bombing destroyed sixty percent of Cologne and almost completely destroyed its central area. By the end of the war, some ninety-five percent of Cologne's population had been killed or had fled the city to escape the bombing.

The British finally landed reinforcements in Egypt and, with the additional firepower and troops, were able to repulse Rommel in late August 1942 at the Battle of El Alamein. By August, Rommel had come close to capturing Cairo and establishing a position on the Nile and Suez Canal, but could not secure victory in light of the valiant British defenders. The struggle for North Africa was vital to the British in order for them to maintain control of the Suez Canal and access to British shipping from the British Empire in Asia, as well as providing a base from which the British could control the Middle East oil fields which Hitler desperately wanted. By the first week of September, Rommel was forced to withdraw west towards Libya. The R.A.F. now controlled the skies over north Africa and launched countless attacks against Rommel's retreating forces. The relentless British attacks had Rommel reeling. By early November, his forces had retreated to Libya hundreds of miles to the west. On November 8, 1942, the Allies made amphibious landings far to the west in Algeria and Morocco. While the British were attacking Rommel's forces from bases in Egypt, the Allied landings in Algeria and Morocco placed Rommel under pressure from the west.

The Allies were rolling back the German conquests in North Africa. They planned to use North Africa as a platform for an invasion of Sicily and then the Italian mainland. The landings in Africa also gave the Allies, in particular the Americans, an opportunity to become battle-hardened and test their amphibious landing capabilities before they attempted the formidable task of trying to breach

German defenses when the eventually attacked the European continent directly.

At the same time, the Nazi armies that had swept across the Soviet Union and come so close to seizing Moscow and Stalingrad were soon to face disaster. The German attempts to seize Stalingrad had bogged down in the brutal Russian winter. The German supply lines were disastrously over-extended, and the Wehrmacht's progress had stalled in the face of fierce Soviet resistance. On November 19, 1942, the Soviets unleashed a huge counterattack that included thousands of battle tanks. The Soviets attacked westward both north and south of Stalingrad in an effort to encircle the Wehrmacht's Sixth Army that had been pressing the Nazi attack on the city. The Wehrmacht attempted to save the Sixth Army from the west, but it was unable to break through the encirclement. The troops involved in the futile rescue effort soon began to retreat in the face of the withering Soviet counterattack.

Hitler forbade any attempt by the trapped Sixth Army to break out of Stalingrad toward the west in order to retreat. He ordered the Sixth Army to fight to the last man. The Wehrmacht eventually was unable to supply the Sixth Army, even by air drops, as the Soviets tightened the noose around the tiny enclave still held by the Sixth and destroyed more and more of the Sixth army's men and material. By January, the Germans' predicament was critical. By February 2, 1943, the Soviets completed their destruction of the Sixth Army, causing hundreds of thousands of German casualties and taking hundreds of thousands of prisoners.

The Third Reich was suffering tremendous defeats in North Africa and Russia and was losing hundreds of thousands of dead and injured German soldiers, along with tremendous amounts of war material. As the Allies mopped up the German forces in North Africa, the Allies had the beachhead they needed to attack Italy and take the war to Germany with ground forces in Europe. That effort would be in addition to the enormous Allied bombing raids that continued to pummel German cities and munitions manufacturing. While the Reich would manage to launch a few more major offensives, from this point on it was fighting a defensive, losing war.

Germany Is Judenrein

IN 1943, TRUDE SET ABOUT TRYING TO RECOVER PROPERTY she and Max had left in Germany as well as property her parents owned. She wrote to Karl Dülken, a cousin on Trude's mother's side, to obtain guidance on how to go about this and for help determining what types of property were eligible for compensation.

Karl replied that registering foreign property was an American construct and did not constitute a basis for claims against the Nazi regime. Rather, registration was a process to determine how much American capital was at work overseas. Nevertheless, he felt it wise to register Trude's property claims in the event registration might be used for some beneficial purpose later on. Karl explained that Trude could not register property the Nazis had confiscated prior to her emigration to the United States because it occurred at a time when she was not subject to the United States' administration of justice.

As to any securities Trude and Max had owned, Karl recommended Trude register them. If she and Max had left the stock certificates behind, Karl suggested Trude use her best estimate of their number and value. As to any securities accounts in Max's name, he believed Trude should register them listing herself as Max's heir. The "Jewish tax" the Nazis had levied when Trude and Max emigrated was a confiscation that occurred after they had left Germany, so Karl believed Trude could register property lost as a result of that confiscation.

Karl did not believe Trude could register Sigmund's property because her mother Martha was Sigmund's heir. Karl wrote that even though her father had been "relocated," that did not, in Karl's understanding, give Trude the right to "appropriate" Sigmund's property by registering it in her name. Further, it is not clear that Trude knew whether either of her parents were still alive, which would have been an obstacle to making a claim to their property.

Karl continued by explaining that:

> After Jews were declared stateless persons, their entire property may have been appropriated. Therefore, register your entire property that you had when you emigrated and that was not confiscated before you emigrated. Under E2 of the registration form, you should write "All properties were seized under the expropriation decree of November 25, 1942." On this day Jews were declared stateless and their property was confiscated.

As time went by, Trude, Renate, and Erica got to know the Pelta family, who were the only other Jewish family living in Deer Park. The girls became close friends with Edmund Pelta, who was the same age as Renate. Renate, Erica, and Edmund played tennis on nearby public courts. They went to the movies in Silverton, the town next door to Deer Park. They walked to the theater from their homes. Twenty-five cents covered the cost of admission, a coke, and a box of candy with change left over. The typical Saturday afternoon matinee included a double feature, newsreel, cartoon, serial, and another short subject. Leading movie stars included Alice Faye, Don Ameche, Esther Williams, and Deanna Durbin. After the movies, the teens went to a burger joint in Silverton named the Hop Off Inn. The Hop Off was so named because it was the last stop on the streetcar line; at that point you had to "hop off." Hamburgers cost fifteen cents.

The area on three sides of Deer Park was undeveloped. Edmond occasionally went into the surrounding forests to hunt rabbits for dinner. Meat was expensive during the war, so the rabbits he bagged were a welcome addition to their diet. On special occasions, they went to family-style Jewish restaurants in nearby Avondale. There were several German restaurants in town whose menus included familiar dishes such as sauerbraten with spaetzle, bratwurst, schnitzel, with strudel for dessert.

On the other side of the world, death continued to stalk members of the Moses family. On January 1, 1943, Lene and Max Berlin were put on Train Da 103 and deported from Theresienstadt to the Auschwitz-Birkenau extermination camp where they were killed. Max Berlin was fifty-five when he was deported; Lene was fifty-two. The Nazis murdered these parents of two children, this owner of a stationery store and his wife.

On April 19, the Warsaw Ghetto uprising began. For nearly a month, groups of Jews who had been able to smuggle small arms into the Ghetto fought the German army to a standstill. Knowing the fate that awaited them if they were deported to camps, the Jews fought fiercely to save their lives and show the world that not all Jews were willing to go quietly to their deaths. In addition to firearms, the fighters improvised other weapons such as Molotov cocktails. They used the firebombs to immobilize the Panzer tanks that were trying to force their way into the ghetto. In the end, the Germans were unable to defeat the rebels through sheer firepower. Instead, they set fire to the ghetto, forcing out its last defenders. On May 16, the Nazis finally put down the Warsaw uprising. As a final touch, the Nazis blew up the Warsaw synagogue.

On May 19, 1943, Germany declared itself *Judenrein,* meaning clean of Jews. Germany also used the word *judenfrei*—free of Jews—to describe its new status.[303]

While Hitler may have taken satisfaction in Germany being Judenrein, the German war effort was crumbling. In July 1943, the Allies landed in Sicily. This was to serve as their springboard for landings in Italy. In late July, Italy's King Victor Emmanuel III ordered the Duce to the royal palace where the Fascist leader was arrested. On September 3, the Allies landed in southern Italy, which led Marshal Badoglio of the Italian armed forces to form a government and negotiate an armistice with the Allies. On September 8, word of the armistice leaked. Hitler immediately sent troops to occupy all of Italy and forestall Allied progress north towards Germany.

---

303 *History of the Jews in Cologne*, Jesse Russel, Ronald Cohn, p. 37, 2012.

The Wehrmacht also launched an enormous attack against the Soviets, trying to recapture the initiative and knock the Soviets out of the war. Instead, the Soviets inflicted a decisive defeat on the Nazi war machine. They repelled the German attack and counterattacked across an enormous front. The Nazi intelligence forces had grievously underestimated the number of troops and the amount of weaponry the Soviets could muster. The Nazis were overwhelmed by the Soviets; the Reich could not replace the tremendous losses its armed forces suffered during operation Barbarossa. Further, the main Soviet battle tank was more than a match for the Nazi Panzers.

By the end of the year, the Soviets had driven the Reich almost completely from Russian soil. The war, which so far had been visited upon Germany only from the air, was now getting closer to German soil by means of Allied ground attacks. The Allies were slowly rolling back the German conquests in southern and eastern Europe and were working their way towards the Fatherland.

THE DEATH CAMPS ARE LEFT
TO DO THEIR WORK

E VIDENCE OF NAZI ATROCITIES AND THE REICH'S MASS MUR-
der of Jews was widely known around the world as early as 1942.
Yet the United States took no action to interdict the deportation and
murder of Jews, nor did it increase the number of Jewish refugees it
would accept. By 1943, as evidence of the magnitude of the murders
became known, pressure built for action.

In November 1943, the Emergency Committee to Save
the Jewish People of Europe introduced a rescue resolution in
Congress. When the State Department continued to refuse to act,
Henry Morgenthau, the Jewish Secretary of the Treasury, met with
President Roosevelt to discuss a report his department had prepared
documenting the State Department's obstruction of Jewish immigration. The report was originally titled "Report to the Secretary on
the Acquiescence of This Government in the Murder of the Jews."
Roosevelt finally acted and issued an executive order creating a War
Refugee Board "to take all measures within its policy (sic) to rescue
victims of enemy oppression in imminent danger of death." By this
time, the Reich had already murdered millions of Jews. With Europe
still engulfed in war, there was no way to effect further immigration from Germany let alone the death camps in the east. Roosevelt's
action was nothing more than window dressing. It had no impact
on the millions of victims whom the Nazis continued to ship to the
death camps.

On December 16, 1943, the SS assigned Ernst to forced labor in the Messelager concentration camp in Cologne. Messelager was a subcamp of the Buchenwald concentration camp in central Germany, east of Cologne. The prisoners dealt with the aftermath of Allied bombing raids, including cleaning up rubble and recovering corpses. The SS also used the prisoners to remove "duds" in bomb detonators, a task likely assigned to prisoners because, even though the bombs were duds, there remained a risk that a wrong move might set them off.

In January 1944, Trude wrote to the World Jewish Congress in New York regarding a letter Trude had received from a friend (her letter to the Congress does not identify the friend):

> My dear Miss Hilb:
>
> Thank you for forwarding my friend's letter to me.
>
> May I ask you for some information:
>
> Can I not communicate with my friend in Geneva directly? Can you find out my mother's address in Theresienstadt, that I can send her pakages (sic)? Or send a Red Cross message? Her name is: Martha Sara Moses, nee Oberlander, born Nov. 13, 1980 in Mannheim, Germany, last residence in Cologne.
>
> Which are the ways to send packages to Jewish camps?
>
> Enclosed please find a letter to my friend in Geneva, which I hope you will be able to forward to her through your representative abroad.
>
> Thank you,
>
> Very sincerely yours,
>
> Mrs. Trude Houser

Trude obviously believed Martha was still alive. Martha was, but, tragically, only for a few months more. On May 15, 1944, two years after the world became aware of the Nazi program of exterminating Europe's Jews, the SS deported Martha Moses from Theresienstadt to Auschwitz, where they murdered her, likely during the first assessment of the prisoners as they exited the transport trains. Martha Oberlander Moses, a loving mother and grandmother who enjoyed supervising her kitchen and cooking for her family, who displayed a warm smile in every photograph and who sat with her granddaughters as they as they tried to finish their dinners, was sixty-four years old when she was killed.

The Summer of 1944

ON JUNE 6, 1944, THE ALLIES LAUNCHED THE D-DAY invasion known as Operation Overlord. The invasion force involved 156,000 troops storming a fifty mile stretch of Normandy beaches under cover of a withering barrage by Allied naval forces. The Nazis were caught unprepared, as they had expected the landings to take place further north in France near Calais. The Allies also controlled the skies. Allied fighter planes raked German defenders from the air while the Allied ships' massive guns bombarded the German coastal fortifications. By the time the Germans realized the invasion at Normandy was the main invasion force and rushed reinforcements to the area, the Allies had established a position on the beaches and were slowing working their way inland.

By early July, Soviet troops crossed the eastern Polish border and began their drive towards Germany. The Reich now faced desperate battles on two fronts but lacked the manpower and equipment to withstand either. In late July, the Allies finally were able to smash their way through the murderous hedgerows in Normandy that had impeded their progress. They quickly swept eastward across France. On August 25, the Allies liberated Paris. The Germans were in full retreat across France. By early September, the Allies were sweeping through Belgium. By the second week of September, they had reached Germany's western border.

In the summer of 1944, Renate took a job as a waitress at Star Lake, a resort in upstate New York situated in the Adirondack

Mountains of St. Lawrence County. Renate had grown into a beautiful young woman with deep brown eyes and long, dark hair that cascaded over her shoulders.

Since Renate was in New York, Trude decided to take the opportunity to visit relatives there. She stayed with one set of relatives, while Erica stayed with another. While the elderly couple with whom Erica stayed was perhaps not an ideal fit for a high school girl, it left Erica with lots of free time. She quickly became comfortable with New York's subway system and spent much of her time at New York's Museum of Natural History. Erica had written to NBC in advance of the trip to inquire about attending a live performance of a half-hour classical music radio program to which the family listened every week. She was lucky enough to get a ticket to see Ezio Pinza, a well-known opera tenor, perform.

Later that summer, Erica spent her last session at Camp Livingston. She helped publish the camp newspaper and devised crossword puzzles for it. When she told her bunkmates the next school year would be her last in high school, they were skeptical since that meant Erica would be entering her senior year at the tender age of fourteen.

Renate graduated from Deer Park High School in the spring of 1944 at age sixteen. She secured a scholarship to attend the University of Cincinnati, where she began her studies as an Applied Arts Major after returning from Star Lake at the end of the summer. Each weekday, Trude drove Renate part way to the University en route to Trude's job at the clothing factory. Renate took a bus the rest of the way to the University's campus in Cincinnati's Clifton neighborhood. As part of her studies at U.C., Renate joined Delta Phi Delta, a national art honorary society. Trude picked Renate up at the University on Trude's way home from work at the end of the day.

In the autumn of 1944, Erica took English III and IV in addition to social studies and chemistry. The fifth subject she needed in order to graduate the next spring was biology. However, she ran into scheduling conflicts such that she could not take the course at Deer Park. Instead, she took the class by means of a correspondence course. While she managed her course work without too much trouble, it was, nevertheless a difficult year for her. Attending classes with seniors who were two to three years older than she was (Erica was only fifteen) left Erica feeling like an outsider. Erica had been an outsider as a Jewish girl in Cologne and she, no doubt, had felt at least somewhat like an outsider at the Catholic school in Harrow Weald. Now, once more, she did not fit in. Nevertheless, she put her head down and forged ahead with her studies and her music.

Hitler launched the last, great Nazi offensive of the war in December 1944. He did so by means of a massive attack west through the Ardennes Forest. The offensive came to be known as the Battle of the Bulge because the Nazi troops pierced the Allied front and established a salient that extended west through the Allied front lines. The German attack force was made up of troops cobbled together from Nazi divisions throughout Europe and tanks scrounged from various units. After several weeks of fierce fighting, the Wehrmacht's offensive collapsed. There was now little to impede the Allies' march through Germany to Berlin. Soviet troops captured Warsaw on January 17, 1945. By late January, the Soviets had crushed the German armies in the east and were streaming west across Poland and East Prussia. They were soon only one hundred miles from Berlin.

MARTHA

TRUDE AND THE GIRLS HAD FOUND THEIR FOOTING. THEY were making their way in their new home. Their financial situation, although precarious, had stabilized. Renate was well on her way towards getting the education she needed to pursue a career employing her substantial artistic talent. Erica was on the verge of finishing high school before beginning the next phase of her education.

However, they pursued their lives from 1942 through 1944 not knowing what had happened to Ernst, David, Sigmund, and Martha other than the few lines in the farewell card Martha had sent prior to being deported to Theresienstadt. Sigmund had died in Cologne in March 1942, but mail service had ended in 1941. There is no evidence that Trude and the girls knew of Sigmund's passing, or that they knew of David's death in Theresienstadt. As to Ernst, they had heard nothing from him for well over three years; all they knew was their last communication from him had been in 1941. After that, there had been only silence.

Then, one aspect of the uncertainty was broken. The Czechoslovak Jewish Representative Committee sent a letter to Trude in January 1945:

Dear Friend:

We hereby are glad to inform you that we just received from a neutral country a list of persons interned in Terezin (Theresienstadt). The name of Mrs. Martha Moses residing in

468

TEREZIN at Rathausgasse 9 appears on this list. Should you wish to communicate with the party please get in touch with your local Red Cross Chapter.

There are <u>no other</u> details except those mentioned above. We therefore do not know whether or not this is the person in whom you are interested.

Very truly yours,

Dr. Fred Fried—Prof. Hugo Perutz

Czechoslovak Jewish Representative Committee.

Should you wish to apply for Palestine Certificates, please fill the enclosed forms and return them. The National Council of Jewish Women, 1819 Broadway, New York will give you information as to possibilities to make out affidavits after you have become a citizen. (Emphasis in the original.)

The letter must have made Trude's heart soar, suggesting as it did that Martha was alive in Theresienstadt. After almost three years with no contact, Trude's mother appeared to be alive. Given Trude's antipathy towards religion, it would not be appropriate to say her prayers had been answered since she likely did not resort to prayers. But without question, she must have been delirious with joy to learn that her mother had survived the Holocaust. For Renate and Erica, the loving grandmother who had helped manage their home in Cologne and who sat with them when they could not finish their meals, was alive.

Family records contain a translation of a brief letter to Trude from an Ernst Jacobi:

Feb. 17, 1945

Dear Mrs. Houser:

I received two letters from my sister. Both arrived yesterday.

The *Aufbau* today published a list of people from Theresienstadt who arrived in Switzerland and are quartered in the refugee camp in St. Gallen. Among them is Mrs. Klara Caro (the wife of Cologne's rabbi). Since I do not know the family name of Frau "Martha," I could not search for her name, but I assume that you can get the Aufbau in Cincinnati, too.

Ernst Jacobi

Research has not disclosed the significance of the reference to Mrs. Caro. Presumably, the reference to Martha was to Martha Moses. However, Martha Moses had not escaped to Switzerland.

On January 26, 1945, Soviet troops attacking from the east on their drive towards Germany liberated Auschwitz. They were stunned by what they found. They made their way past piles of bodies the SS had not had time to burn or bury. They were met by walking skeletons, that is, the skeletal inmates who were still alive, but alive only in a manner of speaking. Many of the surviving inmates were physically too far gone to save. Their bodies, having been starved for so long, could not accept food. They soon died despite efforts to feed them. Many were ill and succumbed to their ailments. Despite having been liberated, thousands of inmates at Auschwitz died without having a chance to return to the world of the living, which as a practical matter they had left long ago.

From January through March 1945, the Allies liberated Holland and Belgium. They then attacked and occupied the Rhineland and Germany's Ruhr Valley, depriving the Reich of most of its industrial heartland. On March 7, the Allies, attacking from the west, crossed the Rhine at Remagen on their drive towards Berlin. The road to Berlin was now open with no further natural barriers to impede the Allied armies. By the middle of April, Nuremberg, scene of the gargantuan early Nazi rallies and namesake for the abominable Nuremberg laws, fell to the Allies. One week later the Soviets entered the outskirts of Berlin from the east.

Meanwhile, March 26, 1945, was a momentous day in Cincinnati. On that day, Trude became a naturalized United States citizen. Her naturalization certificate pegged her at five feet one and one-half inches tall with brown hair and brown eyes. The ceremony was conducted by the United States District Court for the Southern District of Ohio located in Cincinnati:

Be it known that a term of the U.S. District Court of the Southern District of Ohio held pursuant to law at Cincinnati, Ohio on March 26th, 1945 the court having found that Gertrude Houser then residing at Cincinnati, Ohio, intends to reside permanently in the United States (when so required by the Naturalization Laws of the United States), had in all other respects complied with the applicable provisions of such naturalization laws, and was entitled to be admitted to citizenship, thereupon ordered that such person be, and (s)he was admitted as a citizen of the United States of America.

In testimony whereof, the seal of the court is hereunto affixed this 26th day of March in the year of our Lord nineteen hundred and forty-five and of our independence the one hundred and sixty-ninth. (Trude's Naturalization Certificate, March 26, 1945.)

Renate became a United States citizen that same day. (Presumable Erica did as well, but the author has not been able to find documentation confirming such was the case.) Renate's certificate of citizenship stated that she, "having applied to the Commissioner of Immigration and Naturalization for a certificate of citizenship pursuant to Section 339 of the Nationality Act of 1940, having proved to the satisfaction of the Commissioner that she is now a citizen of the United States of America, became a citizen thereof on March 26, 1945 and is now in the United States and had taken the prescribed oath of allegiance..." The District Court issued a Certificate of Citizenship to Renate on June 22. Renate obtained citizenship through Section 339 of the 1940 Nationality Act, which allowed her to claim citizenship through Trude, who had become a naturalized U.S. citizen.

Over the course of the war, Allied bombing destroyed sixty percent of Cologne and almost completely destroyed its central area. "When the U.S. troops occupied Cologne on 6 March 1945, between 30 and 40 Jewish men who had survived in hiding were found."[304] Those desperate men were all that remained of the 15,000 Jews who had made up Cologne's Jewish community before Hitler

---

304 Jguideeurope.

came to power. They were all that was left of the roughly 11,000 Jews who were still in Cologne immediately prior to war, virtually all of whom, by 1945, had emigrated, been deported to death camps, or been killed by the Nazis in some other fashion. Gone were the thousands of merchants, doctors, lawyers, judges, civil servants, craftsmen, musicians, and artists who had made up that community. Gone among those 11,000 souls were children and parents, brothers and sisters, uncles and aunts, grandparents and grandchildren. The Nazis had destroyed all six of the city's synagogues. Judenrein indeed.

By this time, Hitler was sheltering in a bunker far below ground under the Chancellery in the center of Berlin. He could not understand how his Thousand Year Reich was coming to an end. True to deranged form, he blamed the incompetence and cowardice of his generals and the nefarious work of world Jewry for his defeat and the destruction of the Third Reich. Unable to face reality, he shot himself in his bunker on April 30, 1945. Two of his guards took his body and that of his mistress Eva Braun, whom Hitler had married the night before and who had taken her own life that night by swallowing poison, to a spot in the rubble above ground. The guards drenched the two bodies with gasoline and set them afire.

On May 5, 1945, Soviet troops liberated Theresienstadt, but far too late to save David, Martha, and Lene and Max Berlin.

Trude received another letter regarding Martha in May 1945, this time from the Palestine Bureau of the Zionist Organization of America:

> Dear Mrs. Houser:
>
> Please be advised that in accordance with a cable received by us from the Jewish Agency for Palestine, dated 4/24/45 the Palestine Government has approved Palestine Immigration Certificates, on Exchange Basis, in behalf (sic) of
>
> Martha Moses
>
> located in Theresienstadt.

The names have been included in list #TR/20 and dispatched to the British Government in London with a view to be delivered to the protecting power (Swiss Government), who will take the necessary steps to inform the people concerned in Theresienstadt accordingly.

As soon as we have further word about this case, we shall communicate with you.

Sincerely yours,

Dr. S. Bernstein,

Director Palestine Bureau

(Case #288) (May 6, 1945, letter from the Zionist Organization of America [ZOA] to Trude Houser.)

This was further evidence that Martha was alive. Why else would the ZOA write to Trude telling her that arrangements were being made for Martha to emigrate to Palestine? Martha had a case number, her immigration certificate had been approved, and the authorities in Theresienstadt were being notified so they could proceed with Martha's emigration. Whether Martha stayed in Palestine or eventually emigrated from there to join Trude in the United States was immaterial at the moment. What mattered was that Martha was alive.

But Martha was not alive. The ZOA and Czechoslovak Jewish Committee were working with incomplete, outdated lists of inmates at Theresienstadt. Perhaps there was another Martha Moses at the camp who survived the war and the organization mistakenly wrote to Trude. But the stubborn fact was that Trude's mother, Martha Moses, was dead.

How does a person survive, emotionally, going from not knowing a loved one's fate and fearing the worst, to learning the loved one had survived, to, at some point, learning the loved one had been killed? How many head-snapping, heart-stopping turns of events can a person handle? It is difficult to imagine what went through Trude's mind when she learned the awful truth. There are no records revealing how or when Trude learned of Martha's fate. Family records do not show how she reacted or what she told her daughters when their hopes of a reunion with their grandmother were dashed. The organizations in charge of trying to locate survivors made grievous mistakes when it came to Martha Moses, with unimaginable emotional impacts on her surviving family in Cincinnati.

On May 7, 1945, Germany unconditionally surrendered. The Allies declared victory in Europe on May 8, 1945. The war in Europe was over; only the destruction, casualties, and deaths remained.

TRUDE, ERICA, AND RENATE
MOVE FORWARD

NOTWITHSTANDING THE CHALLENGES ERICA FACED BEING by far the youngest member of her high school class, the spring of 1945 provided a highlight to Erica's senior year; she attended her senior prom. The number of boys in the senior class was quite small given the fact that many of them had enlisted. Renate stepped in on Erica's behalf. She asked a male acquaintance to be Erica's date, telling him that Erica's previous, but in truth nonexistent, date had been drafted and was in basic training. Erica was forever grateful to Renate for arranging for her participation in this rite of passage.

By the spring of 1945, Renate had completed her first year at the University of Cincinnati. She decided to return to work as a waitress at Star Lake over the summer. She loved the warm days, swimming in the lake, and sleeping on her cabin's screened-in porch on nights when it was too hot to sleep comfortably inside.

Erica graduated from Loveland High School at the ripe age of fifteen. Someone suggested that she talk to Jewish Family Services in Cincinnati to see if the agency could help her find a summer job. The agency sent her to be interviewed by a couple who needed someone to take care of their two-year old son, Jimmy. Jimmy's mother, an actress, was pregnant and could not be as active as she needed to be to keep up with a two-year old. Jimmy's father had been a band leader and singer in Los Angeles before returning to Cincinnati to work in the family clothing business. The couple hired Erica; she accompanied them to their summer home in Michigan. They paid her $60 for the summer. It turned out that Jimmy's family was the same family who owned the dress factory where Trude worked as a seamstress.

Erica and Jimmy had a small cottage to themselves. Jimmy's parents and several sets of their friends and relatives occupied the main cabin. Erica was responsible for bringing breakfast to Jimmy each morning, feeding and playing with him and staying in the cabin with Jimmy after lunch while he took his nap. Erica took her meals with the cook and the two girls who worked in the kitchen and served meals to the guests.

Erica taught Jimmy to sing songs and nursery rhymes. She was impressed that, as a two-year old, he was able to sing perfectly in tune. One of the songs she taught Jimmy was the Deer Park fight song—"Onward Deer Park"—which was sung to the tune of "On Wisconsin." At age two, Jimmy started picking out tunes on his family's Chickering piano, so he was indeed quite precocious.

Years later, Erica learned more about Jimmy. He had pursued music and at the age of ten became a piano soloist with the Cincinnati Symphony Orchestra, playing Mendelssohn's Piano Concerto No. 1. A dozen years later he was making a name for himself as a conductor. Eventually, Jimmy, that is, James Levine, became famous as the conductor and music director of the Metropolitan Opera in New York City. But to Erica, he would always be Jimmy.

In the autumn of 1945, Erica enrolled at the University of Cincinnati to study chemistry. She also wanted to be part of the University band. However, she did not own an instrument and needed money to buy one. Trude decided to sell one of the two accordions they owned. Renate likely offered hers to be sacrificed, as she had never enjoyed playing the instrument. Trude used the proceeds to purchase a French horn that Erica toted to band practice twice a week during football season. One year, she traveled with the band by train to El Paso where the team played in the Sun Bowl. As might be expected, the train ride was, in Erica's words, "like one non-stop party." One evening, Erica and several friends took advantage of

El Paso's location on the U.S.-Mexican border and crossed the Rio Grande River to have dinner in Mexico.

Erica initially found it difficult to make friends at the university. She ate most of her lunches alone in the cafeteria, where she purchased four side dishes at six cents each. That allowed her to save more than half of her three dollars a week lunch allowance. Fortunately, during her sophomore year, she discovered the Association of Independent Students, a social group for students who were not in a fraternity or sorority. The group had a room in the basement of the Student Union where members gathered for lunch. Erica decided to join them and school suddenly became much less lonely for her.

Trude continued working as a seamstress. She derived great satisfaction from the fact that she had managed to raise the girls, send them to college, and keep their home. Now that the war was over, she began the heart-rending task of trying to determine what had happened to the many family members and friends who had fallen from view during the war. Tragically, many of them were dead. They were victims of the Nazis starving them with inadequate rations, dead from the Nazis' refusal to provide medical care, or dead by virtue of the Nazis murdering them.

On August 6, 1945, a United States B-29 Superfortress bomber named the Enola Gay dropped an atomic bomb on Hiroshima at 8:15 a.m. When Japan failed to surrender, the United States dropped an atomic bomb on the city of Nagasaki on August 9. Six days later, Emperor Hirohito announced that Japan had surrendered. The Japanese emissaries signed the formal surrender documents on the teak decks of the mammoth battleship U.S.S. Missouri on September 2, 1945, which was deemed VJ Day (Victory over Japan Day). The signing of the surrender documents on the Missouri's deck marked the end of hostilities in the Pacific theater of war. The last of the Axis powers had been defeated, but only after tens of millions of people around the world had perished from combat, starvation, disease, or had been murdered in cold blood by the Axis Powers.

We Were All Aware That
Our Final Hour Had Come

T HE NAZIS OPERATED SIX DEATH CAMPS IN EASTERN EUROPE
from late 1941 through 1944: Chelmno, Belzek, Majdanek,
Treblinka, Sobibor, and Auschwitz.[305] Auschwitz, the most notorious
and deadly of the concentration camps, was located in the Polish
town of Oswiecim, forty miles west of Cracow. The camp, near the
prewar German-Polish border, was comprised of forced labor camps,
a concentration camp, and a ruthlessly efficient killing center that
was responsible for the deaths of approximately 1.1 million Jews
and others during its several years of operation. In 1941, Himmler
ordered the original camp be expanded by the construction of a
larger, adjacent camp known as Birkenau, also known as Auschwitz
II, which contained the crematoria. The gas chambers at Auschwitz
killed up to 20,000 victims a day. The SS used the crematoria to dispose of their victims' bodies and cover up the Nazis' crimes against
humanity.

Auschwitz was "surrounded by electrically charged four-meter-
high barbed wire fences, guarded by SS men armed with machine
guns and rifles. The two camps were further closed in by a series of
guard posts located two thirds of a mile beyond the fences. In March

---

305 *Gilder Lehrman Institute of American History*—Immigration Policy during
World War II.

1942, trains carrying Jews commenced arriving daily."[306] The camp had an extremely high mortality rate due to starvation, hard labor, and disease, in addition to the Nazis' daily organized murders of tens of thousands of inmates.

Upon arrival at the camp, most prisoners were designated to be murdered in the gas chambers that same day.[307] Those not marked for extermination were sent to forced labor. The SS shaved the inmates' hair, gave them striped prisoner uniforms, and tattooed an identification number onto each prisoner's left arm.[308] Life expectancy for those in forced labor was a few months. During morning and evening roll call, the prisoners were made to stand for hours in freezing cold; anyone who stumbled or fell was immediately killed.[309] This was the hell on earth to which the SS sent Ernst. While the SS had put Ernst into forced labor in Cologne-Deutz in December 1943, they decided to deport him to Auschwitz in May 1944. Whether the SS deported Ernst because it no longer needed him in Cologne or as part of the Final Solution is unknown.

The SS divided into work groups those inmates who were not selected for murder upon arrival. An SS officer oversaw each work group. The SS selected an inmate—a "kapo"—to preside over each work group. "The SS leaders chose kapos whom they considered the most willing to carry out SS orders. Toward this end, the SS gave the kapos practically unlimited power over the inmates—including beatings. If an inmate died, no questions were asked of the kapo who was in charge; the kapo was only required to report the death and to keep track of the number of inmates."[310] Even though many kapos were Jewish or were members of other groups condemned to Auschwitz,

---

306 WWW.MYJEWISHLEARNING.COM/ARTICLE/AUSCHWITZ-BIRKENAU.

307 WWW.MYJEWISHLEARNING.COM/ARTICLE/AUSCHWITZ-BIRKENAU.

308 WWW.MYJEWISHLEARNING.COM/ARTICLE/AUSCHWITZ-BIRKENAU.

309 WWW.MYJEWISHLEARNING.COM/ARTICLE/AUSCHWITZ-BIRKENAU.

310 *Anatomy of the Auschwitz Death Camp*, Ed. by Yisrael Gutman and Michael Berenbaum, Indiana University Press in association with the United States Holocaust Museum, 1994, Chapter 14—The Auschwitz Prisoner Administration, by Danuta Czech, at 363.

the kapos own survival depended in large measure on how badly they treated their compatriots.

> On top of the shock of arrival, the separation from loved ones at selection, and the eventual awareness that they had been killed in the gas chambers, new inmates had to take up the ruthless fight for survival. Courage and hope were shattered, respect for human life trampled; the question "Will I survive this" found no room in the shadow of the crematoria and was replaced by "How will I die?"[311]

By the middle of January 1945, as Soviet forces began to close in on Auschwitz, the SS had stark issues to confront. It needed to determine how to hide the crimes against humanity its forces had committed. The SS also was not sure what to do with the tens of thousands of unfortunate souls still alive at Auschwitz, since they were victims of and witnesses to the Nazis' crimes. Throughout the war the Germans had taken advantage of their victims by using them as slave labor. While the Nazis wanted to continue to do so even as the war seemed lost and close to conclusion, they also wanted to ensure there were no witnesses to the Third Reich's crimes. The SS faced the dilemma of, on the one hand, trying to move tens of thousands of weak and debilitated prisoners to continue using them as slave laborers and keep them from falling into the Allies' hands as witnesses to the Nazis' crimes, or, on the other hand, continue killing the inmates in Auschwitz and increase the magnitude of their crimes while the Soviets fought their way closer to the camp with each passing day.

The SS debated whether to evacuate the prisoners to another location to continue using them as slave laborers and murder them there or dispose of the prisoners at Auschwitz, even if that meant the SS might not have time to hide the evidence of these late-war murders. The SS decided to evacuate the camp. They forced the inmates to walk towards Germany in the dead of winter, but only after the SS had culled the prison population as if it were eliminating lame livestock before driving the rest to a slaughterhouse. The SS murdered

---

311 *Anatomy* at 370.

thousands of prisoners in Auschwitz in a last pathological, blood-thirsty spree.

On January 18, 1945, the SS began to evacuate the 66,000 prisoners at Auschwitz-Birkenau and its sub-camps. The inmates were forced into the death march in the middle of winter. They went with little clothing, rags for shoes, and no more food than the worthless gruel they had previously been forced to subsist on. Those rations, grievously inadequate to sustain life and energy in Auschwitz, were grossly inadequate to fuel the prisoners as they marched mile after mile through the snow and bitter cold. The result was the roadsides were littered with victims who died from cold and/or starvation, or who were shot by the SS to prevent them from delaying the rest of the evacuees. By the time the prisoners reached their destinations such as Gross-Rosen, Buchenwald, Dachau, and Mauthausen, more than 15,000 of them had either died or been murdered by the guards along the way.[312] The Allies found hundreds of mass graves alongside the route of the death march from Auschwitz, as well as along the paths of similar marches from other camps.[313] Carl Spier died during the death march on February 1, 1945.

The Soviet army entered Auschwitz on January 27, 1945, liberating some 7,000 prisoners, most of whom were ill, dying, and largely beyond saving due to their desperately poor physical condition. Of the 1.3 million people whom the Nazis sent to Auschwitz, they murdered more than 1.1 million. By the end of the war, "95% of German Jewry had either died of natural causes or suicide, had been murdered, or had emigrated."[314]

However, the Nazis had not murdered Ernst; miraculously, he had survived the war. Ernst had survived living underground in Cologne, imprisonment in Klinglepütz, and the rigors of forced labor in the Messelager subcamp in Cologne-Deutz. After all of that, the SS deported him to Auschwitz in May 1944 where Ernst survived for

---

312 WWW.ENCYCLOPEDIA.USHMM.ORG/CONTENT/EN/ARTICLE/DEATH-MARCHES-1.

313 *The Holocaust Encyclopedia*—Death Marches.

314 *Jewish Immigrants of the Nazi Period* at xvii.

nine months. In a letter to Trude, Ernst recounted what happened to him from 1942 to 1945.

> December 21, 1945
>
> Blankenheimerstrasse 55, Köln
>
> Dear Trude,
>
> I wrote to you on the 16th via Bergen-Belsen [family records do not contain this letter]; now I have an opportunity tomorrow to give this letter to someone, and will use it, to send you the report of the worst years. I am wondering which letter will arrive sooner. I wrote to Dülkens via Bergen-Belsen via Frau Rosenfelder. Otherwise, I have nothing new to report today, the weather has turned mild again. If it stays this way, we are lucky, because our furnace doesn't work properly, and coal is in short supply. Love to you and Renate and Erica, your Ernst.
>
> As you may know, we all had to live crowded together in Fort V and the adjoining barracks camp in Müngersdorf. This occurred on June 12, 1942 at 12:30 at night, ordered by the police under the supervision of the Gestapo. Men, women, old people and children, everyone was chased out of their beds and ordered to prepare for deportation. You can only imagine the upset and confusion. (Your dear mother, Dear Trude, was not affected by this, she lived in the [old age] home on Rathenauplatz) which is so called again now.
>
> I myself was [to be] put into a transport to Minsk, which never arrived there, it disappeared on the way without a trace, that means, it was detoured, and the people murdered and buried in a pit. I fear that Uncle Sigmund [balance of sentence missing from translation.] Since I wanted to prevent that dear father would have to go with this transport, I tried to get him from our barrack into the Fort V-situated hospital room. This attempt succeeded, he remained in the hospital room and from there into the home on Beethovenstrasse 16, but unfortunately later on, the same as all the others, he was taken to Theresienstadt. On the return from the hospital room, I saw an opportunity, and I succeeded in avoiding the transport. I lived underground in the city, also a nerve-wracking experience, as the air attacks already made housing hard to find. In the first five weeks, I was in eight different places. Any attempts, made previously, to get

to the country or into Switzerland failed. Some people went, but I heard of no one who arrived there, they were arrested on the way and [missing word]. On October 12, 1942, the house in which I was forced to hide with several other Jews, was betrayed, and found by the Gestapo. (As it turned out later, this once again saved my life, I was assigned to a room in the Thieboldgasse, which I was supposed to move into later. With the next air raid, the entire Thieboldgasse went up in flames, in the assigned house no one escaped.) I then came via Klingelpütz,[315] SS Baubrigade 3 Köln-Deutz prison Köln-Deutz,[316] to the KZ Auschwitz, which as you know was absolutely an extermination camp for Jews. About the treatment by the Gestapo and in the KZ, I needn't elaborate, there has been enough reported and made known.

In Auschwitz I worked mostly in heavy construction; they were building an immense concrete canal there, which was to supply the industries in Upper Silesia, which suffered from water shortages, with water from the Weichsel [the Vistula river watershed in central Poland]. This canal was finished all but 150 meters, but whether the Russians completed it is not known. In between, I was hospitalized once more and other commandoes... [portion missing]

At the end, I landed in one of the worst, if not the worst, commandoes—DAW lumber works.[317] We had to carry, from morning till late at night, the heavy logs from the arriving train cars to the places where they were used; this, [we did] under-nourished, clad in thin cotton, with defective shoes; all this in the winter cold in ice and snow, with the snow sticking to the wooden soles in great clumps.

With all this, our kapo was a bastard, who felt the unloading and carrying was going too slowly, and without care beat us with whatever came into his hands, boards, clubs, bats, pieces of wood. Again, this was my salvation:—on January 8, '45, I once again was hospitalized, on Jan. 18, everyone in the camp who was still able to march, (previously there had been constant

---

315   Klingelputz was a central Cologne prison at which, starting in 1933, the Gestapo detained thousands of prisoners.

316   A division of the KZ (Konzentrationslager) Buchenwald.

317   Deutsche Arbeitswerkstatten means German workshop.

transports departing, in order to minimize the size of the camp, as the Russians were approaching) there were still about 13,000 people called up and marched off. Of these, only very few arrived, almost all of them succumbed either to starvation or beatings, into this category falls the rumored "hunger march" to Belsen. The tension in the camps was at its peak, we could hear, if the wind was right, the long-awaited but still too distant thunder of the guns, and we knew that the next five minutes would be the most critical.

With this transport, the SS disappeared from the camp. But we couldn't leave the blocks; in other words, we couldn't leave the camp, there were patrols everywhere, also within the camp, and anyone who was seen outside the building, was shot. The SS then returned, shot several people to death, then disappeared again, then returned, then disappeared once more.

On January 25, the SS returned once again, and everyone in the camp, even those who were seriously ill, had to appear. We were separated into Jews and non-Jews, those able to march and those unable. We were all aware that our final hour had come. I was put with those able to march but was able to switch over to those who were not, since I told myself, the march (which was supposed to be 100 KM with only very brief rest periods) I would not be able to endure anyway, so why should I make myself miserable, let them kill me here and now. (Whoever was left behind on one of these marches, whether, man, woman or child, was just simply gunned down.) Evidently, though, the Russians were already too close, and the SS was afraid for their own necks:—suddenly one heard the command, "back in front of the blocks." Instead, everyone streamed back into the blocks. The SS disappeared with such speed, that they left two brand new Panzers behind.

The following night there was much shooting and the day after that, Saturday, Jan. 27, 3:30 in the afternoon, the first Russian soldiers marched into the camp. The rejoicing was tremendous, most of the people fell into the arms of the soldiers, hugged and kissed them. The battles it turned out had been more severe than we had thought, several blocks, fortunately already empty, had been hit by grenades, the camp fences (barbed wire fences, electric fences and walls) had been shot up in various places, so that one could go in and out without using the main entrance to the camp.

So, we were freed, but not yet rescued, we were afraid the Germans would bombard the camp, or drop some bombs on our heads, also we feared that the Germans might counter-attack and try to retake the camp. But nothing of the kind occurred, but as amazing as our rescue was, it remained absolutely inconceivable that the entire immense factory with the huge supplies which were all undamaged, would fall into the hands of the Russians. In April, I was sent with others to Katlowitz, and in June released from Sagan. Our life with the Russians is another chapter altogether, about which I will report later.

Your Ernst (Ernst letter to Trude, December 21, 1945.)

Ernst survived nine months in Auschwitz, from May 1944 until the Soviets liberated the camp in January 1945. After liberation, he was hospitalized for three months from January 28, 1945 to May 8, 1845, recovering from the abuse and starvation he had suffered in the camp. Ernst had survived four years in the German army during WWI. He had avoided death during the Allies' thousand bomber attacks on Cologne. He cheated death by refusing to board the train on which he was to be deported to Minsk. He did not succumb to three years of slave labor in Cologne and Auschwitz and avoided near-certain death by refusing to participate in the death march to Belsen.

He was a survivor.

We Had a Nice Passover Celebration

IN 1946, ERNST WAS LIVING IN THE JUDEN FLÜCHTLINGSHEIM (Jewish Refugee Home) at 55 Blankenheimerstrasse in Köln-Sulz. Ernst wrote to Trude in early April. He noted Trude's most recent letter had arrived fairly quickly, so they seemed to have found a mail route that would work satisfactorily. (Ernst letter to Trude, April 2, 1946.) He was pleased to learn Renate and Erica were developing so well. "I was particularly pleased to read that your daughters are such lovely girls and are making their way. Child raising and independence must be quite different there than they were here. Drawing and chemistry are both talents which have always had their roots in our family, I can remember as a youngster, how I would mix all kinds of stuff together, to see what would ignite. I am convinced the girls will both succeed, and then things will be easier for you."

Trude had experienced several health issues recently—a hysterectomy and a severe burn on one of her hands from a grease fire. Ernst wrote he hoped she would have an easier time soon. He reported further about his experiences:

> One thing we learned in the camp: just how little man requires to survive, when he has to. And another thing we know, that the downfall of the Nazis would also be our downfall (Goebbels said that no concentration camp inmate would be able to rejoice at Germany's downfall) but in spite of this, we wished with every fiber of our being for the defeat of the Nazis, because we knew that at least our families overseas had been rescued.

486

Ernst reported that Ernst Dülken and Karl Dülken had been very kind to him, writing to him and updating him about their situations. Further:

> Conditions here are still very muddled. Nothing has been returned of my bank accounts and other Estate assets, the Allies have however, if I am not mistaken, in Teheran, decided on complete restitution for the Jews, but to date there is not the least sign of anything; but one hopes for laws pertaining to this. I have enough money to get along, I earn something from my lumber business even if it isn't much yet. The property in Ehrenfeld you recall we sold about the middle of 1938 to Mahlhens, the property on Merovingerstrasse belongs to the Dülkens, it goes all the way through to Mariahilfstrasse, or properly stated the other way around. Aachenerstrasse 412 [Max and Trude's house] is almost undamaged; while Lindenthal and Braunsfeld [the neighborhoods surrounding the house] are entirely destroyed, the stretch of Aachenerstrasse between Burtscheiderstrasse and Paulistrasse miraculously escaped. (Ernst letter to Trude, April 2, 1946.)

Ernst reported that the people who had purchased the house on Aachenerstrasse were still living there. Ernst mused that, in light of the laws regarding compensation, it might be possible to regain possession of the home.

By the time the war was over, Ernst felt he had lived much of his life; he was in his mid-fifties by then. He decided it was too late for him to start life over in a new country. He decided to stay in Germany and try to rebuild a life there. This was made easier by another development.

Ernst reported what he called "some real news." Ella Goldschmidt had been employed in the congregation office (presumably the synagogue Ernst had attended) in Cologne for many years. In 1941, the Nazis deported her to the Kaiserwald camp in Riga, Latvia, and from there to other camps. She was rescued when the camps were liberated. She and Ernst ran into one another in Berlin. They traveled to Cologne together and lived in the same community center. They were, Ernst wrote, well-suited to one another and were "as good as engaged" with a shared desire to marry soon.

In closing, Ernst thanked Renate and Erica for the notes they had sent to him and praised them for doing well in college. "Best regards and kisses for you and the children, your Ernst."

Ernst wrote again a few weeks later. "The girls have turned out wonderfully well and look dazzling." (Ernst letter to Trude, April 19, 1946.) Ernst reported further on friends and family, most of whom had been deported to various camps with no news of them since. He promised to visit Sigmund's grave to make sure it was maintained properly. Since Martha and David had perished in camps, they had no graves to tend.

"And please let me know your and Renate's and Erica's birthdays and don't be cross with me that I forgot them, but I've had too many things going on in my head or banging me on the head these past few years and as for my papers, not a shred of them is left—the Gestapo, on the one hand, and the bombs, on the other, took good care of that."

On a brighter note, Ernst described the Seder at the Refugee Center where he lived:

> We had a nice Passover celebration. The first two evenings we had a service here at the home, after that a beautiful Seder, that went on until late into the night. It was our first Seder not only since our liberation, but in many years, and for us, who have in the true sense of the word been liberated from the "house of slaves," it had a very special meaning. Even wine had been provided for the first evening; everyone received half a bottle of French red wine. When we had emptied them all, we were told that they were provided to us courtesy of the Americans, matzos were plentiful courtesy of the Dutch. On those evenings, we had many visitors at the home, including English soldiers from the Jewish Legion.

And so, in 1945, Ernst Ichenhäuser, a descendant of Isachar Bar aus Ichenhausen, escaped slavery. He had cheated death time and again to become a free man. Ernst had lived the Passover story.

In German, "ichen hausen" means "I live."

Ernst lived. And so, too, did Trude, Renate, and Erica.

Each of them could say "Ichen hausen"—"I live."

Max and the girls with the family car in front of their home
at 4247 Amity Road, Deer Park, Ohio, 1940

Renate (second from left) and Erica (far right) with friends
by the sign for Max's practice on the front lawn of the family
home. Deer Park School is visible in the background

Newly minted All-American girls sitting on the family lawn
listening to the radio and reading Life magazine

Erica and Renate with Timmy, 1939

The Ichenhäusers' home on Amity Road (later renamed Galbraith Road)

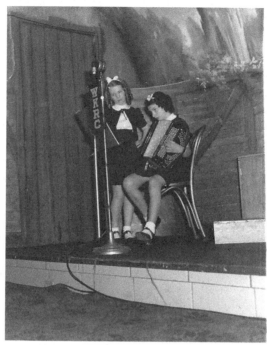

Renate playing the accordion on
a WKRC talent show

Max and the girls in late 1940

City of Cincinnati

OFFICE OF THE MAYOR

JAMES GARFIELD STEWART
MAYOR

MAY STAPLETON, SECRETARY

June 14, 1940

TO WHOM IT MAY CONCERN:

This letter will introduce Doctor Max Houser, who has been a resident of Cincinnati since his arrival in America the first of this year. He was a distinguished physician in Cologne, Germany, for sixteen years, and was the personal physician of the American Consul General in that city, as well as the Vice-Consul, and their families.

Doctor Houser has recently passed the State medical examination in Ohio and is now visiting various places with the idea of picking a location for his permanent residence where he may practice his profession.

He is a man of character and attainments and I feel certain would make a valuable contribution to any community of which he may become a citizen.

I shall appreciate it very much if any one to whom he may present this letter will give him considerate attention and advice.

Very sincerely,

James Garfield Stewart

James Garfield Stewart
Mayor

June 14, 1940, letter of recommendation for Max
from Cincinnati's Mayor James Stewart

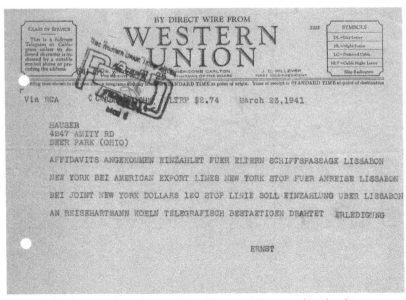

March 23, 1941, telegram from Ernst to Max regarding booking
passage for Trude's parents from Lisbon to New York

DEPARTMENT OF STATE

WASHINGTON

In reply refer to
VD

Max I. Houser, M. D.
    4247 Amity Road,
        Deer Park, Ohio.

Sir:

In reply to your letter of July 11, 1941, regarding the visa cases of your parents and brother-in-law now residing in Germany,

I have to inform you that no consular action may be taken in this case at present because there are no American consular offices operating in the district under reference.

In the event that the alien or aliens in whom you are interested proceed to a territory in which they may appear at an American Consulate, you should notify the Department immediately in order that appropriate advice may be given regarding your further procedure; or, if you have any definite grounds for believing that these aliens have reasonable expectation of being able to proceed at an early date to a district where American consular visa services are available, you may wish to communicate any facts in this connection for the consideration of the Department.

In the absence of reasonable expectation of such departure by the alien or aliens in whom you are interested, it is not believed that any useful purpose will be served by further correspondence in this matter.

Very truly yours,

Enclosure:
    Stamp

A. M. Warren
Chief, Visa Division

Visa Form A-2

August 2, 1941, letter from the U. S. State Department telling Max that further communication regarding Max and Trude's efforts to help Ernst and Trude's parents escape would likely not serve "any useful purpose"

NLT ERNST LOWENHAUSER

409 AACHENERSTR

COLOGNE (GERMANY)

BOOKING TEMPORARILY DISCONTINUED. PERHAPS POSSIBLE THROUGH

HILFSVEREIN SHALL AUTHORIZE JOINT TO PAY WALTER TRIES TO MAKE

RESERVATION.

MAX HOUSER

ACCEPTED SUBJECT TO DELAY AND SENDERS RISK

1941 telegram from Max to Ernst advising that the
shipping lines had stopped booking passage

Sigmund Moses, 1941

"Vacations Not All Play"

Very happy to be Americans are Renate Houser, 13, left, and her sister, Erica Houser, 11, children of Dr. and Mrs. Max Houser, 4247 Amity Road, Deer Park, pictured as they practiced on their accordions in the yard of their home. Vacation is not all play for the sisters, for they spend much time perfecting their accordion music and often in preparing for programs that they are called on to give.

The sisters were born in Cologne, Germany, and have been in this country only a year and eight months. Their parents, foreseeing troubled conditions ahead in Germany about five years ago, determined to quit Germany. They went with their two little girls to Eng-land and were located there for three years. Two months after the war broke out, Dr. and Mrs. Houser determined to come to America, where they felt the future was the brightest for the family.

The children both are enrolled at the Deer Park High School. They have been playing the accordions since they were 8 and 7 years old. Both are gifted in drawing, which is an inheritance, as their two parents are similarly gifted. Renate, who has the greatest ability in drawing, will picture any near-by objected and often, seated in front of her home, draws buildings opposite or trees near by. The sisters look forward to the opening of school, both being close students.

Article about Renate and Erica in the
Cincinnati newspaper, mid-1941

Am 17. Septenrber 1941 ist mein
innigstgeliebter Mann, unser unver-
gesslicher Vater

Max Houser, M.D.

(früher Köln)

im Alter von 48 Jahren nach mo-
natelanger Krankheit von uns gegangen.

In tiefstem Schmerz:

**Trude Houser, geb. Moses;
Renate und Erica Houser.**

Deer Park-Cincinnati, Ohio
4247 Amity Road.

Max's obituary in the Aufbau newspaper

300438 BN

UNITED STATES OF AMERICA
OFFICE OF PRICE ADMINISTRATION

WAR RATION BOOK FOUR

Issued to *Gertrude Houser*
(Print first, middle, and last names)

Complete address *4247 Amity Rd*

Cincinnati, Ohio

READ BEFORE SIGNING

In accepting this book, I recognize that it remains the property of the United States Government. I will use it only in the manner and for the purposes authorized by the Office of Price Administration.

Void if Altered *Gertrude Houser*
(Signature)

It is a criminal offense to violate rationing regulations.

OPA Form R-145   16—35570-1

The cover of Trude's ration book. The United States began rationing after it entered WWII following the Japanese attack on Pearl Harbor

Kathleen Goff in her WAAF
uniform in 1941

Renate (L) with a friend at Star Lake, 1945

Renate and Erica on the lawn at the family home, 1945

Czechoslovak Jewish Representative Committee

Affiliated with the
WORLD JEWISH CONGRESS

1834 BROADWAY, ROOM 267
NEW YORK 23, N. Y.

January 1945

Dear Friend !

We hereby are glad to inform you that we just received from a neutral
country a list of persons interned in Terezin (Theresienstadt). The
name of

MR.   _____

MRS.   Martha Moses,   _____

residing in
TEREZIN at   Rathausgasse 9   _____

appears on this list. Should you wish to communicate with the party
please get in touch with your local Red Cross Chapter.

There are no other details except those mentioned above. We therefore
do not know whether or not this is the person in whom you are interested.

Very truly yours,

Dr. Fred Fried   Prof. Hugo Perutz
CZECHOSLOVAK JEWISH REPRESENTATIVE COMMITTEE

Should you wish to apply for Palestine Certificates, please fill the
enclosed forms and return.
The National Council of Jewish Women, 1819 Broadway, New York will
HF:iw   give you information as to possibilities to make
I.24.45.290.   out affidavits after you have become a citizen.

January 1945 letter from the Czechoslovak Jewish Representative Committee
telling Trude that her mother, Martha Moses, was alive in Theresienstadt

ZIONIST ORGANIZATION OF AMERICA

PALESTINE BUREAU
Zionist Organization of America
41 East 42nd Street
New York City   May 6, 1945

Mrs. M. I. Houser
4247 Amity Rd.
Cincinnati 13, Ohio

Dear Mrs. Houser,

Please be advised that in accordance with a cable received by us from the Jewish Agency for Palestine, dated 4/24/45 the Palestine Government has approved Palestine Immigration Certificates, on Exchange basis, in behalf of

MARTHA MOSES

_____

_____

located in Theresienstadt.

The names have been included in list #TR/20 and dispatched to the British Government in London with a view to be delivered to the protecting power (Swiss Government), who will take the necessary steps to inform the people concerned in Theresienstadt accordingly.

As soon as we have further word about this case, we shall communicate with you.

Sincerely yours,

Dr. S. Bernstein,
Director Palestine Bureau

Case # 288

Letter from the Zionist Organization of America to Trude
indicating that Martha was alive in Theresienstadt and that papers
were being prepared for her to emigrate to Palestine

Ghetto Theresienstadt **212.** No.
Der Ältestenrat

T O D E S F A L L A N Z E I G E

| Name bei Frau-en auch Mädchenname | *Ichenhäuser* | Vorname | *David* | Tr.Nr. *803* |

Geboren am *24.9.1854* in *Fürth* Bez.

Stand *Witwer* Beruf Relig. Geschl. *männl.*

Staatszugehörigkeit Heimatsgemeinde

Letzter Wohnort /Adresse/ *____*

Wohnhaft in Theresienstadt Gebäude No. *L 211* Zimmer No. *118*

Name des Vaters
Be-ruf Letzt. Wohnort

Name der Mutter /Mädchenname/

Sterbetag *9/8 1942* Sterbestunde *5h* Sterbeort: Theresienstadt

Genaue Ortsbezeichnung /Gebäude, Zimmer/ *L 211 III 118*

Verwandte	Name	Tr.Nr.	Verwandt-schaftsgr	Wohnadresse /b.Gatten u.Kindern auch Geburtdaten:/
in Theresienstadt				
im Protektorat				

Tag der letzt. Eheschliessung
Ort der letzt. Eheschliessung
Zahl d.Kinder aus letzt.Ehe

Art des Personalausweises No. Ausge-stellt von

Behandelnder Arzt: *Dr Roth Emierin*

Krankheit /in Blockschrift/ *Marasmus Myocarditis*

Todesursache /in Blockschrift/ *Myocarditis Herzmuskelschwäche*

Totenbeschau führte durch *Dr Pick Me* Tag u.Stunde *9/8 1942* der Totenbeschau *5h*

Ort der Beisetzung Tag u.Stunde der Beisetzung

Theresienstadt, am *9/8 1942*

Der Totenbeschauer	Der Amtsarzt:	Der Chefarzt:

David Ichenhäuser's Death
Certificate from Theresienstadt

American Red Cross

FEB 2 8 2000

Reference: ISS-H-65302

The Holocaust and War Victims
Tracing and Information Center
4700 Mount Hope Drive
Baltimore, Maryland 21215-3231
(410) 764-5311
Fax (410) 764-4638

Dear Ms. Harlan,

A reply has been received from the Czech Red Cross Society regarding your inquiry:

ICHENHÄUSER David, born 24 September 1854, was deported 28 July 1942 from Köln am Rhein to Terezin with the transport III/2. He died in Terezin ghetto on 9 August 1942.

If your case is currently pending with other Red Cross agencies or organizations, your chapter will keep you informed of the search results as they become available. Furthermore, please be aware that information is regularly being discovered and added to archives throughout the world. Therefore, your case will remain open and you will be notified immediately if any new information is received. If you have any questions, please contact your local American Red Cross Chapter.

Sincerely,

Linda C. Klein

Linda Klein
Director

Letter from the American Red Cross to Renate in 2000 regarding
David Ichenhäuser's Deportation to and death in Theresienstadt

July 1, 1942, message from Martha Moses to Trude wishing her a happy birthday and commenting that their friend Hedy had been "released from suffering"

The first page of one of Martha's letters to Max and
Trude, written on tissue thin, onion skin paper

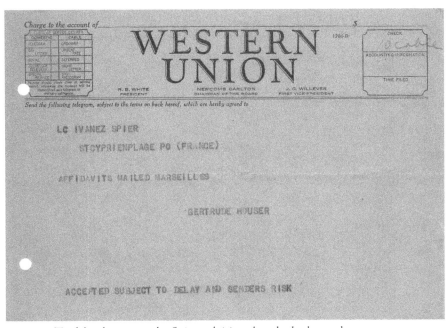

Trude's telegram to the Spiers advising that she had sent the support
affidavits to Marseille as part of her efforts to help the Spiers escape
from the camp where they were being held in Vichy France

Helene – Lene – Berlin, circa 1930   Max Berlin, circa 1930

Gerhard Robert Berlin in Bristol, England, 1943. Gerhard changed his first
name to Robert when he emigrated to the United States after the war

Peter, Anne, and Hannah Rothschild
in Quito, Ecuador, August 1942

Wedding of Anne Rothschild and Gerhard Anker at the British
Embassy in Quito on September 1, 1945. Lene is at the far left; the
British ambassador is next to Lene; Hans is in the center, wearing
glasses; and Peter Rothschild stands second to the right

Cousins Walter and Chelly Emanuel in Amsterdam after the liberation

Clothilde Hahn and Sigbert and Edith Wachs in Havana, November 29, 1945

Renate's Certificate of Citizenship, June 22, 1945

Ella and Ernst, 1945

Ernst and Ella's wedding, 1945

—Photo by Brand Studio.

WHO IS FAIREST OF THEM ALL—Miss Phyllis Livesay, U. C. co-ed, is crowned queen of the Junior Prom at Castle Farm Friday midnight by Jim Alexander, 'Oklahoma" star. The queen's court includes, left to right, Miss Ronnie Hauser, Women's Group System representative; Miss Jean Humphrey, Kappa Delta; Miss Betty Winn Hamilton, Theta Phi Alpha, and Miss Lora Igler, Delta Delta Delta. The queen is a Chi Omega.

February 27, 1947, newspaper article about the University of Cincinnati Junior Prom. Renate, far left (Renate went by "Ronnie" in the United States—the newspaper mispelled "Houser"), was a member of the Prom Queen's court

Ernst Ichenhäuser   Köln-Sülz, 19. April 1946
                          Jüd. Flüchtlingsheim
                          Blankenheimerstr. 55.

Liebe Trude,

       Mit Deinem Brief vom 29. März freute ich mich sehr und besonders mit dem Bildchen der Kinder, die Mädels haben sich ja prachtvoll herausgemacht und sehen blendend aus. Ich hoffe, es geht Dir und ihnen weiter gut. Ich möchte leiden, das Auto, auf welchem sie sitzen, wäre das Deinige, aber ich fürchte, dieses ist nicht der Fall. Auch Dein Brief vom 18. Febr. kam über das Joint Distribution Comitee kam heute, zwei Tage nach obigem Briefe noch an. Man kann ja jetzt direkt schreiben, von England habe ich schon Briefe mit der direkten Post gehabt, sie waren 10-12 Tage unterwegs, ein Brief von mir nach Holland kam durch ein Versehen der Post zurück. Ich ziehe es deshalb vor, diese Briefe nicht mit der gewöhnlichen Post zu senden. Frl. R. darf keine Briefe mehr für uns absenden, was uns sehr arg ist, aber ankommende Sendungen erhalte ich nach wie vor ausgehändigt, Du kannst also weiter an sie senden. Irene Kaufmann wohnt c/o Miss Elly Gottschalk, 448 Central Park West, New York, N.Y., einem Briefe von Dir lag ein Schreiben von ihr bei, worin sie ihren Schwager Rechtsanwalt Dr. Brammertz hier in Köln suchte, ich habe diesen zrZt. aufgesucht und sie stehen jetzt in Verbindung miteinander. Bei uns im Heim wohnt ein Herr Stock aus Stommeln, ich habe mich bei diesem sowohl wie anderweitig nach Anna Katz erkundigt und erfahren, dass sie mit ihrem Töchterchen zusammen mit ihrer Schwester auf Transport gekommen ist, wohin wusste man nicht mit Bestimmtheit zu sagen, man glaubt nach Litzmannstadt. Es ist wohl leider keine Hoffnung mehr, wenn noch einer von ihnen lebte, hätte er sich schon gemeldet. Max Leiser, Spichernstrasse, ist nach Riga gekommen, von dort nach Stuthof und ist dort umgekommen. Über Johanna Frank und Max Spiegel habe ich trotz meiner Bemühungen noch nichts erfahren können, ich forsche weiter nach. Für das Grab Deines lb. Vaters werde ich selbstverständlich sorgen, ich hatte mich schon danach umgesehen, in den nächsten Tagen werde ich wohl wieder zum Friedhof hinauskommen. Gratuliere Tante Clärchen bitte zu ihrem 80. Geburtstage nachträglich noch herzlichst von mir und grüsse sie und alle Verwandten von mir, leider konnte ich ihr nicht mehr rechtzeitig gratulieren, da Dein Brief vom 18. Febr. jetzt erst ankam. Ist es eine grosse Feier gewesen? Schreibe mir doch bitte Deinen und Renate's und Erica's Geburtstage, sei bitte nicht böse, dass ich sie verschwitzt habe, aber in diesen Jahren habe ich zuviel in und auf den Kopf gekriegt und von meinen Papieren ist kein Schnippelchen mehr vorhanden, dafür hat auf der einen Seite die Gestapo und auf der anderen Seite die Bomben gesorgt. Pessach haben wir sehr schön gefeiert, an den beiden ersten Abenden hatten wir bei uns im Heim Gottesdienst, anschliessend schönen Seder, der bis spät in die Nacht hinein dauerte. Es waren nicht nur seit unserer Befreiung sondern seit vielen Jahren der erste Seder und für uns, die wir im wahren Sinne des Wortes aus dem Sklavenhause befreit worden sind, waren sie von besonderer Bedeutung. Sogar für Wein war für den ersten Abend gesorgt worden, jeder erhielt eine halbe Flasche französischen Rotwein, nachdem wir sie ausgetrunken hatten, wurde uns gesagt, sie hätte für den zweiten Abend mitreichen sollen. Hagadahs hatten wir von Amerika gestiftet bekommen, Mazoth hatten wir reichlich von Holland. An diesen Abenden war viel Besuch bei uns im Heim, auch mehrere englische Soldaten von der jüdischen Legion. Ich hoffe, auch Ihr habt die Feiertage gut verbracht und Du hast Dich auf Ostern einmal ordentlich ausruhen können. Was haben Josef und Anna Simons bisher getan? Du hattest doch noch Verwandte drüben, welche eine Farm hatten, oder sind es diese? An Henry Cooper habe ich geschrieben und hoffe bald Antwort zu erhalten. Dass Chelly den Terror überlebt hat, freut mich, ich werde ihr schreiben, ist sie allein oder hat noch einer ihrer Angehörigen überlebt? Für Affidavits ist es noch zu früh, für das britische Gebiet arbeiten die Konsulate noch nicht, für das amerikanische wohl vorerst nur in Ausnahmefällen. - Geschäftlich hat man uns hier einen echten Schildbürgerstreich gespielt: man hatte uns Holzeinkaufscheine für das britische Gebiet gegeben, also für ein Gebiet, in welchem es kaum Holz gibt und

in welchem wir früher niemals eingekauft haben. Nachdem es uns in einer Gemeinschaftsaktion mit viel Mühe und Arbeit und Kosten gelungen war, die Scheine einzudecken, hat man sie für verfallen erklärt, so dass die ganze Arbeit jetzt für die Katz ist. Dieses nennt man hier "planvolle Lenkung". Der Hauptleidtragende ist die Stadt Köln, welche nun ohne Holz dasitzt. Aber das kann uns nicht mehr erschüttern, die Parole hier ist: "nicht ärgern, nur wundern!"
Dass die Pakete an Jacobs an Dich zurückgekommen sind, ist sehr schön, so sind sie doch wenigstens nicht verloren gegangen.
Ernst Dülken schrieb mir von seiner Fabrik und ich freue mich, dass es ihm gut geht. Hat Karl D. nicht die Absicht, wieder etwas anzufangen? Alles Gute, die herzlichsten Grüsse und Küsse für Dich, Renate und Erica
                       Dein
                       Ernst.

Ernst's April 19, 1946 letter to Trude

Leni Rothschild with two of her grandchildren in Quito, February 1948

Edmund Pelta, Erica, Renate, and Allan Wasserman, whom Renate married in 1948

Ella, Ernst, and Trude in Frankfurt, 1954

Ella, Ernst, and Renate, July 2, 1960

Trude (standing) collecting fossils with Trude's son-in-law Allan Wasserman
and granddaughter Margie Wasserman (now Margie Kessel)

A small portion of Trude's mineral and fossil collections

Ernst Ichenhäuser, 1963

Ella Ichenhäuser, 1968

Trude, 1970

Trude showing a mineral specimen to a guest visiting Trude's
display at the Cincinnati Main Library, 1976

POSTSCRIPTS

D URING THE SUMMER OF 1946, RENATE AND ERICA WORKED
as waitresses at Star Lake. On their nights off, they went into
the nearby town for sodas. The girls occasionally met some of the
young men who were attending a forestry school nearby. Renate
and Erica joined the forestry students for trips to the town's diner
where they ate hamburgers and danced to swing music on the diner's
jukebox. The top song of 1946 was "A Fine Romance" by Martha
Tilton and Johnny Mercer, along with "Candy" by Johnny Mercer,
Jo Stafford and The Pipers, "Prisoner of Love" by Perry Como, and
"Five Minutes More" by Frank Sinatra. They enjoyed swimming in
Star Lake during breaks from waitressing, lying on the camp's wooden
dock to warm up after swimming in the lake's chilly water.

RENATE HOUSER WASSERMAN HARLAN

In 1946, when she was seventeen, Renate met Allan Wasserman, a
medical student at the University of Cincinnati. Allan, in addition to
studying medicine, was president of the Sigma Alpha Mu fraternity
and a member of the Omicron Delta Kappa honorary leadership
society at U.C. Renate and Allan became engaged in May 1947 and
were married in 1948. They lived in Cincinnati with Allan's mother
Anna Wasserman until they finished their studies.

Renate graduated from U.C. in 1948 with a bachelor's

degree in applied arts. She took a job at Shillito's, which had been Cincinnati's first department store. However, after a few months Renate applied for a job at Fashion Frocks, a womenswear manufacturer in Cincinnati. The company needed someone to draw the artwork for Fashion Frocks' womenswear catalog, as well as write the ad copy. While Renate had never written a line of copy, she did not let that stop her. She told the interviewer that, of course, she could write copy in addition to doing the artwork. Fashion Frocks hired her, and Renate had a wonderful experience over the next three years creating the sales catalogs. By the time she left the company in 1951, she was earning fifty dollars a week, which was their main support since Allan was doing his internship and residency.

Renate and Allan had a daughter, Marjorie, in 1952. Allan was drafted into the United States army in 1953 and was stationed in Murnau, a small town in southern Germany. Renate and Margie soon joined him. Renate was pregnant and, in February 1954, gave birth to their second child, Steven. Their joy soon turned to despair. Six weeks after Steven was born, Renate lapsed into a coma. She was hospitalized in Munich and was soon transferred to a larger hospital in Frankfurt. After weeks in the hospital with no definitive diagnosis, she seemed to have recovered. However, three weeks later she lapsed back into a coma and was not expected to live. The army flew her to Walter Reed Hospital in Washington D.C. where the physicians diagnosed her with tubercular meningitis, which had a mortality rate of ninety-five percent.

Allan soon flew home, leaving Trude, who had flown to Germany after Renate relapsed, to close the family's home in Murnau and bring Steven and Margie back, where they stayed with Allan's sister Hilda and her husband Joe Cohen in Hamilton, Ohio. By now it was late 1954. The Army wanted to send Renate to the Letterman army hospital in San Francisco. She refused and insisted that Allan take her to Dayton, where their close friends Ilse and Leon Stein helped them set up an apartment. Their German nanny, Inge Hedeker, came to join them and take care of Steven and Margie while Renate recovered. It took three years before Renate was fully able to return normal activities.

Renate, Allan, and their children lived good lives in Dayton and frequently visited Trude and "Granny" Wasserman in Cincinnati. However, in a heart-breaking echo of Renate's loss of her father, Allan died of a heart attack in 1968 at age forty-four. And so Renate, like her mother, was left to raise two children on her own, with Steven being fourteen and Margie sixteen. With the help of Allan's and Renate's friends, Renate was able to keep their home and send their children to college.

Several years later, Renate married Roy Harlan, a chemist who worked at the Wright-Patterson Air Force Base outside of Dayton. They lived in Dayton for many years, enjoying travel and gardening. After Roy passed away, Renate moved to Cincinnati to be near Marjorie.

Renate never forgot what her family went through at the hands of the Nazis. As a result, she was a tireless supporter of Israel, understanding that the Jewish people needed a homeland of their own where they could live and defend themselves. Renate knew only too well that Jews could not rely on any nation to protect them or give them a home. Jews around the world learned they should not rely on anyone else for their safety, because when they most needed help, the nations of the world turned their backs on them.

Renate also never forgot what it was like to be a stranger in a new land trying to establish a new life. When the exodus of Jews from the Soviet Union occurred in 1989, Renate became deeply involved in resettling Russian refugees in the United States. She worked with local agencies in Dayton to help emigres find housing, furniture, and jobs. She hosted Russian refugees at her home for holidays such as Rosh Hashanah, Passover, and Thanksgiving. When South Vietnam fell to the North Vietnamese, Renate worked with local agencies to help resettle Vietnamese refugees in southwestern Ohio.

Renate continued to use her skill as an artist, but as an avocation. She painted hundreds of watercolors, specializing in landscapes, including many paintings of the iconic red barns that dotted the Ohio countryside. Renate also was an avid gardener and superb cook. She was a loving and supportive wife, mother, and grandmother.

Renate's community service work in these and many other regards has been widely recognized:

Jewish Community Council: Presented to Mrs. Allan Wasserman for distinguished leadership and community service in 1965 as winner of the Dorothy B. Moyer Leadership Award given by the Dayton Jewish Community Council.

United Jewish Campaign of the Dayton Jewish Community Council: Citation of recognition for devoted volunteer service to help secure and strengthen Jewish life.

Hadassah: Two-time recipient of Hadassah's Presidential Award for "devoted service to the Jewish people in Israel and the United States, for accepting as a sacred trust the burdens and joys of leadership, for fostering freedom and the ways of peace, for honoring the Jewish heritage which teaches that the blessing of the deed is in the doing thereof."

The United States Department of State: Invitation to Dr. and Mrs. Allan Wasserman to a Seminar on International and Domestic Issues in Washington, D.C., February 22-24, 1967.

United Jewish Appeal, March 5, 1972: The National Women's Division of the United Jewish Appeal recognized Mrs. Allan Wasserman for her significant contribution to the cause of Jewish survival.

United Jewish Appeal: Award of Merit present to Mrs. Roy Harlan "for outstanding achievement on behalf of the people of Israel."

Jewish Federation of Dayton, Ohio: "To Renate Harlan for devoted leadership as an officer of the Jewish Federation of Greater Dayton, 1978-83," presented on June 29, 1983.

Jewish Family Services: "To Ronnie Harlan (Renate) in appreciation of your dedication, leadership and devoted energy 1984-87," from the Board of Jewish Family Services, Dayton, Ohio.

Jewish Federation of Dayton, Ohio: "To Ronnie Harlan in recognition of decades of service, 1970-1993," by the Jewish Federation of Greater Dayton, Ohio, June 22, 1993.

Chairperson, United Jewish Appeal Educational Institute program, January 25, 1965.

Chairperson: Hadassah "Sonia Riskin Vocational Education Luncheon" Feb. 22, 1965.

President: Dayton, Ohio, chapter of Hadassah and Treasurer for Hadassah's Central States Region.

Dayton Art Institute: "Certificate of Appreciation awarded to Ronnie Harlan for her many hours of devoted service," by the Dayton Art Institute, May 1999.

Montgomery County Mental Health Services Board: Recognized Renate for her service on the Mental Health Services Board of Directors.

The Dayton Daily News: Named Renate as one of Dayton's "Top Ten Women" in 1983.

Montgomery County United Appeal (predecessor to the United Way): Certificate of Appreciation for Outstanding Volunteer Service.

Renate passed away on November 4, 2016 at age eighty-eight. A stolperstein has been placed outside Renate's childhood home at 412 Aachenerstrasse. Stolpersteine, literally "stumble stones," are cobblestones placed in front of the location where a Holocaust victim last lived voluntarily. Each stone is topped with a brass plaque stating the name and fate of the victim. Renate's stone reads: "Here lived Renate Ichenhäuser, born 1928, fled to England in 1938 and in 1939 to the United States."

ERICA STUX SHORE

Erica obtained her Bachelor of Science degree in 1949. She continued her studies at U.C. and received a master's degree in chemistry in 1950 at age twenty-one. She married Paul Stux, a Viennese-Jewish refugee, in 1955. They lived in Akron, Ohio, where they raised three children: Lydia, Ted, and Arnie. Erica first worked as a chemist in Cincinnati from 1950-56. She worked from 1978-84 as a technical writer for Pittsburgh Plate Glass Company, a global producer of paints, coatings, optical products, specialty materials, and fiber glass. After Paul died, Erica married William ("Bill") Shore, a Czech-Jewish survivor of Auschwitz. They enjoyed one another's intellect and played doubles ping-pong in the Senior Olympics.

Erica was a prolific author. She wrote dozens of plays, books, and poems. She composed songs and played accordion for decades in a klezmer band. Erica also played the French horn, piano, and recorder. She wrote a musical entitled "Aloha" which was produced in Los Angeles. She wrote other musicals: *Rainbow Days*, *Let It Out*, *Rain*, and *From Shepherd to King*. She also enjoyed birdwatching and playing bridge. In addition to speaking German and English, Erica developed a working knowledge of Russian and French.

BOOKS BY ERICA STUX

Landlady (a novel)
Eight Who Made a Difference: Pioneer Women in the Arts
Writing for Freedom: The Story of Lydia Maria Child
Sequins and Sorrow
Enrico Fermi, Trailblazer in Nuclear Physics
The Achievers: Great Women in the Biological Sciences
The Wonder of Wings
Incredible Insects
Expressions of Nature through Photography and Words
Naturally Inspired: Poems of the Great Outdoors
Permutations of the Humble Coffee Bean: Poems of Daily Tasks and Diversions
Who, Me? Paranoid?
Aiming for the Jocular Vein
They Found Order in Nature
Working Where Poems Are Lurking
Strobe Lights (a volume of poetry)

Erica contributed poems and articles to: *Grit, Columbus Dispatch, Philadelphia Inquirer, Saturday Evening Post, Wall Street Journal, Reader's Digest, Canto, Maryland Review of Poetry, Lutheran Digest, Scroll, Haiku, Outdoor, Summit, Chicago Daily News,* and *Gentle Survivalist.* Her contributions to children's publications included: *Climb, Explore, Wee Wisdom, Hopscotch, Adventures in Storytelling, Real Kids, Story Friends, Words of Cheer, Purring in a Pocket, Ohio Woodlands,* and *Young Crusader.*

Erica passed away on December 18, 2018, at age eighty-nine. A stolperstein in her name has been placed at the family home at 412 Aachenerstrasse: "Here lived Erika Ichenhäuser, born 1929, fled in 1938 to England and 1939 to the United States."

TRUDE MOSES ICHENHÄUSER (HOUSER)

Trude made a life for herself after Renate and Erica married and moved away. She worked at Fashion Frocks as a seamstress for several years. She then worked for many years as a seamstress at Pogue's, a Cincinnati department store, making clothing alterations.

Trude developed an interest in mineral and fossil collecting stemming from Max's collection, which he shipped to the United States with their other belongings when they emigrated. She traveled much of the United States to clamber along highway roadcuts and climb into quarries to find fossils and crystals using her rock hammer, chisel, and canvas specimen bag. Trude became President and Program Chair of a Cincinnati fossil collecting club named The Dry Dredgers. Some of her fossils were so significant that the Smithsonian Museum of Natural History asked her to donate portions of her collection to the Museum, which she did. Trude donated more than 3,300 specimens, including many spectacular fossils embedded in black slate. The Smithsonian's Department of Paleontology used many of her specimens for the Museum's Naturalist Center that visitors can access for study and research. The Museum memorialized her collection with a bronze plaque in the Naturalist Center.

Trude also served as the program chair for the Cincinnati Mineral Society. Her collections of fossils and minerals, which she arranged in twenty-five elegant display cases, became so extensive that it filled her basement and several bedrooms on the second floor of her home. She won numerous ribbons and trophies at conventions for fossil and mineral collectors, including five trophies for her display of ammonites (a type of fossil that resembles a nautilus). She even had a display of fluorescent rocks that had to be viewed in a dark room with a fluorescent light in order to see the minerals' beautiful colors.

Trude (who was known as "Trudy" in the United States) was featured in the September-October 1977 issue of *The Mineralogical Record* magazine. Here are excerpts from the magazine's lengthy portrait of her: "'15,000 Fossils…and still counting.' That's the report I received from Trudy Houser, member since 1959 of the Cincinnati Mineral and Dry Dredger Societies…The nucleus of the Houser collection, which, in addition to fossils, includes 2500 catalogued minerals and crystals, was a miscellaneous group of about 350 'insufficiently labeled' minerals and fossils that Trudy's husband, a physician, had gathered on weekend excursions since the age of 12… When her husband died in 1941 there were two daughters, 12 and 13, to raise. For diversion, the doctor's widow began researching the proper identification and labelling of fossils by Phylum, Class, Order, Genus, Species and Location—quite an undertaking for someone untrained in the field, who, three months prior to graduation, had decided to marry, rather than complete her History of Art college major. If, when in Cincinnati, one indicates a desire to view an outstanding local mineral and fossil collection, Trudy Houser's house is where one will usually be taken…and receive the warmest of welcomes—plus a choice of beverages and homemade cakes. In the Cincinnati Mineral Society, Mrs. Houser has filled every office and chairmanship, from publicity to President…To those who ask the question 'Why? What do you get from collecting?' Trudy's answer is, 'consolation, and joy in the earth's beauty; and the fulfillment of a duty—to preserve that beauty for future generations.' And, she smiles fondly, 'pleasant evenings with strangers can grow into lifetime friendships'…Trudy recently delighted Smithsonian paleontologists with a gift of approximately 2000 fossil specimens, over *100* of which were not previously represented in the National Collections. Most of her donation will be housed in the Smithsonian's Naturalist Center…the specimens will have special labels indicating them to be part of the Gertrude Houser collection, and a plaque is also being prepared." R.A. Davis, the Paleontologist and Curator of Collections for the Cincinnati Museum of Natural History, also recognized Trude's collections and generosity.

Trude passed away on May 16, 1982, at the age of eighty.

THE ICHENHÄUSERS' HOME IN COLOGNE

The Kristallnacht mobs did not damage the Ichenhäusers' home at 412 Aachenerstrasse. Renate believed this was because Max's patients loved him. He had an outstanding reputation, which she believed led their neighbors to refrain from damaging the family's home. Ultimately, an Aryan family "purchased" the home, although the purchasers did not actually pay any money to Max and Trude. The home miraculously was not destroyed during the Allied bombing of Cologne, although the neighborhoods all around it were flattened. The Ichenhäusers never regained possession of their home, although long after the war they received a pittance of a settlement that represented a fraction of the home's value. The ground floor where Max had his office has been converted into a pharmacy. The rooftop garden has been converted into a closed room.

Stolpersteine have been placed in front of the house for Sigmund, Martha, Max, Trude, Renate, and Erica.

"Here lived and practiced Dr. Max Ichenhäuser, born 1892, taken into 'protective custody' 1938 in Dachau, fled in 1938 to England and to the United States in 1939, died Sept. 17, 1941. "

"Here lived Gertrude Ichenhäuser, born Moses 1901, fled in 1938 to England and to the United States in 1939."

"Here lived Renate Ichenhäuser, born 1928, fled in 1938 to England and to the United States in 1939. "

"Here lived Erica Ichenhäuser, born 1929, fled to England in 1938 and to the United States in 1939. "

"Here lived Sigmund Moses, born 1859, humiliated/disenfranchised, died March 25, 1942. "

"Here lived Martha Moses, nee Oberlander, born 1880, deported 1942 to Theresienstadt, murdered in Auschwitz 1944. "

Stolpersteine have been placed at 409 Aachenerstrasse where Ernst and David last lived voluntarily:

"Here lived David Ichenhäuser, born 1854, deported in 1942 to Theresienstadt, murdered Aug. 9, 1942. "

"Here lived Ernst Ichenhäuser, born 1889, deported in 1942 to Auschwitz, liberated."

David and Emma Ichenhäuser gravestones say:

"Emma Ichenhäuser Nee Dülken, Dec. 19, 1860—Feb. 23, 1938, Love, kindness and generosity crowned her actions and life."

"David Ichenhäuser, September 24, 1854—August 9, 1942 in Theresienstadt."

ERNST AND ELLA

Ernst and Ella submitted claims in Germany to recover property they lost during the war. Ella sought to recover items she left at her home at 368 Zulpicherstrasse in Cologne, such as furniture and clothing. She stated that "most of the assets had to be forcibly left in our last apartment." She explained that her family's belongings "were, as was customary at that time, taken over by Nazi organizations and sold in favor of them. Unfortunately, I cannot give you any witnesses because they are murdered or dead." The Nazis sent Ella's mother to the Asyl; what few belongings she took with her were lost when the SS deported her to a death camp.

Ernst sought to recover his and his family's belongings. When the Nazis evicted Ernst and David from their apartment at 409 Aachenerstrasse and forcibly relocated them to 23 Venloerstrasse, Ernst had their furniture packed by Heinrich Hoffmann, a freight forwarder, who sent their boxes and suitcases to a storeroom in the Roonstrasse synagogue. Ernst took a few items with him when he was forced into the Müngersdorf camp. "After a bomb attack, I fled and left the things there. The camp was disbanded after this attack and the inmates were deported. The camp remained under the administration of the Gestapo." This was when Ernst went into hiding in Cologne. "When I was arrested in 1942, the Gestapo found the warrant [the receipt from the freight forwarder] and the keys with me."

One of the items Ernst lost was a stamp collection he had purchased for 8,000 Reichmarks in 1937-38. Ernst bought the collection to convert currency into objects that might retain value and that he could take with him if he were able to emigrate. Ernst also sought to recover "precious metal objects" that were "sent to Berlin." It is unclear to what he was referring, although it may have related to family silver such as candlesticks and the like. Ernst also listed jewelry: "mother's brilliant necklace was 6 ½ carats brilliants and 6 ¼ carat diamonds."

Ernst's claim file includes notations that: "In the summer of 1941, David Ichenhäuser and his son, who lived together in Aachenerstrasse 409, were forced to leave their home and were taken to the Venloerstrasse…After David Ichenhäuser had been driven from the Pension Mayer-Ettlinger in the Venloerstrasse 23 and in the nursing home of the Israeli Asylum in Cologne-Ehrenfield, Ottostrasse 85, he was forcibly deported in 1942 and brought to the camp Theresienstadt."

Ernst applied for compensation for the time he was imprisoned in Cologne and Auschwitz. Incredibly, his claim was denied, in part because the Gestapo had found him guilty of "economic war crimes" by virtue of Ernst having purchased food stamps on the black market. Of course, the regime had left Ernst no choice but to commit this "crime" since he had no other way to obtain food stamps and, in turn, food on which to survive. Even in the immediate aftermath of the war, there were still irredentist Nazis infected with residual anti-Semitism who sought to inflict further pain on and deny the basic humanity of the Nazis' Jewish victims.

Ernst and Ella lived out their days in Cologne. Ernst passed away on July 7, 1964 at age 74. Ella passed away many years later, on August 8, 1989, at age 97. They were buried in Cologne. Ernst has a stolperstein at 409 Aachenerstrasse in front of the apartment building where Ernst and David Ichenhäuser last lived voluntarily: "Here lived Ernst Ichenhäuser, born 1889, deported to Auschwitz in 1942, liberated."

KATHLEEN GOFF

After the war and demobilization from the WAAF, Kathleen spent some time managing a transport depot in Austria. She eventually went to Uruguay to work at the British embassy in Montevideo. It was there that Kathleen met her husband, Frank Ryan. They married; their daughter Patricia was born in Montevideo. Kathleen and Frank returned to Britain and settled in Hertfordshire where they had another daughter, Kate, and a son, Christopher. They eventually moved to a home on the High Street in Puckeridge.

Kathleen died on October 13, 2010. She was remembered as a woman of high moral standards who brimmed with energy and enthusiasm. Kathleen believed that if a thing was worth doing, "it was worth doing badly." That is to say, she felt that if something were worth doing, a person should not hold back or forego it just because the individual might not do it perfectly. Have a go and give it your best, whatever the outcome may be. Kathleen's daughter Patricia ("Pat") Goff Neate lives in the village of Rosscarbery on Ireland's southwestern coast. Kate Goff Lovell lives in Somerset, outside of London. Pat and Kate's brother Christopher lived in Hertfordshire until he passed away in January 2021.

LENE AND MAX BERLIN

The Nazis deported Lene and Max to Theresienstadt on September 25, 1942. The SS deported them to the Auschwitz-Birkenau extermination camp on January 23, 1943. Lene, age fifty-three when she was deported to Auschwitz, was murdered on January 24, 1943, the day she arrived. Max was fifty-six when the SS sent him to Auschwitz. Max, too, died in Auschwitz, but the date of his death is unknown.

As previously noted, Max and Lene were able to get their children, Lisselotte and Gerhard, out of Germany in 1939 on the Kindertransport. The children spent the duration of the war in England with the Malones, an Irish Catholic family in Bristol. Lisselotte changed her name to Elizabeth (or at least went by Elizabeth) while in Britain because her given name of Lisselotte proved to be difficult for many British to pronounce and because her schoolmates teased her about her name. Elizabeth worked as a seamstress and metal worker during the war. She also attended "Finishing School" in England. Elizabeth left England in 1945 after the war ended and emigrated to the United States on one of the Queen Elizabeth liners.

Gerhard emigrated to the United States in 1946 at age sixteen; he secured passage on a freighter to Philadelphia. Gerhard's Certificate of Identity listed him as just a shade over five feet tall, with fair hair and brown eyes. The photograph on his Certificate shows him wearing a sport coat, tie, and round wire-rim glasses. Once in the United States, Gerhard changed his name to Robert Gerhard Berlin. Robert lived with his Aunt Aanchen (Ana) and her husband Joseph Simons on their farm at 3 Bartlett Drive in Norwich, New York, where Robert finished high school. Robert held many jobs over the years, including as a restaurateur, appliance sales and repairman, plant manager, and more. His son Mark Berlin lives outside Philadelphia.

HILDE AND CARL SPIER

As previously described, the Spiers fled to southern France where the Vichy police moved them among several internment camps. The police eventually released them. They lived for roughly the next two years with friends along the Côte d'Azur before the police interned them again. A relative arranged for Hilde's cousin Angelo Donati to take custody of their children Marianne and Rolf. The Vichy police arrested Carl and Hilde in August 1942 and sent them to the internment camp at Drancy from which the Nazis deported them to Auschwitz on Transport No. 27 on September 2, 1942. Hilde was murdered upon arrival at Auschwitz. Carl was assigned to forced labor in a shoe factory. He survived for two years. In January 1945, the Nazis began evacuating prisoners from Auschwitz in the infamous death march from Auschwitz to the Buchenwald concentration camp in Germany. Carl died on February 1, 1945 during the death march to Buchenwald.[318]

---

318 Return to Erfurt at 135-36.

Angelo Donati fled to Switzerland when the Nazis discovered he was helping thousands of Jews escape from Vichy France and sought to arrest him. Donati was able to save Marianne and Rolf with the help of Donati's butler Francesco Moraldo. Moraldo took Marianne and Rolf to Moraldo's hometown, the tiny village of Creppo in Italy's Liguria region, just east of the French border. Moraldo hid the children there with the complicity of the village, even though German troops were in the area until they retreated northward late in the war. The remote, humble village of Creppo was accessible only by a footpath. It lacked electricity and running water. The poor soil supported only a few grapevines and some potatoes, but the area had an abundance of chestnut trees. Villagers used the chestnuts to make a sort of pancake as a staple food.[319] Moraldo and the children lived with Moraldo's parents in a tiny, stone house whose walls were blackened by decades of smoke.[320]

After the war, Donati returned to Italy and adopted Marianne and Rolf. Donati died on December 30, 1960. Among the awards Donati received for his valor were the Grand Officer of the Italian Crown, Commander of the Order of Sant'Agata of San Marino, and Commander of the Order of the Italian Solidarity Star. In 2004, Italy honored Donati with the Gold Medal of Civic Merit. The President of the Italian Ciampi offered the following in recognition of Donati's actions during the war:

> During the second world war in the area of France occupied by Italian troops, Angelo Donati, with indomitable courage succeeded in saving, in collaboration with Italian civilian and military authorities, thousands of Jews of different nationalities, protecting their lives menaced by deportation in Nazi extermination camps. With generosity of mind and passionate commitment he gave life and coherent affirmation to the values of liberty and justice.

On February 11, 1999, Yad Vashem named Moraldo one of the "Righteous Among the Nations" for the courage he displayed in

---

319   Return to Erfurt at 123-24.

320   Return to Erfurt at 124.

hiding Marianne and Rolf. If the Nazis had found him harboring Jews, they would have executed him on the spot. Moraldo died on April 28, 2001, at age ninety-five.

Marianne Spier's recollections of her childhood are recounted in the stunning, heart-breaking memoir "Return to Erfurt: Memories of a Destroyed Youth," by Olga Tarcali. Renowned Nazi hunter Serge Klarsfeld wrote the foreword.

Stolpersteine for Hilde and Carl have been placed in Cologne-Lindenthal at 163 Gleueler Strasse, their last home in Cologne.

Hilde's plaque reads: "Dr. Hilde Spier, nee Wolff, born 1901. Fled to Belgium 1935, to France in 1940, interned in Drancy, deported in 1942, murdered in Auschwitz."

Carl's plaque reads: "Here lived Carl L. Spier, born 1900, fled in 1935 to Belgium, to France in 1940, interned in Drancy and deported in 1942 to Auschwitz, murdered in the death march from Auschwitz, February 1, 1945."

THE ZADE FAMILY

The Nazis murdered Hugo, Marta, and Ursula Zade in Auschwitz. Stolpersteine have been placed for them at 50 Salierring in Cologne. A stone has also been placed for Hugo and Marta's son Hans.

The town of Langenfeld placed a plaque for Dr. Zade at the Martinus Hospital on Richrath and named one of the town's streets Hugo Zade Way. Dr. Zade established and operated the first pediatric practice in Langenfeld until the Nazis destroyed his practice by stationing S.A. thugs outside his office to "suggest" patients seek treatment elsewhere.

The stolperstein for Hans Zade is incorrect in several respects and will be replaced. Hans was born on June 9, 1907, in Langenfeld-Immigrath. He escaped from Germany in 1938 when he was thirty-one, emigrating to England. No records have been found explaining how Hans obtained a visa to enter Britain. From 1938 to 1946, Hans designed arc welding equipment and extruders for Arc Manufacturing Company in London. The British interned him as a security risk for three months in 1940, but his employer helped secure his release. Hans pursued a career in mechanical engineering and worked as chief engineer and general manager at Rediweld Ltd. in Crawley, a town in West Sussex, south of London. His work included electrical engineering, cathode rays, high voltage issues, and plastics. He authored several articles on welding and plastics which have been published in English, German, French, and Dutch technical journals. Hans died in December 1996 in Crawley.

Anne Lilienfeld, born in Hamburg on December 27, 1909, emigrated to London in 1938 to join Hans. They married and lived at 143 Holland Road in London's Kensington district. Anne worked as a domestic servant from 1938-39. Hans and Anne had a son Steven in 1944. Anne spent ten years as a part-time teacher at the Horsham School of the Arts. Steven became a teacher and relocated from London to Leeds.

HANS AND LENI ROTHSCHILD

Hans and Leni emigrated first to Belgium, then England, and then to Ecuador where they made new lives for themselves and their children Hannah, Anne, and Peter, as described below.

Hannah Rothschild

Hannah married Gunter Engel, who had emigrated to Ecuador from Germany. Gunter's family owned a drapery and carpet business in Dortmund known as "Engel Gardinen und Teppiche," meaning "Engel Curtains and Carpets." The business was prosperous and had approximately two dozen employees. The store featured large display windows fifteen feet high filled with samples of the fabrics and draperies the Engels offered. Gunter fled from Germany to Czechoslovakia and from there to Ecuador; he arrived after the Rothschilds had already settled there. Gunter eventually went by the name Gonzalo in an effort to integrate into Ecuadorian society. His brother Werner, with whom Gunter founded and ran an auto parts and service business in Quito, later emigrated to Israel.

Gunter and Hannah had three children: Ruth, Eva, and Ralph.

In 1954, Hannah and Gunter purchased a small banana plantation where they grew bananas for export. They also grew cocoa beans. Almost everything on the farm was done by hand labor; they did not have any mechanical equipment. While Gunter stayed in Quito to work, Hannah stayed at the farm to oversee operations there. Their workers sun-dried the cocoa beans on large tarps. Hannah and Gunter sold the beans to local chocolate makers who processed the cacao into large bars of semi-sweet chocolate. Their customers included La Universal, one the largest chocolatiers in Ecuador—it is still in business today. As in Germany, the Rothschild family ate a lot of chocolate, including chocolate baked goods that Leni and Hannah made.

Ruth's brother Ralph Engel lived with Ruth and her husband Leo for one year in the United States. Ralph then emigrated to Israel. Ralph lives in Nahariya, where he married an Israeli woman, Raquel. They have eight children.

Anne Rothschild

Anne and her husband Gerardo Anker had two children: Esteban Eugenio and Margarita Silvia.

Esteban married Lucia Cardenas, with whom he had three children: Andres Ricardo, Roberto Filipe, and Gabriela Silvia. Gabriela and Roberto live in Ecuador. Andres lives in London.

Margarita married Patricio Riofrio Polit. Patricio's mother's last name was Polit; his father's last name was Riofrio. In Spain and Latin America, people bear both of their parents' last names. In the case of Patricio Riofrio Polit, his first surname is his father's last name, while the second surname is his mother's last name.

Margarita and Patricio had three children: John David, Adrienne Veronica, and Alexie Danielle. John is a professor at The College of William and Mary in Virginia. Adrienne is a social worker in New Jersey. Alexie is a doctor in Durham. She and her husband are both graduates of Duke University.

Peter Rothschild

Peter Rothschild, who eventually went by Pedro in Ecuador, married Ana Elvira Engel. They had five children: Irene Olga; Daniel Julio; Susan Elizabeth; Silvia Miriam; and Sandra.

Peter's daughter Irene, born in 1958, is the Engels' oldest child. She is the only one who still lives in Ecuador. She is married to Alberto Dorfzaun; they live in Quito. Alberto has done a great deal of research on Jewish exile in Ecuador. His daughter Daniela did original research about Manuel Antonio Munoz Borrero—Ecuador's Consul to Sweden during the Holocaust who was honored posthumously by Yad Vashem, Israel's Holocaust Memorial Museum, for saving Jewish lives. Alberto's father, Kurt Dorfzaun, established the largest Panama hat manufacturer in Ecuador, based in the city of Cuenca. Alberto works in the business.

Susan (Susi) Rothschild (Peter's third child) met Israeli Dan Ohana when Dan was visiting Ecuador. They married and moved to Kfar Saba in Israel. They have three daughters.

EVA AND LORE CAPELL

Joseph Dülken's daughter Eva married Hermann Capell; they settled in Cologne. Hermann and Eva's daughter Else married and had a daughter, Lore. Neither Else nor Lore emigrated before the war. Eva was deported to Theresienstadt and was reported missing after the war. Else and Lore were deported to the Jewish ghetto in Riga. They survived concentration camps and forced labor. After the war, they returned to Cologne for a short period before emigrating to Palestine in 1947. Lore moved back to Cologne in 1957 and opened a butcher shop with her husband. She died in Cologne in 1998 and was buried in the Cologne-Bocklemünd Jewish cemetery.

EDITH AND SIGBERT WACHS

Edith and Sigbert Wachs, whom Trude tried to help emigrate, were able to escape from Germany and emigrate to Cuba.

TONI COHEN

Trude's friend Toni Cohen survived the Holocaust. While research has not disclosed how she survived, family albums contain photographs of her in Geneva after the war.

MAJOR BATTLES IN WHICH MAX PARTICIPATED DURING WWI

? 10—Nov. 3, 1915: Autumn battle in Champagne (Tahure).

Nov. 4, 1915—April 8, 1916: Stationary battles (stationary engagements to hold a position) in Champagne.

April 28—May 16; July 15—July 30; and Aug. 5—Sept. 3, 1916: Battle of Verdun, in particular:

> Battles at Hill 304.
> Battles at "Zwischenwerk Thiaumont."
> Battles at the Maas.

Sept. 15.—Sept. 28, 1916: Battle of the Somme.

April 3, 1916—April 5, 1917: Stationary battles at the Aisne.

April 12—May 27, 1917: Battles at Verdun (Hill 304).

? 14, 1917—Jan. 6, 1918 and Feb. 6, 1918—May 9, 1918: Stationary battles at Reims.

May 27—June 13, 1918: Battles of Soisson and Reims.

June 14—July 14, 1918: Stationary battles at Reims.

July 15—July 17, 1918: Assault battle on the Marne and in Champagne.

July 18—July 25, 1918: Defensive battle between Soissons and Reims.

July 26—Aug. 3, 1918: Mobile defensive battle between Marne and Vesle.

Aug. 4—Aug. 14, 1918, and Aug. 15—Aug. 30, 1918: Stationary
battles at Reims.

Sept. 10—Oct. 14, 1918: Battles on the Front at
Armentières—Lens.

Oct. 15—Oct. 19, 1918: Battles between Deûle Canal and the
Scheldt River.

Oct. 20—Nov. 4, 1918: Battles at the Hermann position on the
Scheldt River.

Nov. 5—Nov. 11, 1918: Retreat battles in front of the Antwerp-
Maas position.

(Nov. 11, 1918: Germany surrendered to the Allies.)

JEWISH SITES IN COLOGNE

A memorial plaque has been placed at the Jewish elementary school
on Lützowstrasse that Renate attended.

A monument has been added to the Jewish cemetery in
Cologne's Bocklemünd district where remnants of Torahs and other
prayer items the Nazis destroyed or defiled have been buried. Cologne
built a museum of Jewish culture on the Rathausplatz (town hall
square) in 2006.

After the war, the military government provided a house at 55
Blankenheimerstrasse to the remnants of Cologne's Jewish community to house refugees. Ella and Ernst lived there for a time.

During Kristallnacht, S.A. mobs destroyed the Roonstrasse
Synagogue where Max was bar mitzvah. On April 29, 1945, in the
ruins of the synagogue, those few Jews still in Cologne, all of whom
had been in hiding, decided to reestablish the congregation. They
held their first service in the ruins of the synagogue; a United States
army chaplain led the service after a seven-year hiatus in prayer at
the site. The Allied forces provided a room at the former Jewish hospital for the nascent congregation to use. Through the cooperation
of the military government, the Jewish Hospital was returned to the
Jewish community. In addition to the prayer room, a number of
community offices were established there to enable the community

to plan reconstruction of Jewish life for the small, frail remnants of the 18,000 Jews who had once lived in Cologne.

The Roonstrasse synagogue was reconstructed in 1959. (www. GERMANSYNAGOGUES.COM.) It houses a Jewish community center, a small museum, and a kosher restaurant. The interior features a stunning blue dome.

FÜRTH

A memorial to the Jewish community of Fürth was established in Geleitsgasse Square. The Nazis destroyed Fürth's Jewish cemetery, which was one of the oldest in Germany, having been established in 1607. The cemetery was restored in 1949; it is now one of the best-preserved Jewish cemeteries in Germany.

ANNE ROTHSCHILD'S ESSAY

What follows is an essay Anne wrote when she was in the seventh grade. It provides a compelling child's eye view of what it was like to have been evacuated from London at the outset of the war and to emigrate to Ecuador:

> Mr. Nolan, the seventh-grade teacher of our school likes exciting and sad stories and therefore asked me to write about the most interesting part of my life. So I will start with the crisis of 1938, the time when Hitler invaded Czechoslovakia and everybody in England was expecting war. I will write it in a diary form or else it would take me ten years to write about everything.
>
> "Shall we evacuate our children?" This was a question which was discussed by the parents every minute in Sept. 1938. After a day or so my parents decided that I should be evacuated with the school. I was supposed to go with my brother who also went to Woodstock School. Bad Luck! I sprained my foot so badly that I had to lie down. How could I be evacuated? Perhaps they could carry me. Mummy got the things ready. One evening

Daddy said, "Mr. Chamberlain has gone to Munich! It is Sept. 28. By Oct. 30 it is all over. All of London is happy again. Peace, Peace! We knew there was not going to be a war. Is Hitler going to stop marching? Time goes on. Who asked if Hitler would stop marching? I? Never! There he has gone again threatening Poland. It's 1939.

Children are to be evacuated! August 29, get your things ready and come to school, we might get notice to leave London. Poor me! No brother to go with me this time because I have changed school. August 30, still waiting, no news. August 31, said good bye to mummy, daddy, brother Peter and sister Hannah, as usual, stayed in school till five. News! We're going tomorrow. Bad luck! It's mummy's birthday on Sept. 1. The first time that we are separated on that day. Still worse, the next day would be my sister's birthday. I went to school by car and tears here and there. In front of the school. No crying allowed. "Goodbye, goodbye see you soon. Come and visit me. Yes I'll write often. Cheer up it's not so bad. Don't worry about me. I'll be alright, yes I've got a hanky. Well, goodbye."

Alone, alone, alone! "Oh no Anne, no crying. Some children don't even have something to eat. You've still got mummy and daddy. Yes you're lucky enough!" There is a group of people laughing. It changes the atmosphere. A bell! What does that mean? We are going, we are going! Goodbye London! Goodbye London! I wonder when I shall see you again. Dry those tears! Miss Potter the headmistress is in a flutter. "Yes girls, no girls, what's the matter girls? Get your things ready girls, are you ready girls? Let's go girls." Girls, girls, girls, girls everywhere but no one I loved, no one I knew well! No mummy, no daddy, but only girls, girls, girls. There is one staring at me. Did she see the tear rolling down my cheek? No, her eyes are glistening too. Whose aren't? And there goes Miss Potter again. "Hurry up girls! Cheer up girls!" Oh that woman, I could kill her. Can't she be quiet once? She knows we are fighting against tears.

There's the station. "Show your tickets. No the train has not arrived yet. Yes it will arrive in about an hour." An hour!

An hour of waiting. Nobody to cheer you up. Shall I pinch that fat girl in front? No, that would be mean at such a time. And Miss Potter: "Girls you may walk around and look at things. Let's sing a song to cheer us up." Oh, the darling, just now I could have kissed her. She broke the dreary atmosphere. We sang "Rule Britannia." The station master passes. "What good girls you have. The school before you cried the whole time."

The train, the train, hurrah! My what an old thing. Suppose it was built sometime in the 18th century. We're off upee [sic]!

The train does not even have a corridor. It only has departments. "Ten green bottles are hanging on the wall," my, everybody is singing that song. Watfort Junction, already? [Watford Junction is a railway station that serves Watford, Hertfordshire, on the West Coast Main Line, 17 miles northwest of London] It can't be true. Yes there is the sign. There comes a man with Wall's ice cream. [Wall's Ice Cream was founded in 1922. First sold in London via horse and cart, it eventually used tricycle carts to sell throughout London.] "I am hungry! Hand me my suitcase, I want to get my sandwiches" "You are lucky, I forgot mine." Alright you can have one of mine. We are moving again. I wonder what my billet is going to be like [a billet is an assigned lodging]. So do I, so do I. Berkhamstead, Berkhamstead. Why, we are at our destination already. What a little station. One hundredth of the size of Victoria Station in London. [Berkhamstead is a market town in Hertfordshire 26 miles northwest of London.)]

There is Miss Potter. "Get in line girls, get in line girls. We are going to the school now. When the other headmistress comes, greet her nicely, and say that you thank her for letting us use her school in the afternoons." "Yes Miss Potter." "Miss Potter why don't we have lessons in the morning from now on?" "Because the other school uses the building in the morning."

There is the school. "What a gray ugly building pooh how awful! "Look, look a swimming pool." How nice, how dirty. Look at all the redworms in it and that dead bird lying on top. I wonder when they cleaned it last. "Come on girls, hurry up, we have to sort you now for the billets." "I wonder what my billet is going to be like? I hope I won't come to some grumpy old person who thinks children have to go to bed at six p.m. "Anne Rothschild!" "Yes Miss Potter." "You will come to Shenstone Court. Pat Hyman you go with Anne. Ellen and Ines you go too." A car is waiting outside. We go up a hill. "You lucky girls you have the nicest billet." Yes, yes, yes you'll have a nice home. Don't look so grave cheer up, cheer up. "Yes cheer up. They don't know how we feel. Cheer up it's alright for them to say. And you'll have a nice home. It can't be nice, how can it be nice away from home? Probably we are going to a nice dirty home. There we see a tiny house. "That's it, that's it. "No says the driver." "No?" There comes a nice house. How enormous. Don't I wish I live there. We are going up the drive. "That isn't the house?" "Yes it is." "How beautiful! It's not much smaller than Buckingham Palace." "Anne what a park. Whose house is it?" "It's Lady Cooper's and Sir Richard's." "A Sir and a Lady! I suppose they won't even look at us. But…There they are both of them with beaming faces. What a welcome, what happiness! They greet us. "I hope you'll be happy here." They kiss us. How different than we expected. How beautiful, what a home! We go upstairs through some long corridors. Our room, how big and a bathroom next door. They leave us. The sunshine has gone. Mummy, mummy I feel so alone! Now the room looks dreary. Shall we go to the park. Yes we go. How beautiful, how nice. [The Cooper Baronetcy of Shenstone Court is in the parish of Shenstone in County Stafford. It was created in 1905 for the agriculturist Richard Powell Cooper.]

Time passes. There are ten children and a teacher. We are happy. Our sadness has gone. Do we quarrel? I should say so. I sleep in a different room now. I sleep together with Hazel in the gardener's cottage. It's night. The sirens go, the sirens go. "Anne wake up, hurry, hurry." We are outside. "Hear the anti-aircraft guns?" We are in the shelter. People have come down in nighties and pajamas. Lady Cooper has pigtails. We wait, wait, wait. Won't the all clear ever sound? Oh no why should it? There comes Bill, Lady Cooper's son. He had been outside. "Hurry folks aren't you ever coming out, the all clear has sounded five minutes ago."

It is July 1940. Mummy has come to visit me. She tells me her secret. We are going to Ecuador and she is taking me home. Home, home, how lovely. Where is Ecuador? Never heard of it before. In South America? No? Really? Goodbye everybody. Goodbye Lady Cooper. I am surprised. I am sad leaving this place. I had thought that I could not like a place far away from home. But I did. I had begun to love Lady Cooper. She and her husband had been so kind, so unearthly kind.

London, London this time I saw it with a smile on my face and not with tears. It had changed a little. Here and there were some bombed houses. This London was not so peaceful anymore. Air raid, Air raid. What's the use of going in the shelter in the daytime? But at night. How beautiful are the searchlights. Look at that airplane coming down, it's burning. Hurrah, it's a German.

We have our Ecuadorian visas. We go to Liverpool. Now we're in the customs. See our boat? It's painted green. How small it is but how nice. We are going, we are going. Look at all those burnt boats around us. What a beginning! Will we be sunk? Of course not. How nice is the journey, how exciting. I'll write about it to my friends. But now my plan is spoilt. There is a notice that you may not tell what happens on the journey. Bad luck! I wanted to show off. 10 days passed, 2 weeks passed, 3 weeks passed, we're there. Hurrah, hurrah! Salinas, what a harbor, but better than I expected.

We get on shore. How nice and quiet. No guns sticking out of the thickets, no airplanes patrolling overhead, no black out! I am going to love this country, this beautiful, quiet piece of land!

ACKNOWLEDGEMENTS

FIRST AND FOREMOST, I WANT TO THANK MY MOTHER FOR serving as an inspiration to me. She survived many hard blows, any one of which might have crippled her, but she persevered. Having suffered prejudice and ostracism and having been forced to flee the country where she was born, she never forgot those experiences. Rather than banish them from thought or stew in anger, they became guideposts that directed her throughout her life. She opened her heart and home to others who were fleeing persecution and unrest. She was kind, generous, and strong. I hope this book, in at least some small measure, honors her and conveys who she was, what she overcame, and commemorates the tremendous number of people she helped through her decades of community service.

I would like to express my thanks to and love for my wonderful wife Sharon for her support throughout this undertaking. She proofread numerous iterations of the manuscript and made suggestions and corrections of things I did not see because my brain was fuzzy after having read it so many times. I appreciate her tolerance of the piles of files, books, and papers I stored throughout our house while working on this project. The surface of our dining room table and much of the floor around it have begun to reappear as I box and store my archive.

I want to thank my sister Margie Kessel, cousin Lydia Stux, and my late aunt Erica Stux for their assistance in researching this family history. They responded to my many requests for information

542

and documents by scouring scrapbooks and sifting through boxes that had been tucked away for years in closets, attics, and basements. They also combed their memories for information that likewise had been in deep storage for years.

I want to thank Sharon's and my dear friend Marlies Bruning for her help. Marlies has been a tremendous resource throughout this endeavor. She translated many documents, helped me understand German idioms, taught me about German customs and practices, and has been an all-around supporter of this project.

I also want to thank Cathy Lara, my translator extraordinaire at Cathy Lara & Associates. Cathy and her colleagues did a marvelous job translating documents, many of which were very difficult to read because they were in cursive handwriting on eighty-year-old onion skin paper. Some documents were faded and quite a few were almost illegible—at least to me. Yet Cathy was able to translate them. In addition, Cathy and her colleagues researched and annotated the documents with a tremendous amount of interesting and useful information.

Filmmaker Eva Zelig has been extremely helpful and generous with her time. Eva identified and put me in touch with distant cousins who had emigrated to Ecuador. Eva's documentary "An Unknown Country" was a fascinating starting point for this part of my research. Eva helped me understand the lives of the immigrants who made homes in a new land that was so different from what they had known. Her comments and suggestions were tremendously helpful. Thank you also to Andres Anker for his help researching this part of the story.

I also owe a debt of gratitude to Marlene Roesberg Strauss and Mark Berlin for their help researching and understanding aspects of my family's history. They have been generous with their time and responsive to my many requests for help understanding what happened to our families and teasing out the branches of my family tree.

I want to acknowledge the special debt my family owes to Walter and Dorothy Goff and their children Kathleen, Josephine, Dorothy, and Bernard for sheltering my mother and aunt in their home. The Goffs opened their home to Renate and Erica and were friends to Trude and Max at a time when they desperately needed shelter and support. The Goffs' extraordinary generosity made the Ichenhäusers' year in Britain much easier to endure. In particular, I want to thank Kathleen's daughter Patricia ("Pat") Neate for her enthusiastic and invaluable assistance reviewing family albums, sorting through old correspondence for information about my family's stay with the Goffs, researching various issues, and sending photographs of my family while they were in England. After decades had passed since our families were in touch, Pat has become both a collaborator and a friend. Thank you, a million times over.

I also want to thank Barbara Klieforth for her help and friendship. Barbara has been generous with her time, researching various aspects of this story and sharing information about her grandfather, Alfred W. Klieforth, the U.S. Consul General in Cologne in 1938. But for Consul Klieforth's intercession, my grandfather Max might well have died in Dachau or another camp. If that had occurred, Trude, Renate, and Erica likely would have been trapped and died in Germany as well.

I hope this book honors the people whose stories I have told and helps keep their memory alive.

Steven Wasserman
September 2021

ABOUT THE AUTHOR

Steven Wasserman is a retired attorney.
He and his wife live in San Francisco.